POSUKA DEMIZU

Even if you know how things are going to go, it's tough to draw the facial expressions of a character making difficult decisions or feeling despair.

But obviously that's a good thing.

The next volume is going to be even more exciting.

See you again soon.

KAIU SHIRAI

Writer Shirai's personal highlights for *The Promised Neverland* fanatics, part 3:

1. A hint about the secret to the system(?) of the neck numbers is hidden somewhere in this volume.

2. Ray had decided at a young age to read all of the books in the house before he turned 12 years old. So the book he's holding in chapter 32 is the final one that he just finished reading.

Okay, please enjoy the volume!

Posuka Demizu debuted as a manga artist with the 2013 *CoroCoro* series *Oreca Monster Bouken Retsuden*. A collection of illustrations, *The Art of Posuka Demizu,* was released in 2016 by PIE International.

Kaiu Shirai debuted in 2015 with *Ashley Gate no Yukue* on the *Shonen Jump+* website. Shirai first worked with Posuka Demizu on the two-shot *Poppy no Negai*, which was released in February 2016.

THE PROMISED NEVERLAND

VOLUME 4
SHONEN JUMP Manga Edition

STORY BY KAIU SHIRAI
ART BY POSUKA DEMIZU

Translation/Satsuki Yamashita
Touch-Up Art & Lettering/Mark McMurray
Design/Julian [JR] Robinson
Editor/Alexis Kirsch

Printed in the U.S.A.

Published by VIZ Media, LLC
P.O. Box 77010
San Francisco, CA 94107

10 9 8 7 6 5 4 3 2 1
First printing, June 2018

viz.com

PARENTAL ADVISORY
THE PROMISED NEVERLAND is rated T+
and is recommended for ages 16 and up.
This volume contains fantasy violence and
adult themes.

shonenjump.com

THE PROMISED NEVERLAND

4

I Want to Live

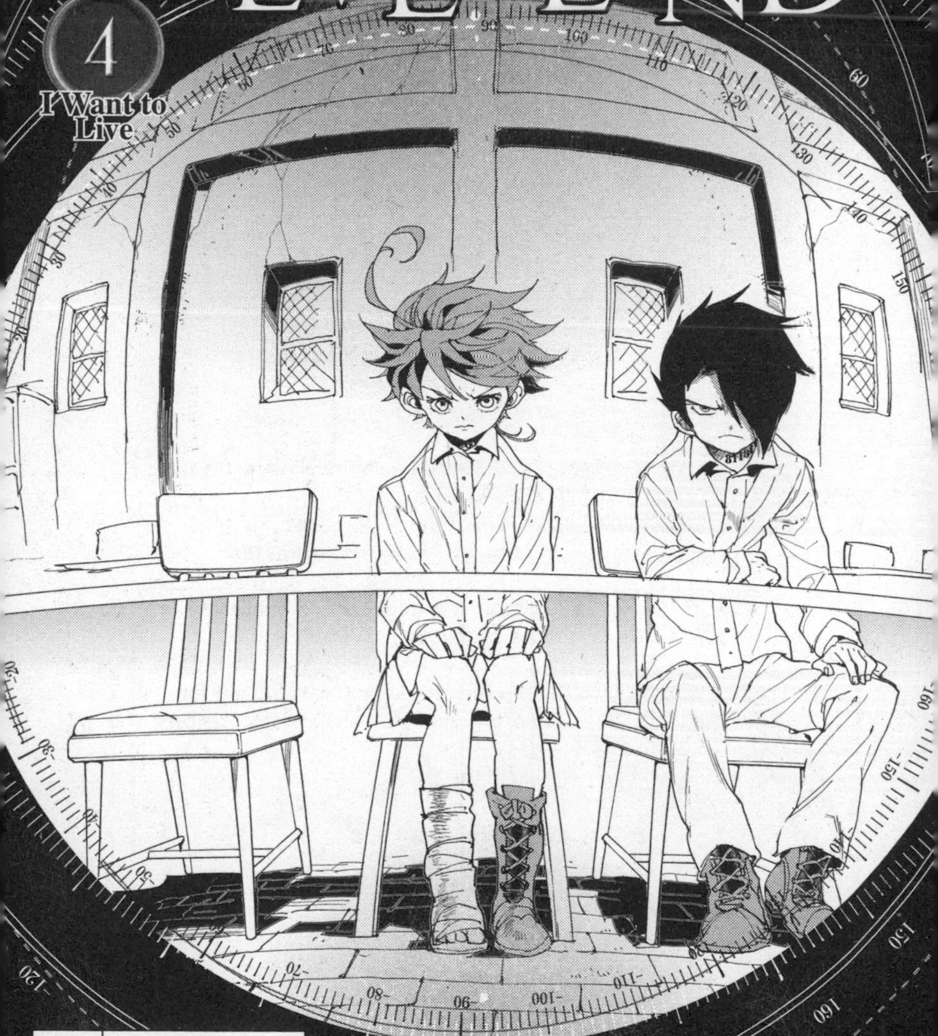

STORY	KAIU SHIRAI
ART	POSUKA DEMIZU

SHONENJUMP MANGA

CHARACTERS

EMMA

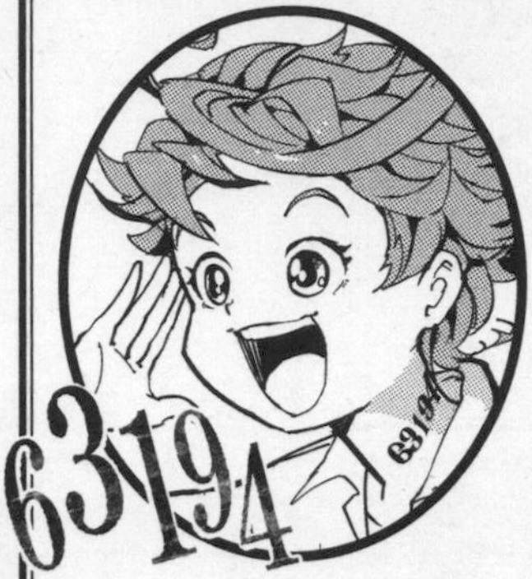
63194

An enthusiastic and optimistic girl with superb athletic and learning abilities.

RAY

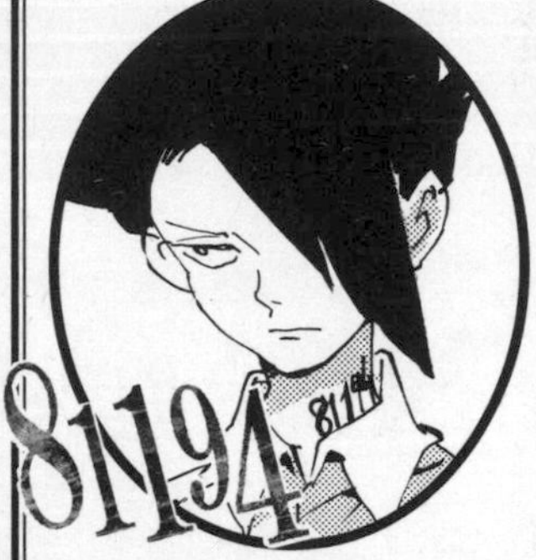
81194

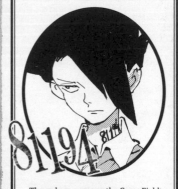

The only one among the Grace Field House children who can match wits with Norman.

NORMAN

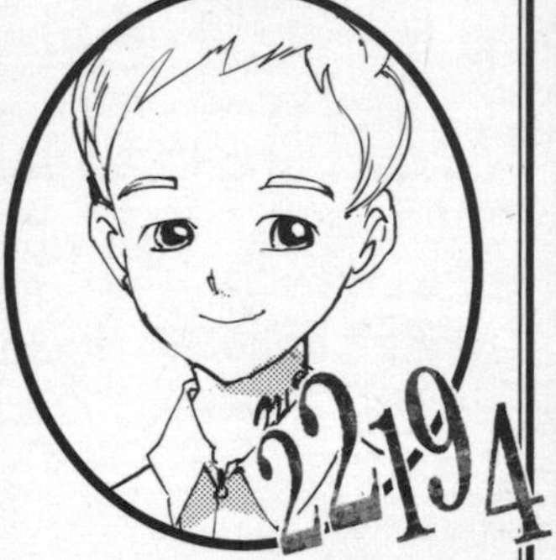
22194

A boy with excellent analytical and decision-making capabilities. He's the smartest child at Grace Field House.

KRONE

Isabella's assistant and a
subordinate of the demons.

ISABELLA

The "Mom" of the children at
Grace Field House.

DON

A carefree boy who is cheerful
but competitive.

GILDA

A girl who is interested in fashion.

The Story So Far

The 38 children of Grace Field House orphanage are all living happily with their "Mom,"
Isabella, treating her as if she were their real mother. One day, one of the children leaves
the orphanage to live with her new foster family. But when Emma and Norman go to
the gate to deliver something she's left behind, they witness her lifeless body and some
terrible demons. In addition, they discover that Mom is raising them as food for the
demons. Emma swears that she'll never lose another family member and starts gathering
information in order to survive. She and Norman figure out that the daily tests they take
are to develop their brains, the demons' favorite part to eat. They eventually get Ray to
join their side, and the three start planning a way to escape.

THE PROMISED NEVERLAND 4

I Want to Live

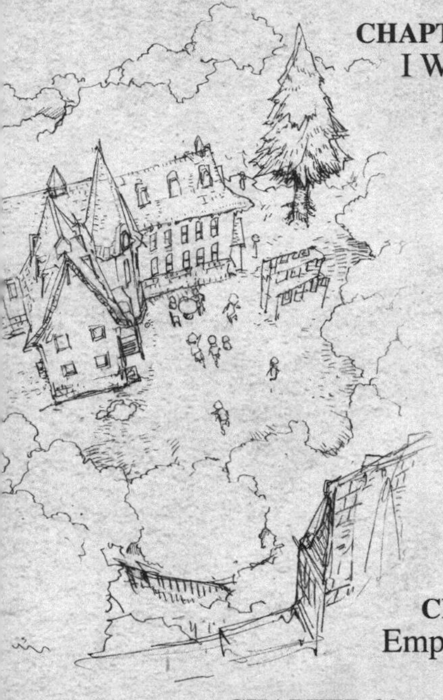

CHAPTER 26: I WANT TO LIVE

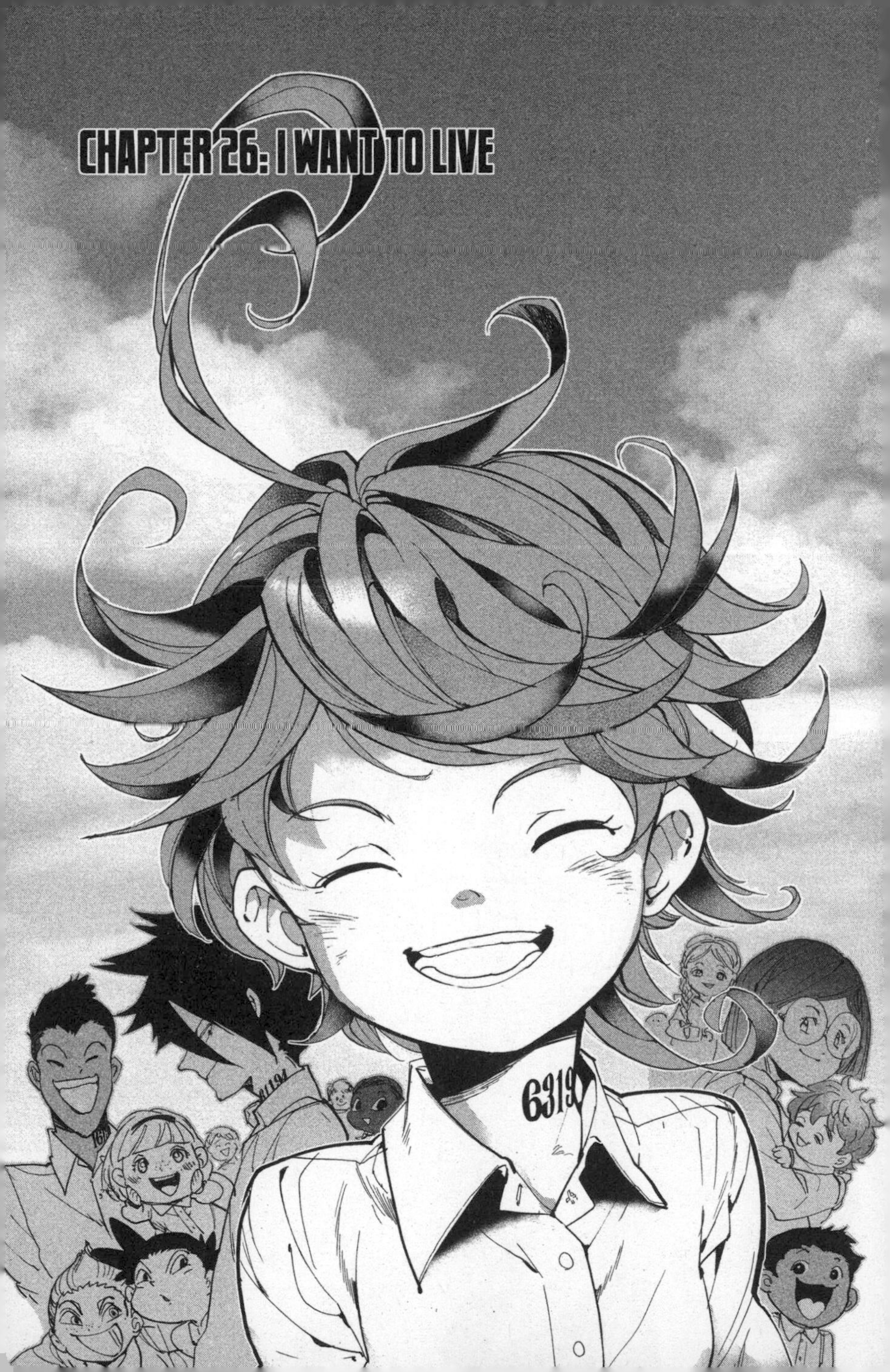
6319

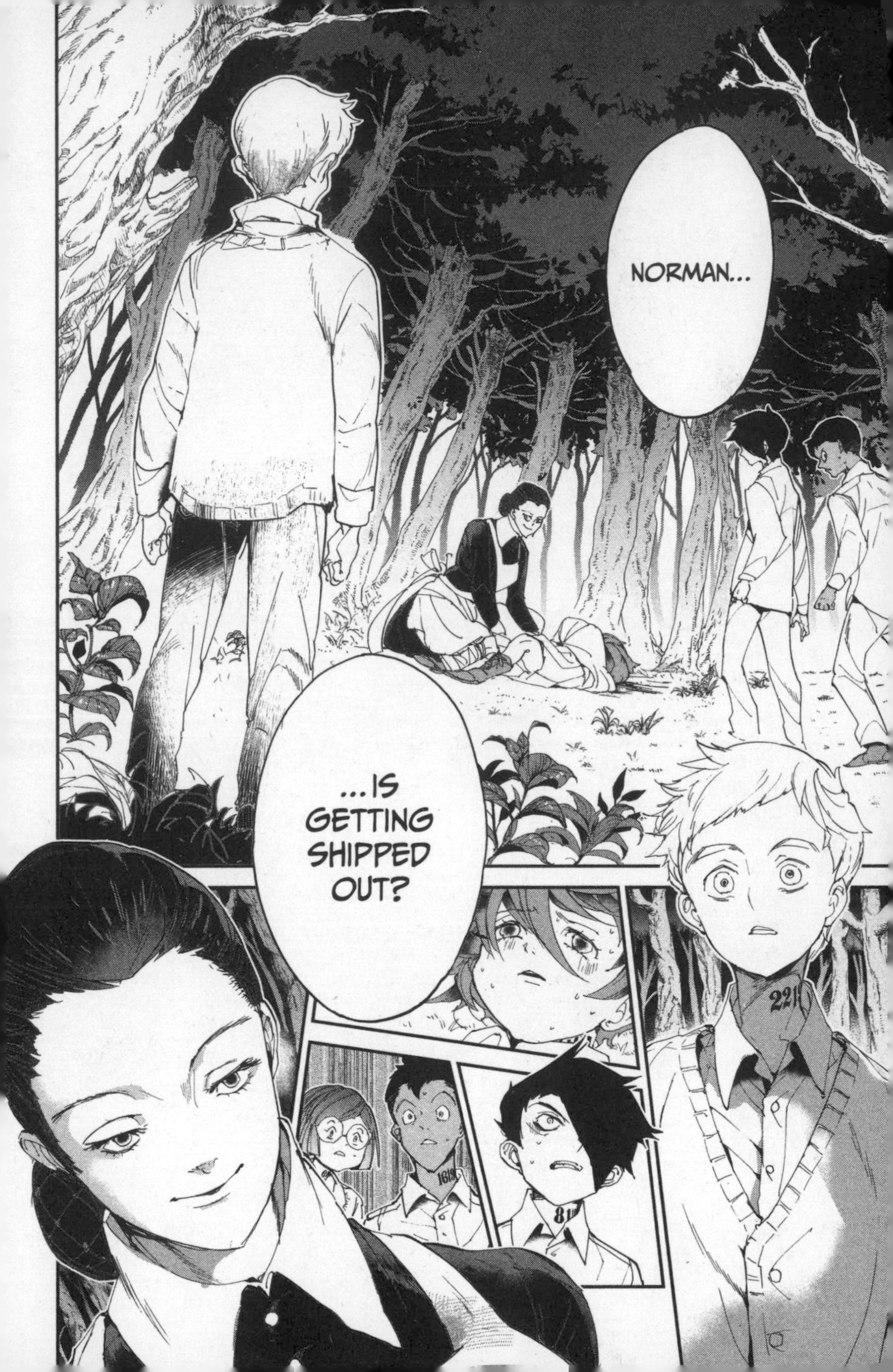
NORMAN...
...IS GETTING SHIPPED OUT?

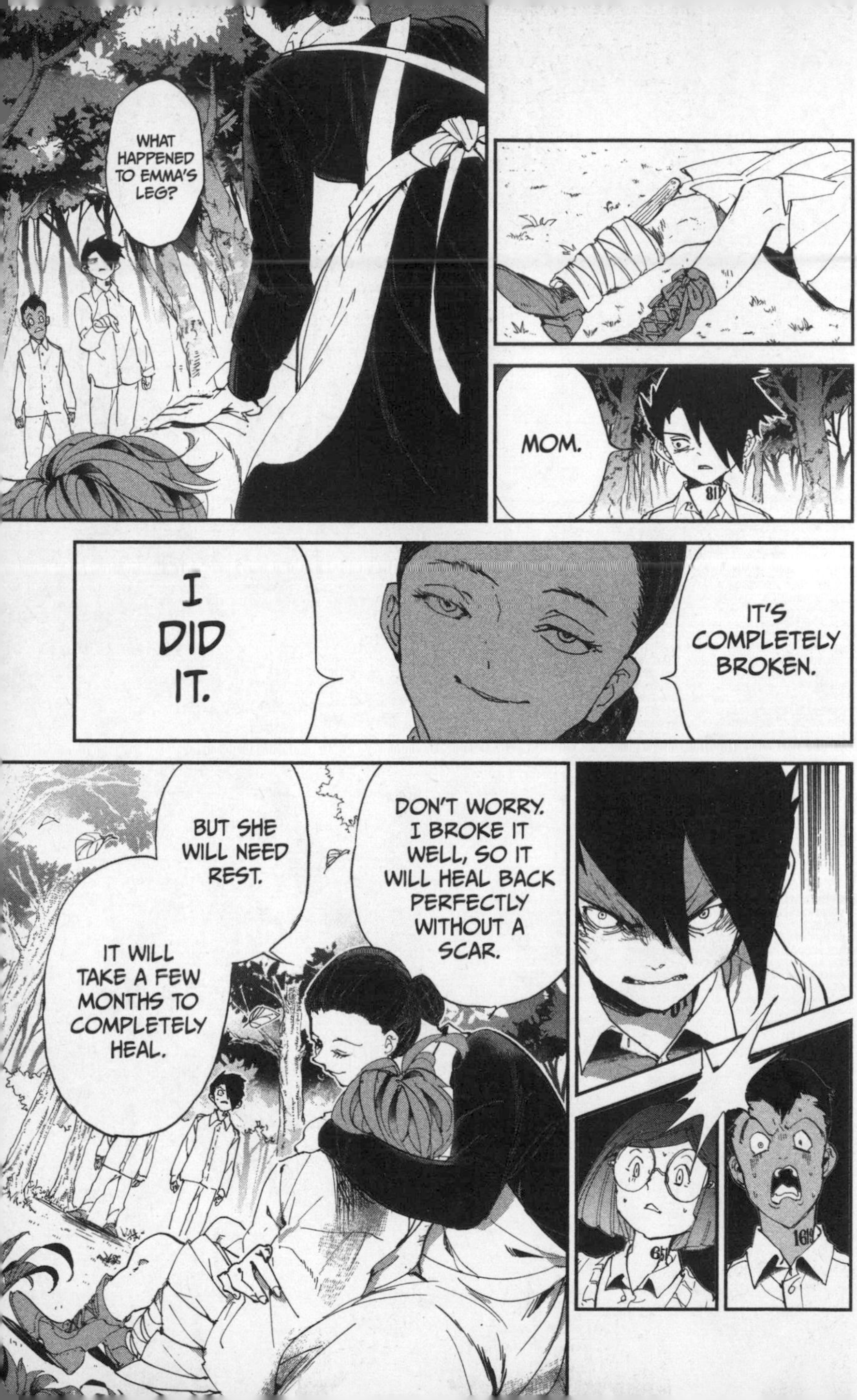
MOM.
WHAT HAPPENED TO EMMA'S LEG?
IT'S COMPLETELY BROKEN.
I DID IT.
DON'T WORRY. I BROKE IT WELL, SO IT WILL HEAL BACK PERFECTLY WITHOUT A SCAR.
BUT SHE WILL NEED REST.
IT WILL TAKE A FEW MONTHS TO COMPLETELY HEAL.

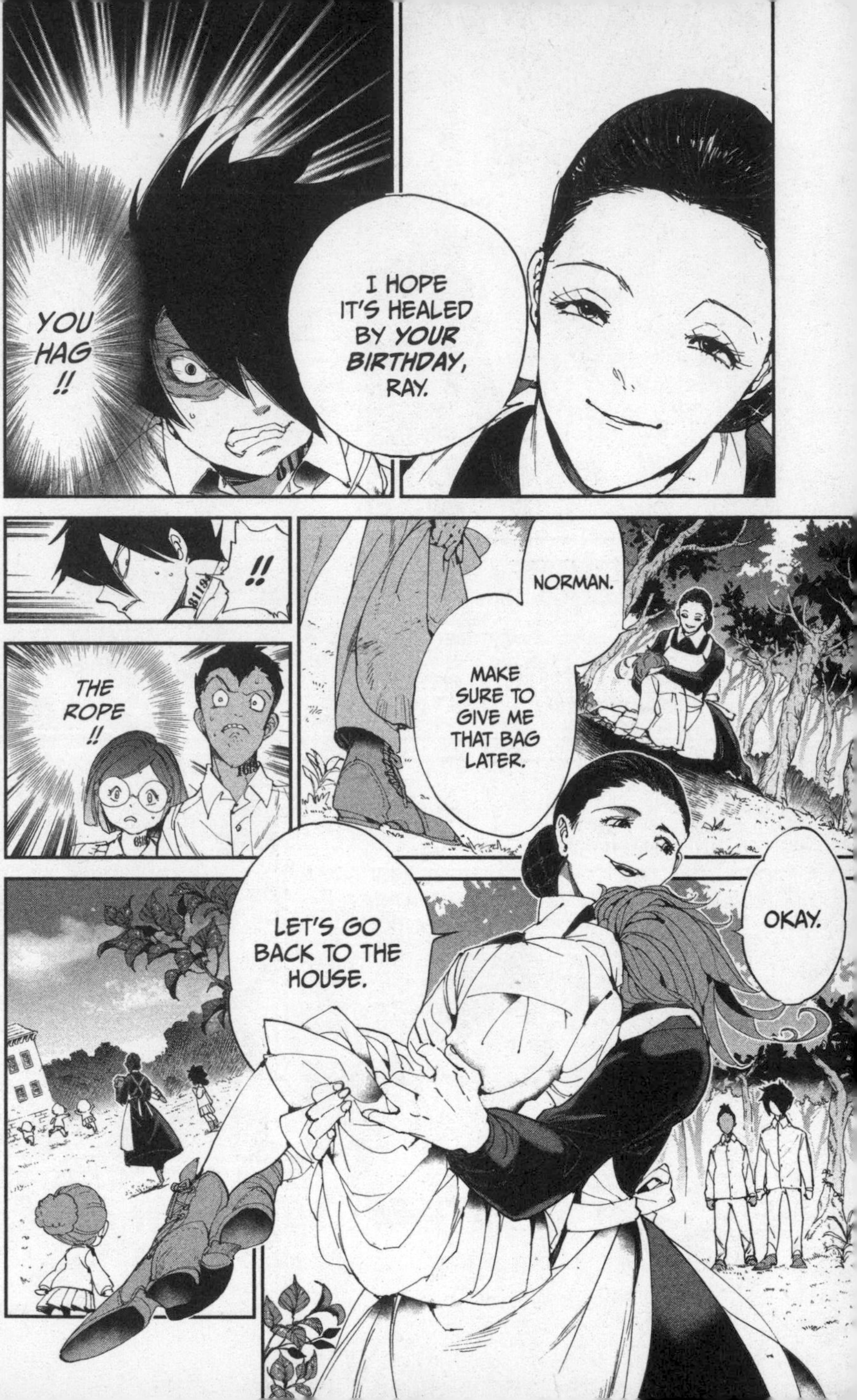
I HOPE IT'S HEALED BY YOUR BIRTHDAY, RAY.
YOU HAG!!
NORMAN.
MAKE SURE TO GIVE ME THAT BAG LATER.
!!
THE ROPE!!
OKAY.
LET'S GO BACK TO THE HOUSE.

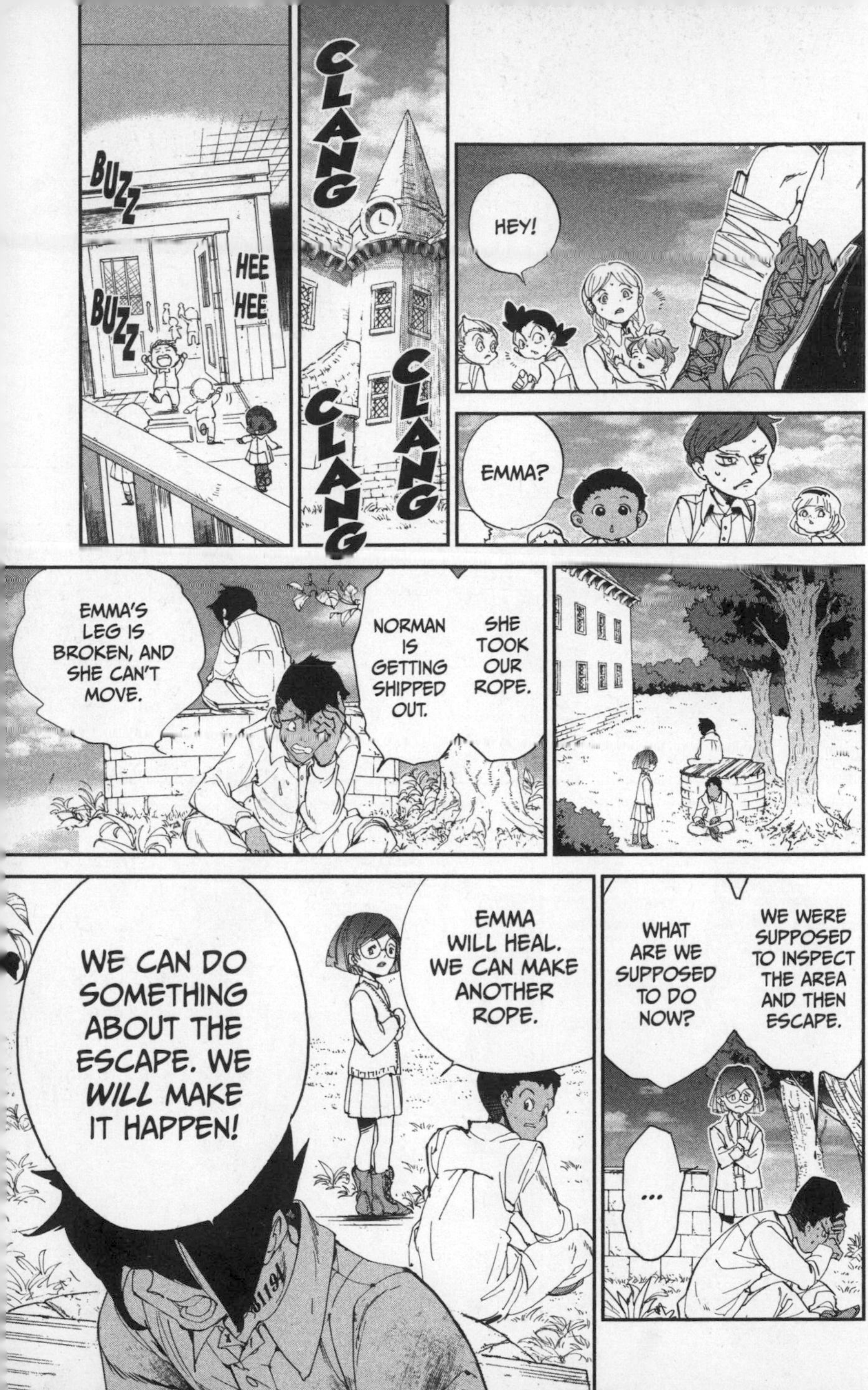
HEY!
EMMA?
CLANG
CLANG
CLANG
CLANG
BUZZ
HEE HEE
BUZZ
SHE TOOK OUR ROPE.
NORMAN IS GETTING SHIPPED OUT.
EMMA'S LEG IS BROKEN, AND SHE CAN'T MOVE.
WE WERE SUPPOSED TO INSPECT THE AREA AND THEN ESCAPE.
WHAT ARE WE SUPPOSED TO DO NOW?
...
EMMA WILL HEAL. WE CAN MAKE ANOTHER ROPE.
WE CAN DO SOMETHING ABOUT THE ESCAPE. WE *WILL* MAKE IT HAPPEN!

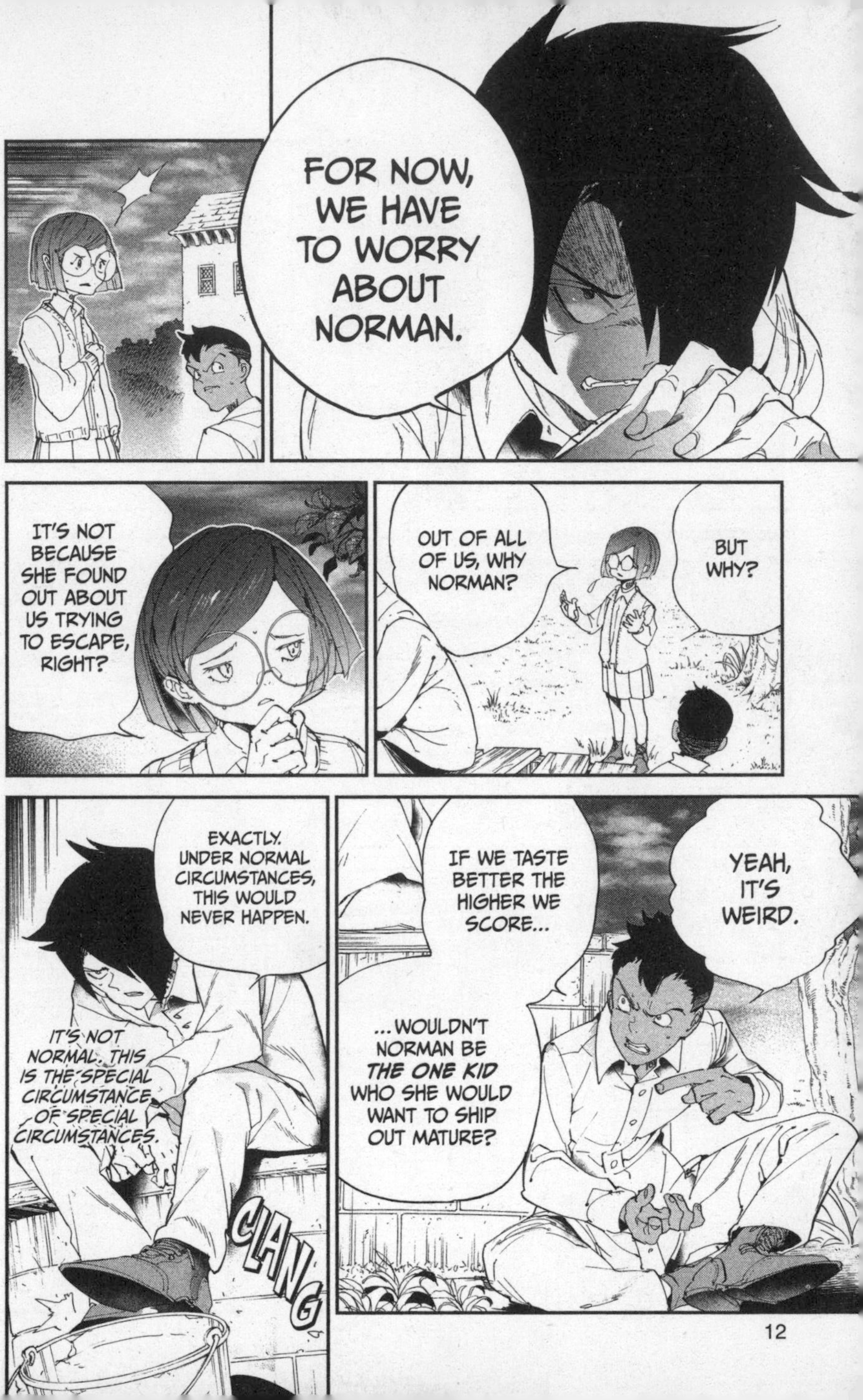
FOR NOW, WE HAVE TO WORRY ABOUT NORMAN.
BUT WHY?
OUT OF ALL OF US, WHY NORMAN?
IT'S NOT BECAUSE SHE FOUND OUT ABOUT US TRYING TO ESCAPE, RIGHT?
YEAH, IT'S WEIRD.
IF WE TASTE BETTER THE HIGHER WE SCORE...
...WOULDN'T NORMAN BE *THE ONE KID* WHO SHE WOULD WANT TO SHIP OUT MATURE?
EXACTLY. UNDER NORMAL CIRCUMSTANCES, THIS WOULD NEVER HAPPEN.
IT'S NOT NORMAL. THIS IS THE SPECIAL CIRCUMSTANCE OF SPECIAL CIRCUMSTANCES.
CLANG

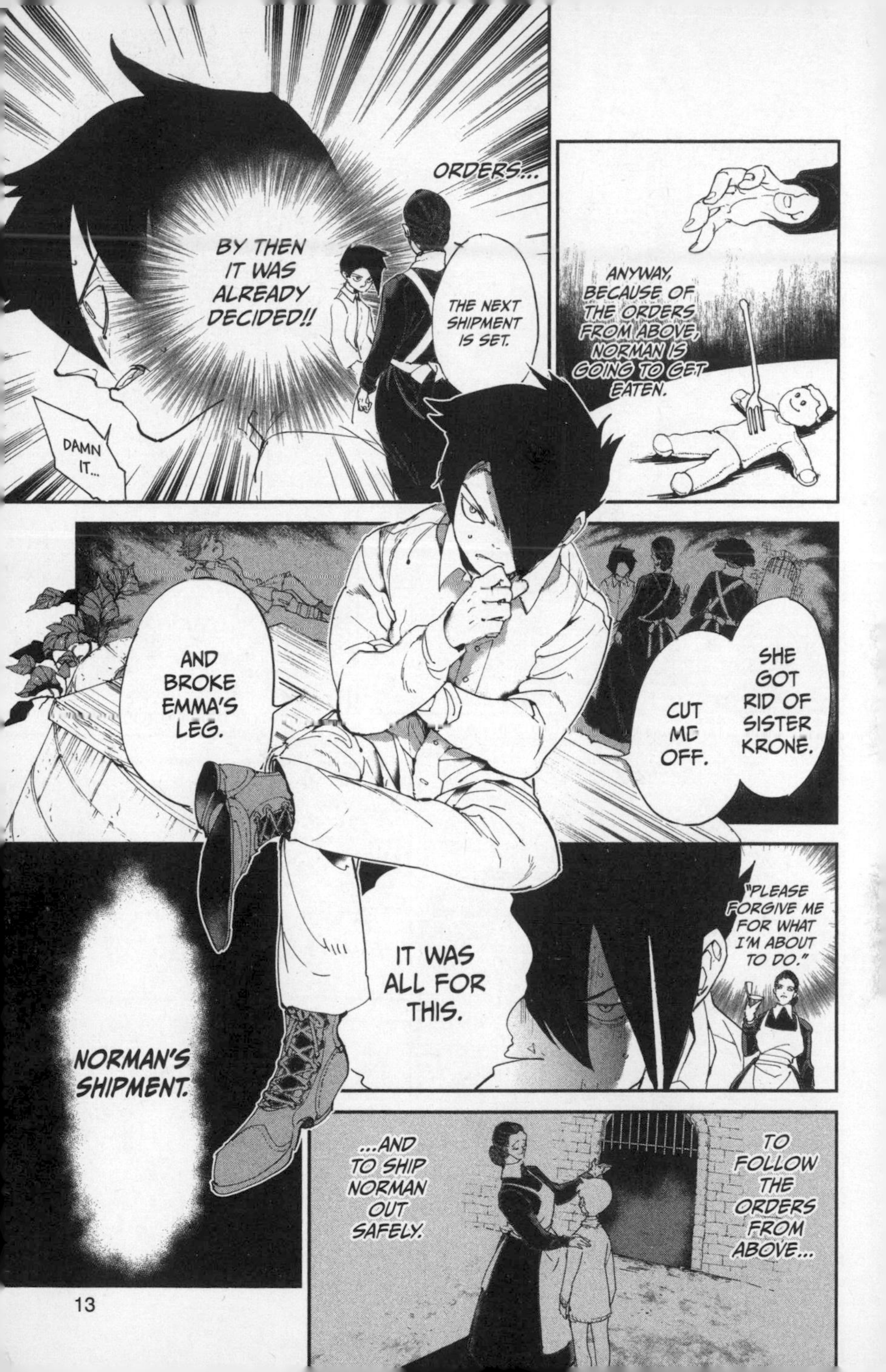
ANYWAY, BECAUSE OF THE ORDERS FROM ABOVE, NORMAN IS GOING TO GET EATEN.
ORDERS...
THE NEXT SHIPMENT IS SET.
BY THEN IT WAS ALREADY DECIDED!!
DAMN IT...
SHE GOT RID OF SISTER KRONE.
CUT ME OFF.
AND BROKE EMMA'S LEG.
"PLEASE FORGIVE ME FOR WHAT I'M ABOUT TO DO."
IT WAS ALL FOR THIS.
TO FOLLOW THE ORDERS FROM ABOVE...
...AND TO SHIP NORMAN OUT SAFELY.
NORMAN'S SHIPMENT.

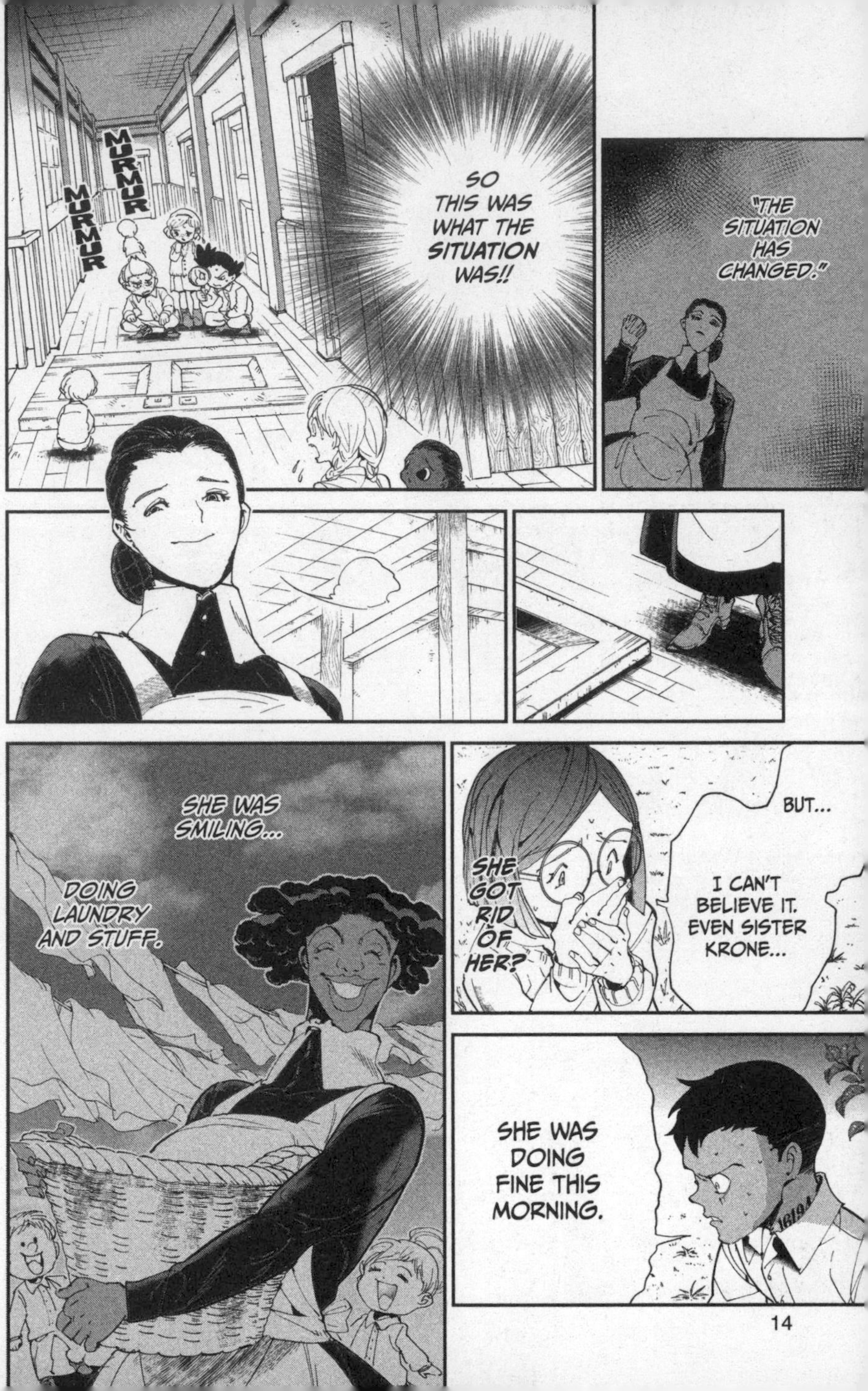
"THE SITUATION HAS CHANGED."
SO THIS WAS WHAT THE SITUATION WAS!!
MURMUR
MURMUR
BUT...
I CAN'T BELIEVE IT. EVEN SISTER KRONE...
SHE GOT RID OF HER?
SHE WAS DOING FINE THIS MORNING.
SHE WAS SMILING...
DOING LAUNDRY AND STUFF.

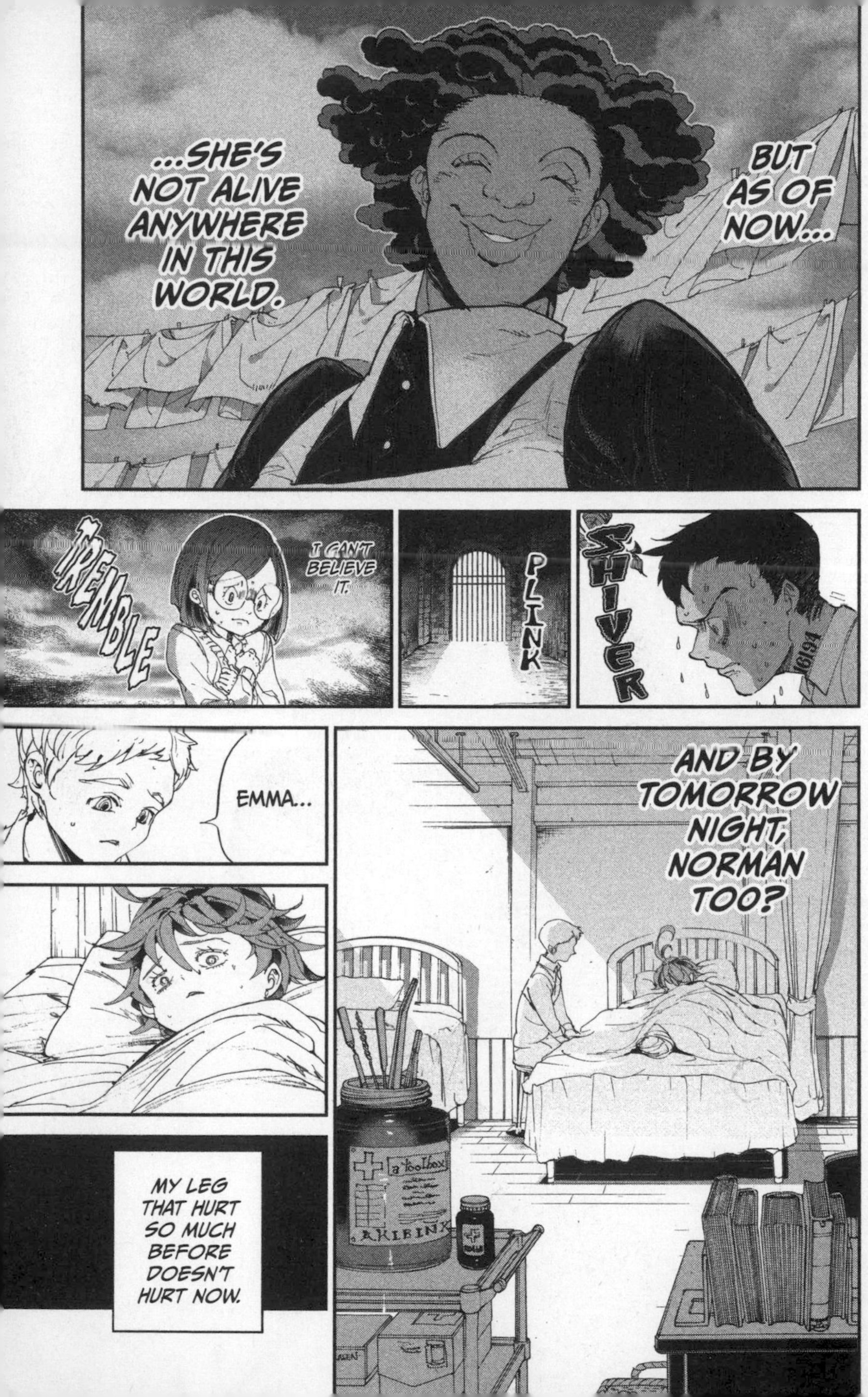
BUT AS OF NOW...
...SHE'S NOT ALIVE ANYWHERE IN THIS WORLD.
SHIVER
PLINK
I CAN'T BELIEVE IT.
TREMBLE
AND BY TOMORROW NIGHT, NORMAN TOO?
EMMA...
MY LEG THAT HURT SO MUCH BEFORE DOESN'T HURT NOW.

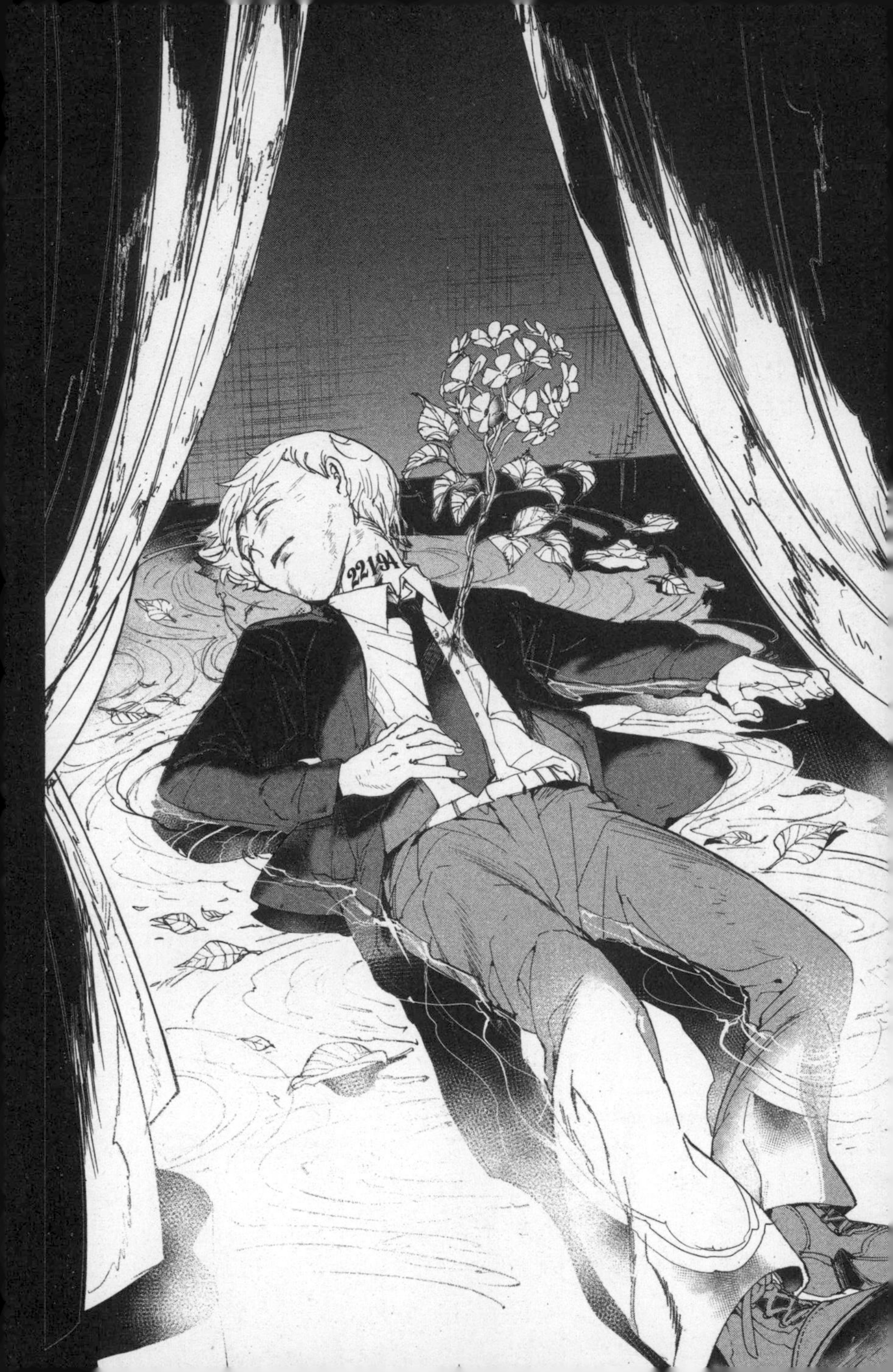
22194

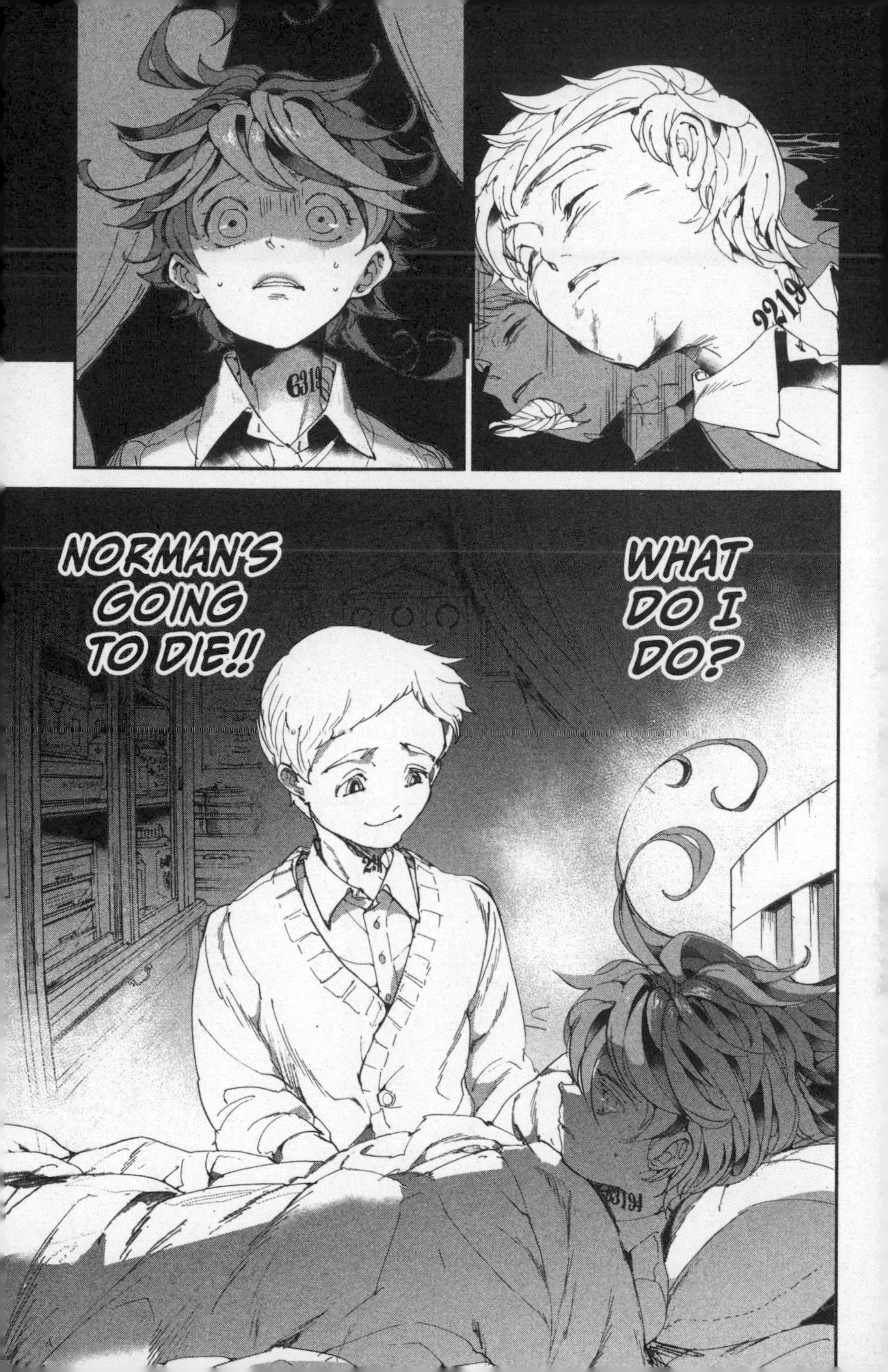
WHAT DO I DO?
NORMAN'S GOING TO DIE!!

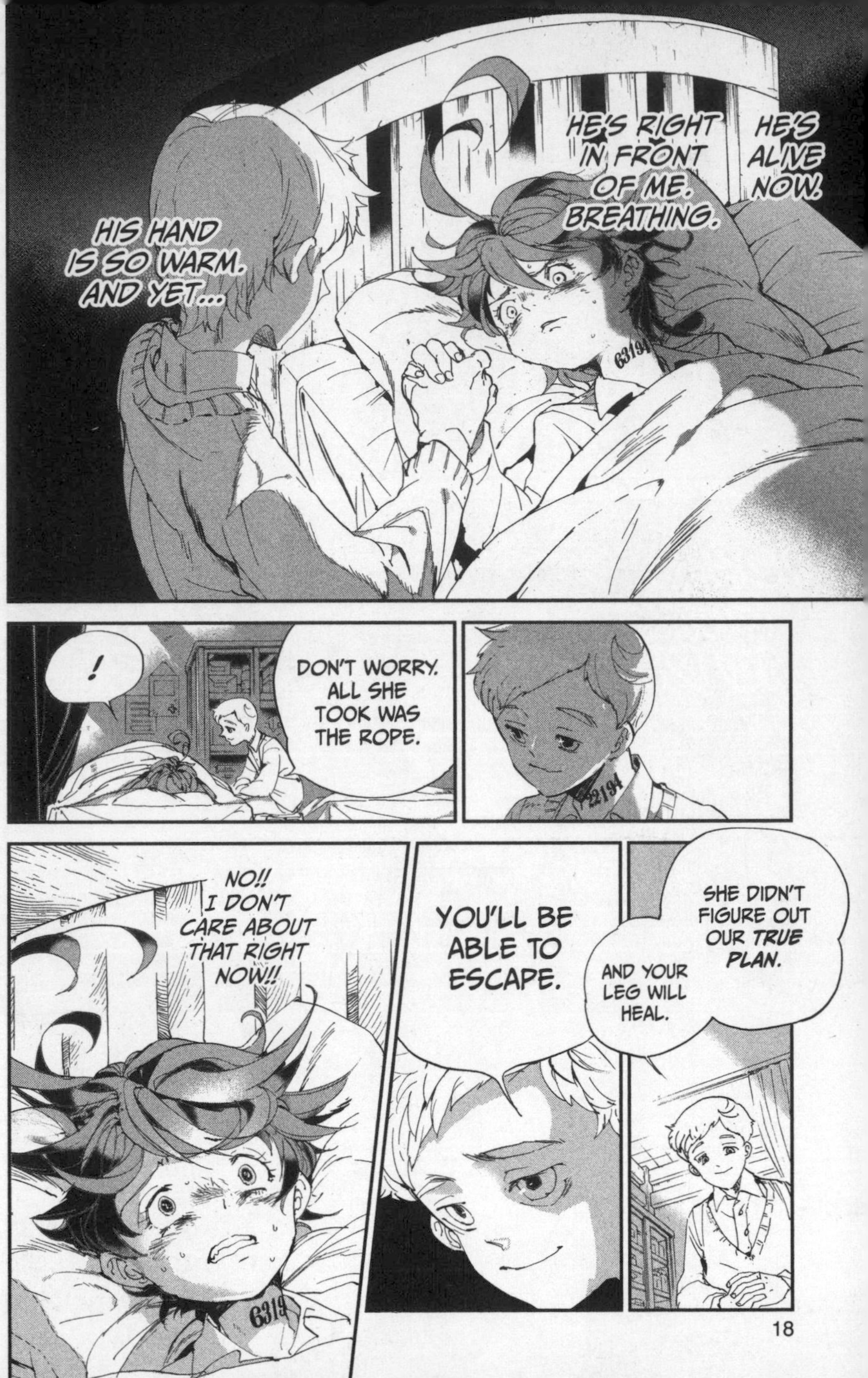

HE'S ALIVE NOW.
HE'S RIGHT IN FRONT OF ME. BREATHING.
HIS HAND IS SO WARM. AND YET...
DON'T WORRY. ALL SHE TOOK WAS THE ROPE.
!
SHE DIDN'T FIGURE OUT OUR *TRUE PLAN.*
AND YOUR LEG WILL HEAL.
YOU'LL BE ABLE TO ESCAPE.
NO!! I DON'T CARE ABOUT THAT RIGHT NOW!!

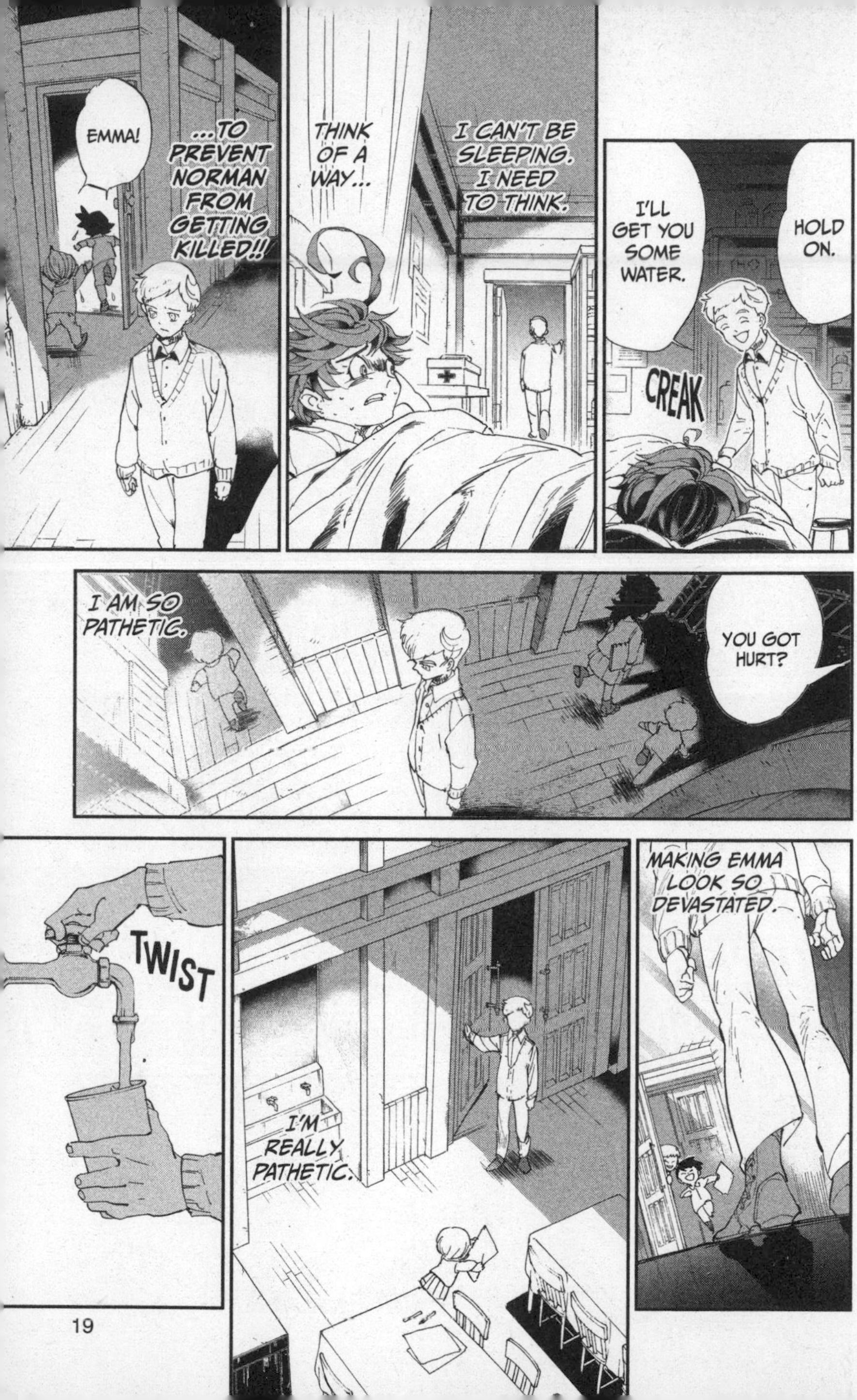
HOLD ON.
I'LL GET YOU SOME WATER.
CREAK
I CAN'T BE SLEEPING. I NEED TO THINK.
THINK OF A WAY...
...TO PREVENT NORMAN FROM GETTING KILLED!!
EMMA!
YOU GOT HURT?
I AM SO PATHETIC.
MAKING EMMA LOOK SO DEVASTATED.
I'M REALLY PATHETIC.
TWIST

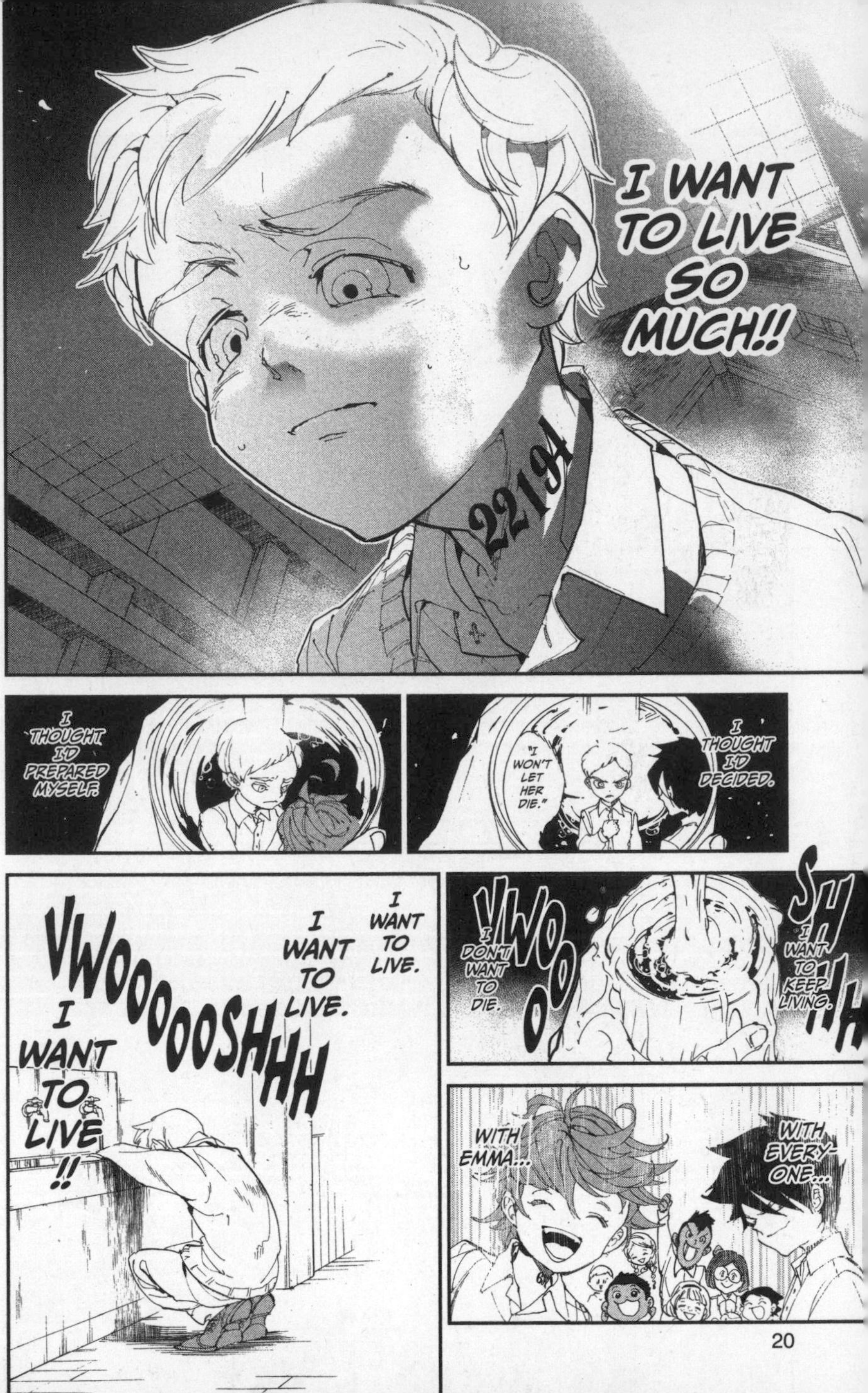
I WANT TO LIVE SO MUCH!!
I THOUGHT I'D DECIDED.
"I WON'T LET HER DIE."
I THOUGHT I'D PREPARED MYSELF.
SHHH
I WANT TO KEEP LIVING.
VWOOOO
I DON'T WANT TO DIE.
WITH EVERYONE...
WITH EMMA...
I WANT TO LIVE.
I WANT TO LIVE.
VWOOOOOSHHHH
I WANT TO LIVE!!

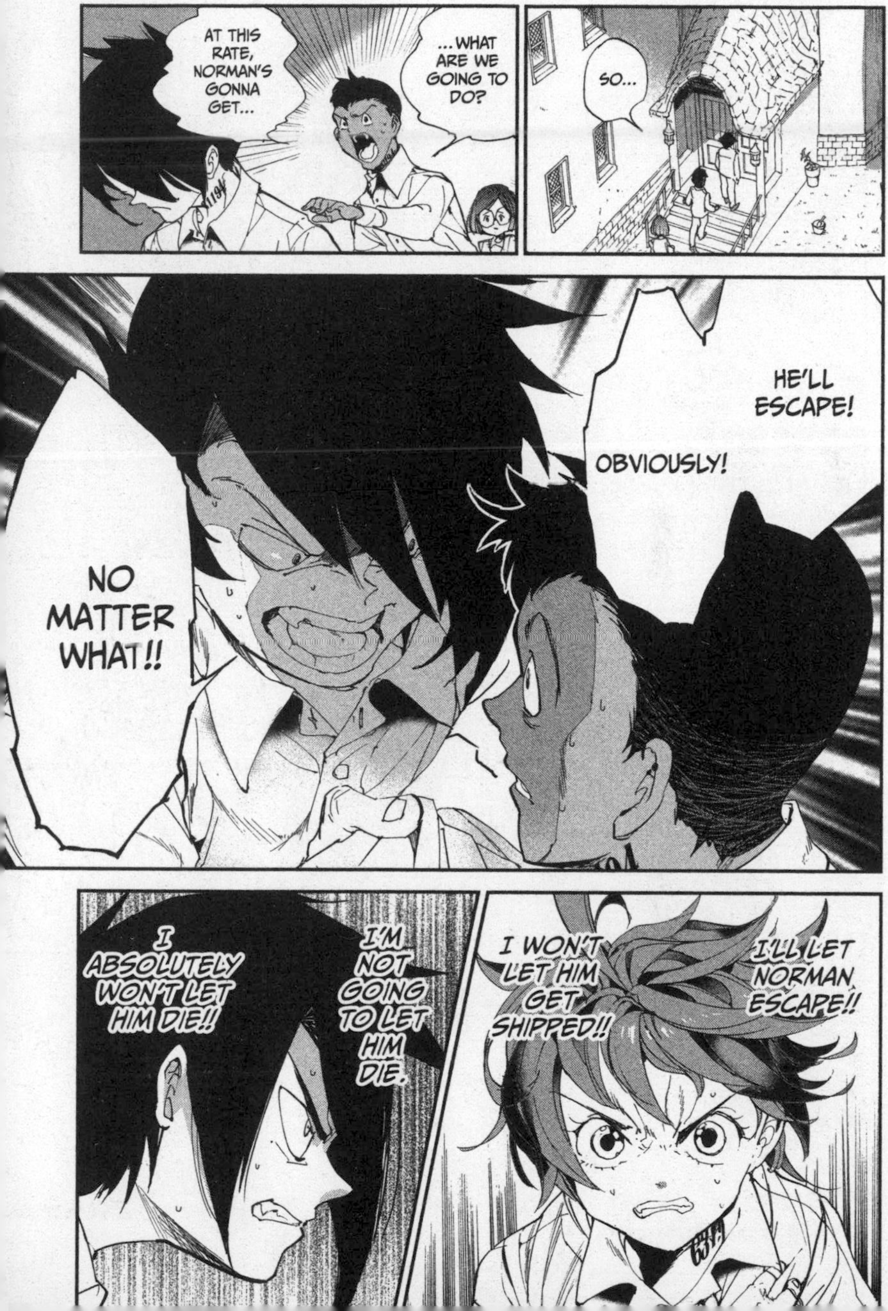
SO...
...WHAT ARE WE GOING TO DO?
AT THIS RATE, NORMAN'S GONNA GET...
HE'LL ESCAPE!
OBVIOUSLY!
NO MATTER WHAT!!
I'LL LET NORMAN ESCAPE!!
I WON'T LET HIM GET SHIPPED!!
I'M NOT GOING TO LET HIM DIE.
I ABSOLUTELY WON'T LET HIM DIE!!

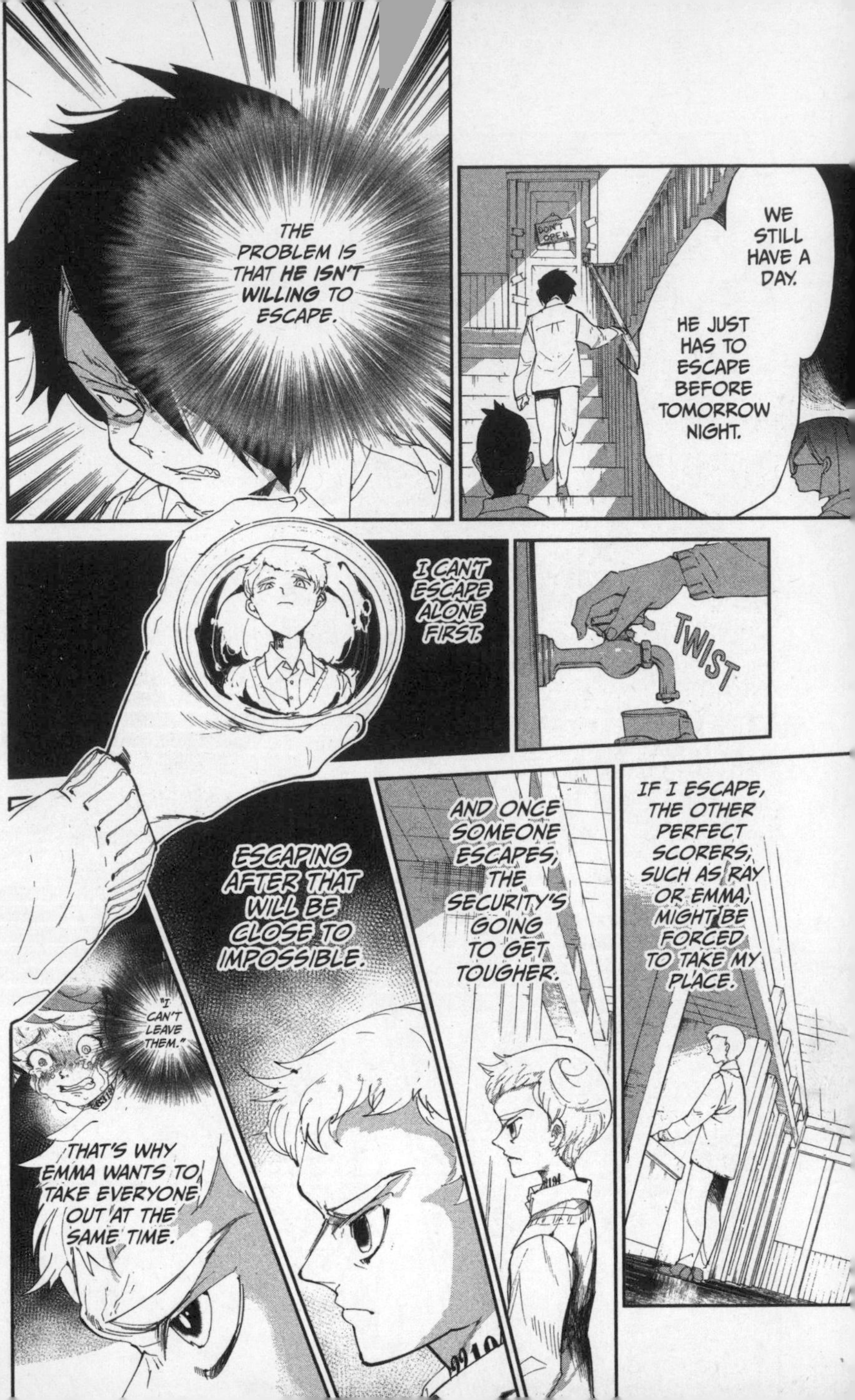
DON'T OPEN
WE STILL HAVE A DAY.
HE JUST HAS TO ESCAPE BEFORE TOMORROW NIGHT.
THE PROBLEM IS THAT HE ISN'T WILLING TO ESCAPE.
TWIST
I CAN'T ESCAPE ALONE FIRST.
IF I ESCAPE, THE OTHER PERFECT SCORERS, SUCH AS RAY OR EMMA, MIGHT BE FORCED TO TAKE MY PLACE.
AND ONCE SOMEONE ESCAPES, THE SECURITY'S GOING TO GET TOUGHER.
ESCAPING AFTER THAT WILL BE CLOSE TO IMPOSSIBLE.
"I CAN'T LEAVE THEM."
THAT'S WHY EMMA WANTS TO TAKE EVERYONE OUT AT THE SAME TIME.

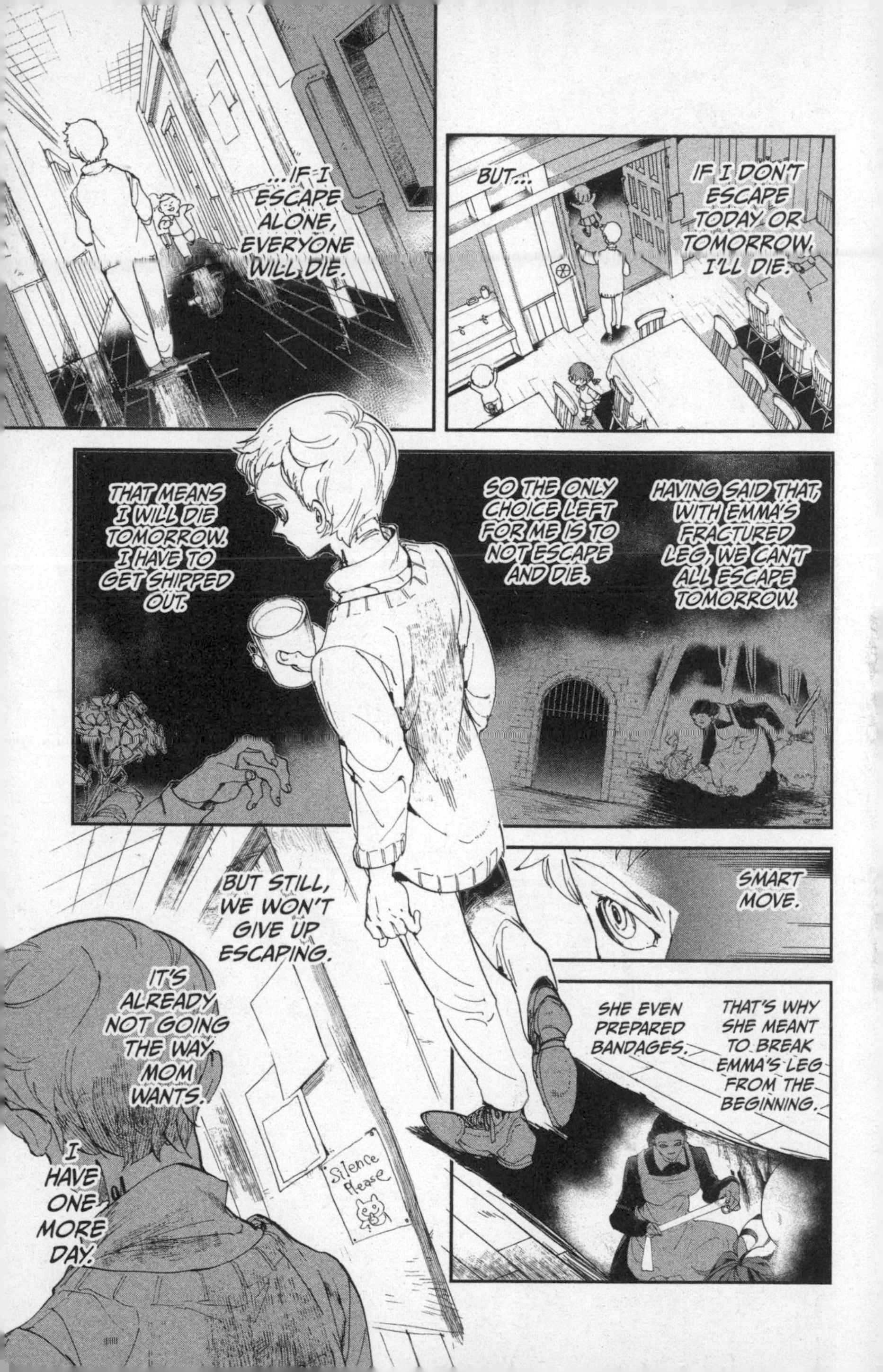
IF I DON'T ESCAPE TODAY OR TOMORROW, I'LL DIE.
BUT...
...IF I ESCAPE ALONE, EVERYONE WILL DIE.
HAVING SAID THAT, WITH EMMA'S FRACTURED LEG, WE CAN'T ALL ESCAPE TOMORROW.
SO THE ONLY CHOICE LEFT FOR ME IS TO NOT ESCAPE AND DIE.
THAT MEANS I WILL DIE TOMORROW. I HAVE TO GET SHIPPED OUT.
SMART MOVE.
THAT'S WHY SHE MEANT TO BREAK EMMA'S LEG FROM THE BEGINNING.
SHE EVEN PREPARED BANDAGES.
BUT STILL, WE WON'T GIVE UP ESCAPING.
IT'S ALREADY NOT GOING THE WAY MOM WANTS.
Silence Please
I HAVE ONE MORE DAY.

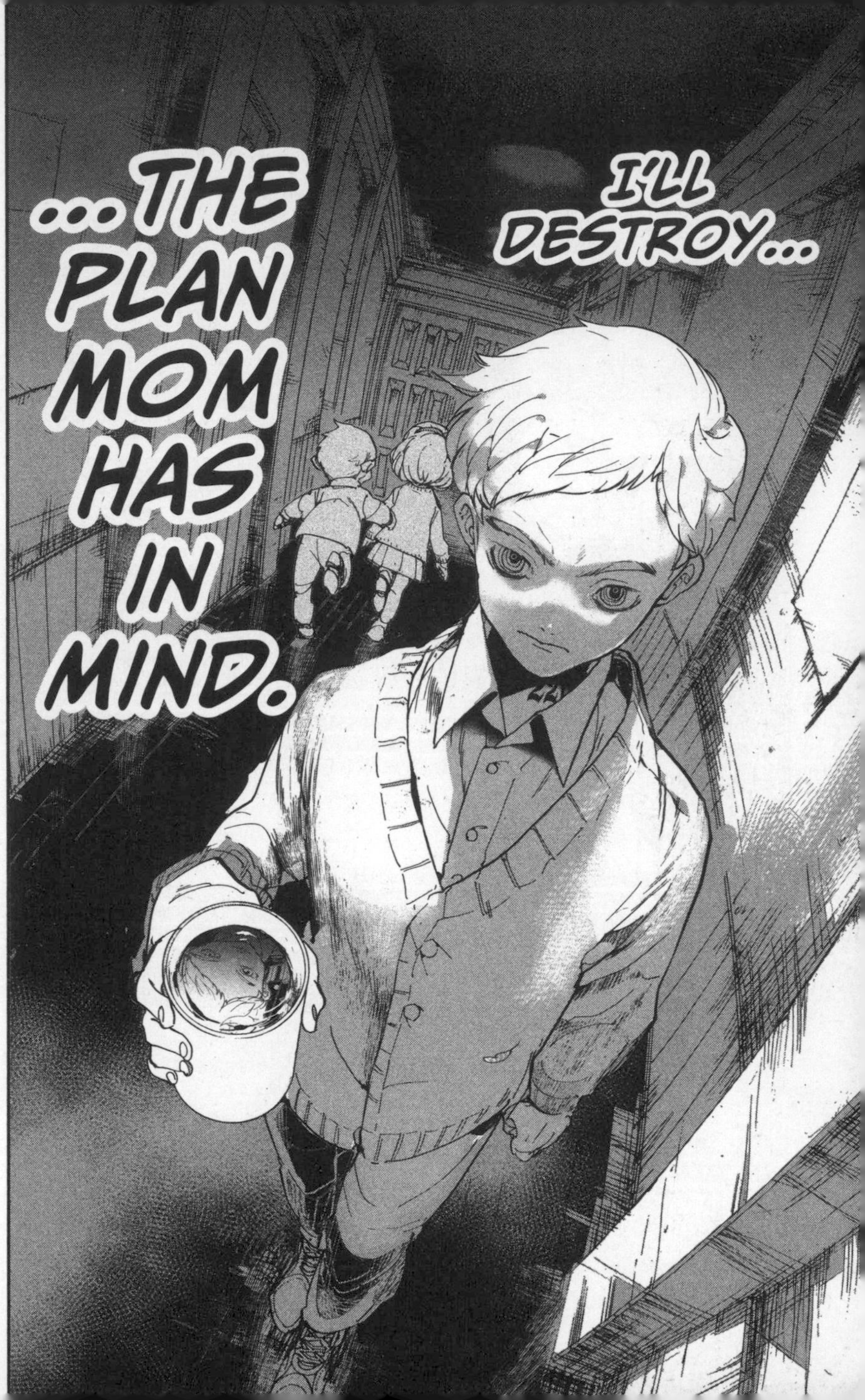
I'LL DESTROY...
...THE PLAN MOM HAS IN MIND.

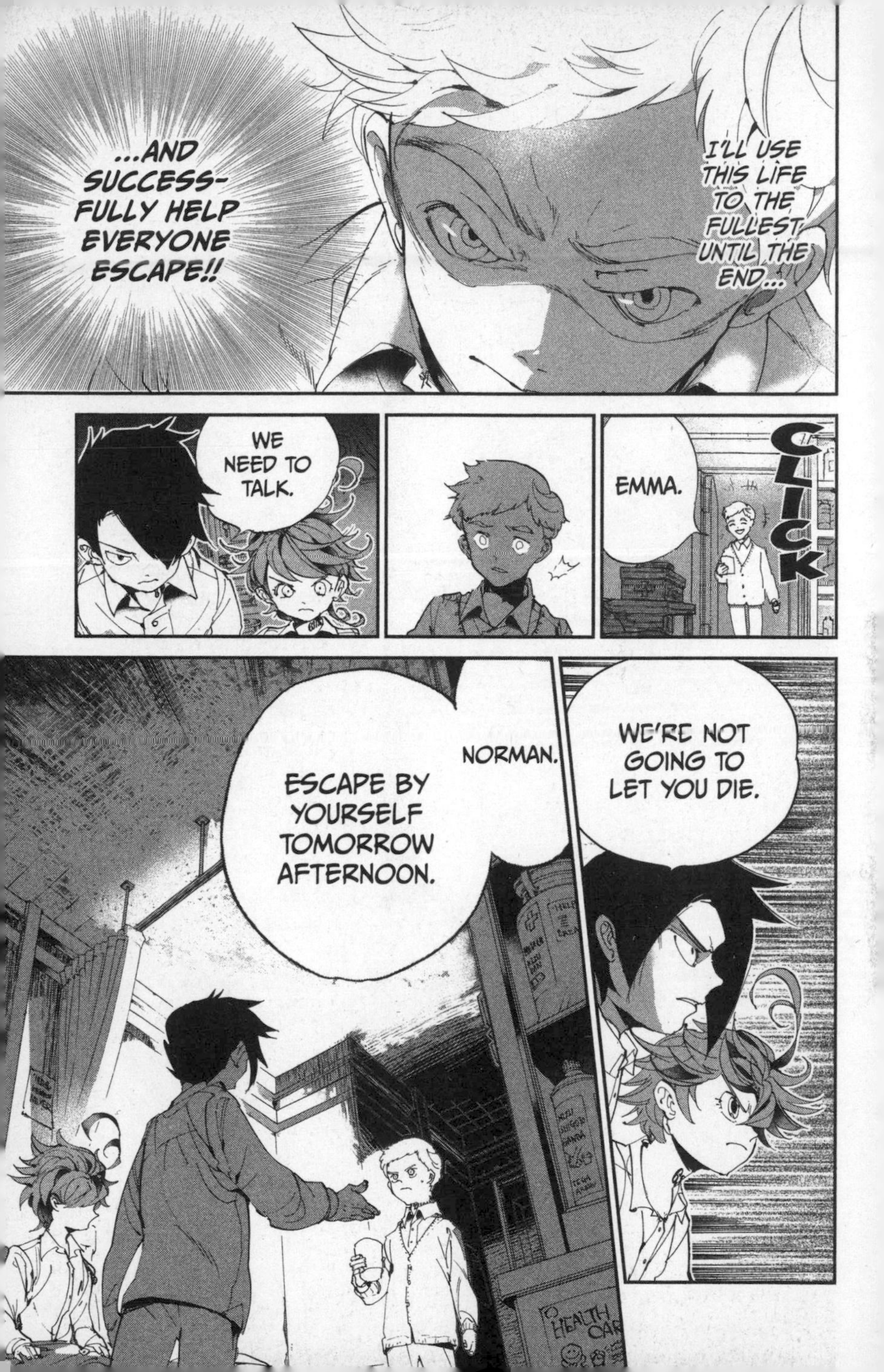
I'LL USE THIS LIFE TO THE FULLEST UNTIL THE END...
...AND SUCCESS-FULLY HELP EVERYONE ESCAPE!!
CLICK
EMMA.
WE NEED TO TALK.
WE'RE NOT GOING TO LET YOU DIE.
NORMAN.
ESCAPE BY YOURSELF TOMORROW AFTERNOON.

GRACE FIELD HOUSE ITEMS

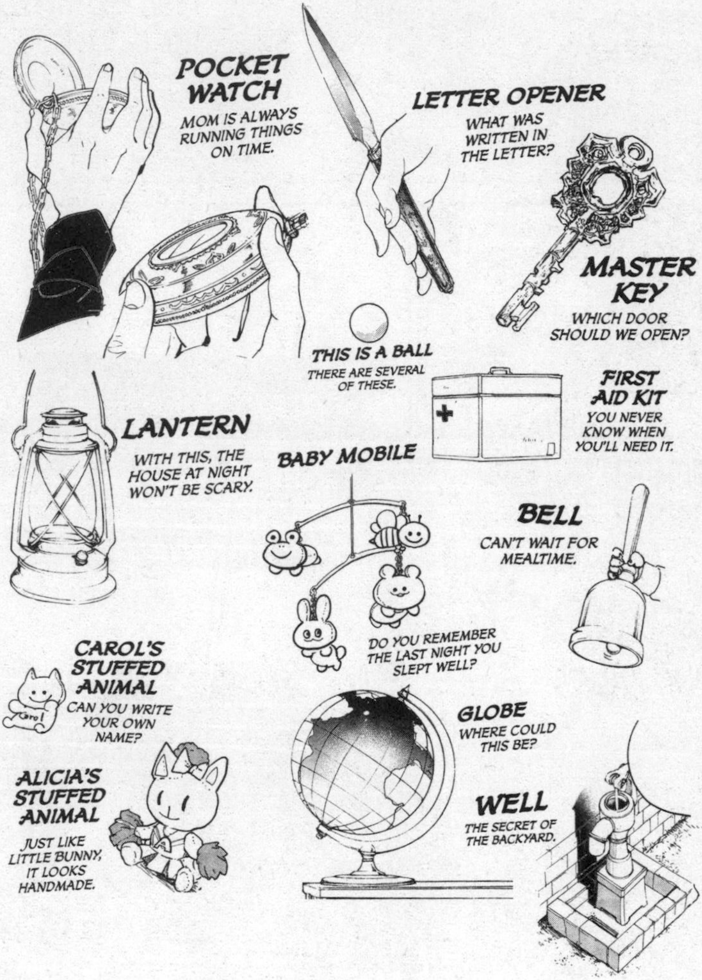
POCKET WATCH
MOM IS ALWAYS RUNNING THINGS ON TIME.
LETTER OPENER
WHAT WAS WRITTEN IN THE LETTER?
MASTER KEY
WHICH DOOR SHOULD WE OPEN?
THIS IS A BALL
THERE ARE SEVERAL OF THESE.
FIRST AID KIT
YOU NEVER KNOW WHEN YOU'LL NEED IT.
LANTERN
WITH THIS, THE HOUSE AT NIGHT WON'T BE SCARY.
BABY MOBILE
DO YOU REMEMBER THE LAST NIGHT YOU SLEPT WELL?
BELL
CAN'T WAIT FOR MEALTIME.
CAROL'S STUFFED ANIMAL
CAN YOU WRITE YOUR OWN NAME?
Carol
GLOBE
WHERE COULD THIS BE?
ALICIA'S STUFFED ANIMAL
JUST LIKE LITTLE BUNNY, IT LOOKS HANDMADE.
WELL
THE SECRET OF THE BACKYARD.

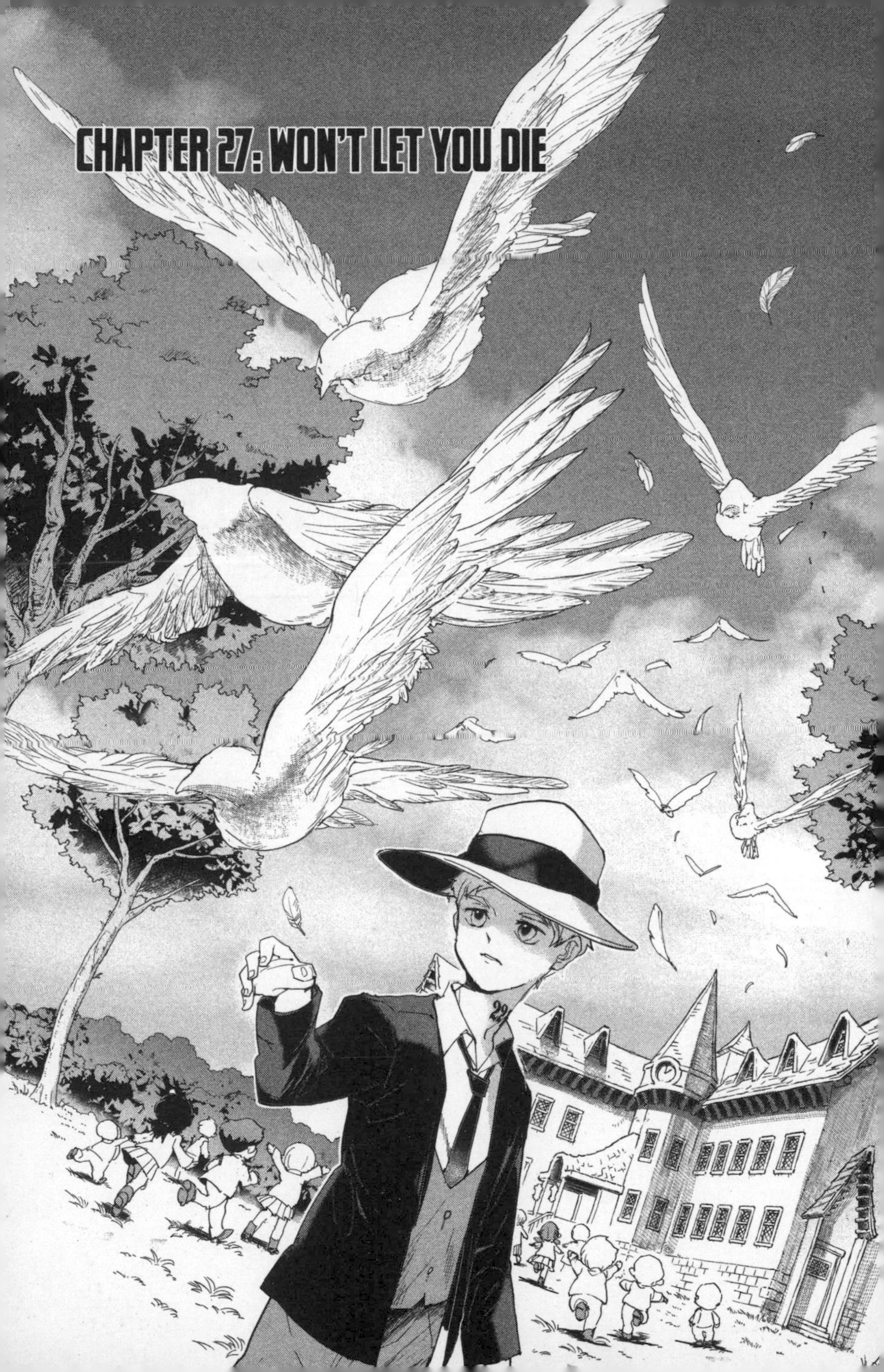
CHAPTER 27: WON'T LET YOU DIE

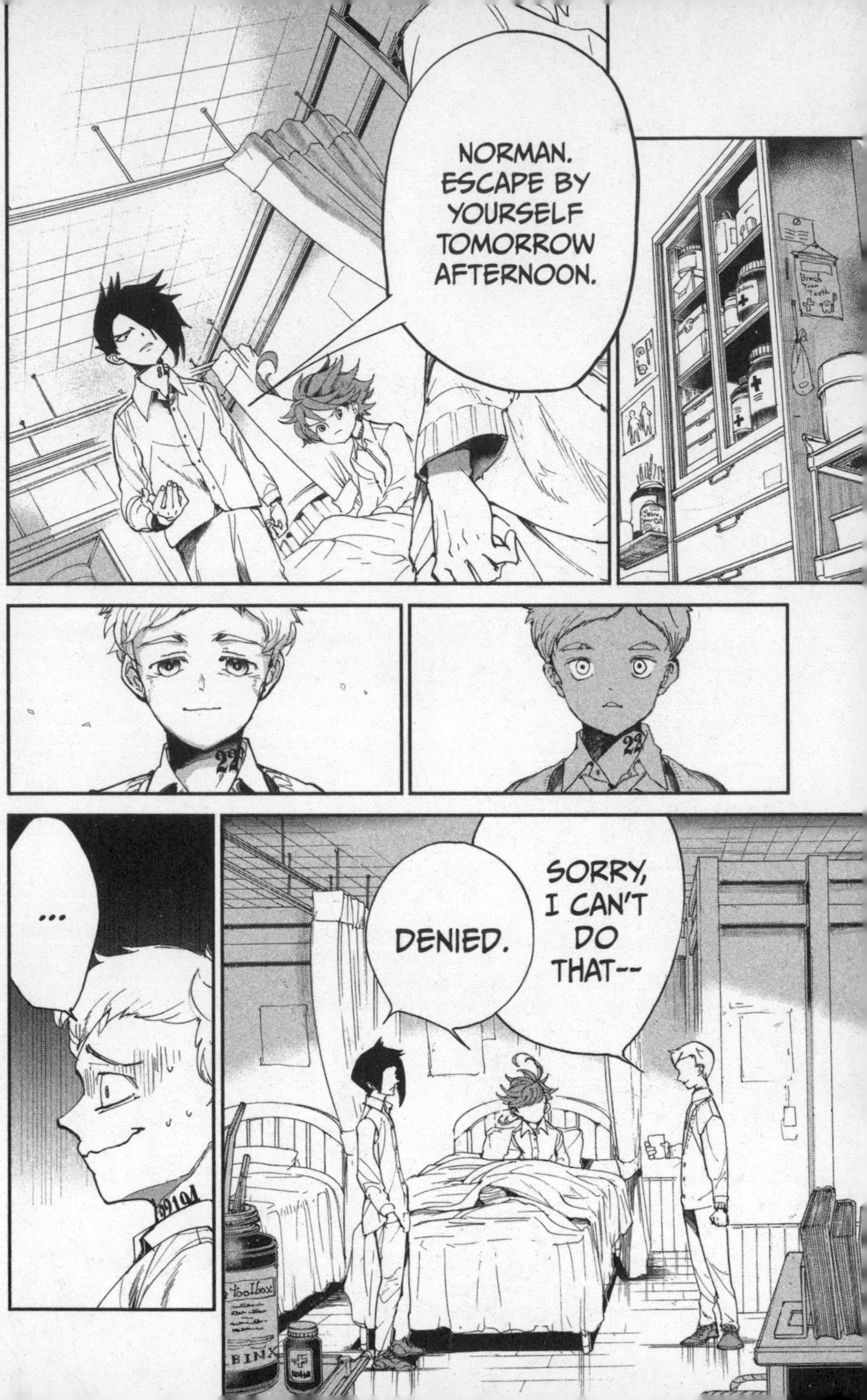
NORMAN. ESCAPE BY YOURSELF TOMORROW AFTERNOON.
SORRY, I CAN'T DO THAT--
DENIED.
...

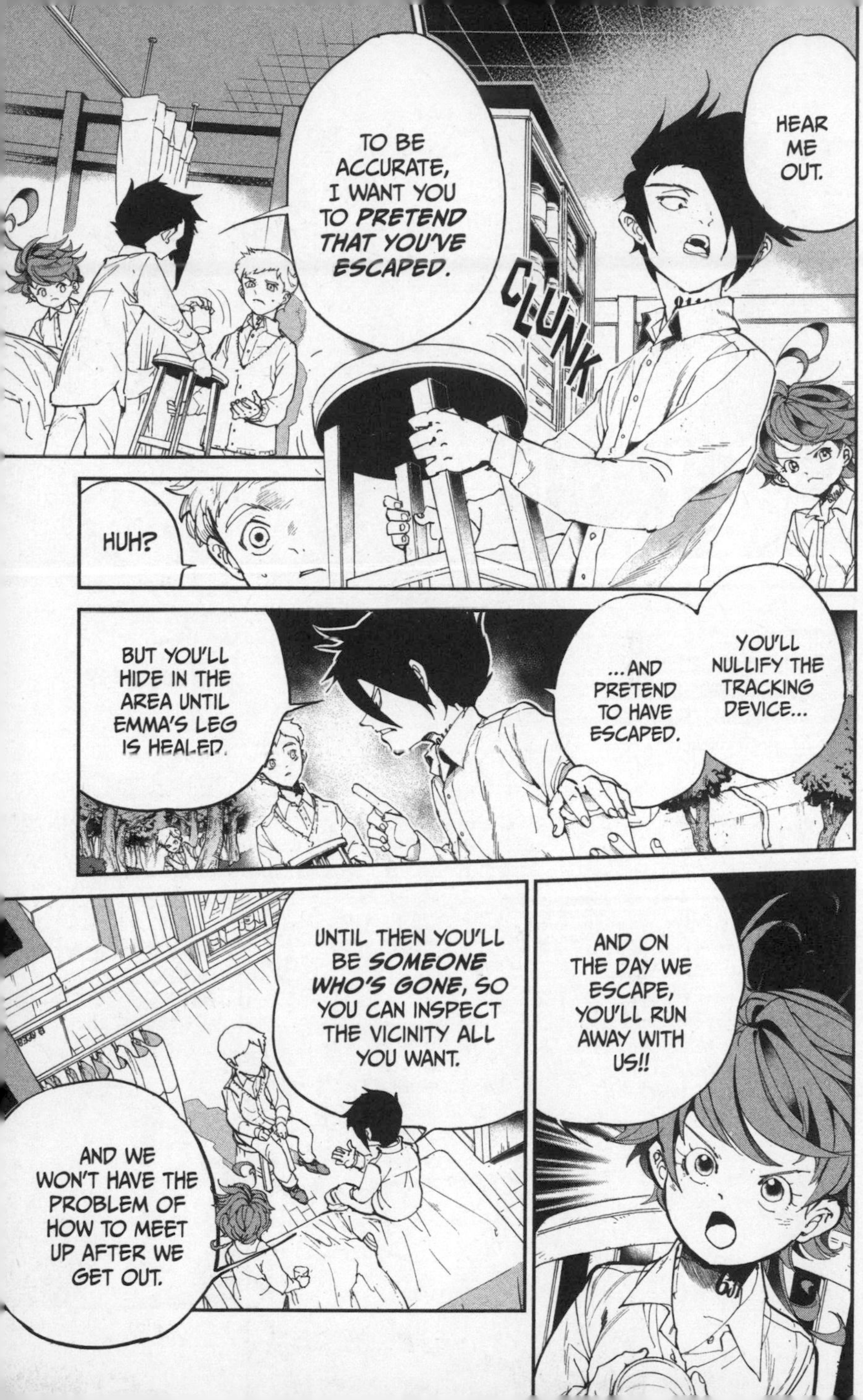
HEAR ME OUT.
CLUNK
TO BE ACCURATE, I WANT YOU TO *PRETEND* THAT YOU'VE *ESCAPED*.
HUH?
YOU'LL NULLIFY THE TRACKING DEVICE...
...AND PRETEND TO HAVE ESCAPED.
BUT YOU'LL HIDE IN THE AREA UNTIL EMMA'S LEG IS HEALED.
AND ON THE DAY WE ESCAPE, YOU'LL RUN AWAY WITH US!!
UNTIL THEN YOU'LL BE *SOMEONE WHO'S GONE*, SO YOU CAN INSPECT THE VICINITY ALL YOU WANT.
AND WE WON'T HAVE THE PROBLEM OF HOW TO MEET UP AFTER WE GET OUT.

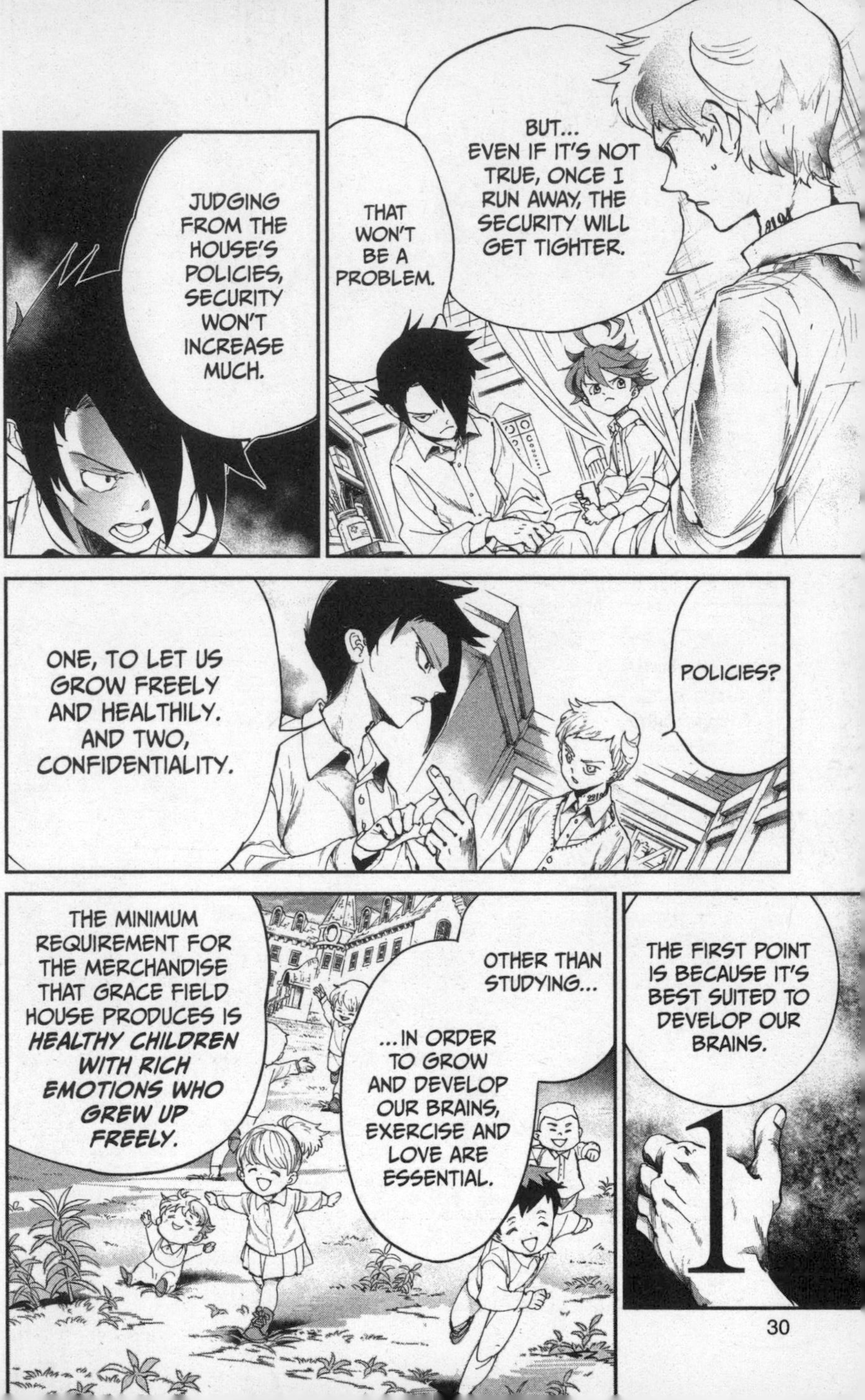

BUT... EVEN IF IT'S NOT TRUE, ONCE I RUN AWAY, THE SECURITY WILL GET TIGHTER.
THAT WON'T BE A PROBLEM.
JUDGING FROM THE HOUSE'S POLICIES, SECURITY WON'T INCREASE MUCH.
POLICIES?
ONE, TO LET US GROW FREELY AND HEALTHILY. AND TWO, CONFIDENTIALITY.
THE FIRST POINT IS BECAUSE IT'S BEST SUITED TO DEVELOP OUR BRAINS.
1
OTHER THAN STUDYING...
...IN ORDER TO GROW AND DEVELOP OUR BRAINS, EXERCISE AND LOVE ARE ESSENTIAL.
THE MINIMUM REQUIREMENT FOR THE MERCHANDISE THAT GRACE FIELD HOUSE PRODUCES IS *HEALTHY CHILDREN WITH RICH EMOTIONS WHO GREW UP FREELY.*

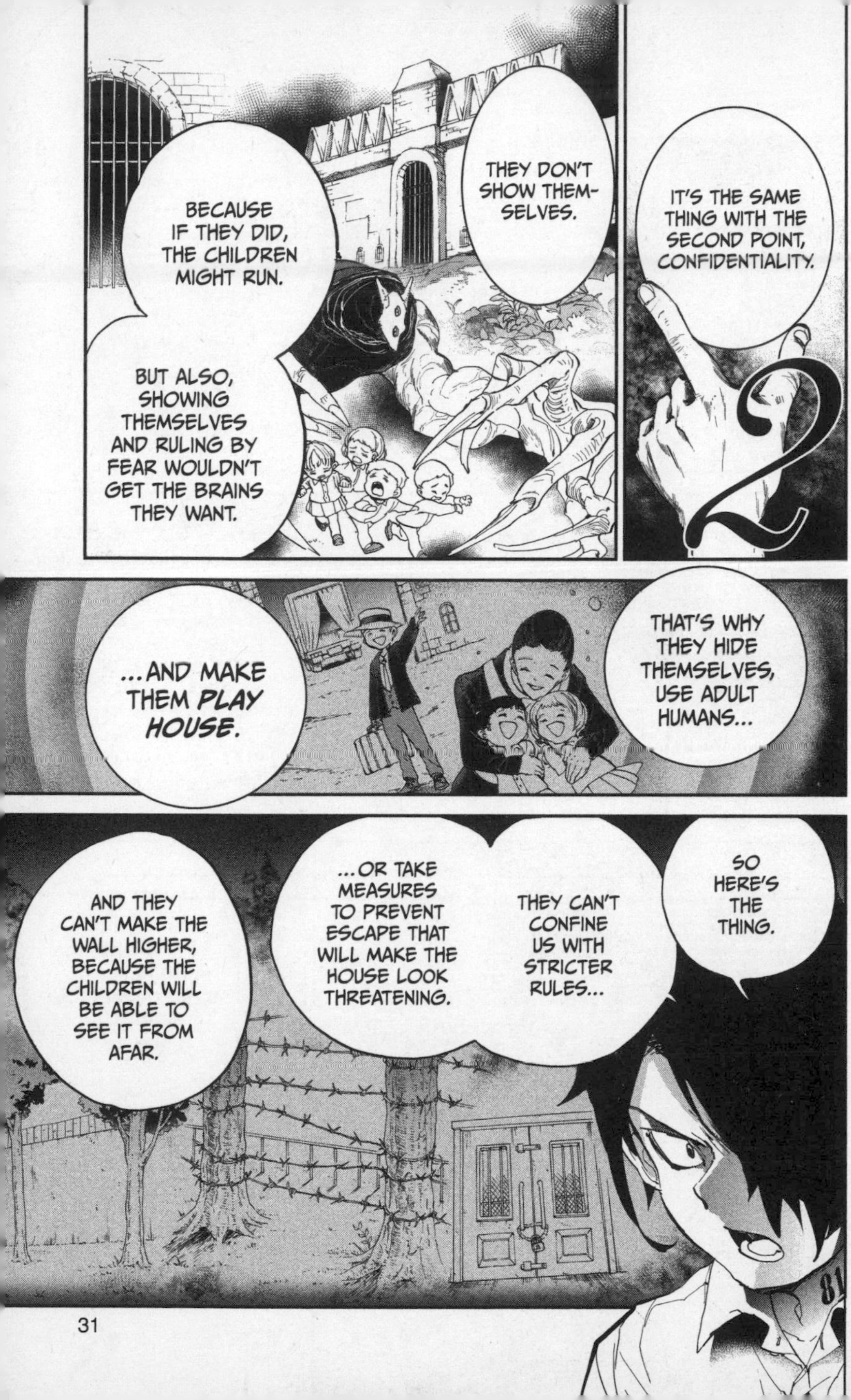
IT'S THE SAME THING WITH THE SECOND POINT, CONFIDENTIALITY.
2
THEY DON'T SHOW THEM-SELVES.
BECAUSE IF THEY DID, THE CHILDREN MIGHT RUN.
BUT ALSO, SHOWING THEMSELVES AND RULING BY FEAR WOULDN'T GET THE BRAINS THEY WANT.
THAT'S WHY THEY HIDE THEMSELVES, USE ADULT HUMANS...
...AND MAKE THEM *PLAY HOUSE*.
SO HERE'S THE THING.
THEY CAN'T CONFINE US WITH STRICTER RULES...
...OR TAKE MEASURES TO PREVENT ESCAPE THAT WILL MAKE THE HOUSE LOOK THREATENING.
AND THEY CAN'T MAKE THE WALL HIGHER, BECAUSE THE CHILDREN WILL BE ABLE TO SEE IT FROM AFAR.
81

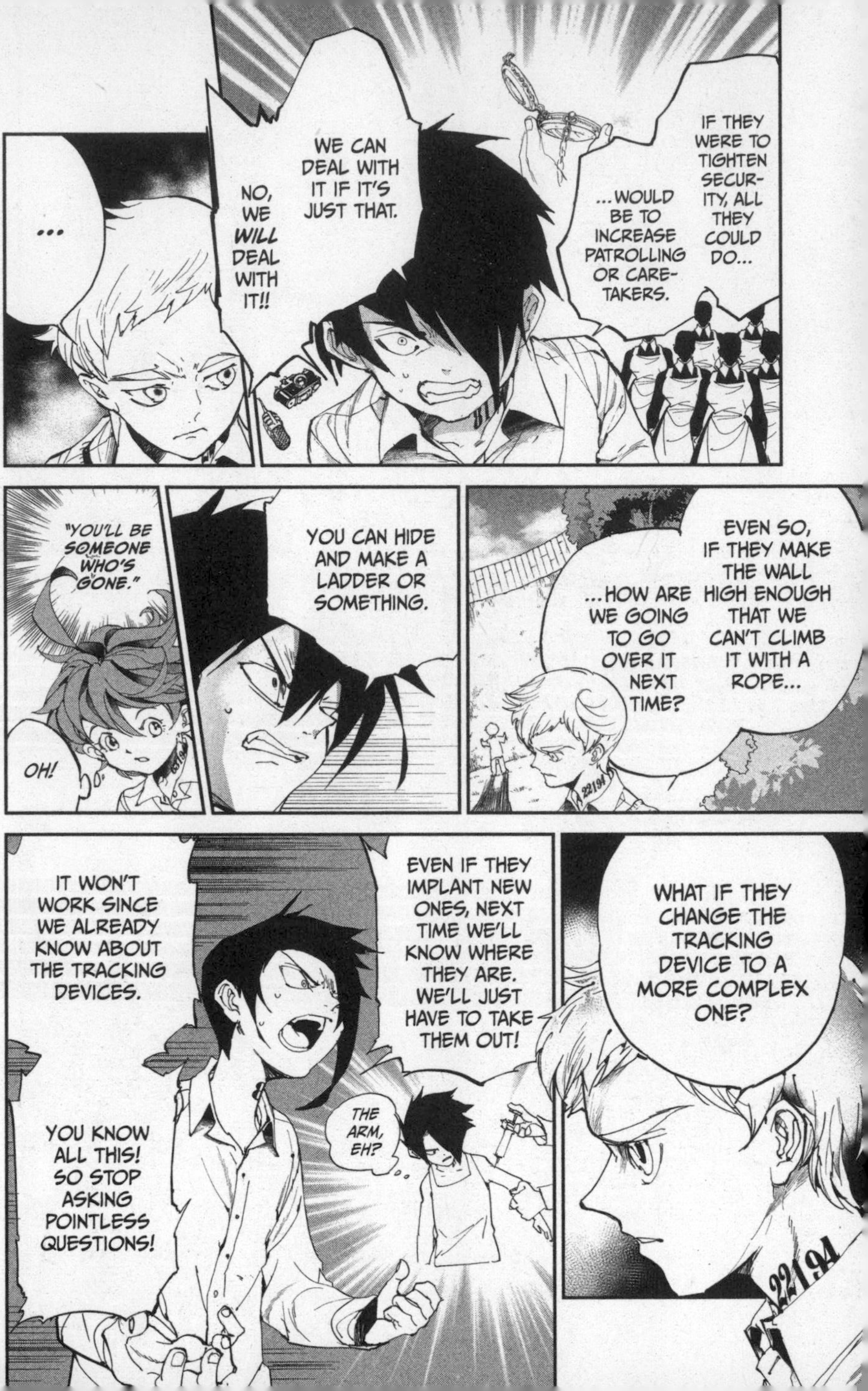
IF THEY WERE TO TIGHTEN SECURITY, ALL THEY COULD DO...
...WOULD BE TO INCREASE PATROLLING OR CARETAKERS.
WE CAN DEAL WITH IT IF IT'S JUST THAT.
NO, WE *WILL* DEAL WITH IT!!
...
EVEN SO, IF THEY MAKE THE WALL HIGH ENOUGH THAT WE CAN'T CLIMB IT WITH A ROPE...
...HOW ARE WE GOING TO GO OVER IT NEXT TIME?
YOU CAN HIDE AND MAKE A LADDER OR SOMETHING.
"YOU'LL BE SOMEONE WHO'S GONE."
OH!
WHAT IF THEY CHANGE THE TRACKING DEVICE TO A MORE COMPLEX ONE?
IT WON'T WORK SINCE WE ALREADY KNOW ABOUT THE TRACKING DEVICES.
EVEN IF THEY IMPLANT NEW ONES, NEXT TIME WE'LL KNOW WHERE THEY ARE. WE'LL JUST HAVE TO TAKE THEM OUT!
THE ARM, EH?
YOU KNOW ALL THIS! SO STOP ASKING POINTLESS QUESTIONS!

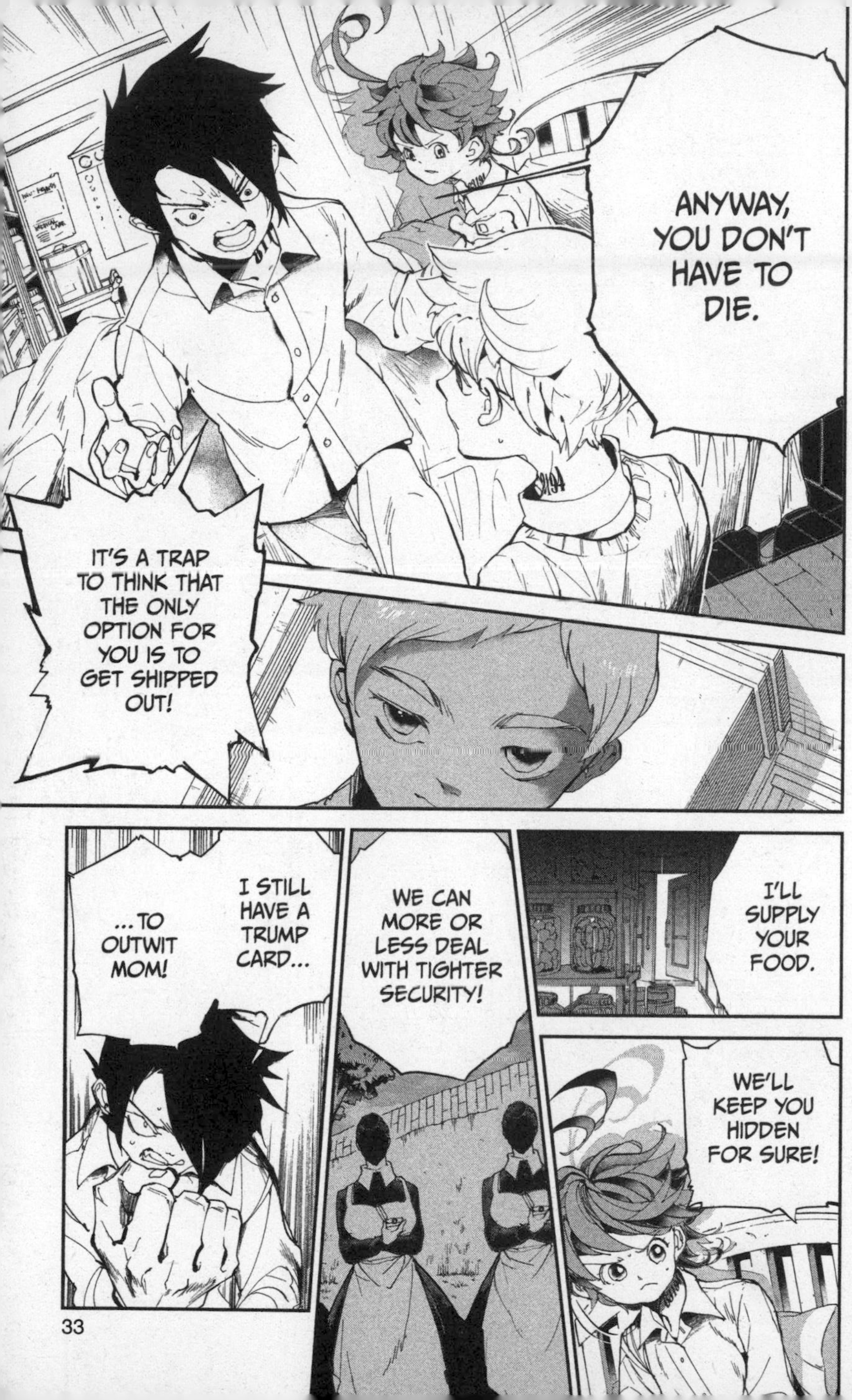
ANYWAY, YOU DON'T HAVE TO DIE.
IT'S A TRAP TO THINK THAT THE ONLY OPTION FOR YOU IS TO GET SHIPPED OUT!
I'LL SUPPLY YOUR FOOD.
WE'LL KEEP YOU HIDDEN FOR SURE!
WE CAN MORE OR LESS DEAL WITH TIGHTER SECURITY!
I STILL HAVE A TRUMP CARD...
...TO OUTWIT MOM!

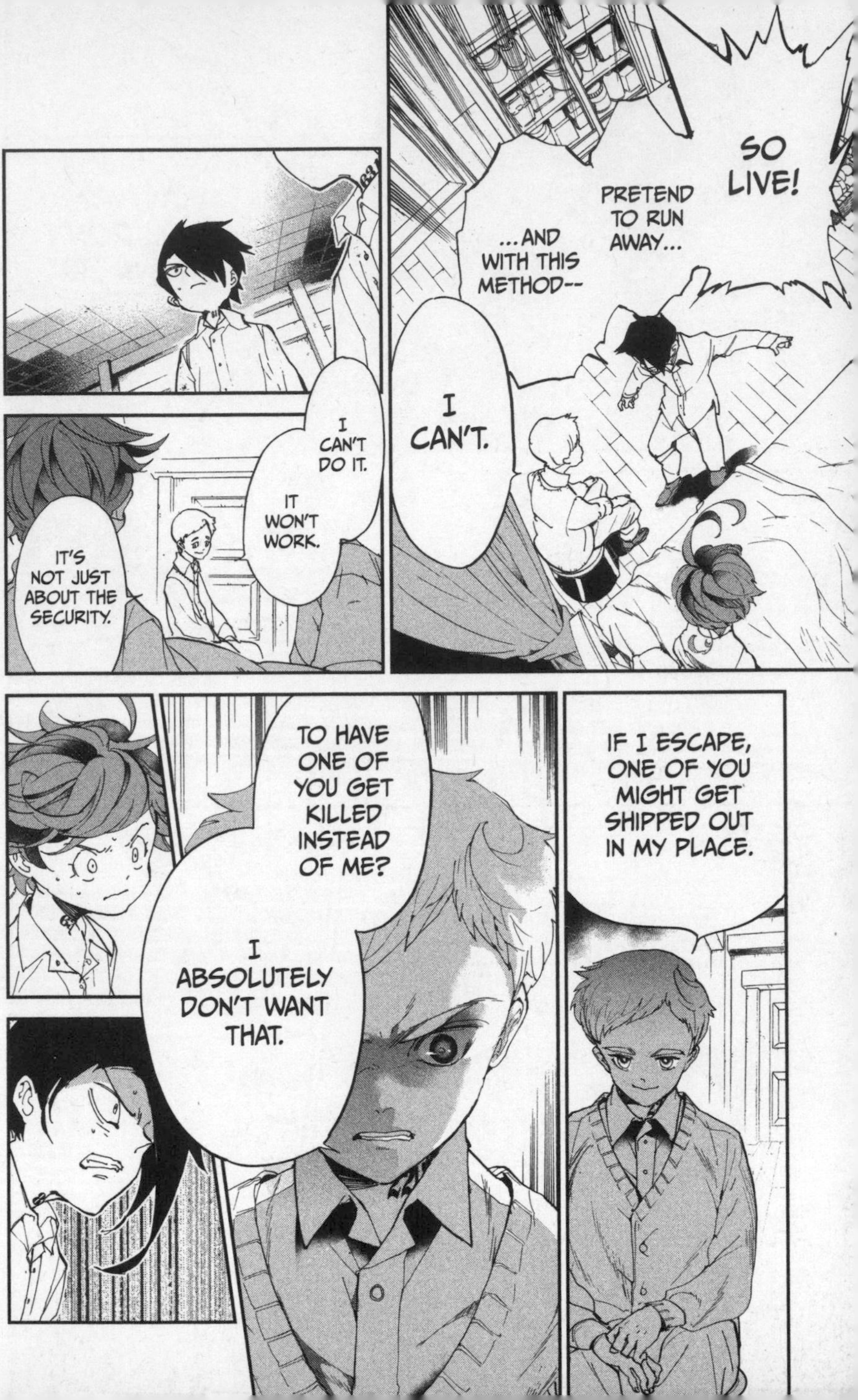
SO LIVE!
PRETEND TO RUN AWAY...
...AND WITH THIS METHOD--
I CAN'T.
I CAN'T DO IT.
IT WON'T WORK.
IT'S NOT JUST ABOUT THE SECURITY.
IF I ESCAPE, ONE OF YOU MIGHT GET SHIPPED OUT IN MY PLACE.
TO HAVE ONE OF YOU GET KILLED INSTEAD OF ME?
I ABSOLUTELY DON'T WANT THAT.

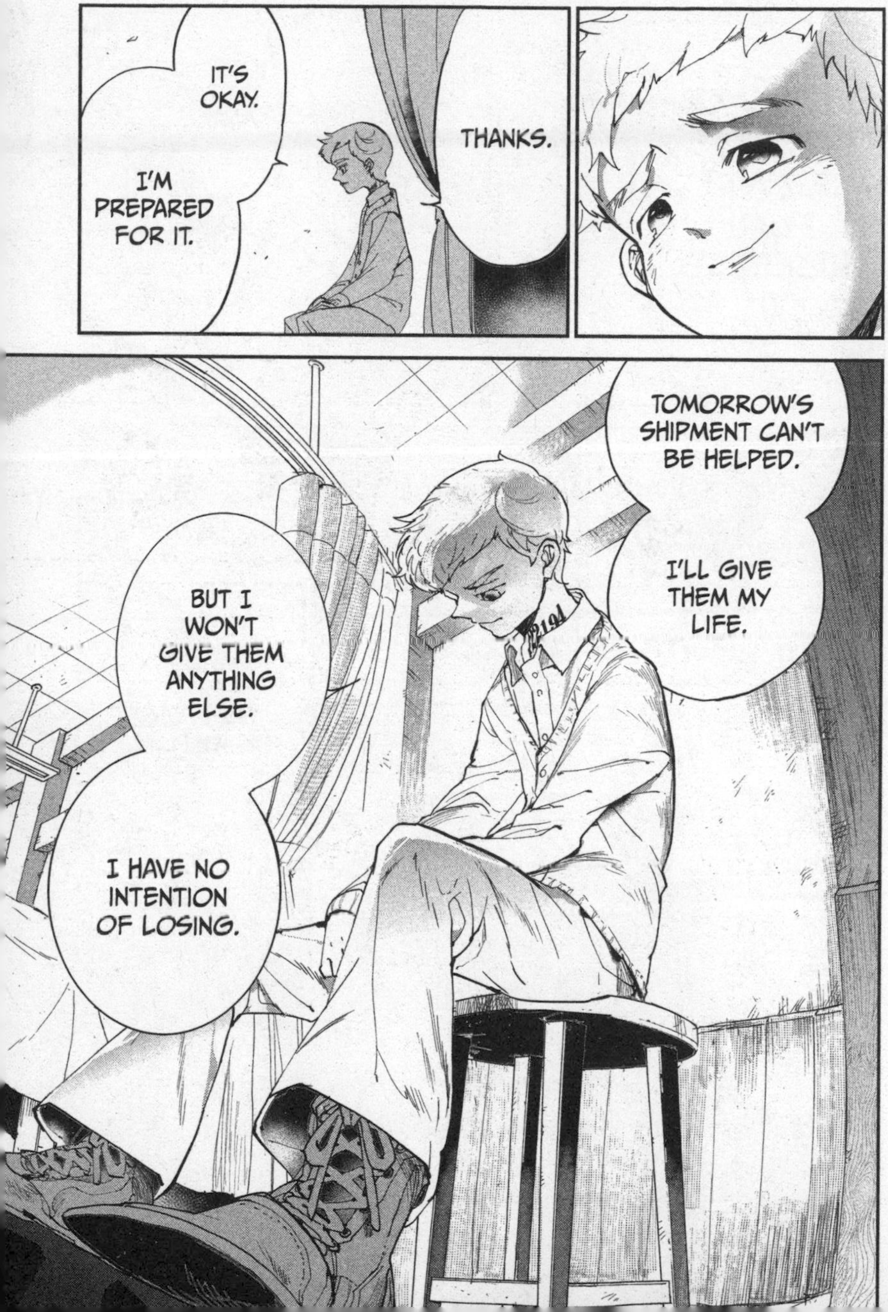
THANKS.
IT'S OKAY.
I'M PREPARED FOR IT.
TOMORROW'S SHIPMENT CAN'T BE HELPED.
I'LL GIVE THEM MY LIFE.
BUT I WON'T GIVE THEM ANYTHING ELSE.
I HAVE NO INTENTION OF LOSING.

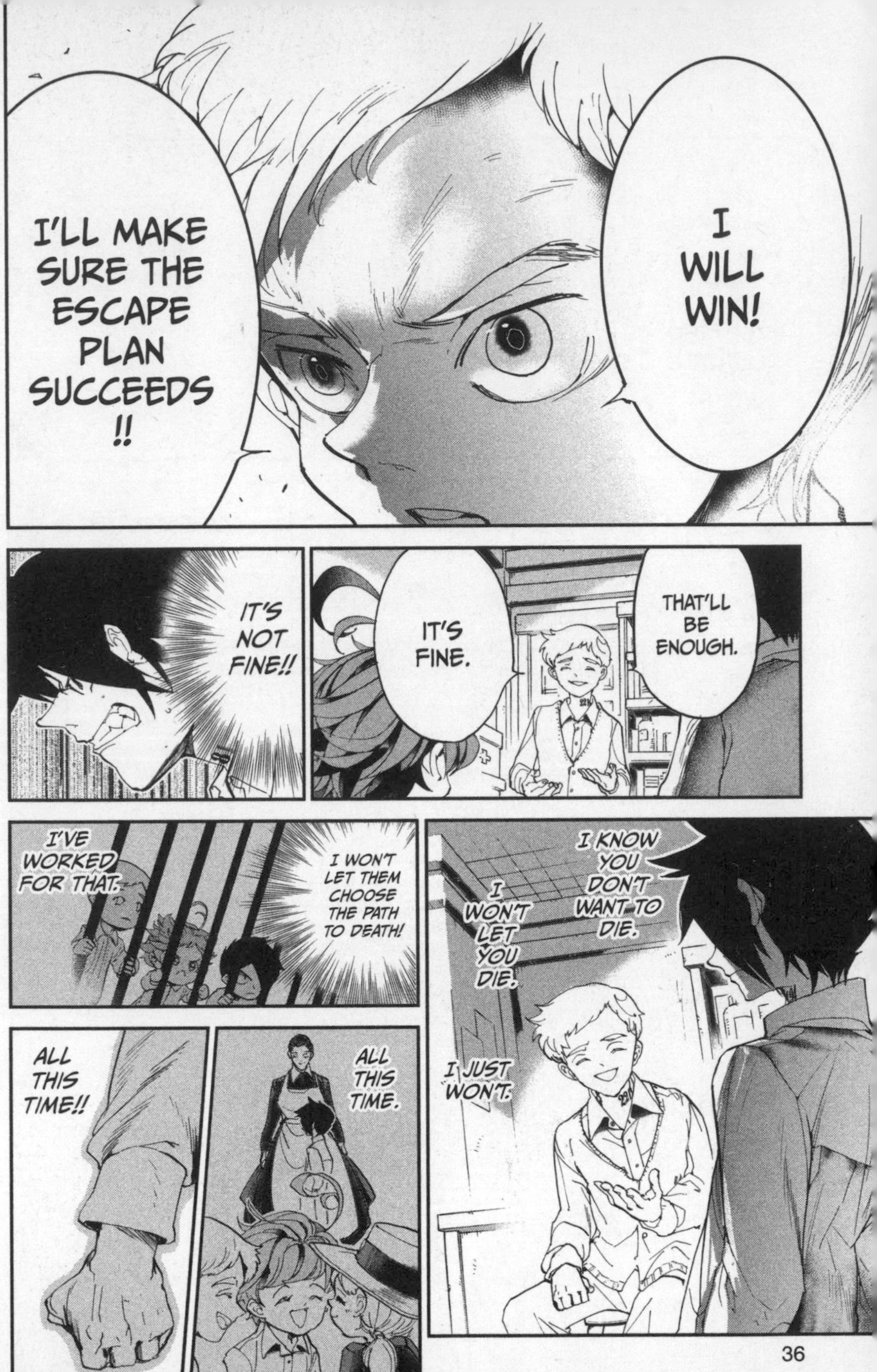
I WILL WIN!
I'LL MAKE SURE THE ESCAPE PLAN SUCCEEDS!!
THAT'LL BE ENOUGH.
IT'S FINE.
IT'S NOT FINE!!
I KNOW YOU DON'T WANT TO DIE.
I WON'T LET YOU DIE.
I JUST WON'T.
I WON'T LET THEM CHOOSE THE PATH TO DEATH!
I'VE WORKED FOR THAT.
ALL THIS TIME.
ALL THIS TIME!!

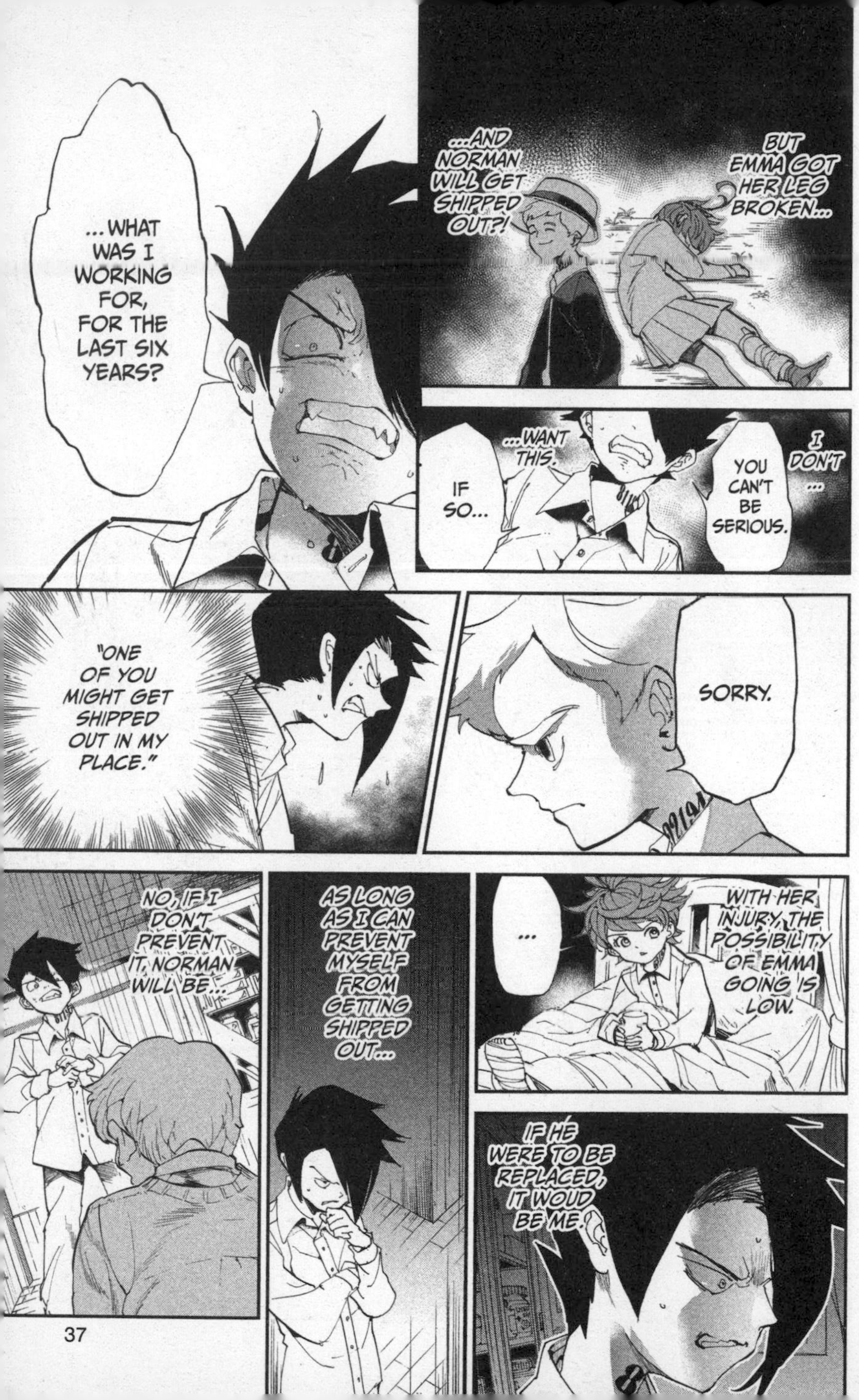
BUT EMMA GOT HER LEG BROKEN...
...AND NORMAN WILL GET SHIPPED OUT?!
I DON'T...
YOU CAN'T BE SERIOUS.
...WANT THIS.
IF SO...
...WHAT WAS I WORKING FOR, FOR THE LAST SIX YEARS?
SORRY.
"ONE OF YOU MIGHT GET SHIPPED OUT IN MY PLACE."
WITH HER INJURY, THE POSSIBILITY OF EMMA GOING IS LOW.
...
IF HE WERE TO BE REPLACED, IT WOUD BE ME.
AS LONG AS I CAN PREVENT MYSELF FROM GETTING SHIPPED OUT...
NO, IF I DON'T PREVENT IT, NORMAN WILL BE...

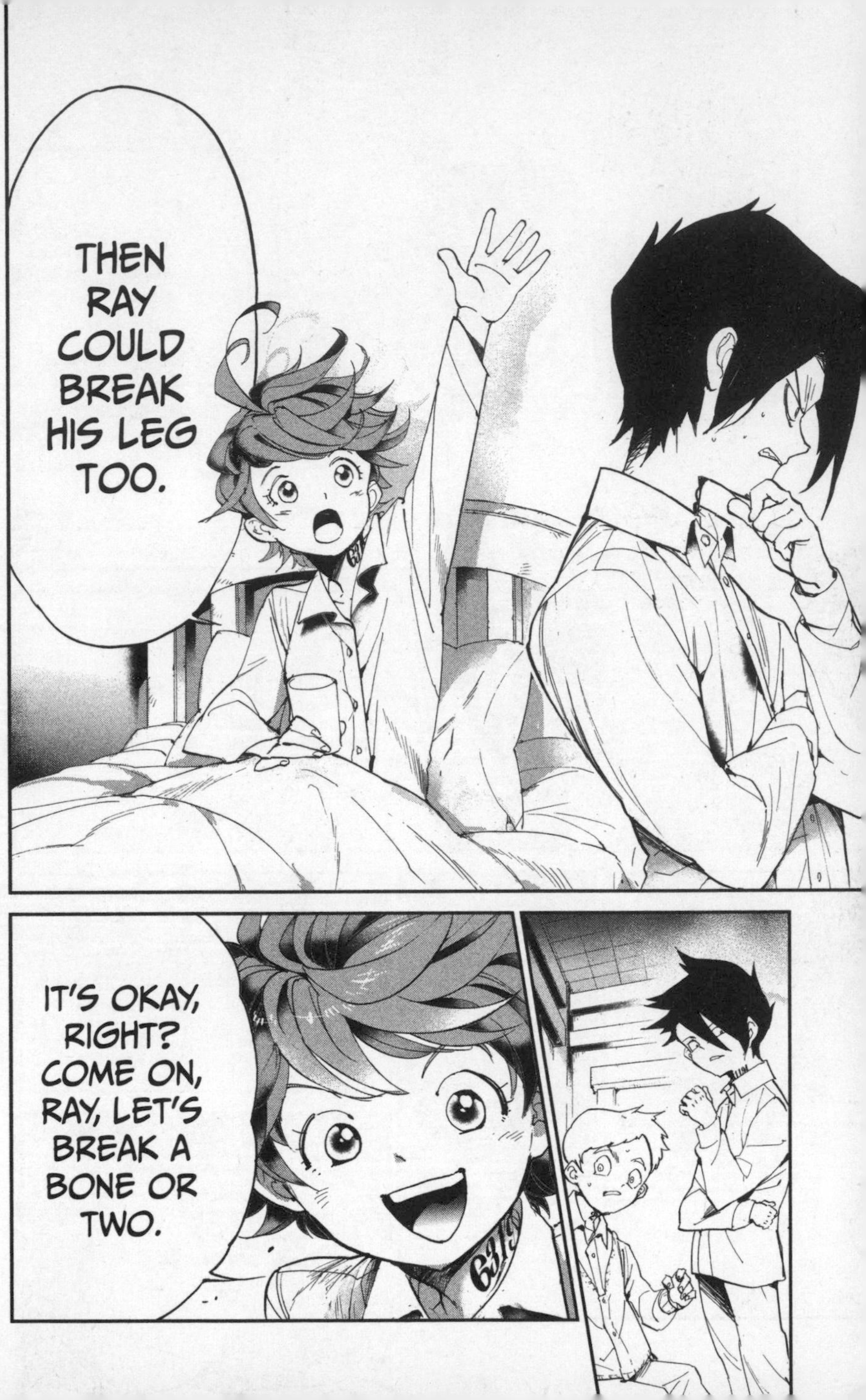
THEN RAY COULD BREAK HIS LEG TOO.
IT'S OKAY, RIGHT? COME ON, RAY, LET'S BREAK A BONE OR TWO.

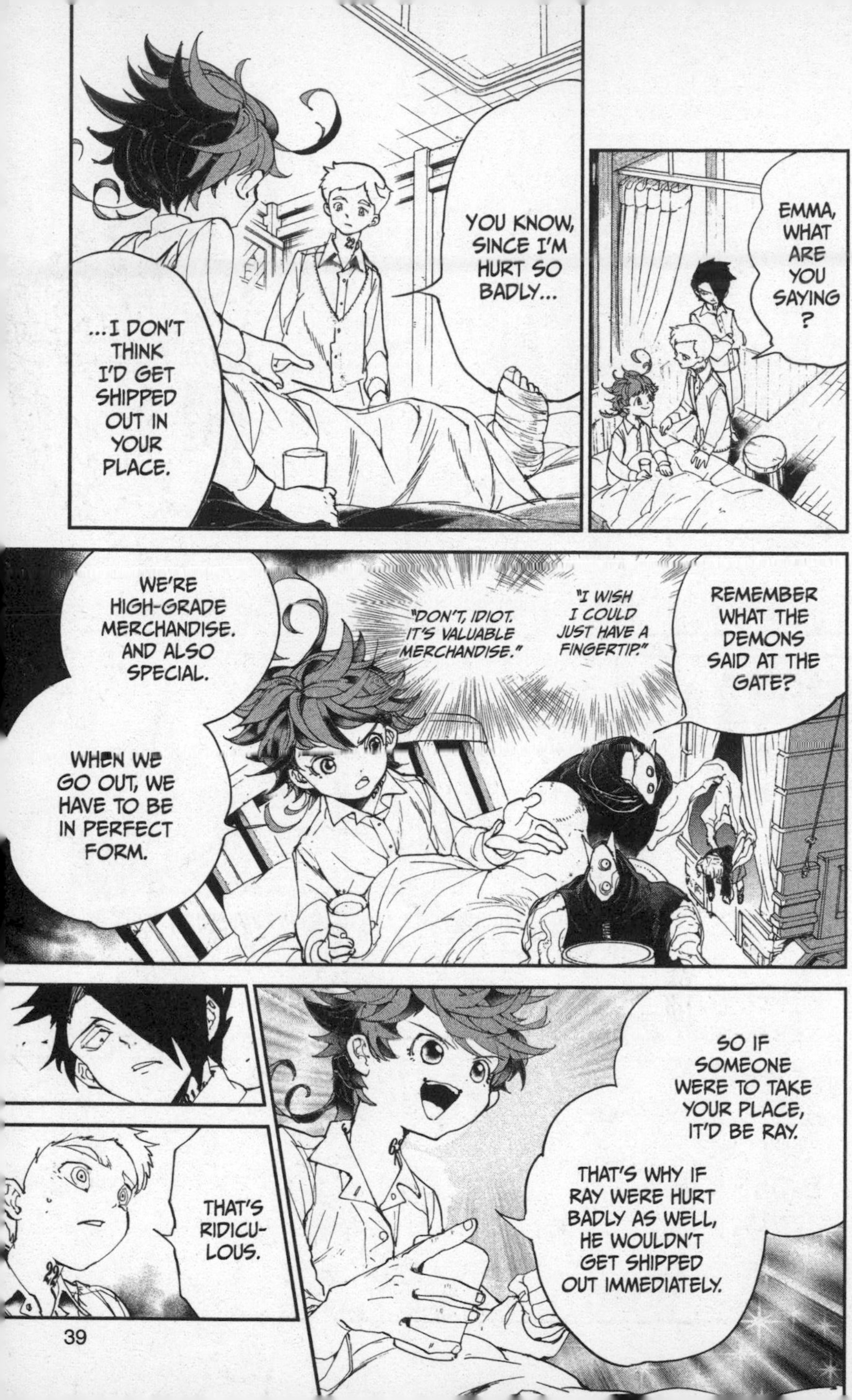
EMMA, WHAT ARE YOU SAYING?
YOU KNOW, SINCE I'M HURT SO BADLY...
...I DON'T THINK I'D GET SHIPPED OUT IN YOUR PLACE.
REMEMBER WHAT THE DEMONS SAID AT THE GATE?
"I WISH I COULD JUST HAVE A FINGERTIP."
"DON'T, IDIOT. IT'S VALUABLE MERCHANDISE."
WE'RE HIGH-GRADE MERCHANDISE. AND ALSO SPECIAL.
WHEN WE GO OUT, WE HAVE TO BE IN PERFECT FORM.
SO IF SOMEONE WERE TO TAKE YOUR PLACE, IT'D BE RAY.
THAT'S WHY IF RAY WERE HURT BADLY AS WELL, HE WOULDN'T GET SHIPPED OUT IMMEDIATELY.
THAT'S RIDICU-LOUS.

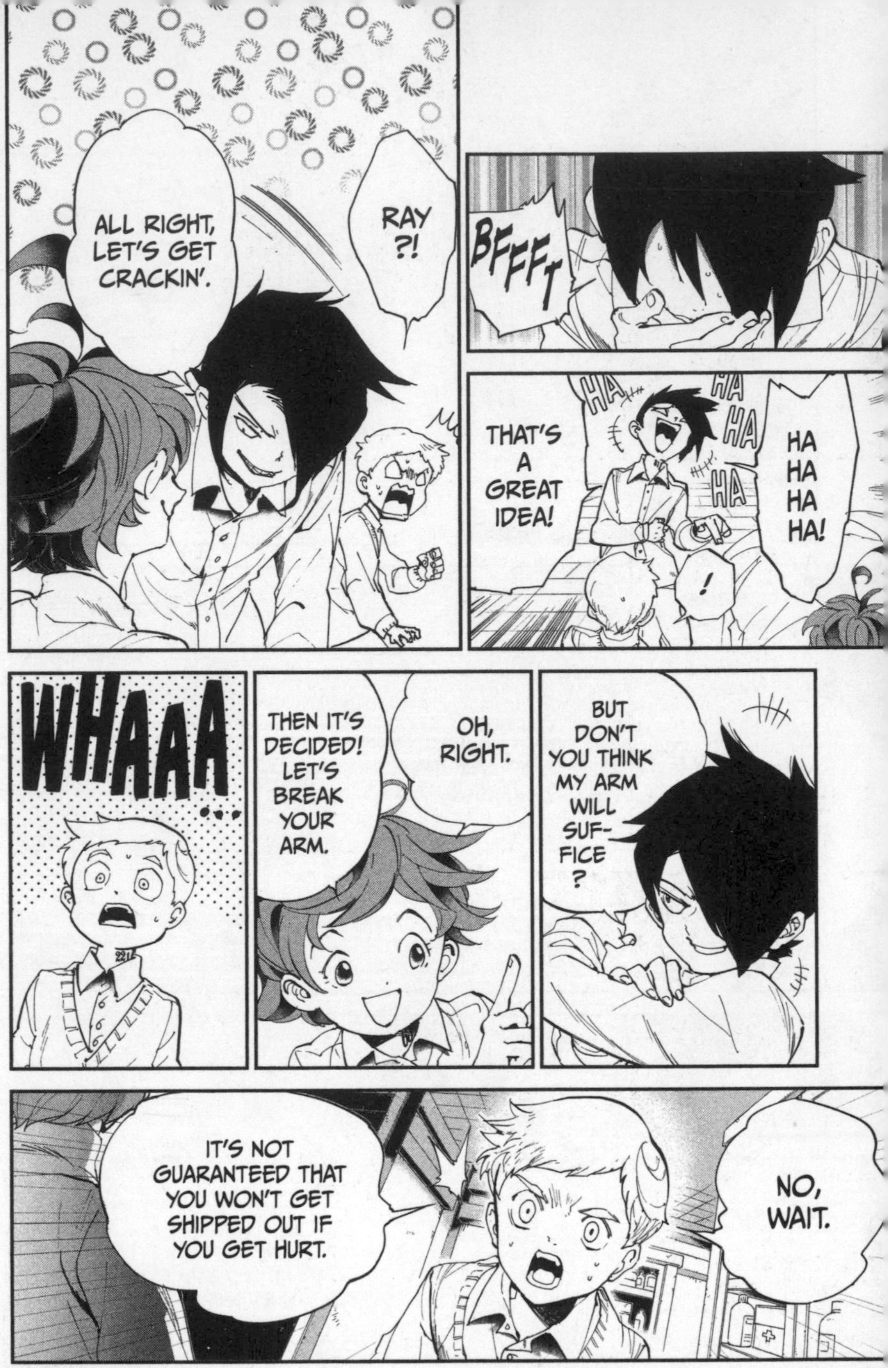
BFFFT
HA HA HA HA!
HA HA HA HA
THAT'S A GREAT IDEA!
!
RAY ?!
ALL RIGHT, LET'S GET CRACKIN'.
BUT DON'T YOU THINK MY ARM WILL SUF-FICE ?
OH, RIGHT.
THEN IT'S DECIDED! LET'S BREAK YOUR ARM.
WHAAA...
NO, WAIT.
IT'S NOT GUARANTEED THAT YOU WON'T GET SHIPPED OUT IF YOU GET HURT.

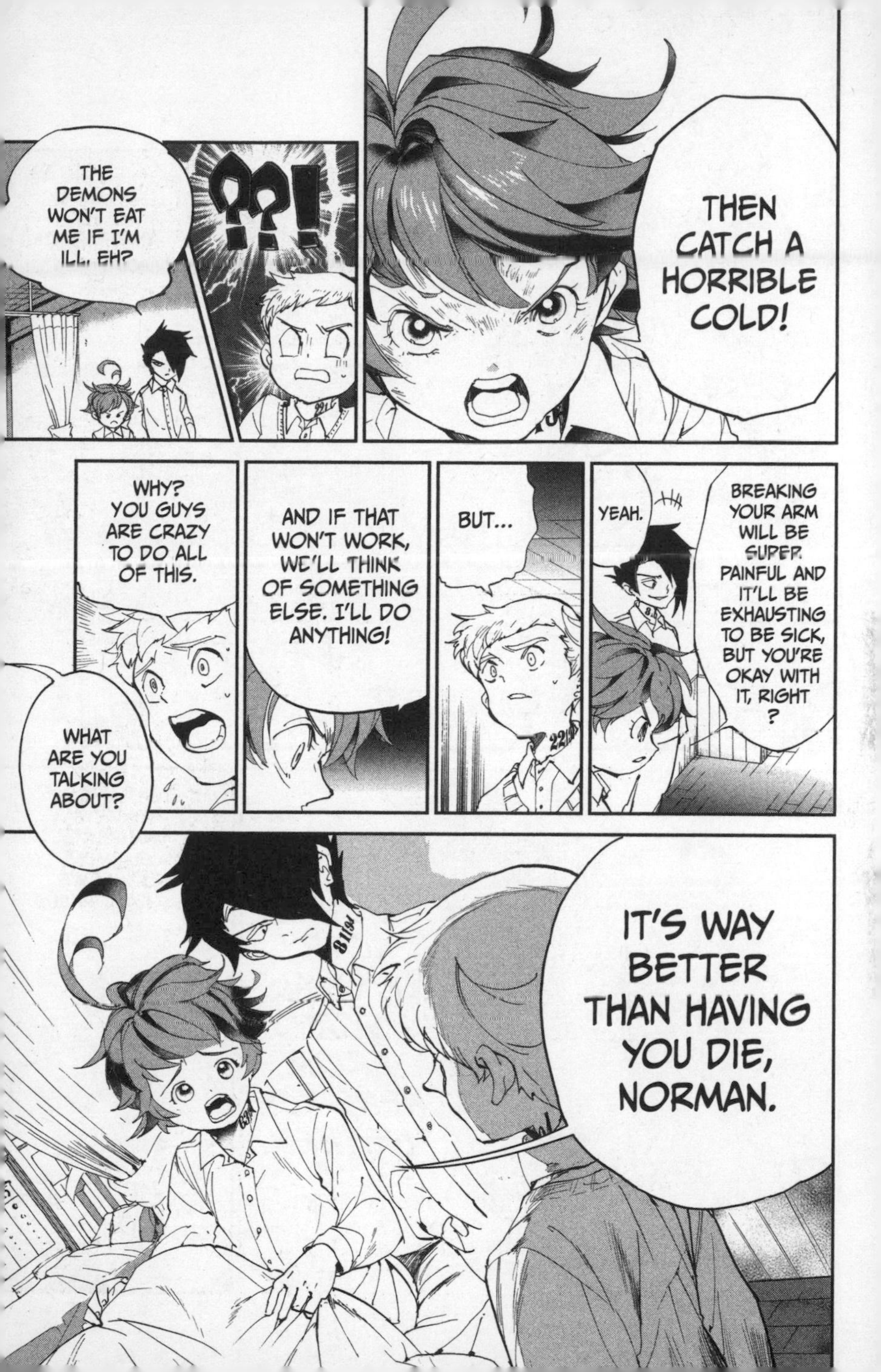
THEN CATCH A HORRIBLE COLD!
??!
THE DEMONS WON'T EAT ME IF I'M ILL, EH?
BREAKING YOUR ARM WILL BE SUPER PAINFUL AND IT'LL BE EXHAUSTING TO BE SICK, BUT YOU'RE OKAY WITH IT, RIGHT?
YEAH.
BUT...
AND IF THAT WON'T WORK, WE'LL THINK OF SOMETHING ELSE. I'LL DO ANYTHING!
WHY? YOU GUYS ARE CRAZY TO DO ALL OF THIS.
WHAT ARE YOU TALKING ABOUT?
IT'S WAY BETTER THAN HAVING YOU DIE, NORMAN.

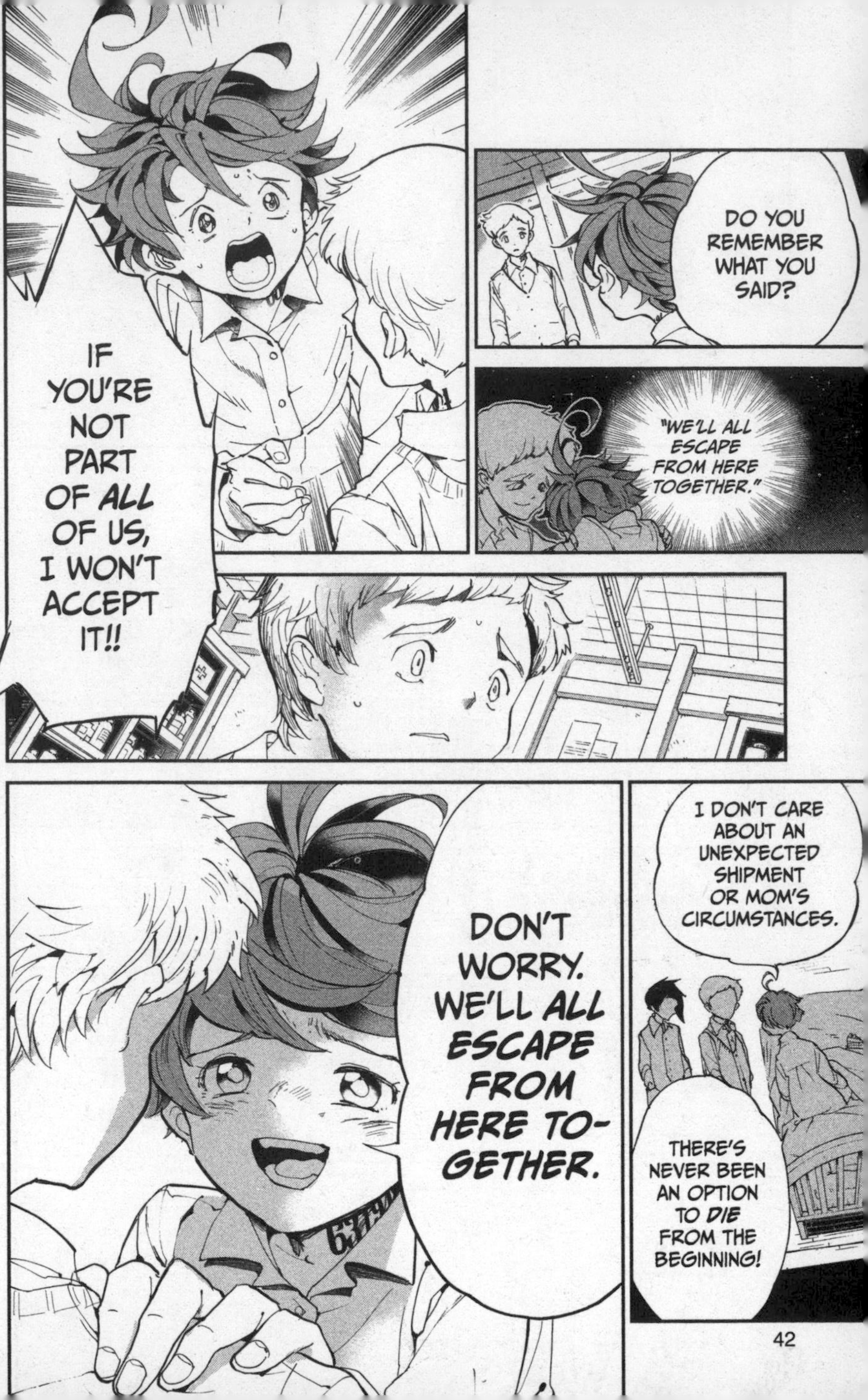
DO YOU REMEMBER WHAT YOU SAID?
"WE'LL ALL ESCAPE FROM HERE TOGETHER."
IF YOU'RE NOT PART OF *ALL* OF US, I WON'T ACCEPT IT!!
I DON'T CARE ABOUT AN UNEXPECTED SHIPMENT OR MOM'S CIRCUMSTANCES.
THERE'S NEVER BEEN AN OPTION TO *DIE* FROM THE BEGINNING!
DON'T WORRY. WE'LL *ALL ESCAPE FROM HERE TO-GETHER.*

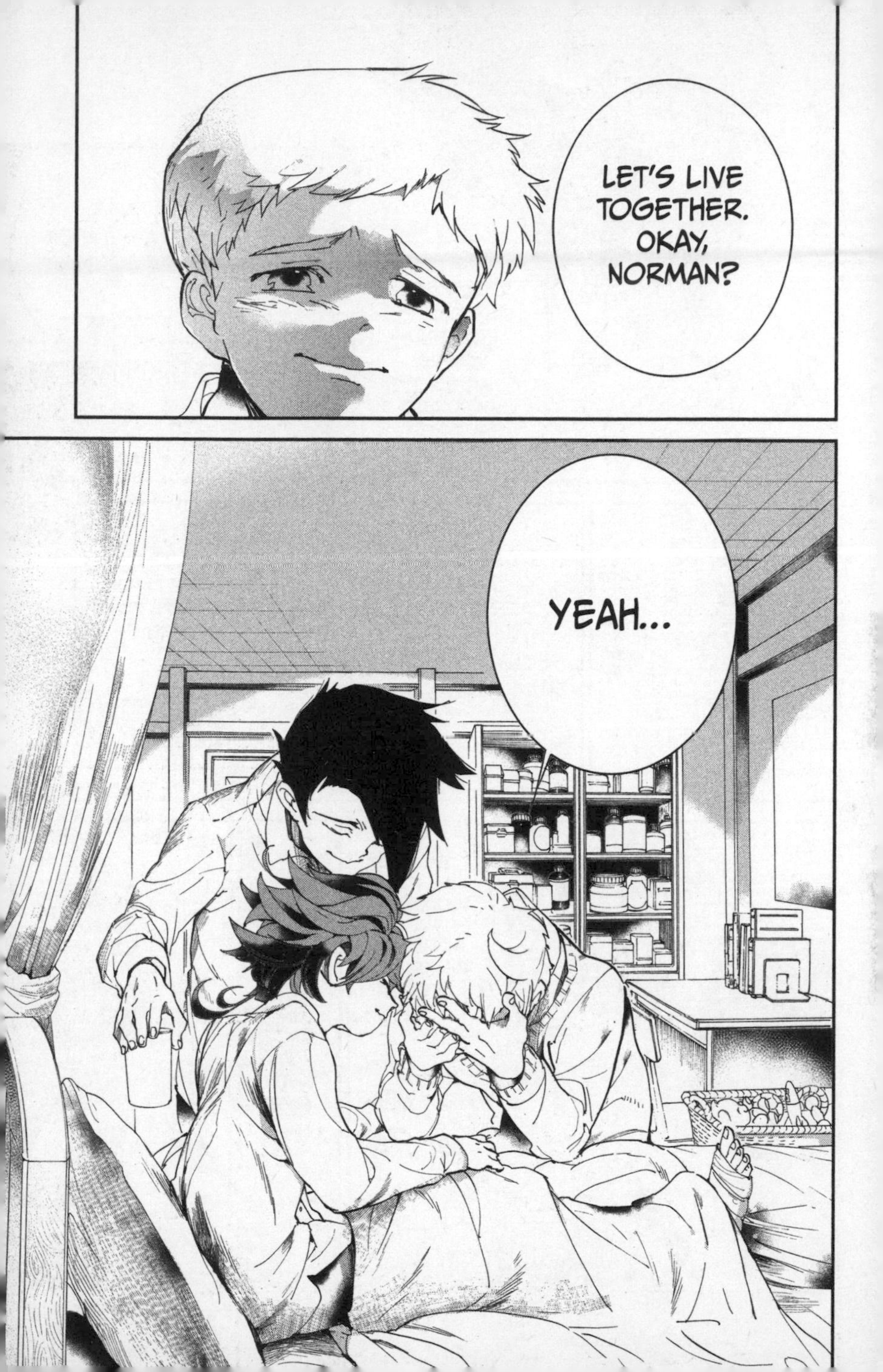
LET'S LIVE TOGETHER. OKAY, NORMAN?
YEAH...

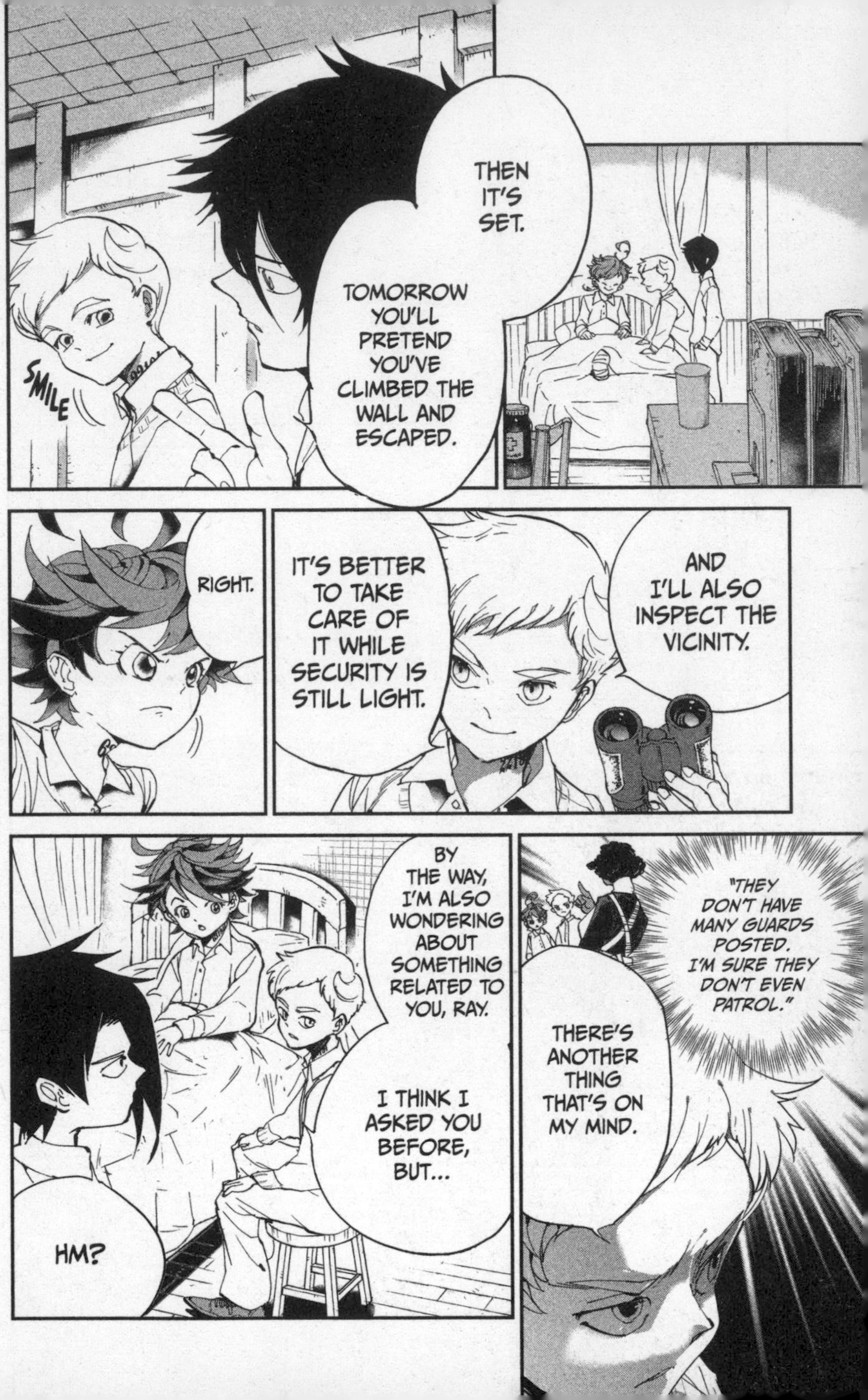
THEN IT'S SET.
TOMORROW YOU'LL PRETEND YOU'VE CLIMBED THE WALL AND ESCAPED.
SMILE
AND I'LL ALSO INSPECT THE VICINITY.
IT'S BETTER TO TAKE CARE OF IT WHILE SECURITY IS STILL LIGHT.
RIGHT.
"THEY DON'T HAVE MANY GUARDS POSTED. I'M SURE THEY DON'T EVEN PATROL."
THERE'S ANOTHER THING THAT'S ON MY MIND.
BY THE WAY, I'M ALSO WONDERING ABOUT SOMETHING RELATED TO YOU, RAY.
I THINK I ASKED YOU BEFORE, BUT...
HM?

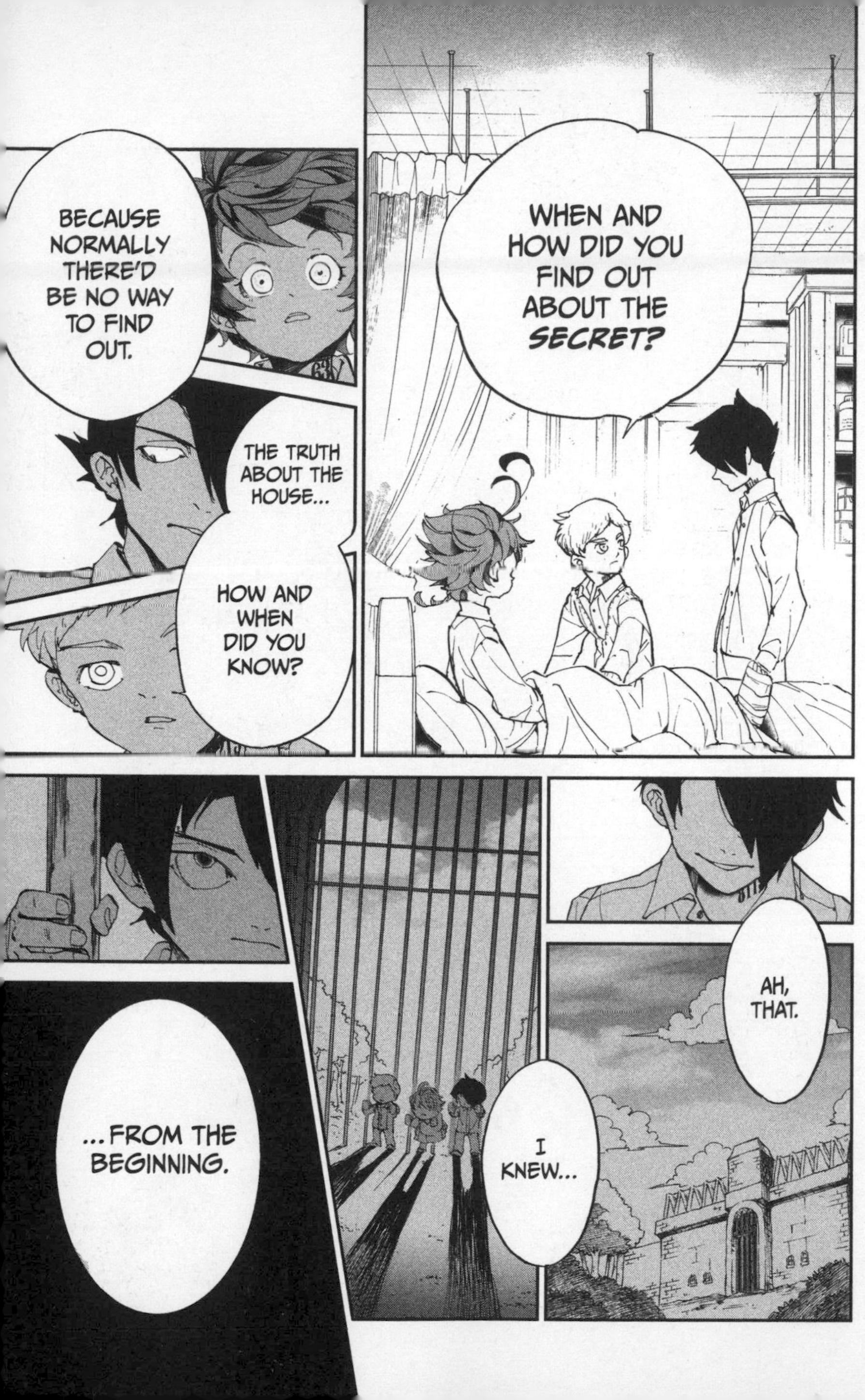
WHEN AND HOW DID YOU FIND OUT ABOUT THE *SECRET?*
BECAUSE NORMALLY THERE'D BE NO WAY TO FIND OUT.
THE TRUTH ABOUT THE HOUSE...
HOW AND WHEN DID YOU KNOW?
AH, THAT.
I KNEW...
...FROM THE BEGINNING.

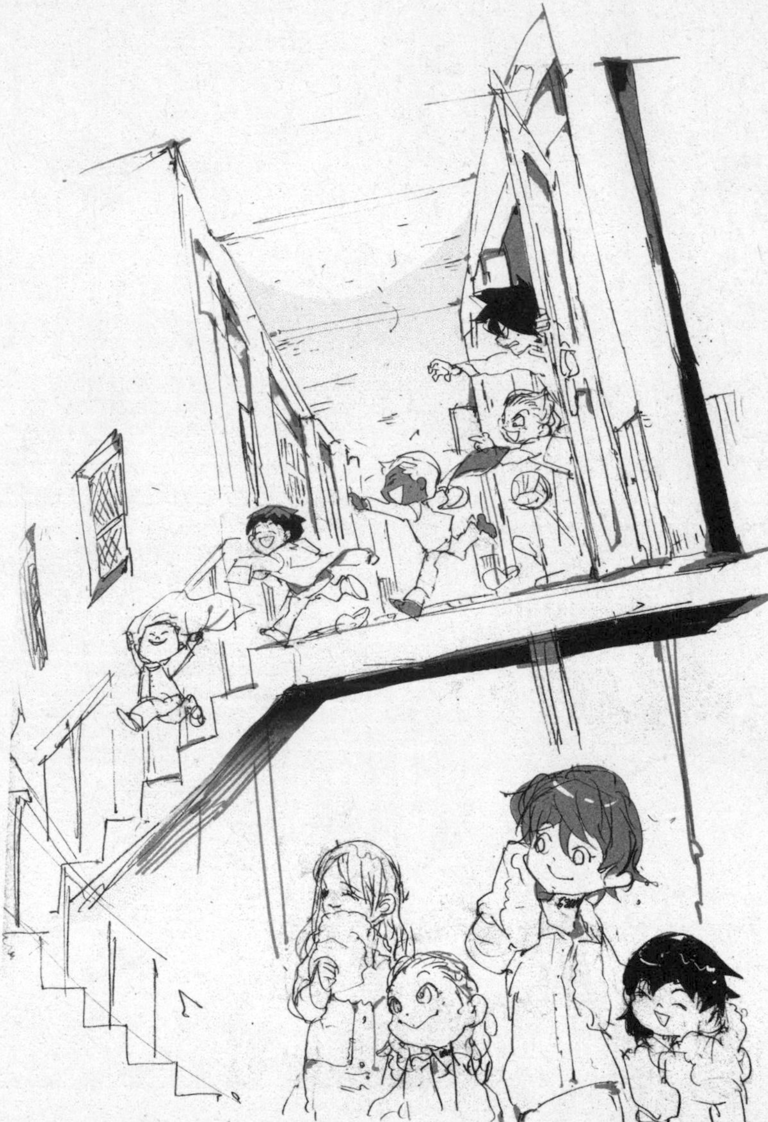

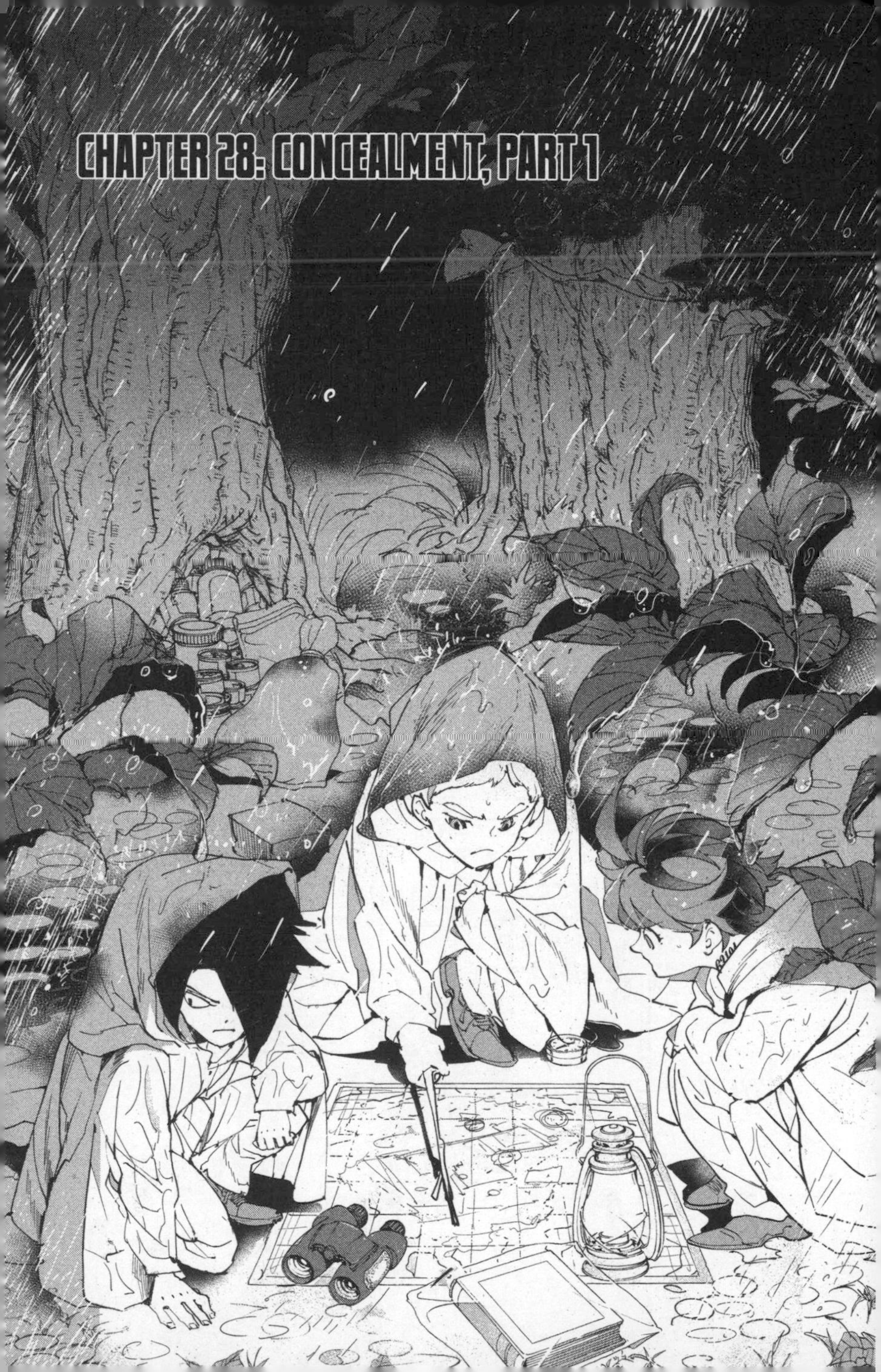
CHAPTER 28: CONCEALMENT, PART 1

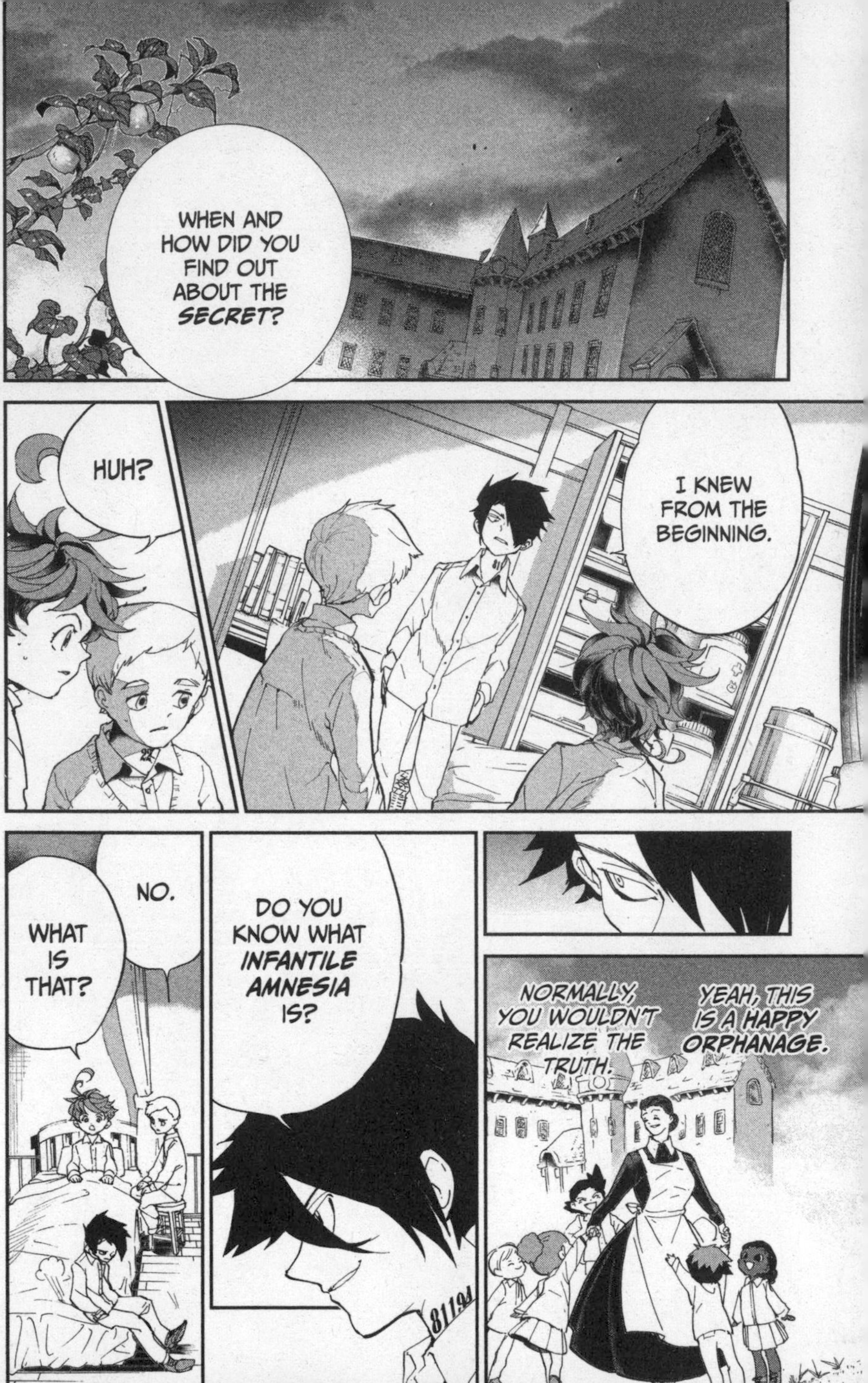
WHEN AND HOW DID YOU FIND OUT ABOUT THE SECRET?
I KNEW FROM THE BEGINNING.
HUH?
YEAH, THIS IS A HAPPY ORPHANAGE.
NORMALLY, YOU WOULDN'T REALIZE THE TRUTH.
DO YOU KNOW WHAT INFANTILE AMNESIA IS?
NO.
WHAT IS THAT?

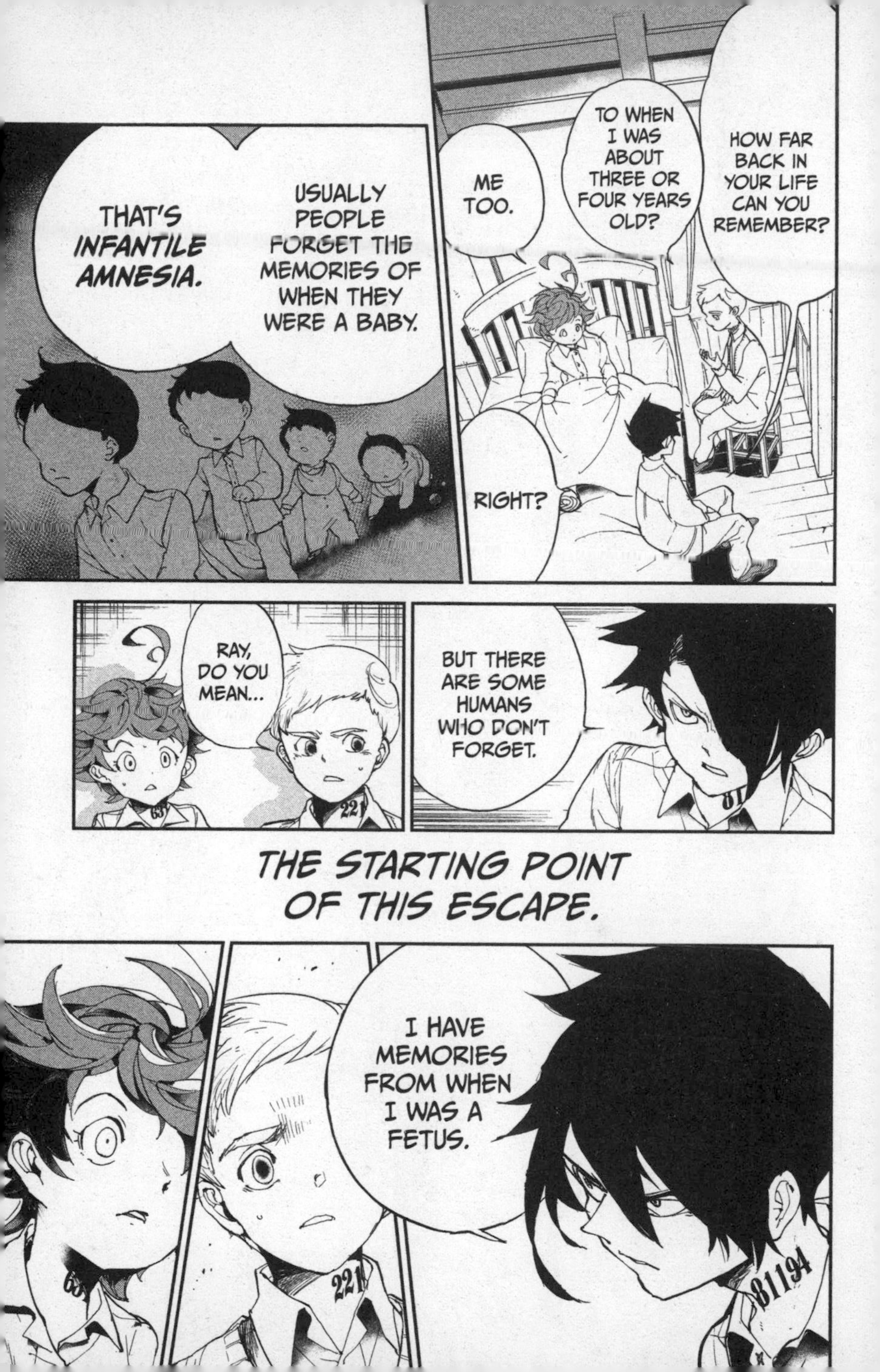
HOW FAR BACK IN YOUR LIFE CAN YOU REMEMBER?
TO WHEN I WAS ABOUT THREE OR FOUR YEARS OLD?
ME TOO.
RIGHT?
USUALLY PEOPLE FORGET THE MEMORIES OF WHEN THEY WERE A BABY.
THAT'S *INFANTILE AMNESIA.*
BUT THERE ARE SOME HUMANS WHO DON'T FORGET.
RAY, DO YOU MEAN...
THE STARTING POINT OF THIS ESCAPE.
I HAVE MEMORIES FROM WHEN I WAS A FETUS.

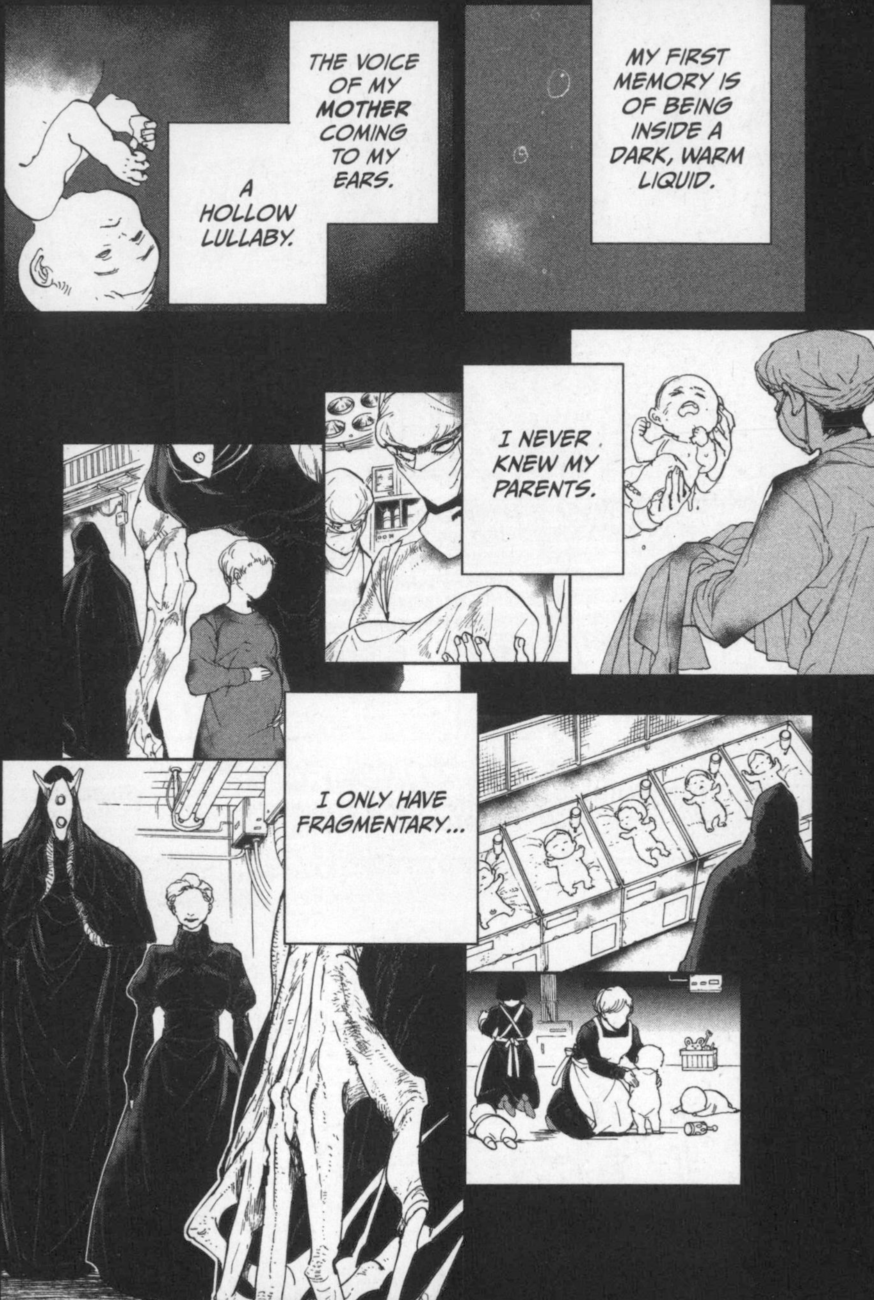
MY FIRST MEMORY IS OF BEING INSIDE A DARK, WARM LIQUID.
THE VOICE OF MY MOTHER COMING TO MY EARS.
A HOLLOW LULLABY.
I NEVER KNEW MY PARENTS.
I ONLY HAVE FRAGMENTARY...

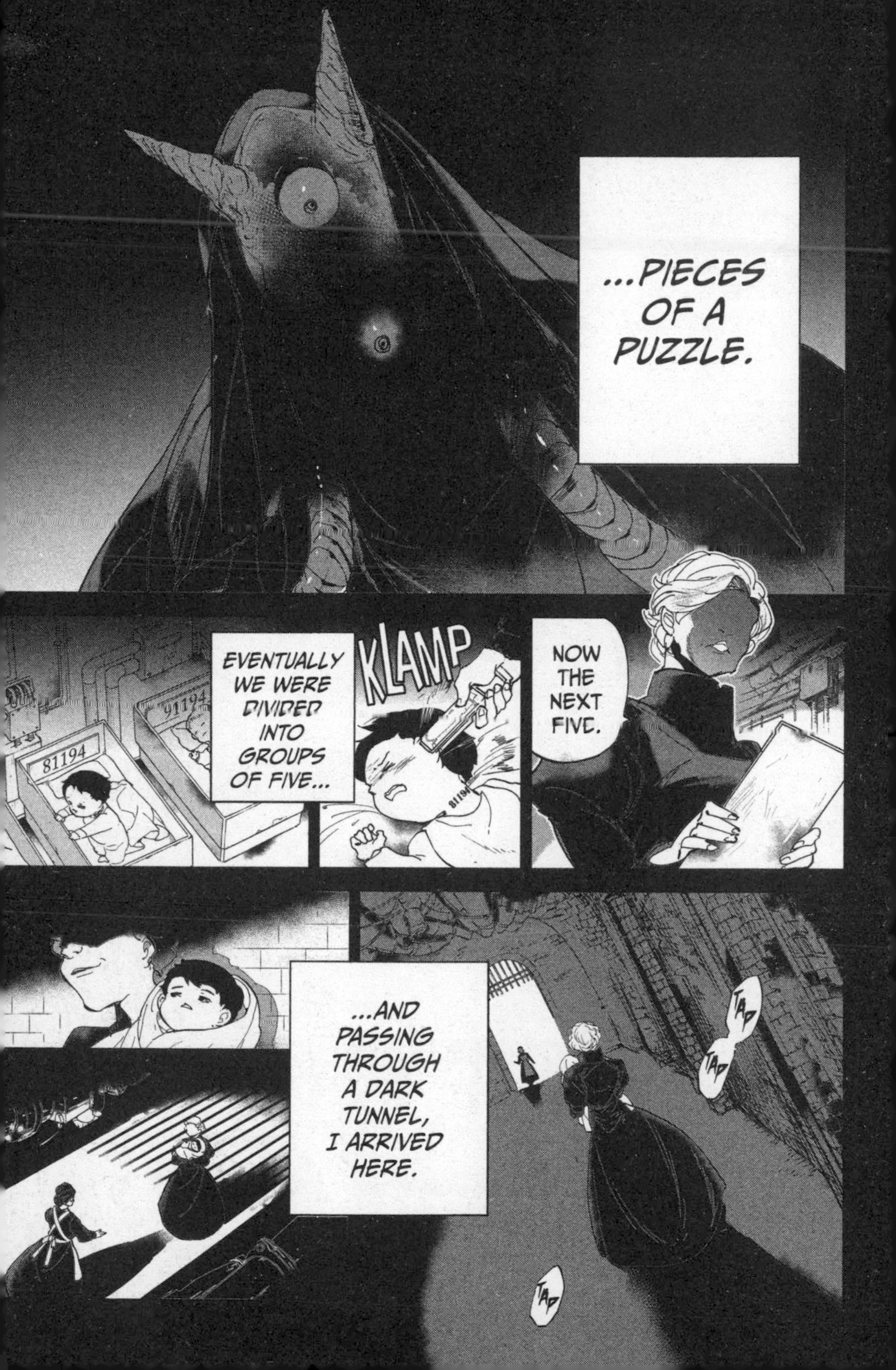
...PIECES OF A PUZZLE.
NOW THE NEXT FIVE.
KLAMP
81194
EVENTUALLY WE WERE DIVIDED INTO GROUPS OF FIVE...
81194
91194
TAP
TAP
...AND PASSING THROUGH A DARK TUNNEL, I ARRIVED HERE.
TAP

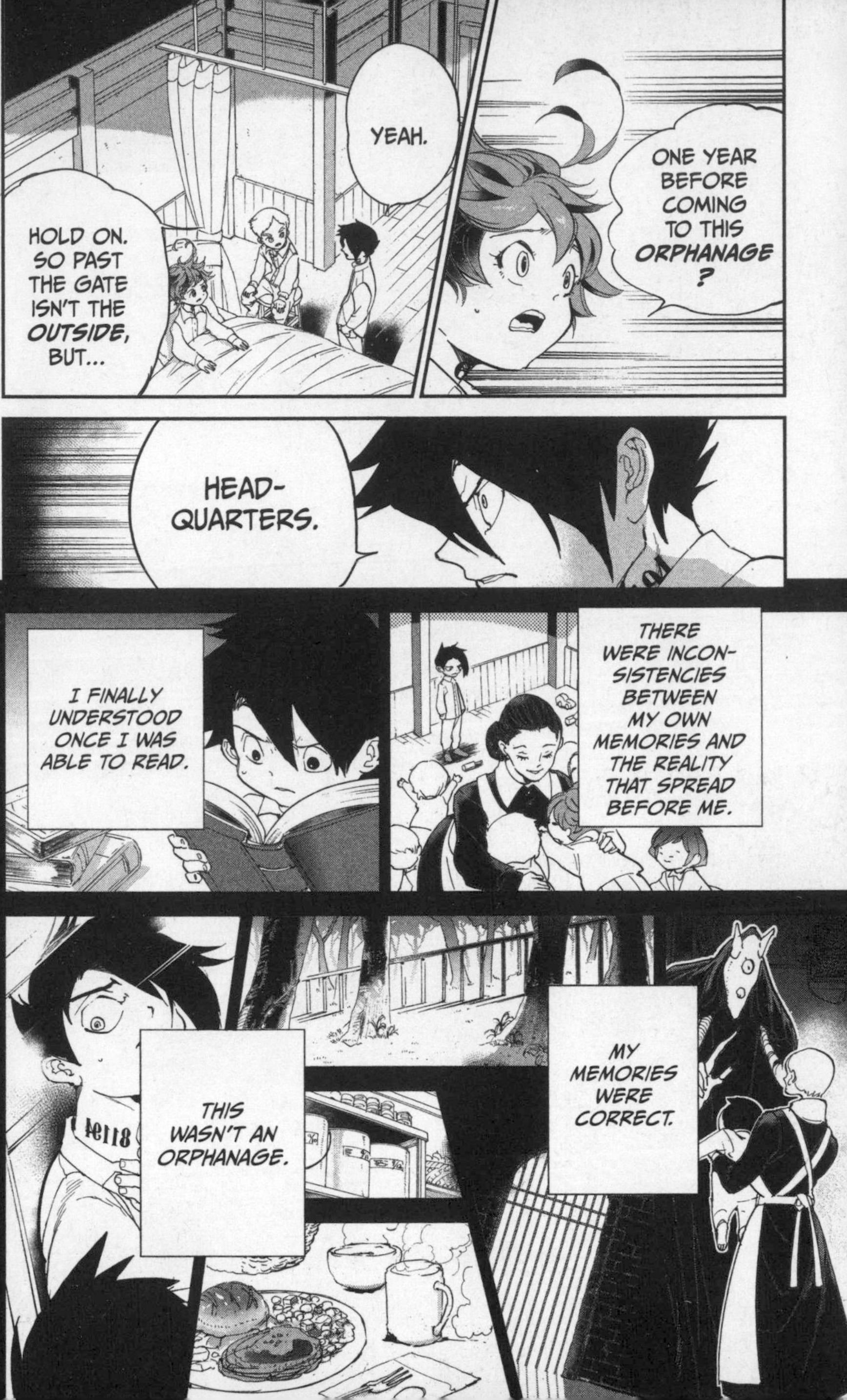
ONE YEAR BEFORE COMING TO THIS *ORPHANAGE*?
YEAH.
HOLD ON. SO PAST THE GATE ISN'T THE *OUTSIDE*, BUT...
HEAD-QUARTERS.
THERE WERE INCON-SISTENCIES BETWEEN MY OWN MEMORIES AND THE REALITY THAT SPREAD BEFORE ME.
I FINALLY UNDERSTOOD ONCE I WAS ABLE TO READ.
MY MEMORIES WERE CORRECT.
THIS WASN'T AN ORPHANAGE.

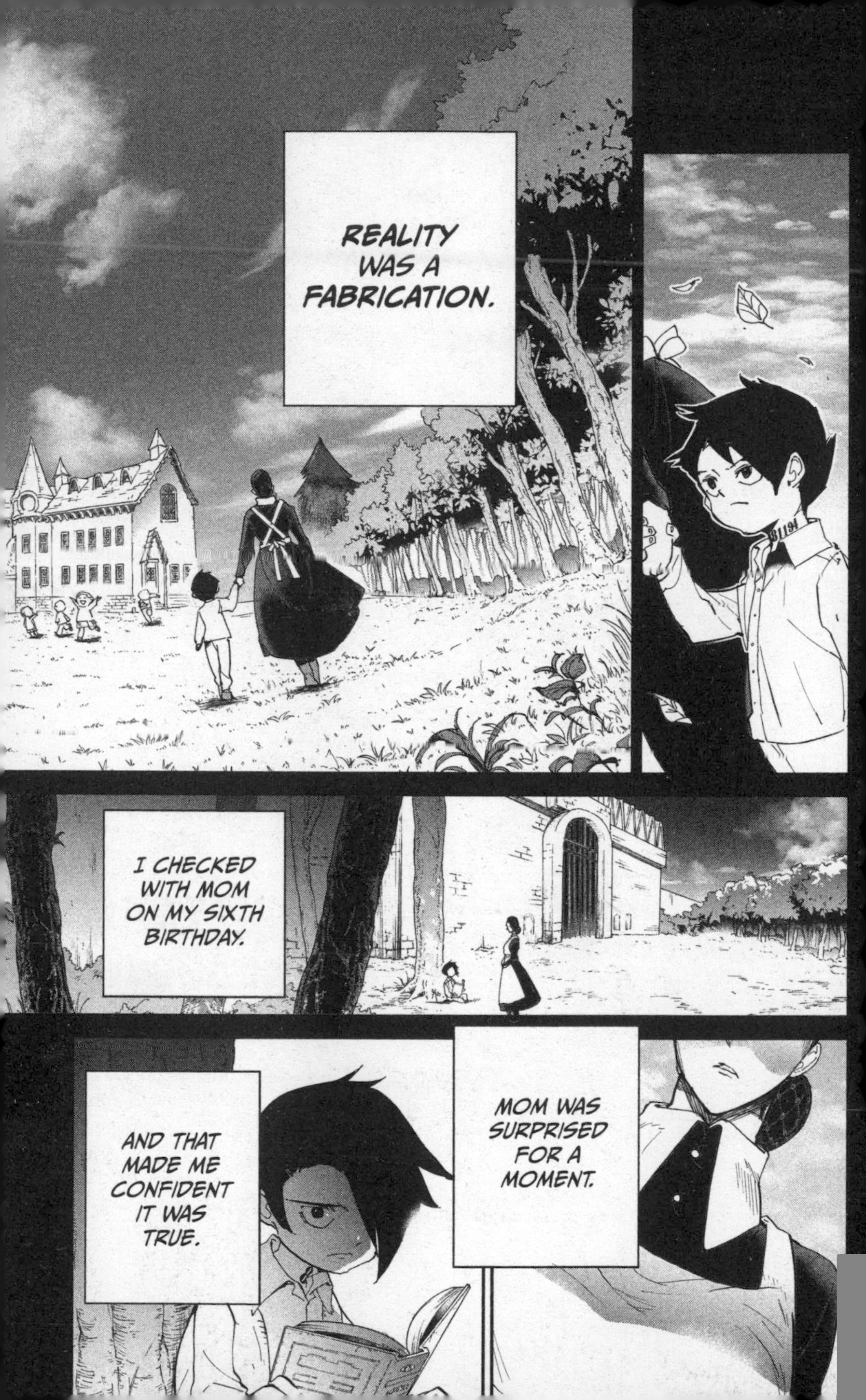
81194
REALITY WAS A FABRICATION.
I CHECKED WITH MOM ON MY SIXTH BIRTHDAY.
MOM WAS SURPRISED FOR A MOMENT.
AND THAT MADE ME CONFIDENT IT WAS TRUE.

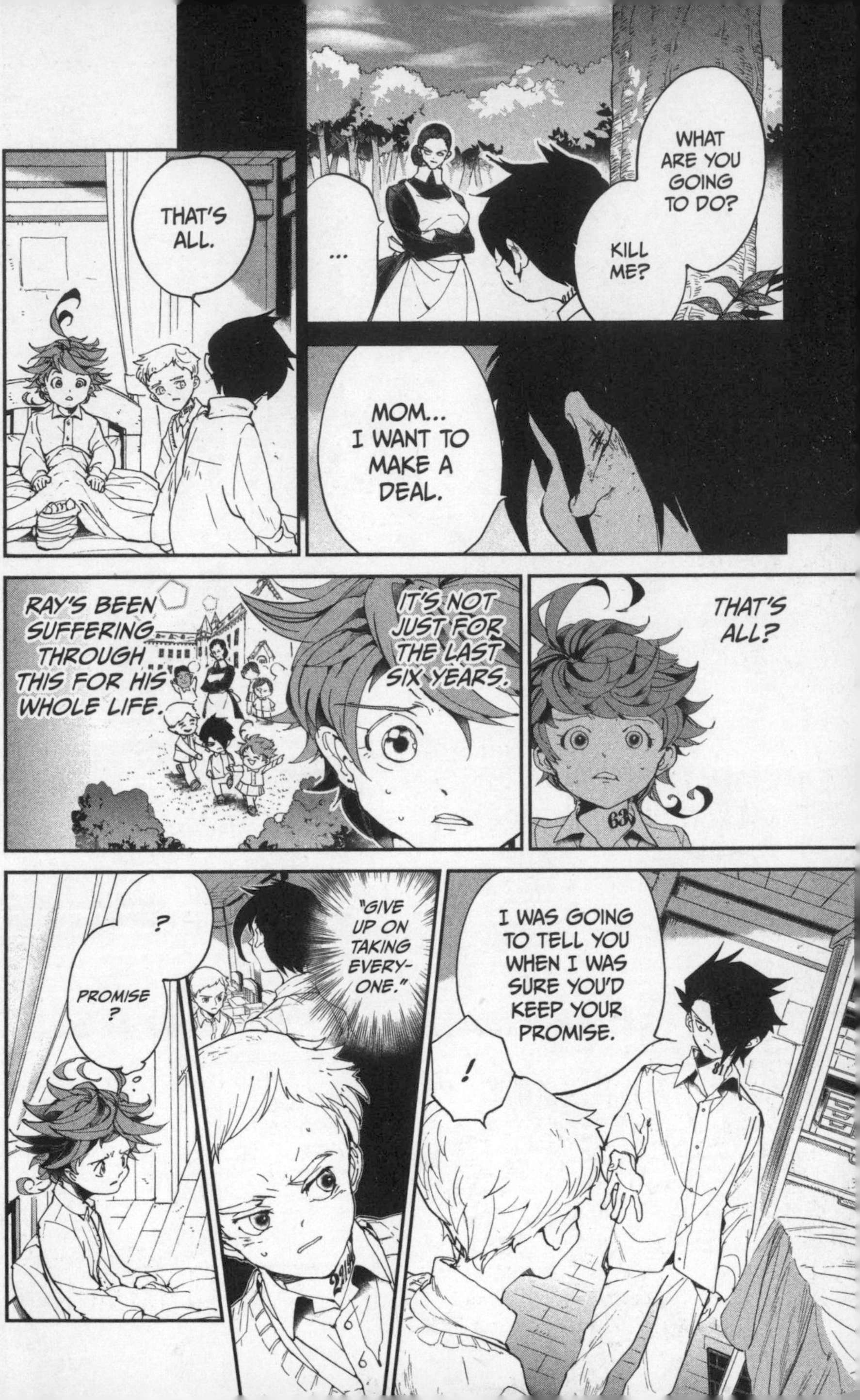
WHAT ARE YOU GOING TO DO?
KILL ME?
...
MOM... I WANT TO MAKE A DEAL.
THAT'S ALL.
THAT'S ALL?
IT'S NOT JUST FOR THE LAST SIX YEARS.
RAY'S BEEN SUFFERING THROUGH THIS FOR HIS WHOLE LIFE.
I WAS GOING TO TELL YOU WHEN I WAS SURE YOU'D KEEP YOUR PROMISE.
!
"GIVE UP ON TAKING EVERY-ONE."
?
PROMISE?

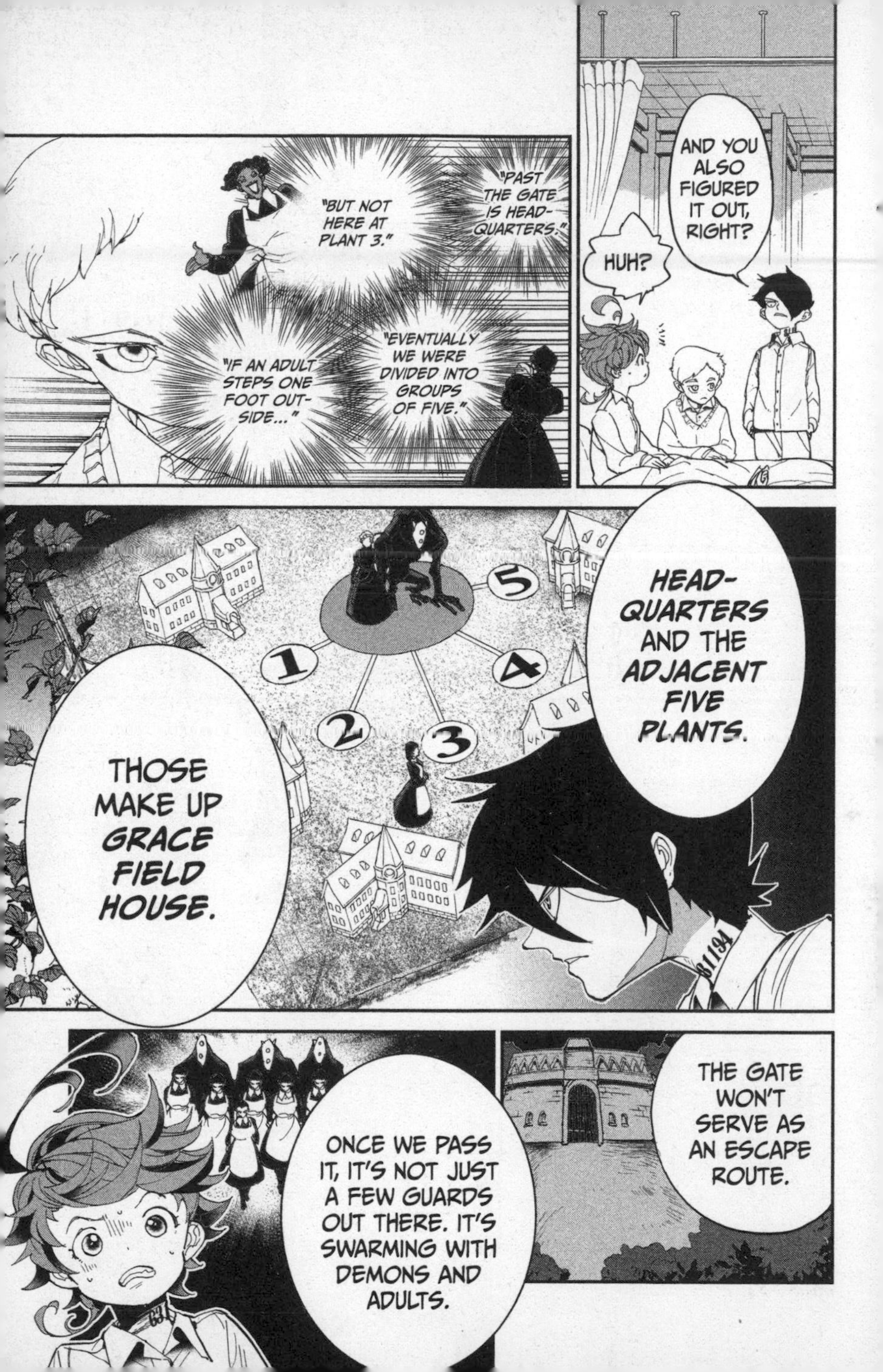
AND YOU ALSO FIGURED IT OUT, RIGHT?
HUH?
"PAST THE GATE IS HEAD-QUARTERS."
"BUT NOT HERE AT PLANT 3."
"EVENTUALLY WE WERE DIVIDED INTO GROUPS OF FIVE."
"IF AN ADULT STEPS ONE FOOT OUT-SIDE..."
HEAD-QUARTERS AND THE ADJACENT FIVE PLANTS.
THOSE MAKE UP GRACE FIELD HOUSE.
THE GATE WON'T SERVE AS AN ESCAPE ROUTE.
ONCE WE PASS IT, IT'S NOT JUST A FEW GUARDS OUT THERE. IT'S SWARMING WITH DEMONS AND ADULTS.

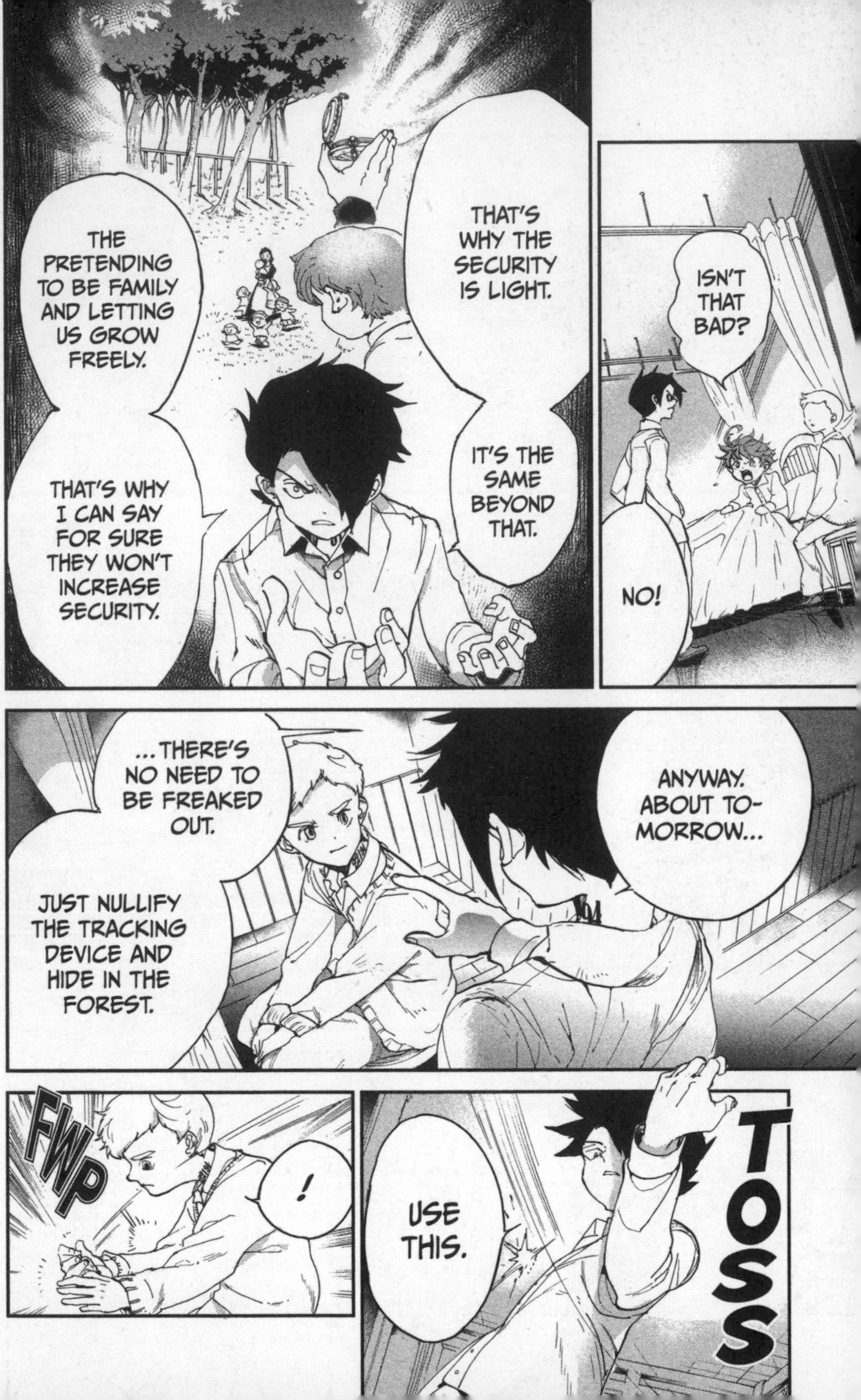
ISN'T THAT BAD?
NO!
THAT'S WHY THE SECURITY IS LIGHT.
IT'S THE SAME BEYOND THAT.
THE PRETENDING TO BE FAMILY AND LETTING US GROW FREELY.
THAT'S WHY I CAN SAY FOR SURE THEY WON'T INCREASE SECURITY.
ANYWAY. ABOUT TO-MORROW...
...THERE'S NO NEED TO BE FREAKED OUT.
JUST NULLIFY THE TRACKING DEVICE AND HIDE IN THE FOREST.
TOSS
USE THIS.
!
FWP

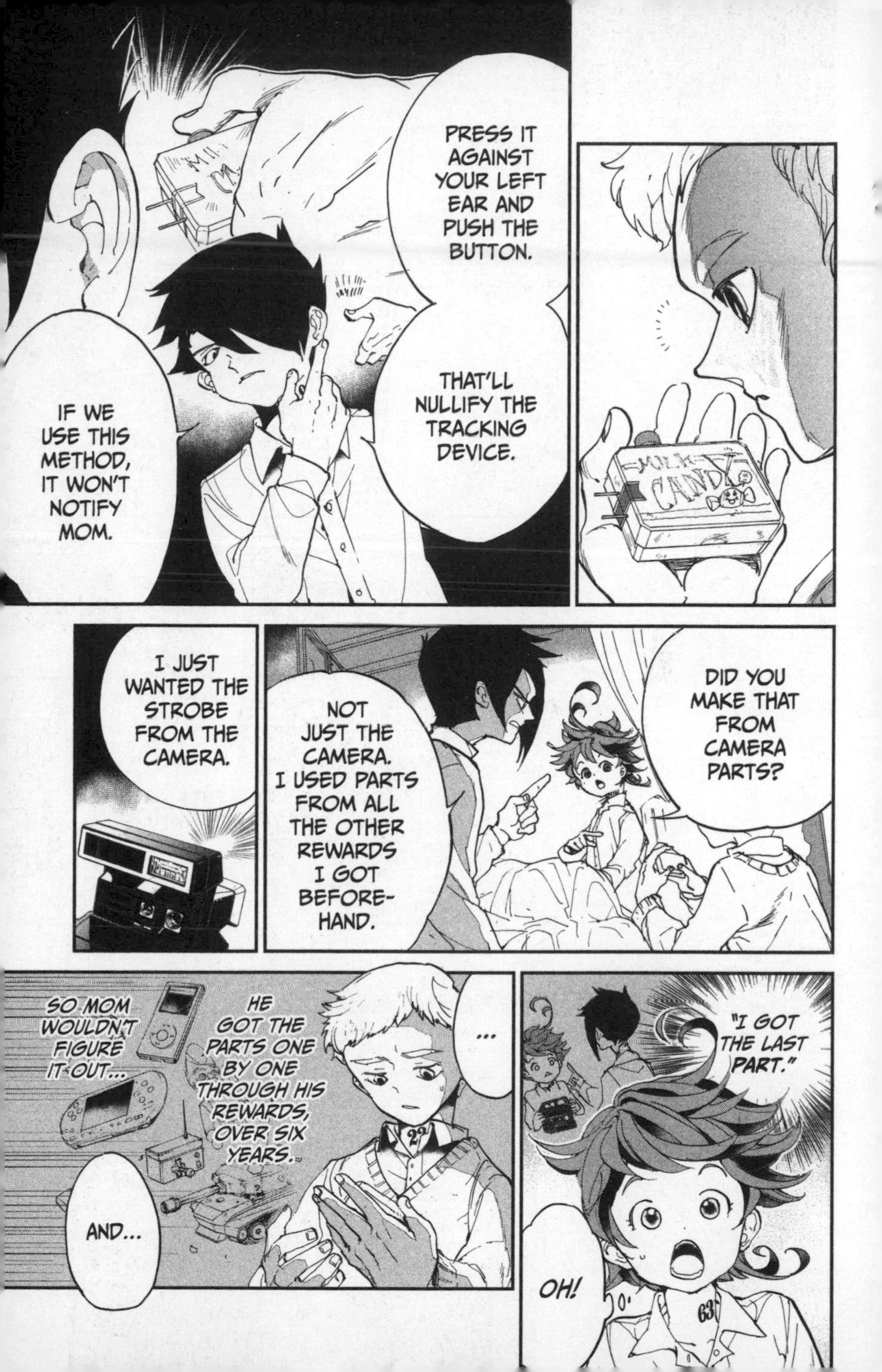
PRESS IT AGAINST YOUR LEFT EAR AND PUSH THE BUTTON.
THAT'LL NULLIFY THE TRACKING DEVICE.
IF WE USE THIS METHOD, IT WON'T NOTIFY MOM.
DID YOU MAKE THAT FROM CAMERA PARTS?
NOT JUST THE CAMERA. I USED PARTS FROM ALL THE OTHER REWARDS I GOT BEFORE-HAND.
I JUST WANTED THE STROBE FROM THE CAMERA.
"I GOT THE LAST PART."
OH!
...
HE GOT THE PARTS ONE BY ONE THROUGH HIS REWARDS, OVER SIX YEARS.
SO MOM WOULDN'T FIGURE IT OUT...
AND...

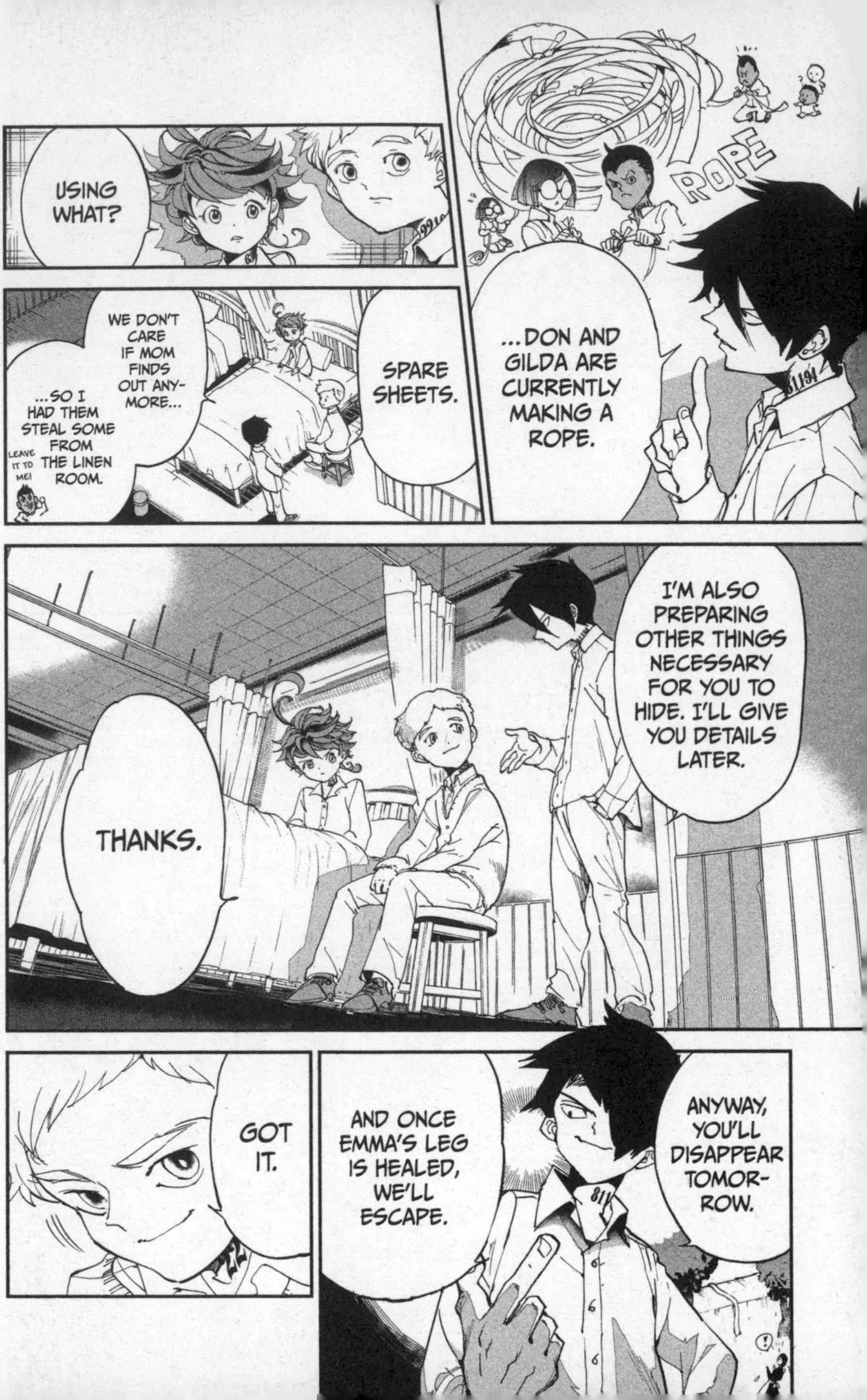
ROPE
...DON AND GILDA ARE CURRENTLY MAKING A ROPE.
USING WHAT?
SPARE SHEETS.
WE DON'T CARE IF MOM FINDS OUT ANYMORE...
...SO I HAD THEM STEAL SOME FROM THE LINEN ROOM.
LEAVE IT TO ME!
I'M ALSO PREPARING OTHER THINGS NECESSARY FOR YOU TO HIDE. I'LL GIVE YOU DETAILS LATER.
THANKS.
ANYWAY, YOU'LL DISAPPEAR TOMORROW.
AND ONCE EMMA'S LEG IS HEALED, WE'LL ESCAPE.
GOT IT.

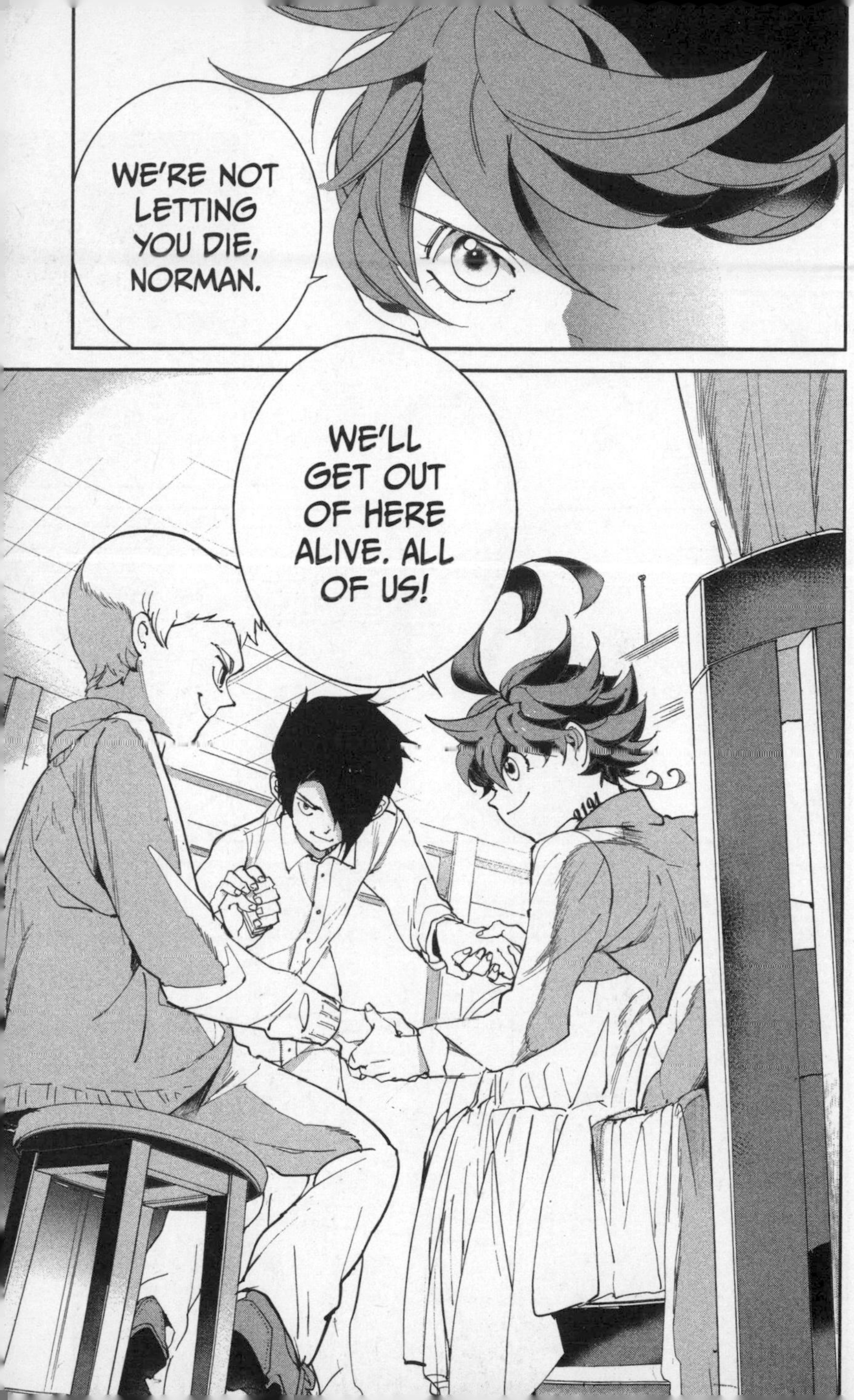
WE'RE NOT LETTING YOU DIE, NORMAN.
WE'LL GET OUT OF HERE ALIVE. ALL OF US!

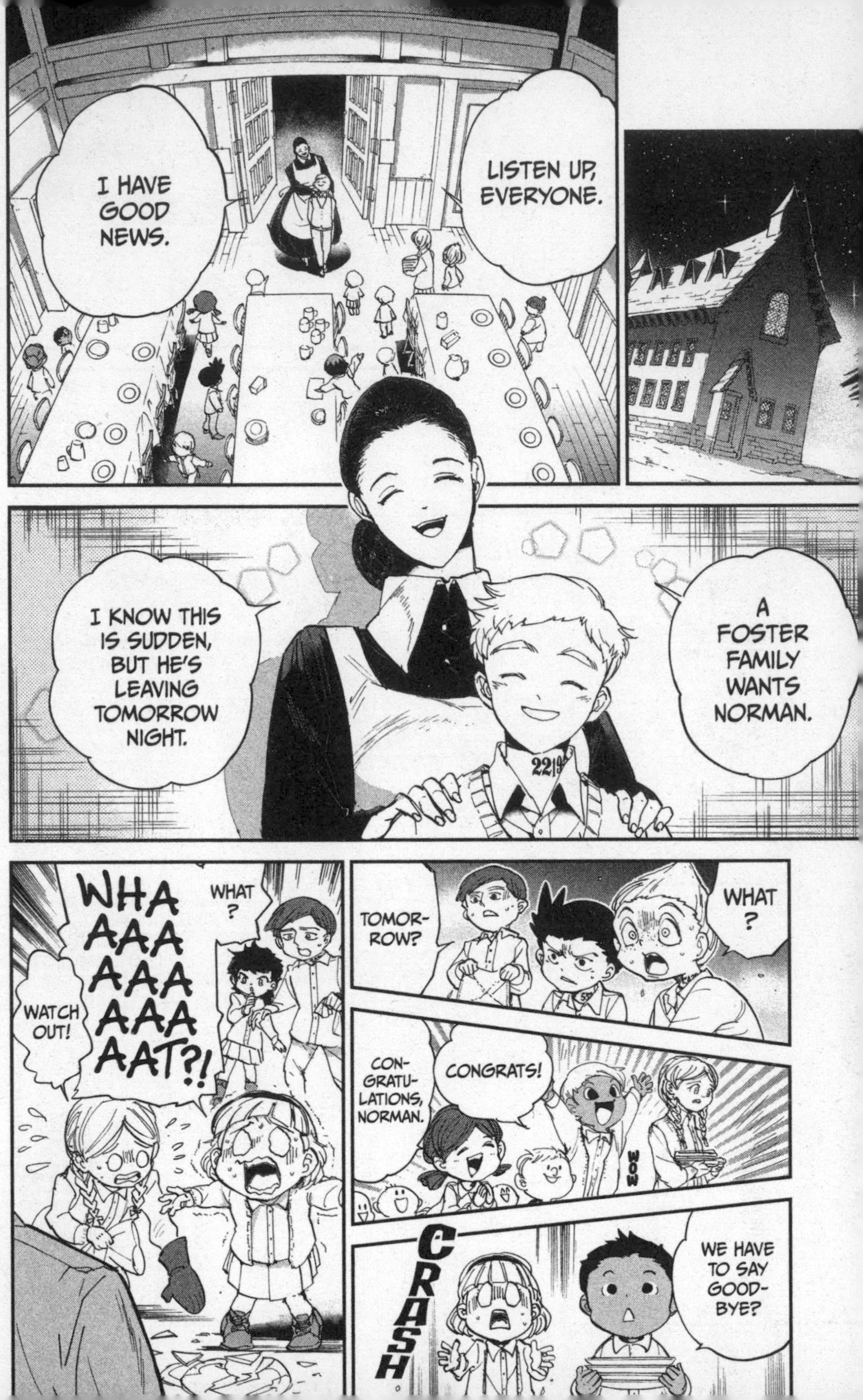
LISTEN UP, EVERYONE.
I HAVE GOOD NEWS.
A FOSTER FAMILY WANTS NORMAN.
I KNOW THIS IS SUDDEN, BUT HE'S LEAVING TOMORROW NIGHT.
WHAT?
TOMOR-ROW?
CONGRATS!
CON-GRATU-LATIONS, NORMAN.
WOW
WE HAVE TO SAY GOOD-BYE?
CRASH
WHAT?
WHAAAAAAAAAAAAT?!
WATCH OUT!

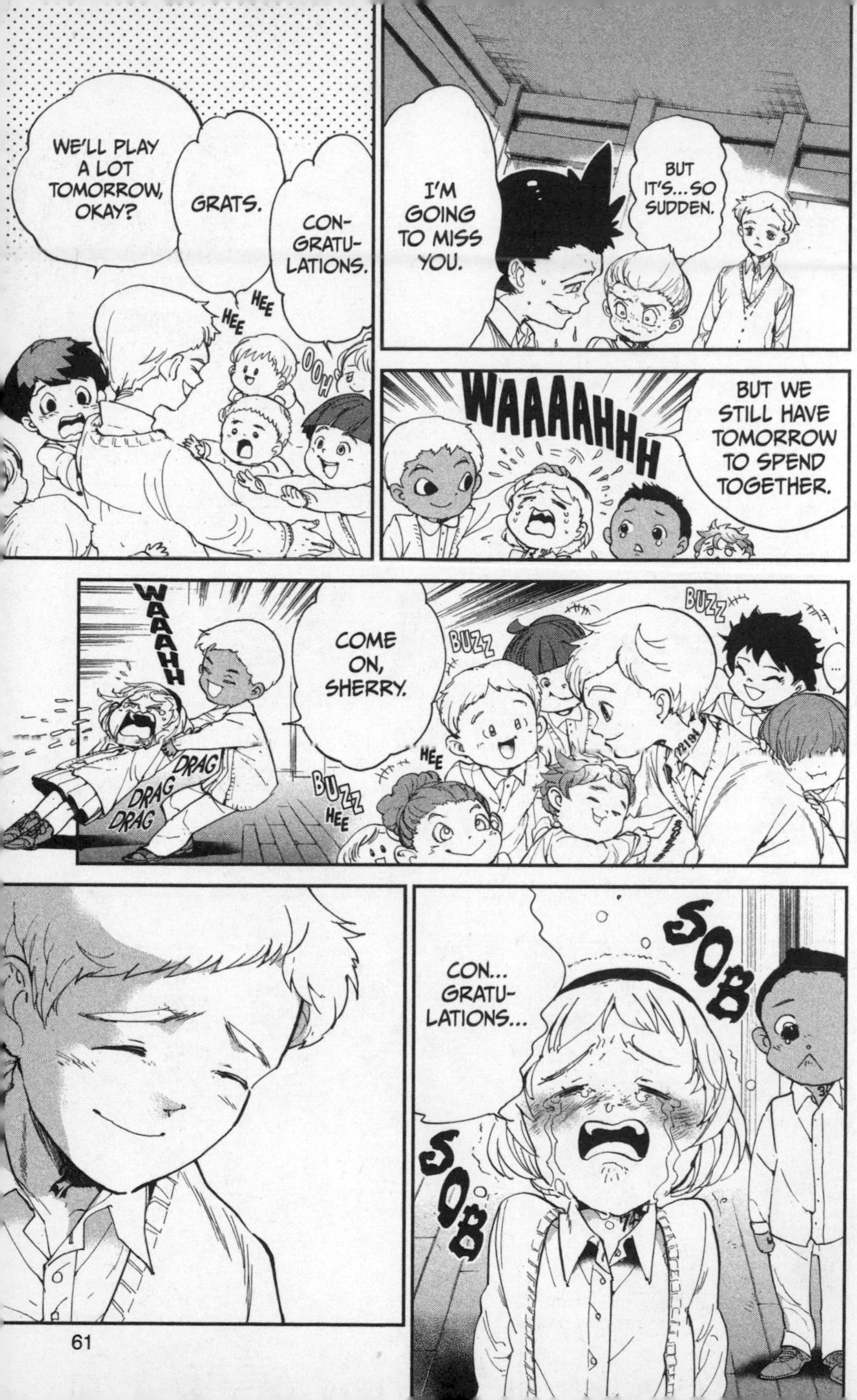
BUT IT'S... SO SUDDEN.
I'M GOING TO MISS YOU.
BUT WE STILL HAVE TOMORROW TO SPEND TOGETHER.
WAAAAHHHH
CON-GRATU-LATIONS.
GRATS.
WE'LL PLAY A LOT TOMORROW, OKAY?
HEE
HEE
OOH
BUZZ
...
BUZZ
HEE
BUZZ
HEE
COME ON, SHERRY.
WAAAHH
DRAG
DRAG
DRAG
SOB
CON... GRATU-LATIONS...
SOB

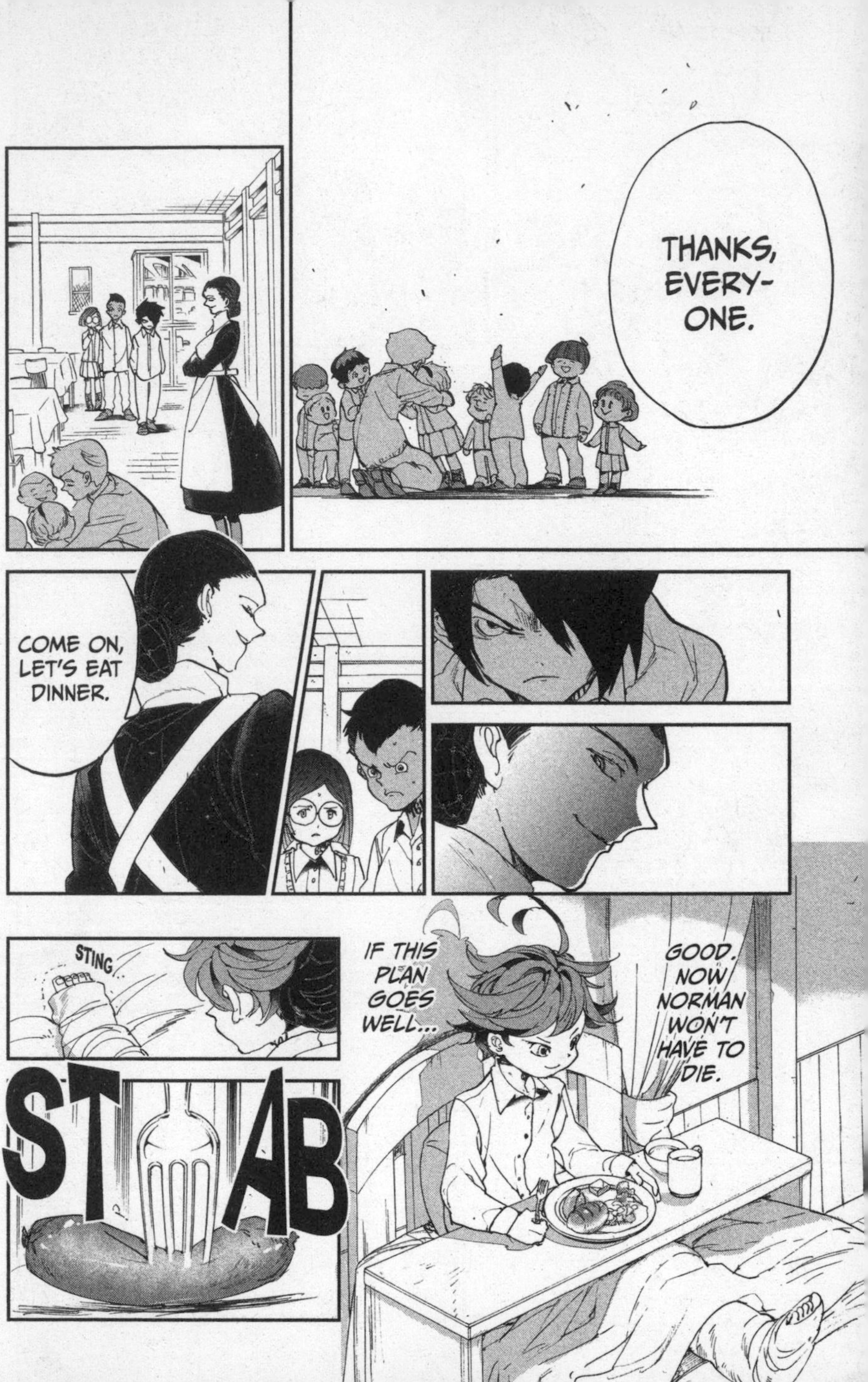
THANKS, EVERY-ONE.
COME ON, LET'S EAT DINNER.
GOOD. NOW NORMAN WON'T HAVE TO DIE.
IF THIS PLAN GOES WELL...
STING
STAB

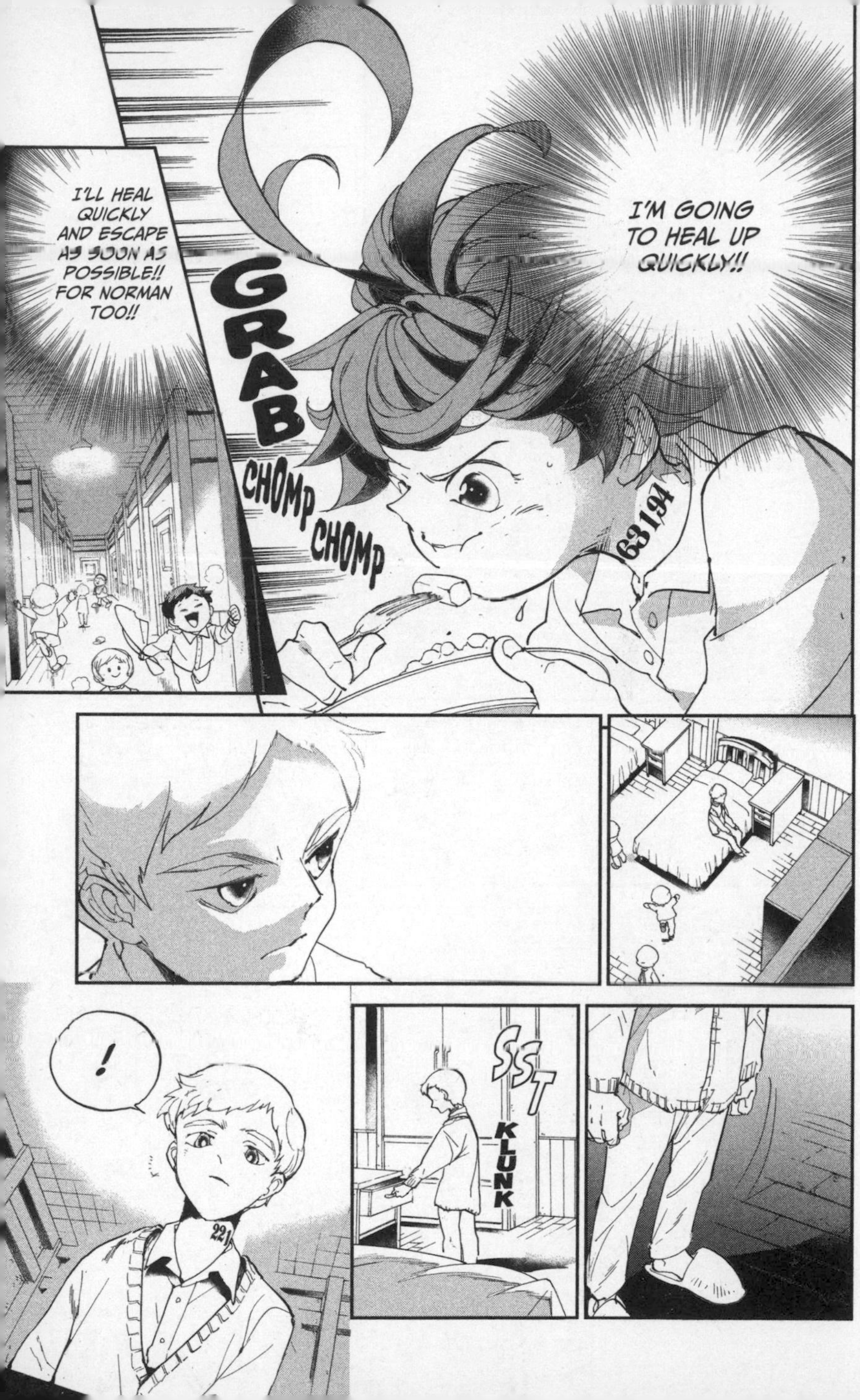
I'M GOING TO HEAL UP QUICKLY!!
GRAB
CHOMP CHOMP
I'LL HEAL QUICKLY AND ESCAPE AS SOON AS POSSIBLE!! FOR NORMAN TOO!!
SST
KLUNK
!

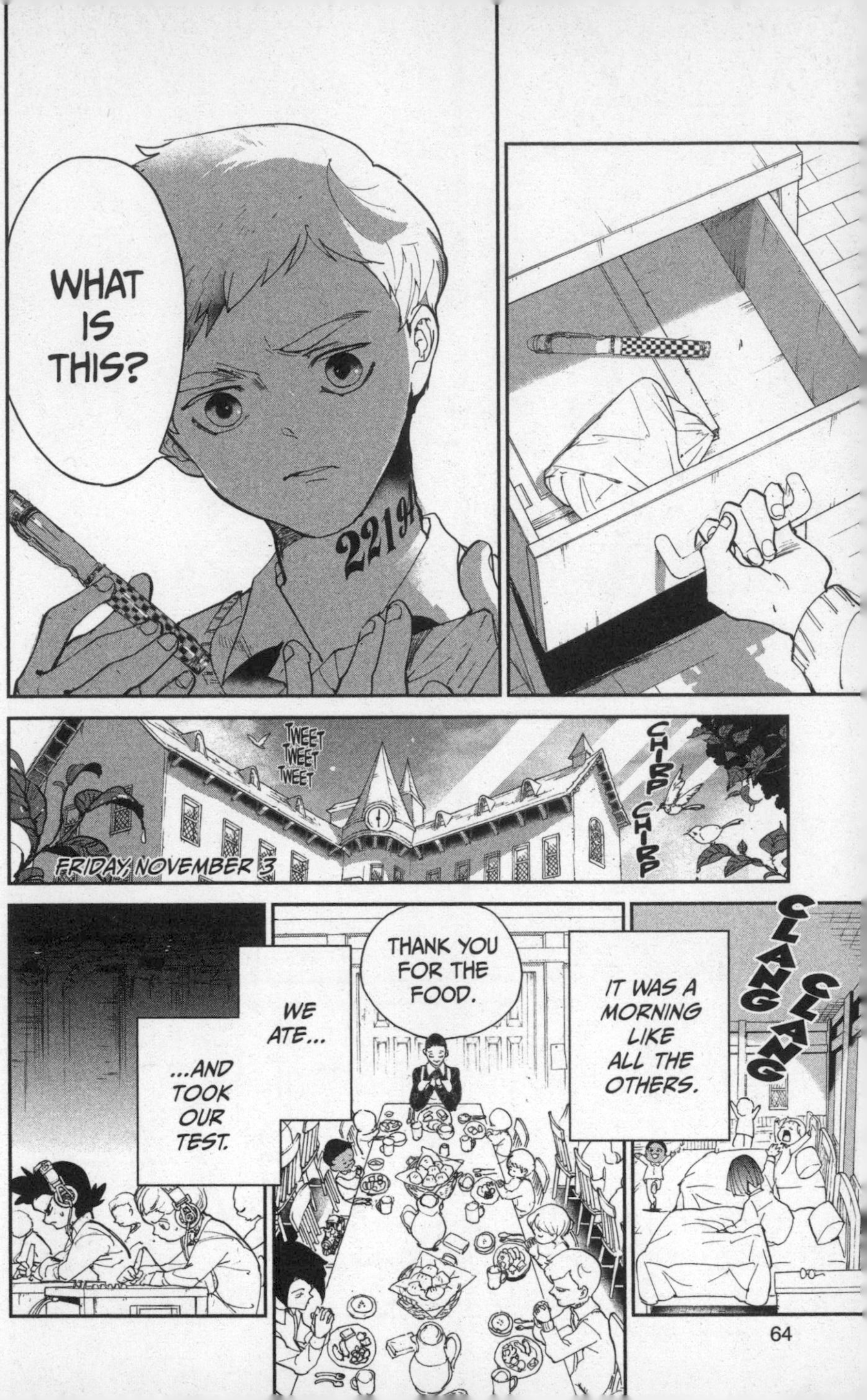
WHAT IS THIS?
CHIRP CHIRP
TWEET TWEET TWEET
FRIDAY, NOVEMBER 3
CLANG CLANG
IT WAS A MORNING LIKE ALL THE OTHERS.
THANK YOU FOR THE FOOD.
WE ATE...
...AND TOOK OUR TEST.

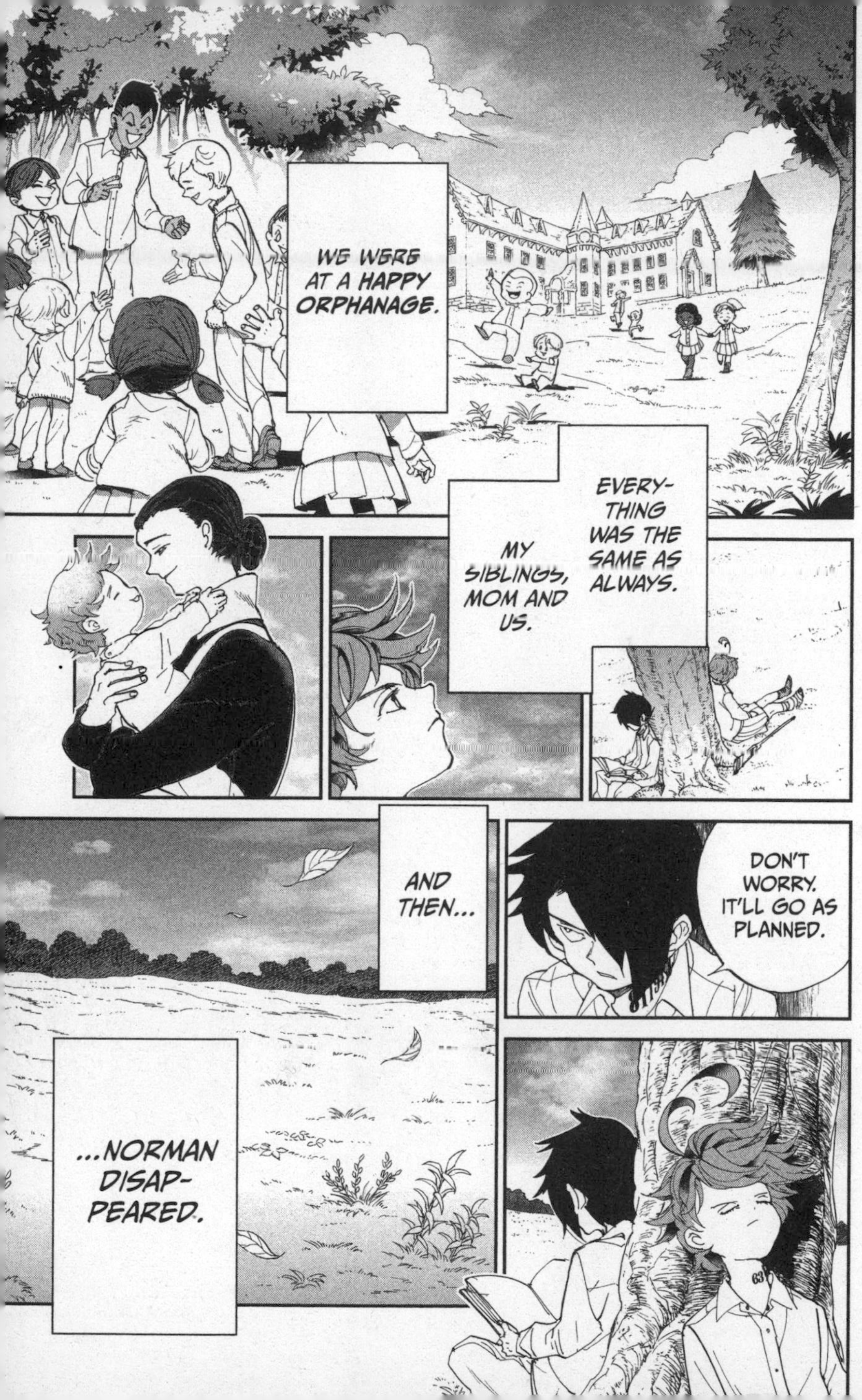
WE WERE AT A HAPPY ORPHANAGE.
EVERY-THING WAS THE SAME AS ALWAYS.
MY SIBLINGS, MOM AND US.
DON'T WORRY. IT'LL GO AS PLANNED.
AND THEN...
...NORMAN DISAP-PEARED.

THE PROMISED NEVERLAND SIDE SCENE 006

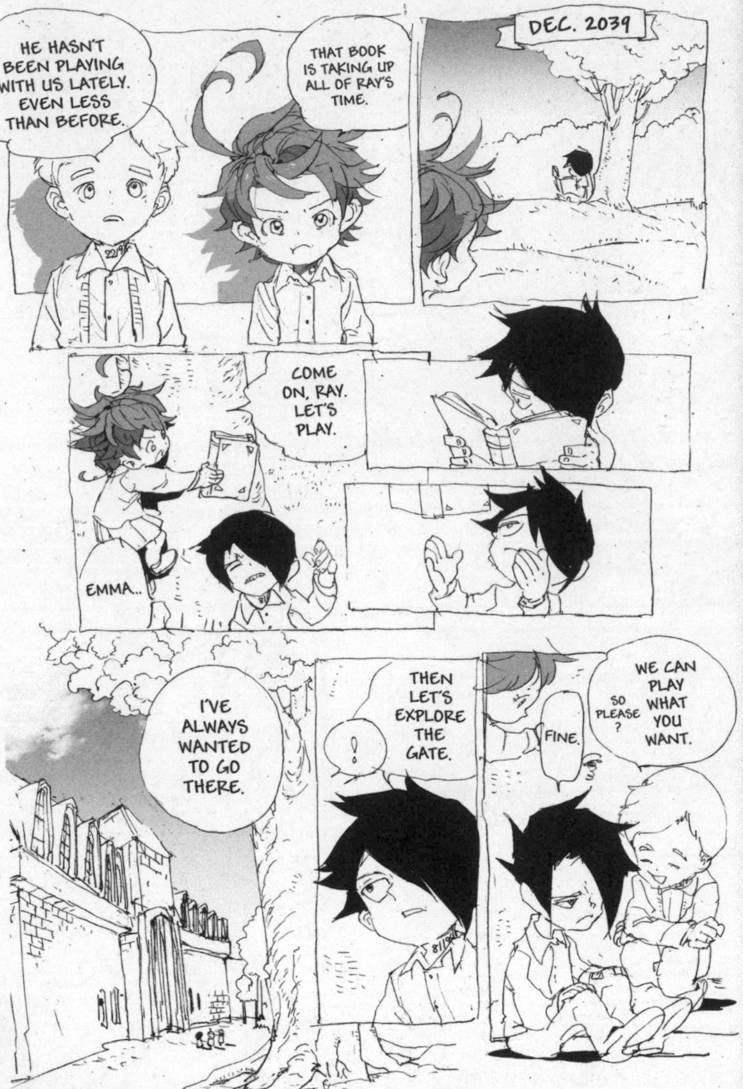
DEC. 2039
THAT BOOK IS TAKING UP ALL OF RAY'S TIME.
HE HASN'T BEEN PLAYING WITH US LATELY. EVEN LESS THAN BEFORE.
COME ON, RAY. LET'S PLAY.
EMMA..
WE CAN PLAY WHAT YOU WANT.
SO PLEASE?
FINE.
THEN LET'S EXPLORE THE GATE.
!
I'VE ALWAYS WANTED TO GO THERE.

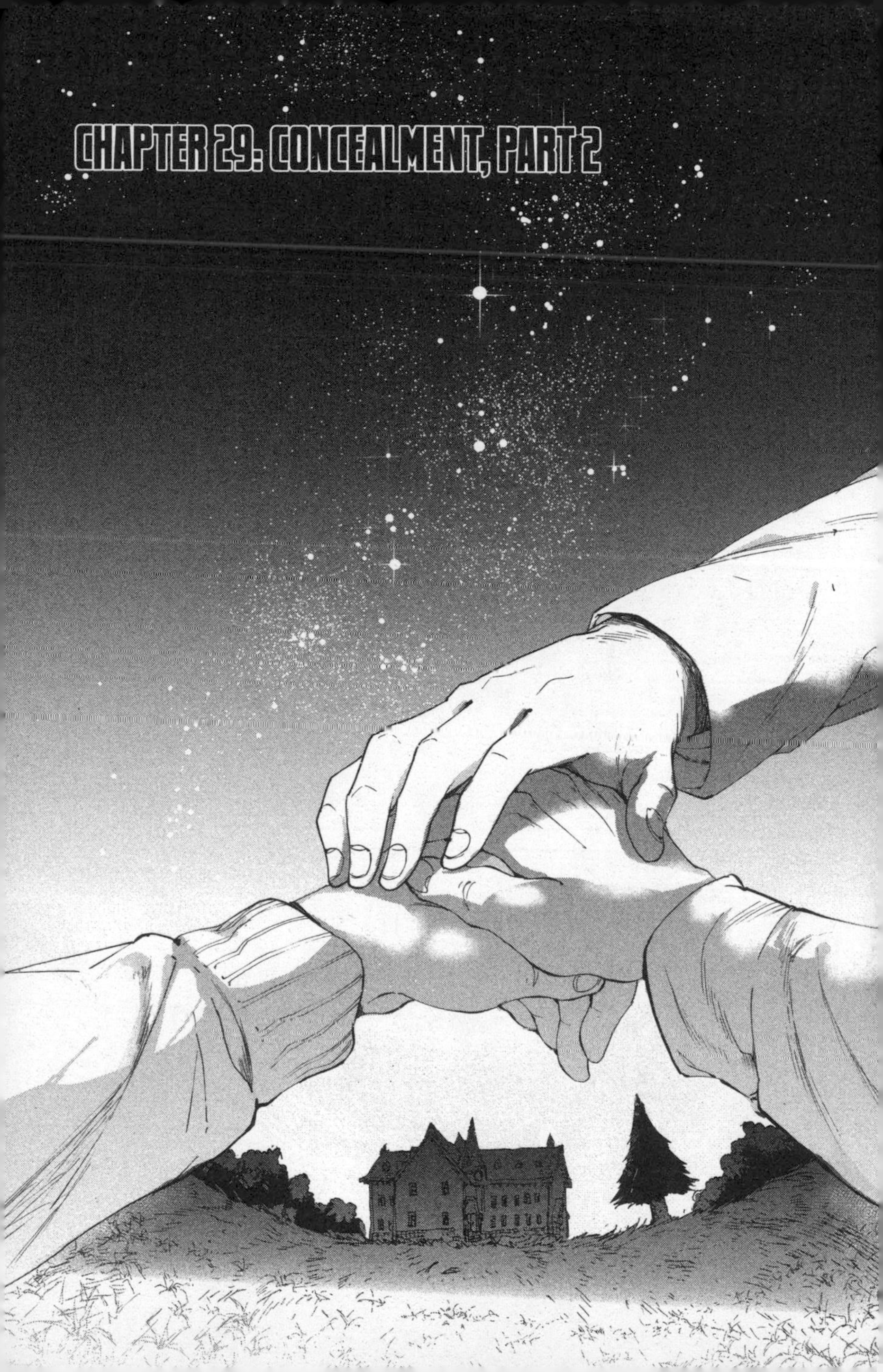
CHAPTER 29: CONCEALMENT, PART 2

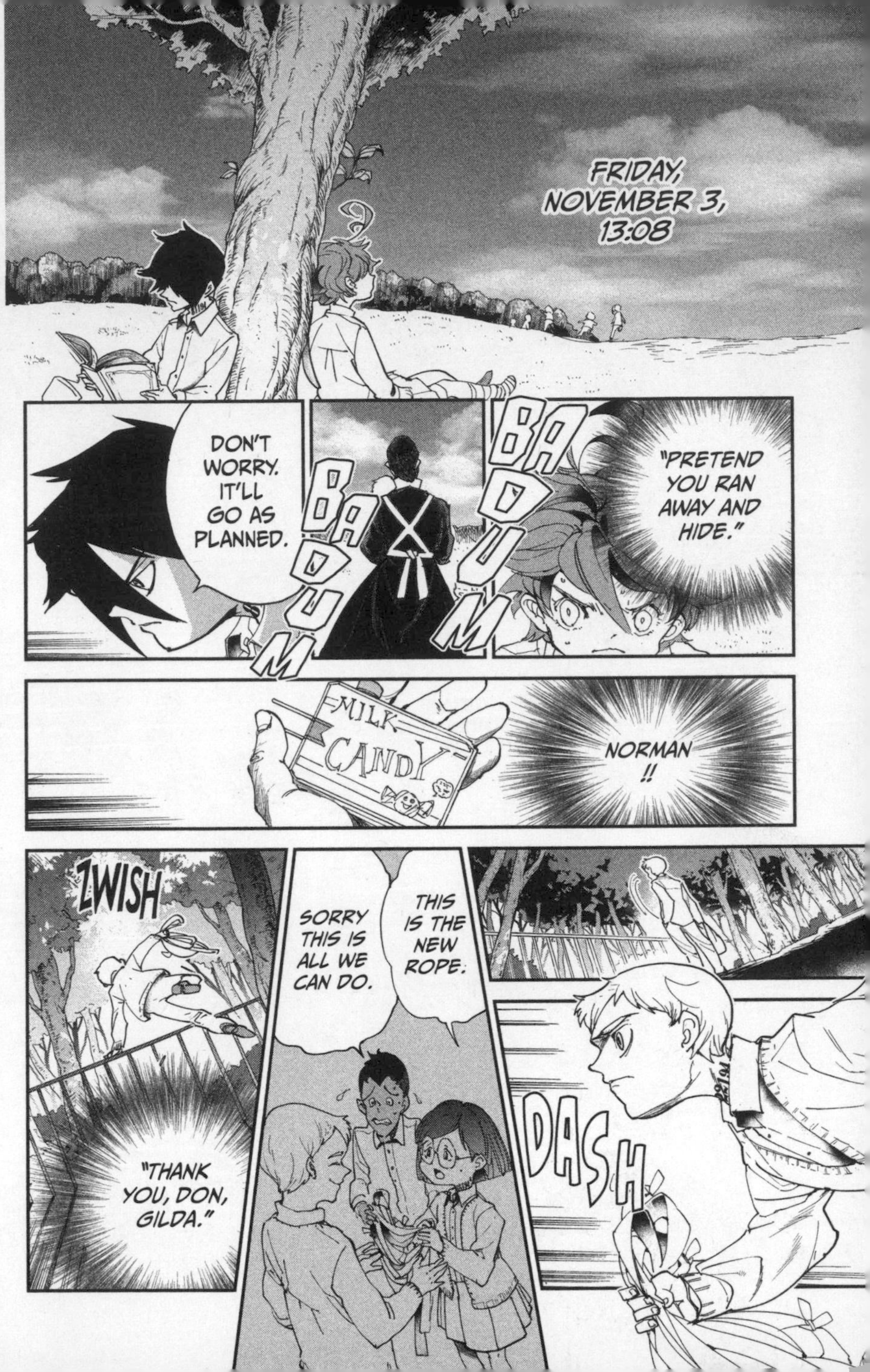
FRIDAY, NOVEMBER 3, 13:08
BADUM
"PRETEND YOU RAN AWAY AND HIDE."
BADUM
DON'T WORRY. IT'LL GO AS PLANNED.
NORMAN !!
MILK CANDY
DASH
THIS IS THE NEW ROPE.
SORRY THIS IS ALL WE CAN DO.
ZWISH
"THANK YOU, DON, GILDA."

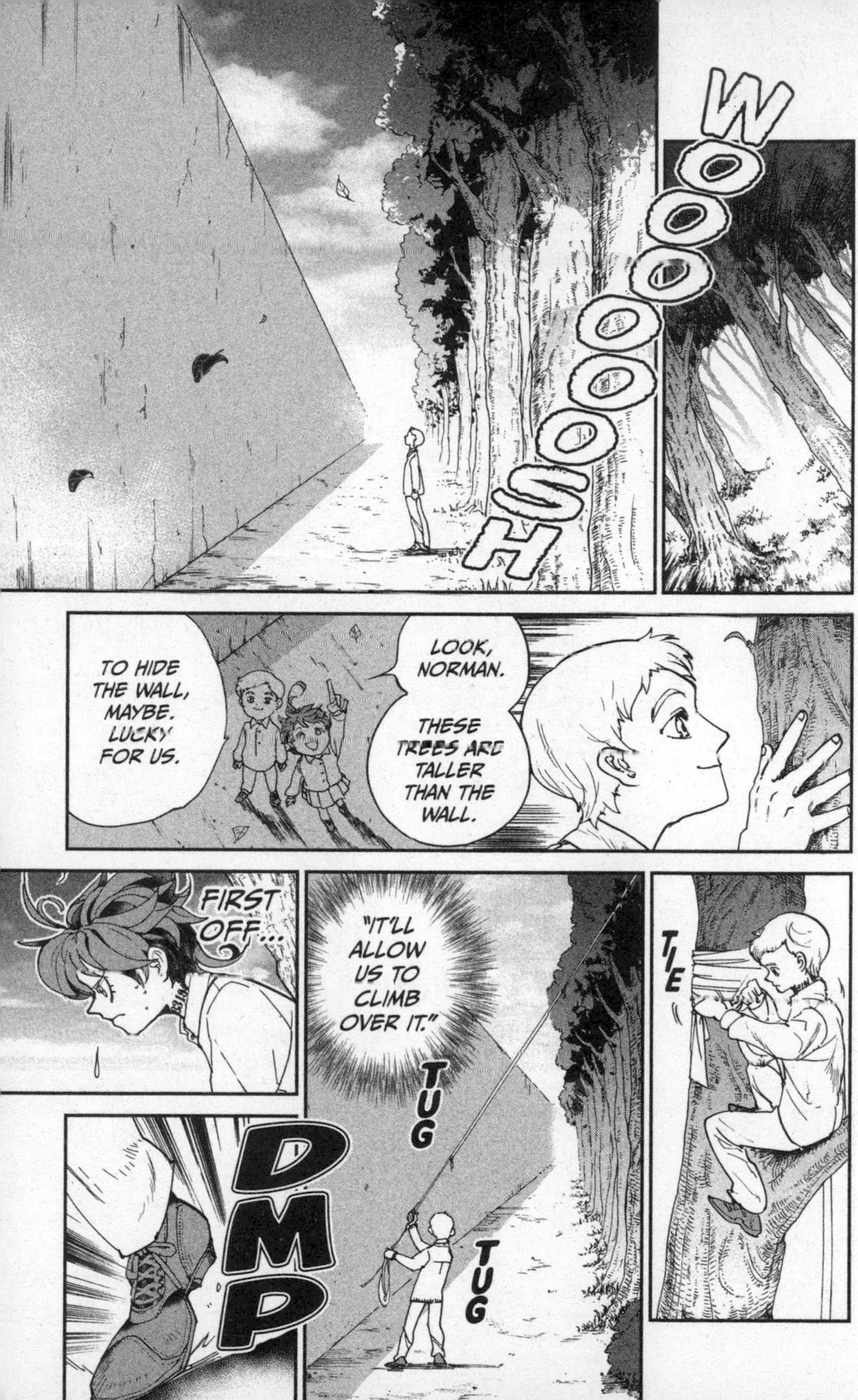
WOOOOOOSH
LOOK, NORMAN.
THESE TREES ARE TALLER THAN THE WALL.
TO HIDE THE WALL, MAYBE. LUCKY FOR US.
TIE
"IT'LL ALLOW US TO CLIMB OVER IT."
TUG
TUG
FIRST OFF...
DMP

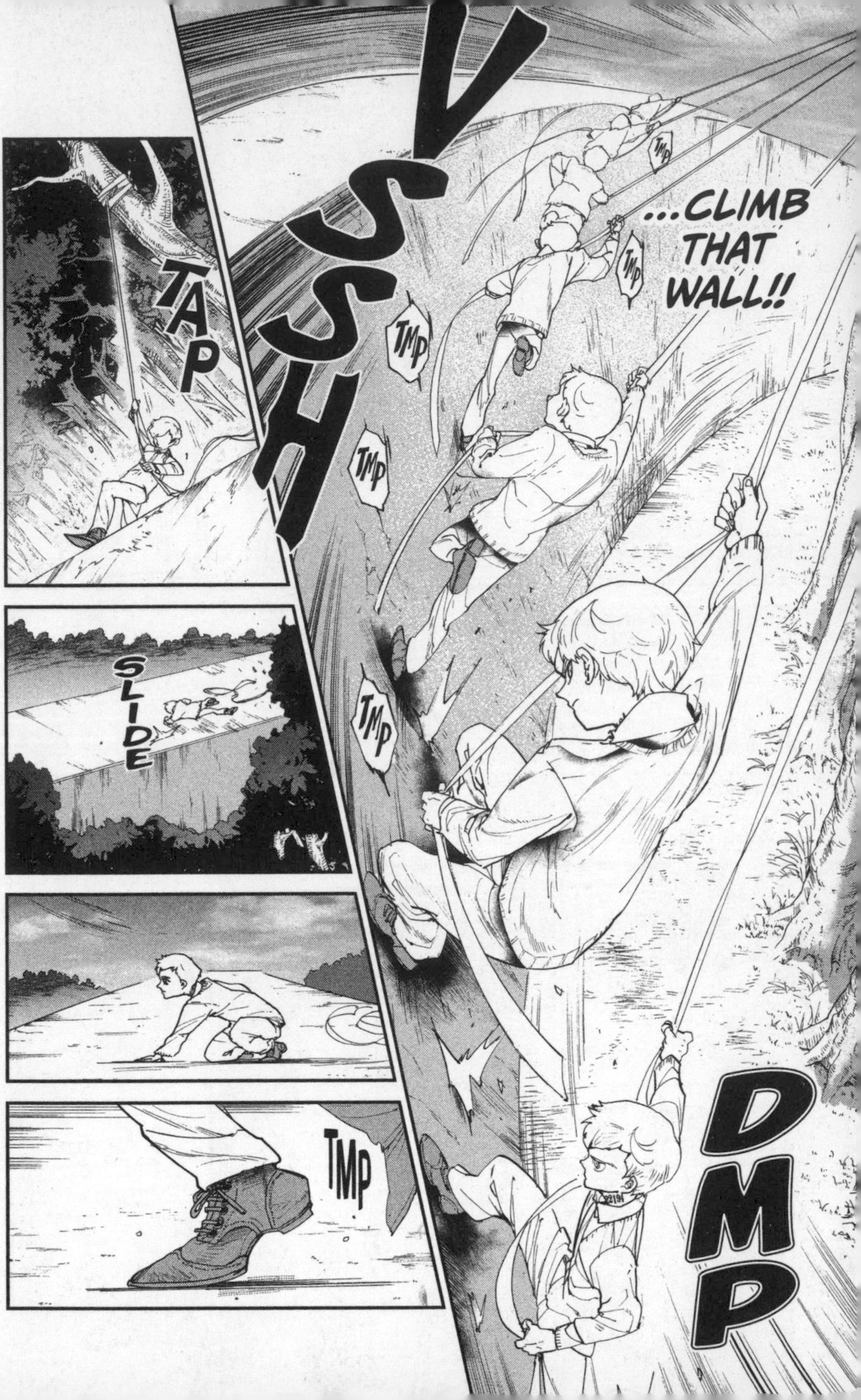
VSSH
TMP
...CLIMB THAT WALL!!
TMP
TMP
TMP
TMP
DMP
TAP
SLIDE
TMP

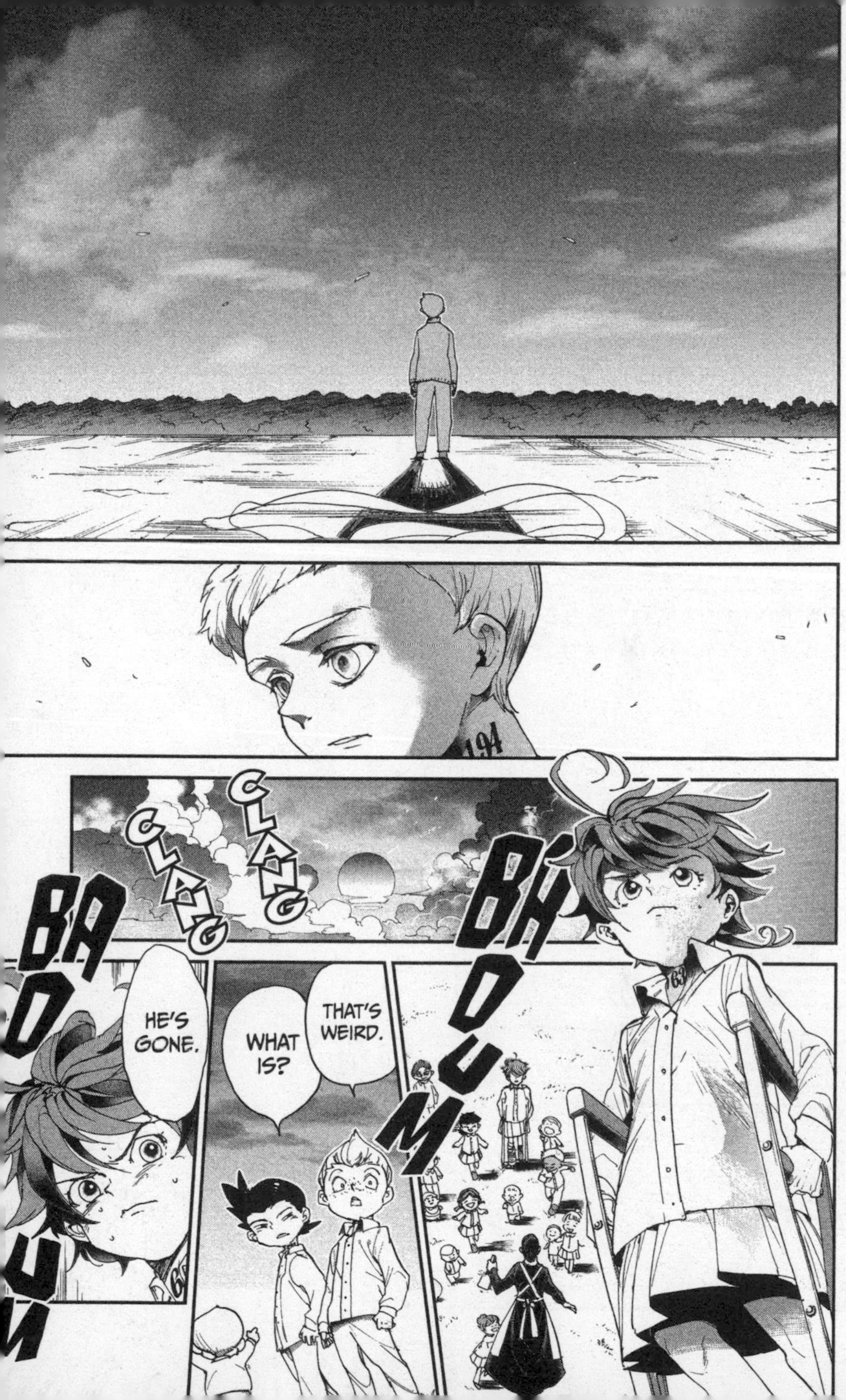
CLANG
CLANG
BA DUM
THAT'S WEIRD.
WHAT IS?
HE'S GONE.
BA DUM

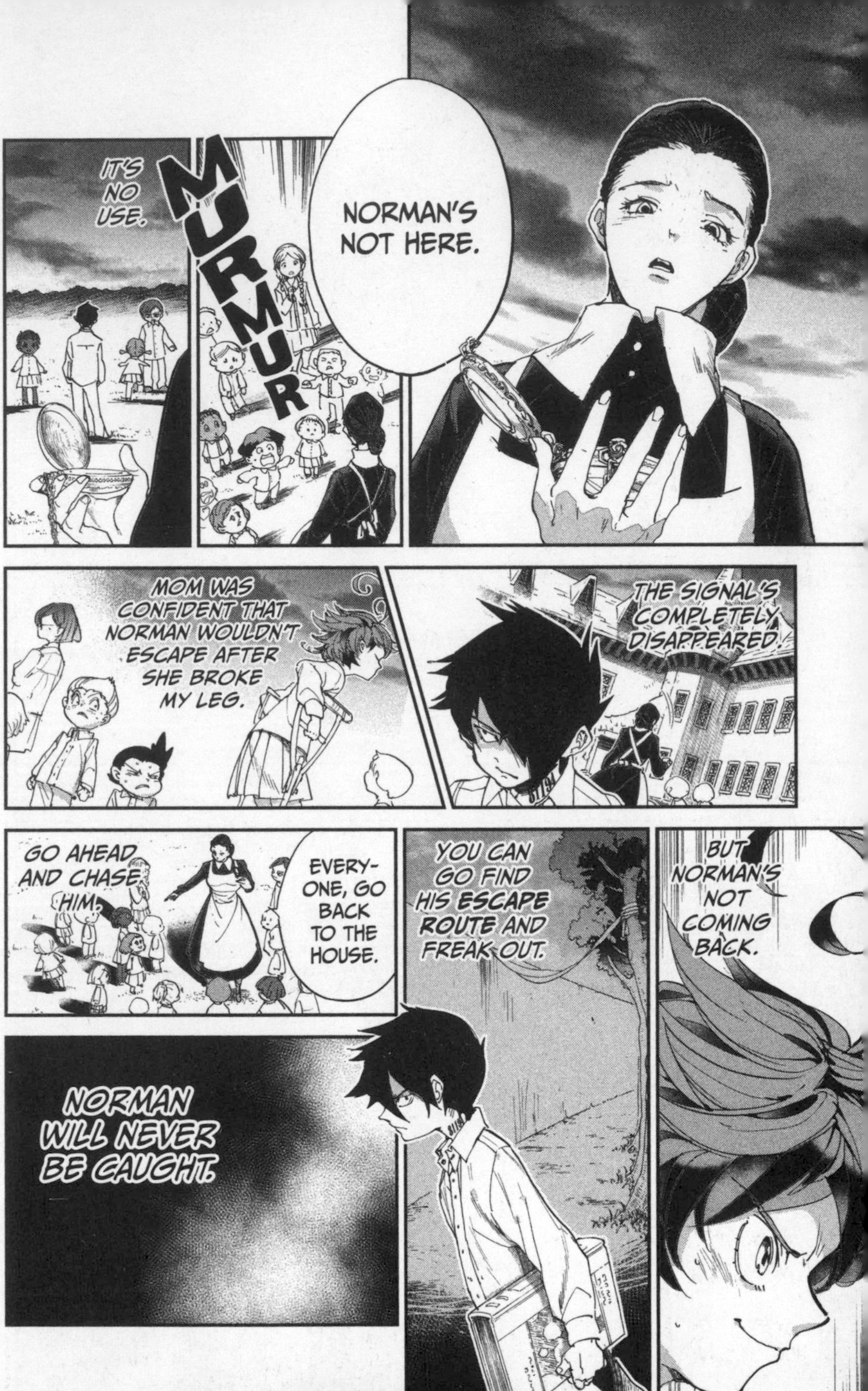
NORMAN'S NOT HERE.
MURMUR
IT'S NO USE.
THE SIGNAL'S COMPLETELY DISAPPEARED.
MOM WAS CONFIDENT THAT NORMAN WOULDN'T ESCAPE AFTER SHE BROKE MY LEG.
BUT NORMAN'S NOT COMING BACK.
YOU CAN GO FIND HIS ESCAPE ROUTE AND FREAK OUT.
EVERY-ONE, GO BACK TO THE HOUSE.
GO AHEAD AND CHASE HIM.
NORMAN WILL NEVER BE CAUGHT.

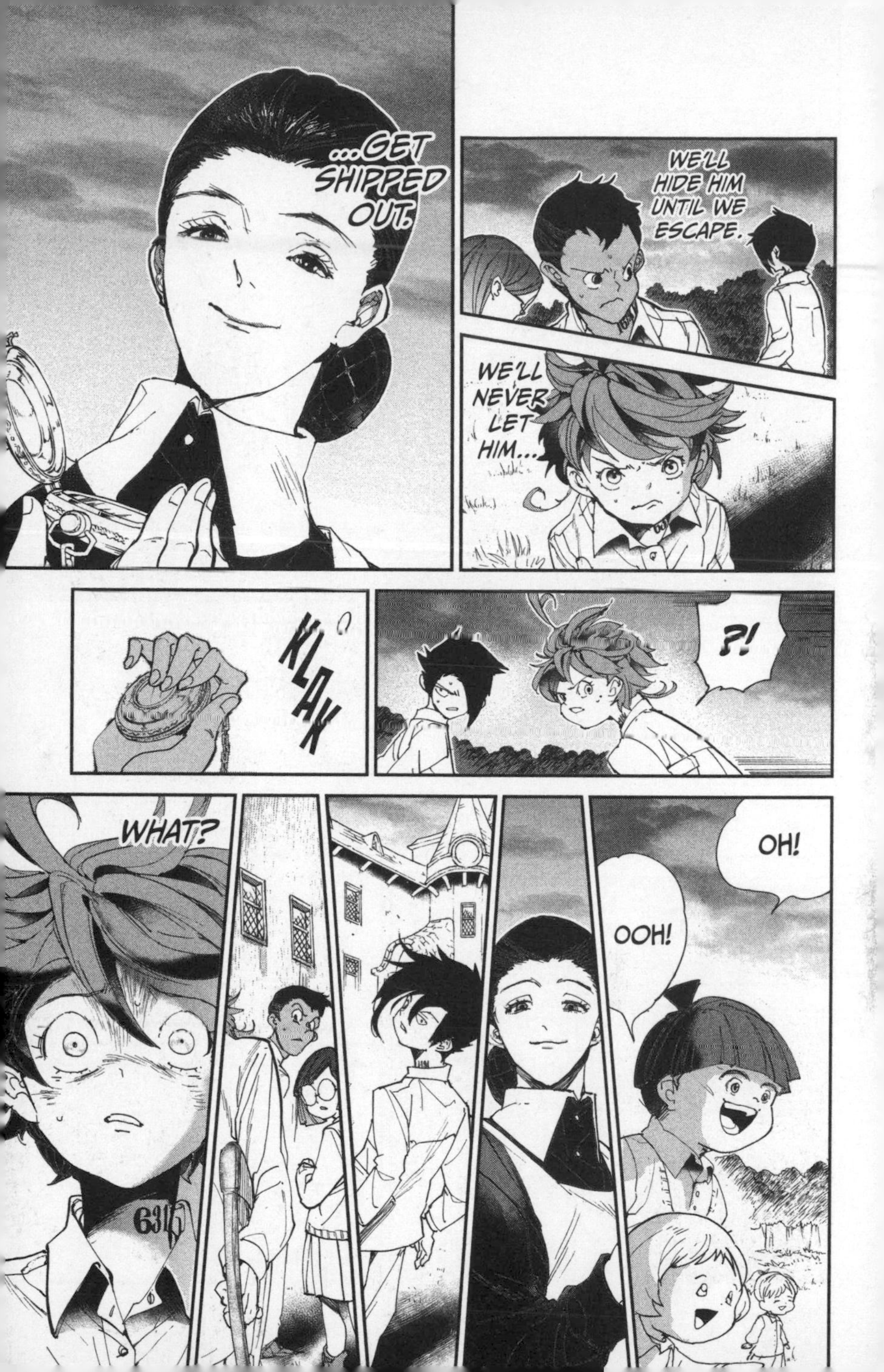

WE'LL HIDE HIM UNTIL WE ESCAPE.
WE'LL NEVER LET HIM...
...GET SHIPPED OUT.
?!
KLAK
OH!
OOH!
WHAT?

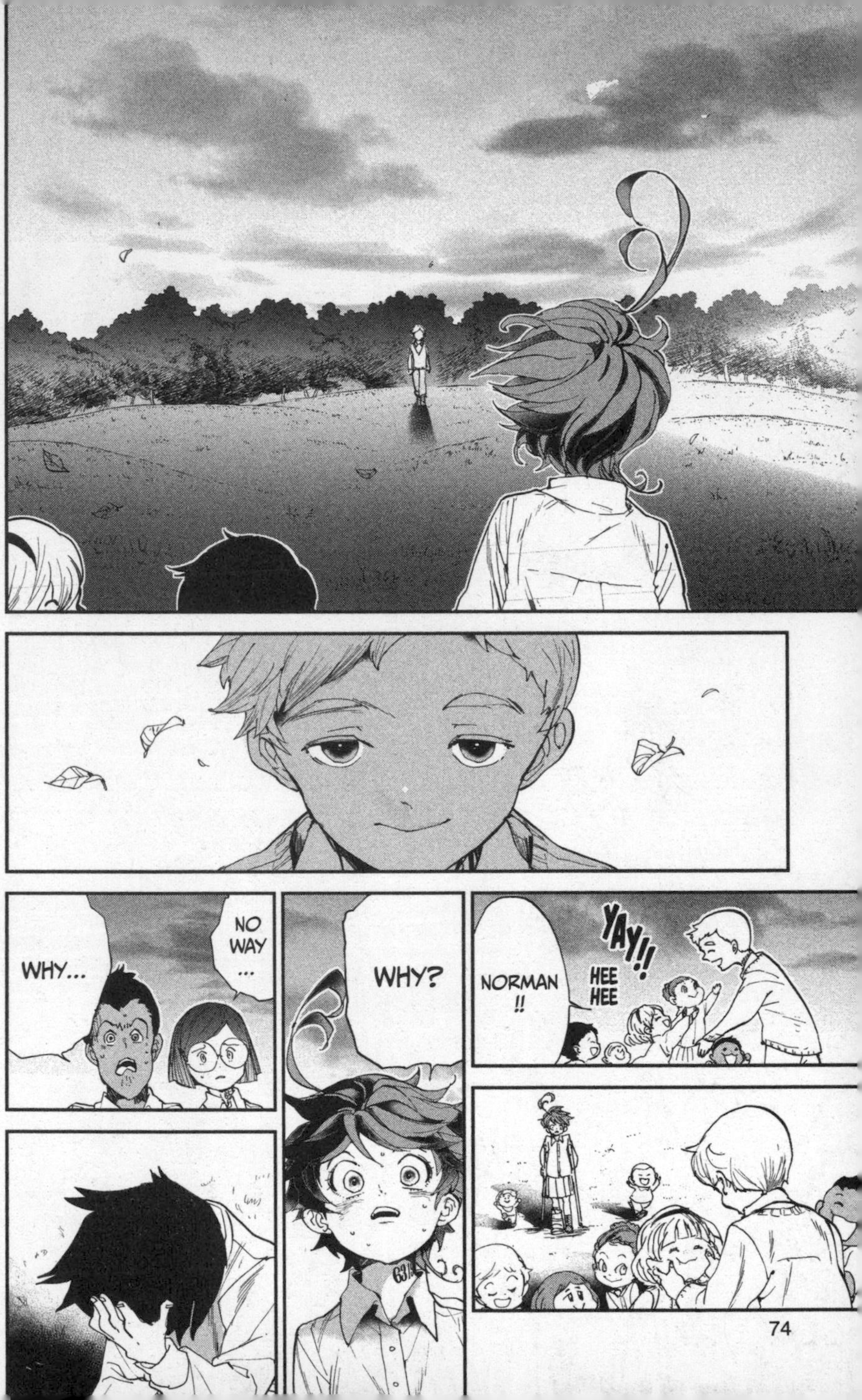

YAY!!
HEE HEE
NORMAN!!
WHY?
NO WAY...
WHY...

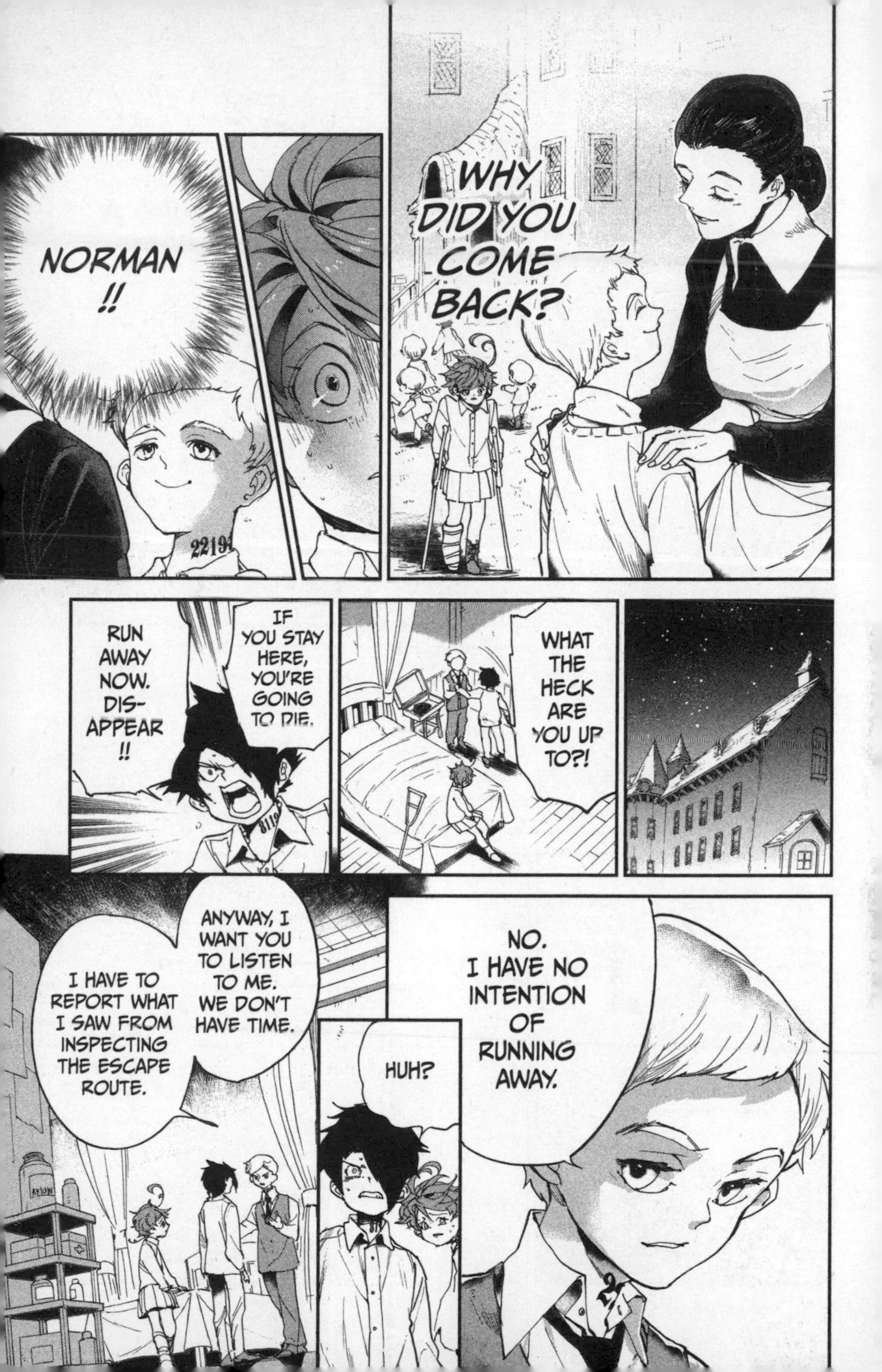
WHY DID YOU COME BACK?
NORMAN !!
WHAT THE HECK ARE YOU UP TO?!
IF YOU STAY HERE, YOU'RE GOING TO DIE.
RUN AWAY NOW. DIS-APPEAR !!
NO. I HAVE NO INTENTION OF RUNNING AWAY.
HUH?
ANYWAY, I WANT YOU TO LISTEN TO ME. WE DON'T HAVE TIME.
I HAVE TO REPORT WHAT I SAW FROM INSPECTING THE ESCAPE ROUTE.

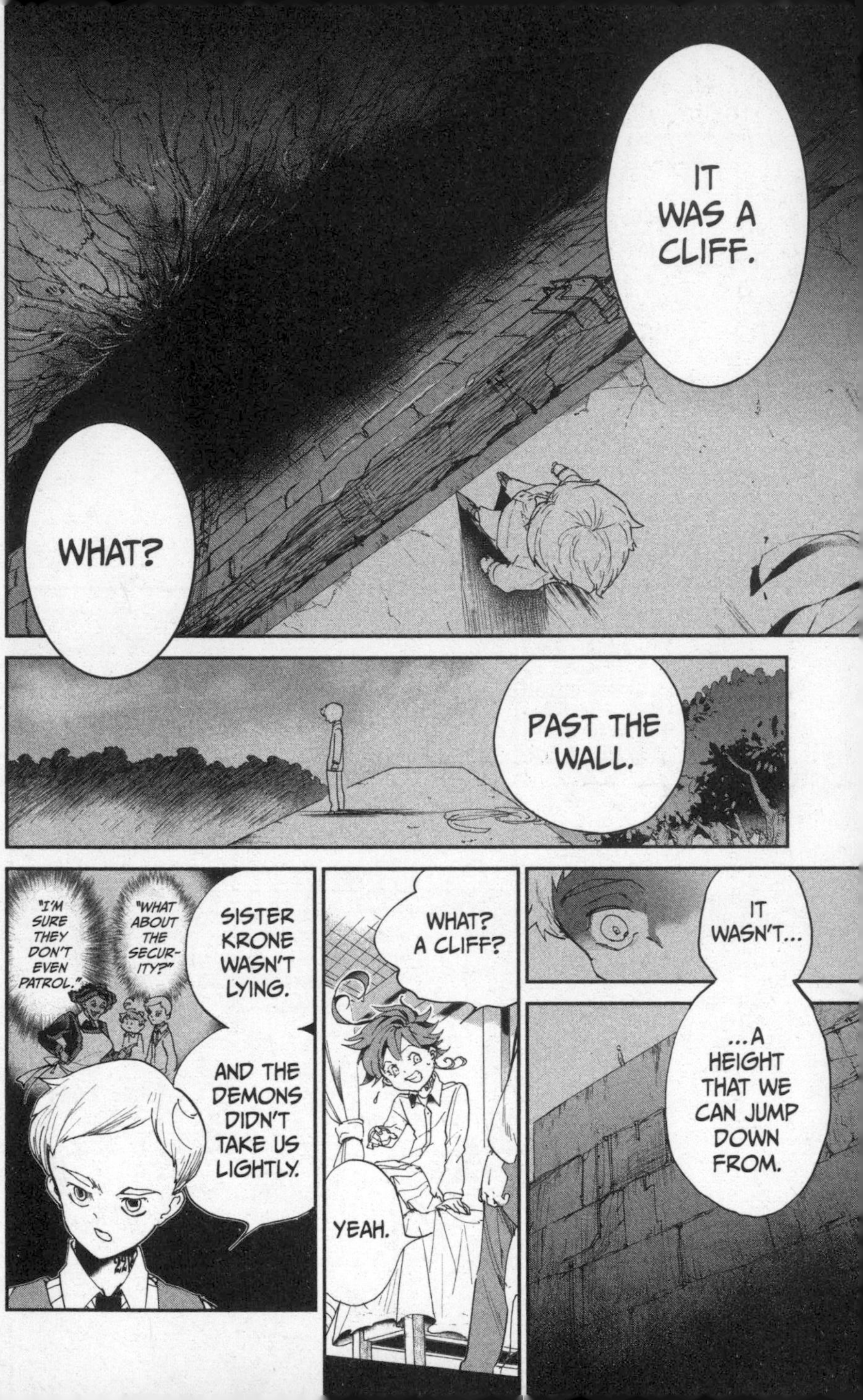
IT WAS A CLIFF.
WHAT?
PAST THE WALL.
IT WASN'T...
...A HEIGHT THAT WE CAN JUMP DOWN FROM.
WHAT? A CLIFF?
YEAH.
SISTER KRONE WASN'T LYING.
"WHAT ABOUT THE SECURITY?"
"I'M SURE THEY DON'T EVEN PATROL."
AND THE DEMONS DIDN'T TAKE US LIGHTLY.

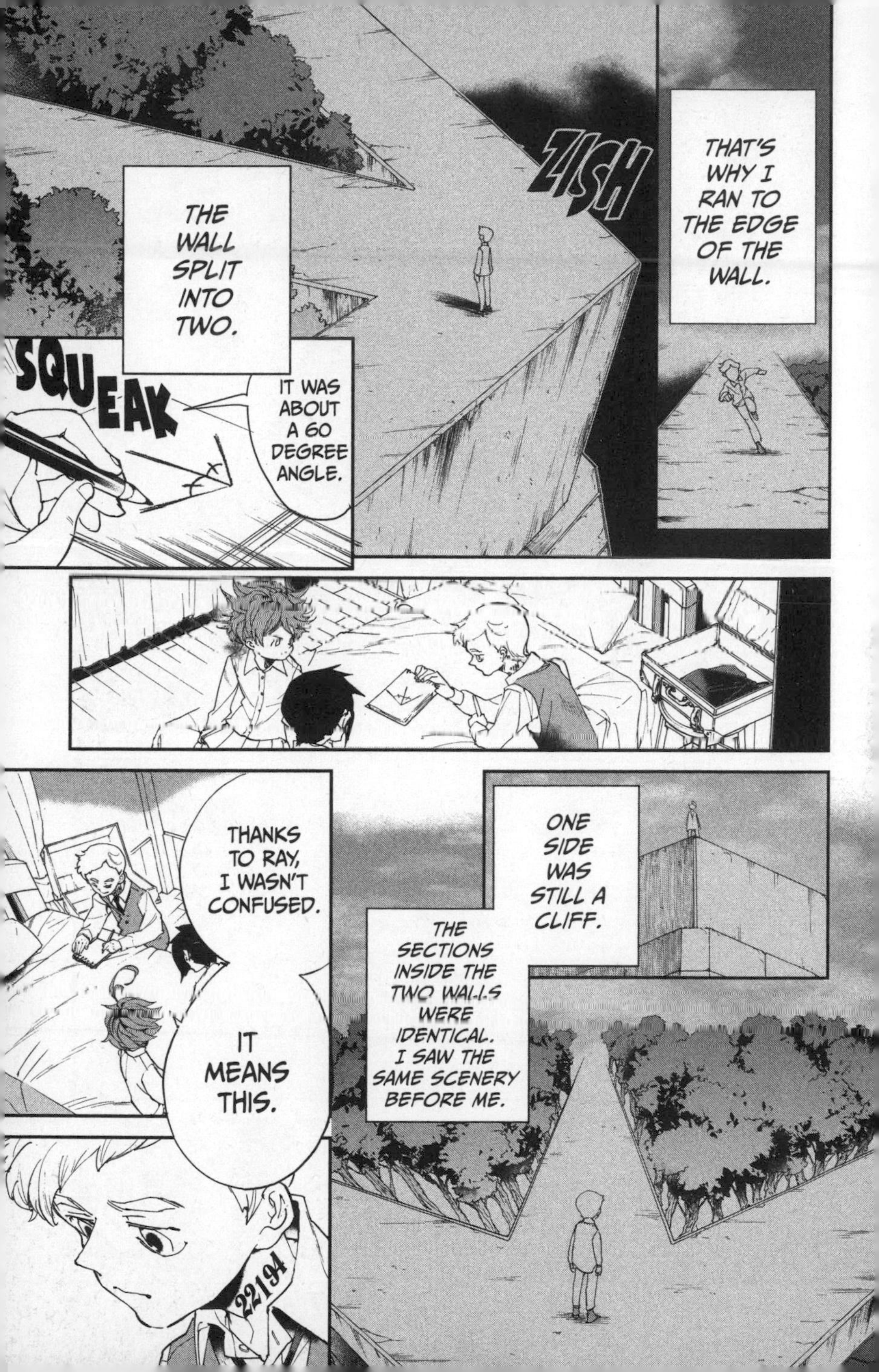
THAT'S WHY I RAN TO THE EDGE OF THE WALL.
ZISH
THE WALL SPLIT INTO TWO.
SQUEAK
IT WAS ABOUT A 60 DEGREE ANGLE.
ONE SIDE WAS STILL A CLIFF.
THE SECTIONS INSIDE THE TWO WALLS WERE IDENTICAL. I SAW THE SAME SCENERY BEFORE ME.
THANKS TO RAY, I WASN'T CONFUSED.
IT MEANS THIS.
22194

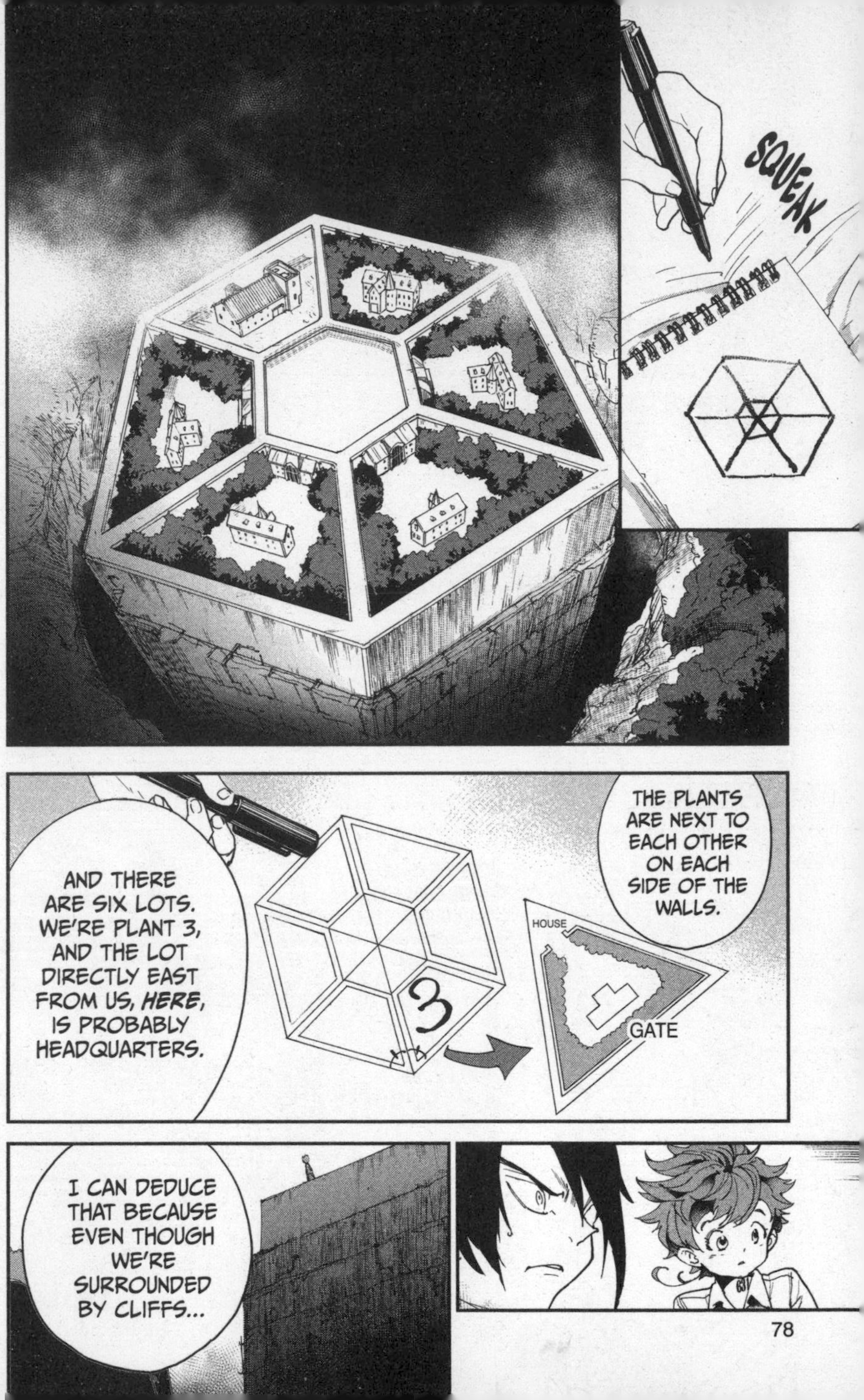

SQUEAK
THE PLANTS ARE NEXT TO EACH OTHER ON EACH SIDE OF THE WALLS.
AND THERE ARE SIX LOTS. WE'RE PLANT 3, AND THE LOT DIRECTLY EAST FROM US, *HERE*, IS PROBABLY HEADQUARTERS.
3
HOUSE
GATE
I CAN DEDUCE THAT BECAUSE EVEN THOUGH WE'RE SURROUNDED BY CLIFFS...

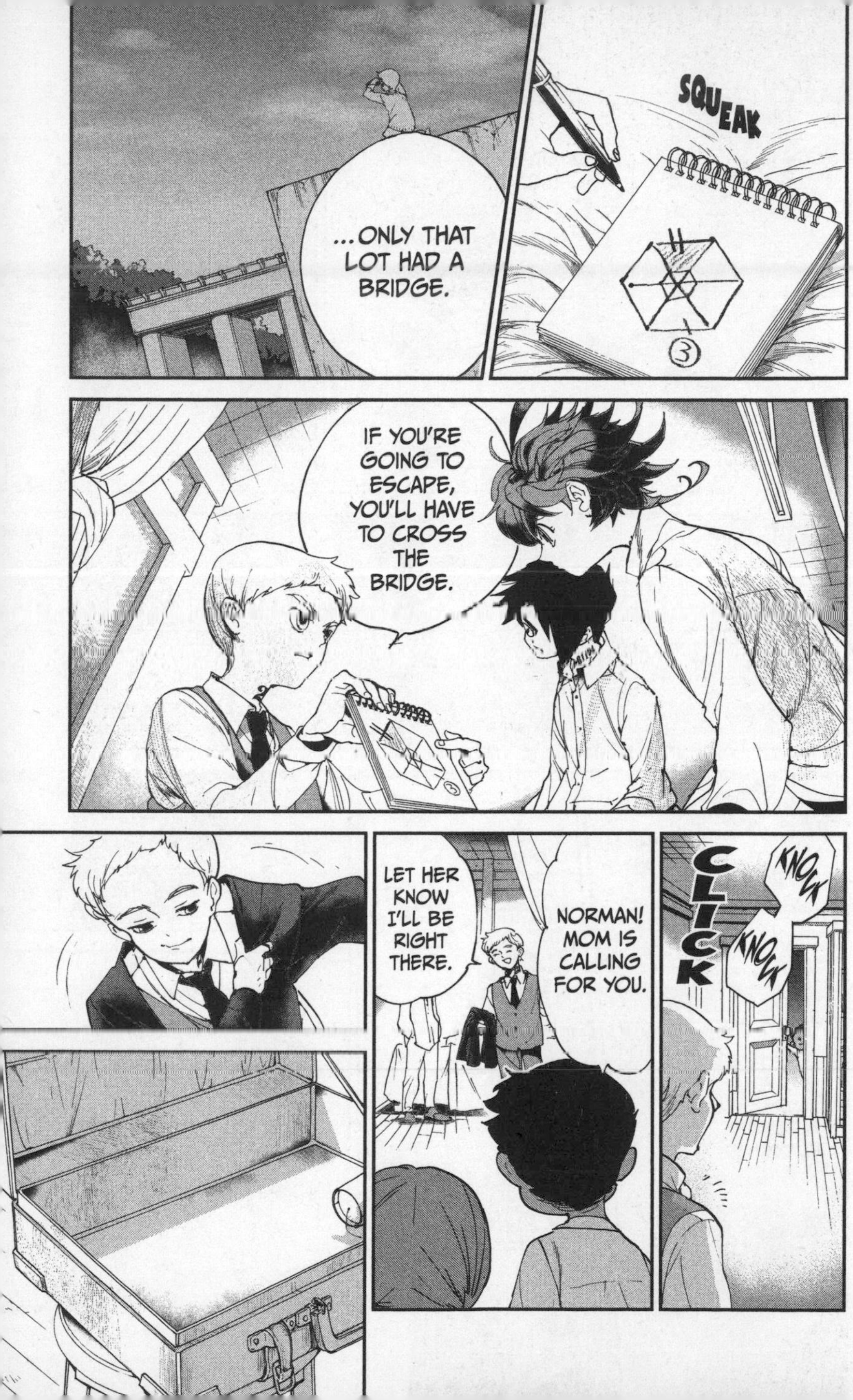
SQUEAK
...ONLY THAT LOT HAD A BRIDGE.
IF YOU'RE GOING TO ESCAPE, YOU'LL HAVE TO CROSS THE BRIDGE.
CLICK
KNOCK
KNOCK
NORMAN! MOM IS CALLING FOR YOU.
LET HER KNOW I'LL BE RIGHT THERE.

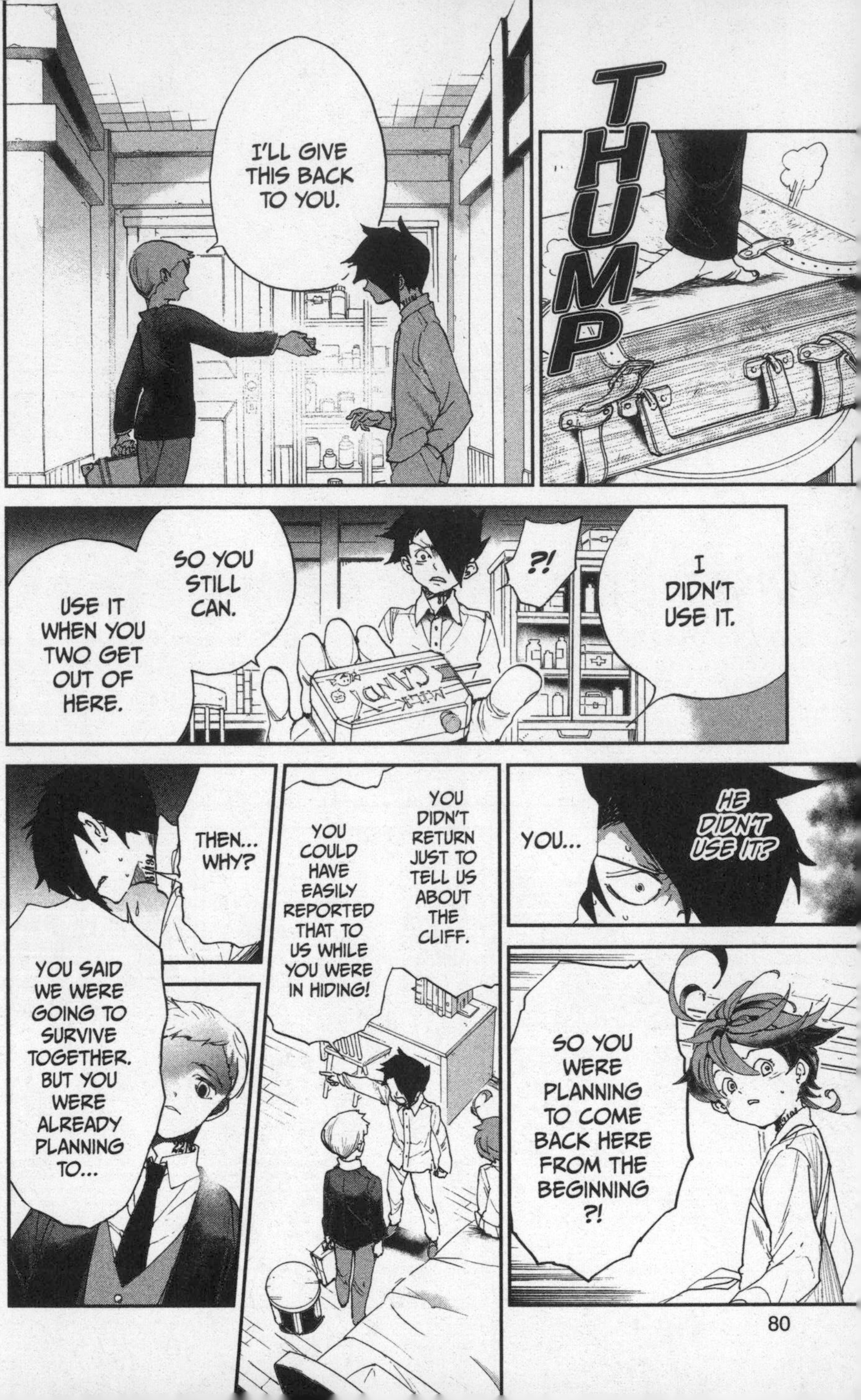
THUMP
I'LL GIVE THIS BACK TO YOU.
I DIDN'T USE IT.
?!
SO YOU STILL CAN.
USE IT WHEN YOU TWO GET OUT OF HERE.
HE DIDN'T USE IT?
YOU...
YOU DIDN'T RETURN JUST TO TELL US ABOUT THE CLIFF.
YOU COULD HAVE EASILY REPORTED THAT TO US WHILE YOU WERE IN HIDING!
THEN... WHY?
SO YOU WERE PLANNING TO COME BACK HERE FROM THE BEGINNING ?!
YOU SAID WE WERE GOING TO SURVIVE TOGETHER. BUT YOU WERE ALREADY PLANNING TO...

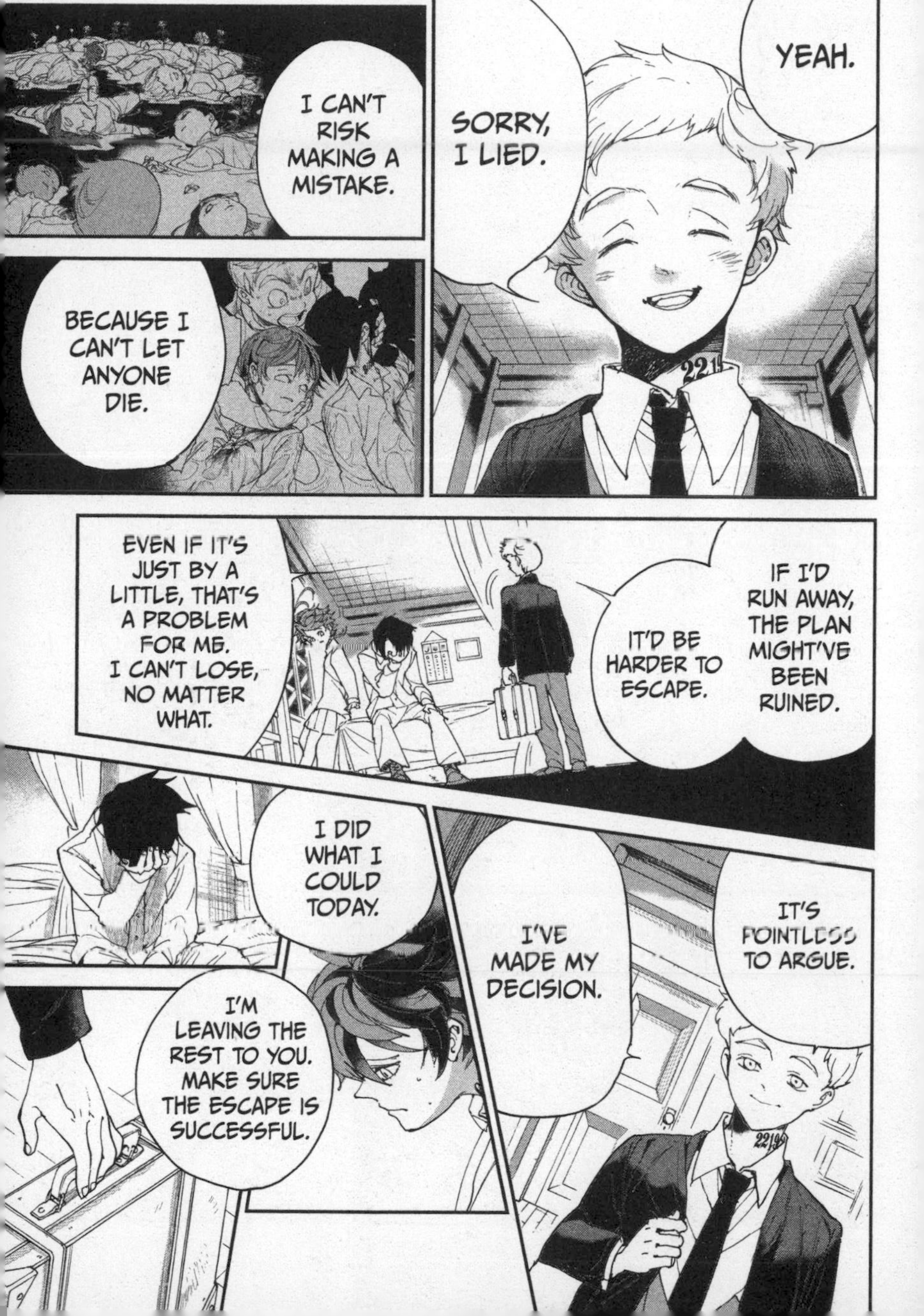
YEAH.
SORRY, I LIED.
I CAN'T RISK MAKING A MISTAKE.
BECAUSE I CAN'T LET ANYONE DIE.
IF I'D RUN AWAY, THE PLAN MIGHT'VE BEEN RUINED.
IT'D BE HARDER TO ESCAPE.
EVEN IF IT'S JUST BY A LITTLE, THAT'S A PROBLEM FOR ME. I CAN'T LOSE, NO MATTER WHAT.
IT'S POINTLESS TO ARGUE.
I'VE MADE MY DECISION.
I DID WHAT I COULD TODAY.
I'M LEAVING THE REST TO YOU. MAKE SURE THE ESCAPE IS SUCCESSFUL.

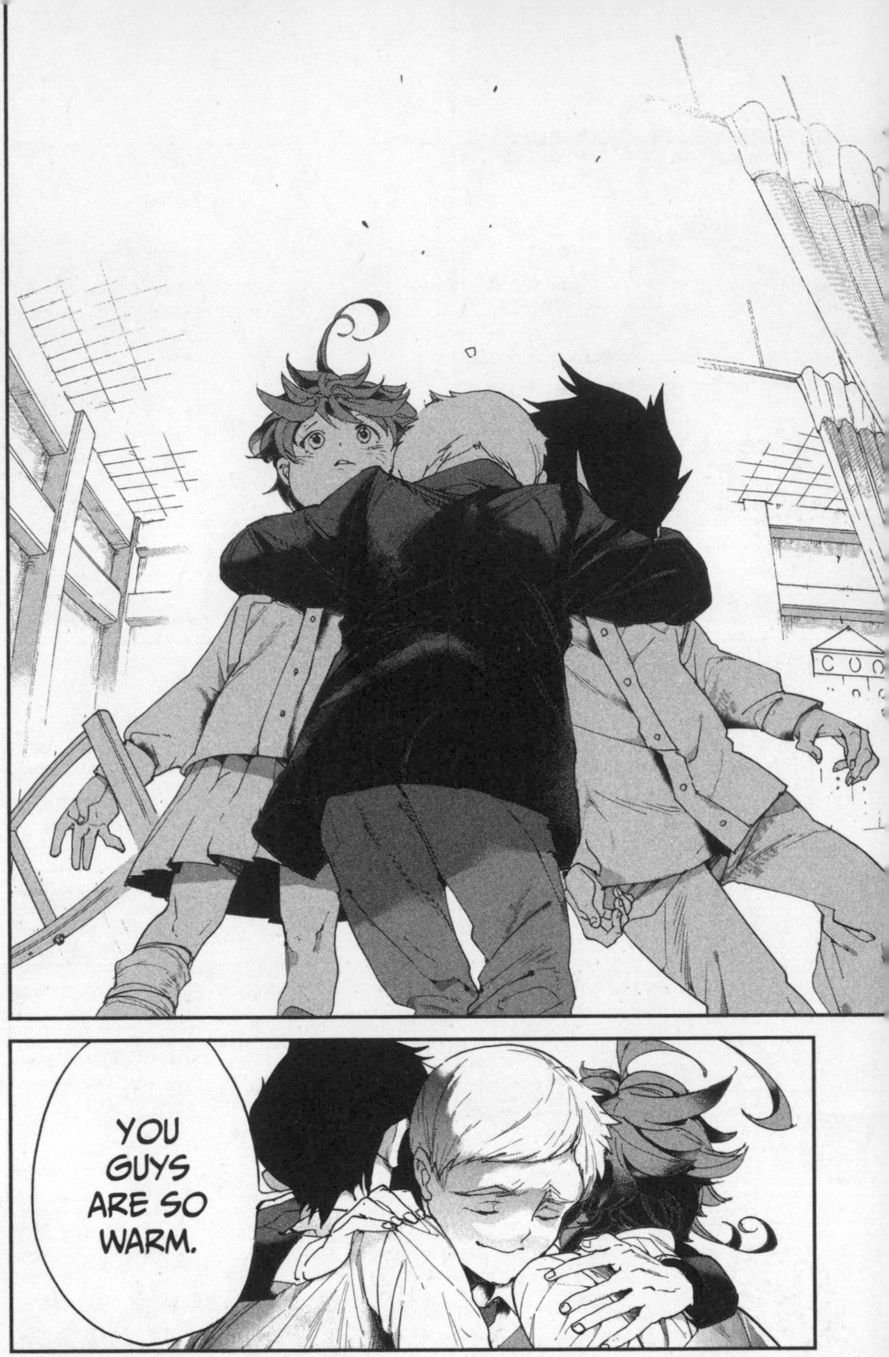
YOU GUYS ARE SO WARM.

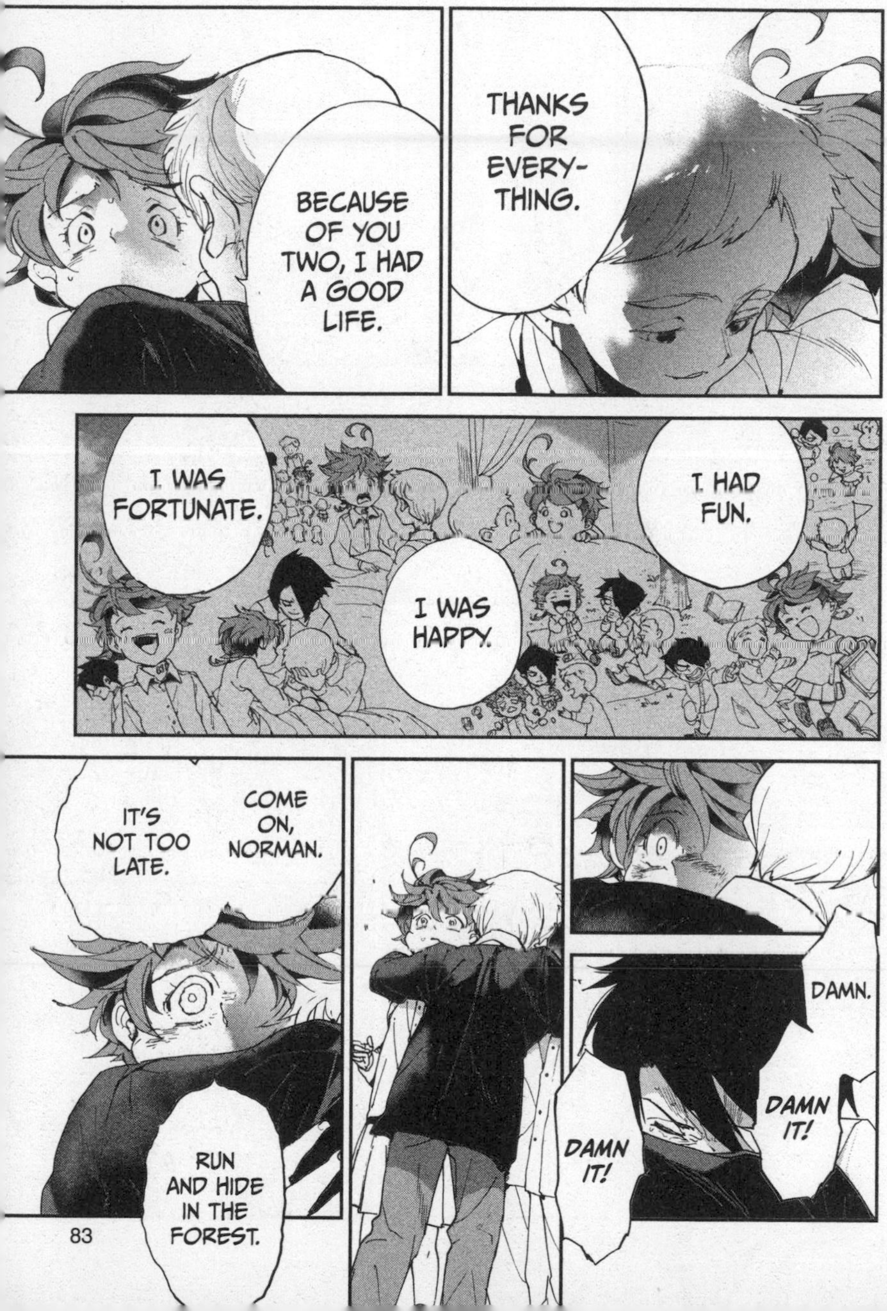
THANKS FOR EVERY-THING.
BECAUSE OF YOU TWO, I HAD A GOOD LIFE.
I HAD FUN.
I WAS FORTUNATE.
I WAS HAPPY.
DAMN.
DAMN IT!
DAMN IT!
COME ON, NORMAN.
IT'S NOT TOO LATE.
RUN AND HIDE IN THE FOREST.

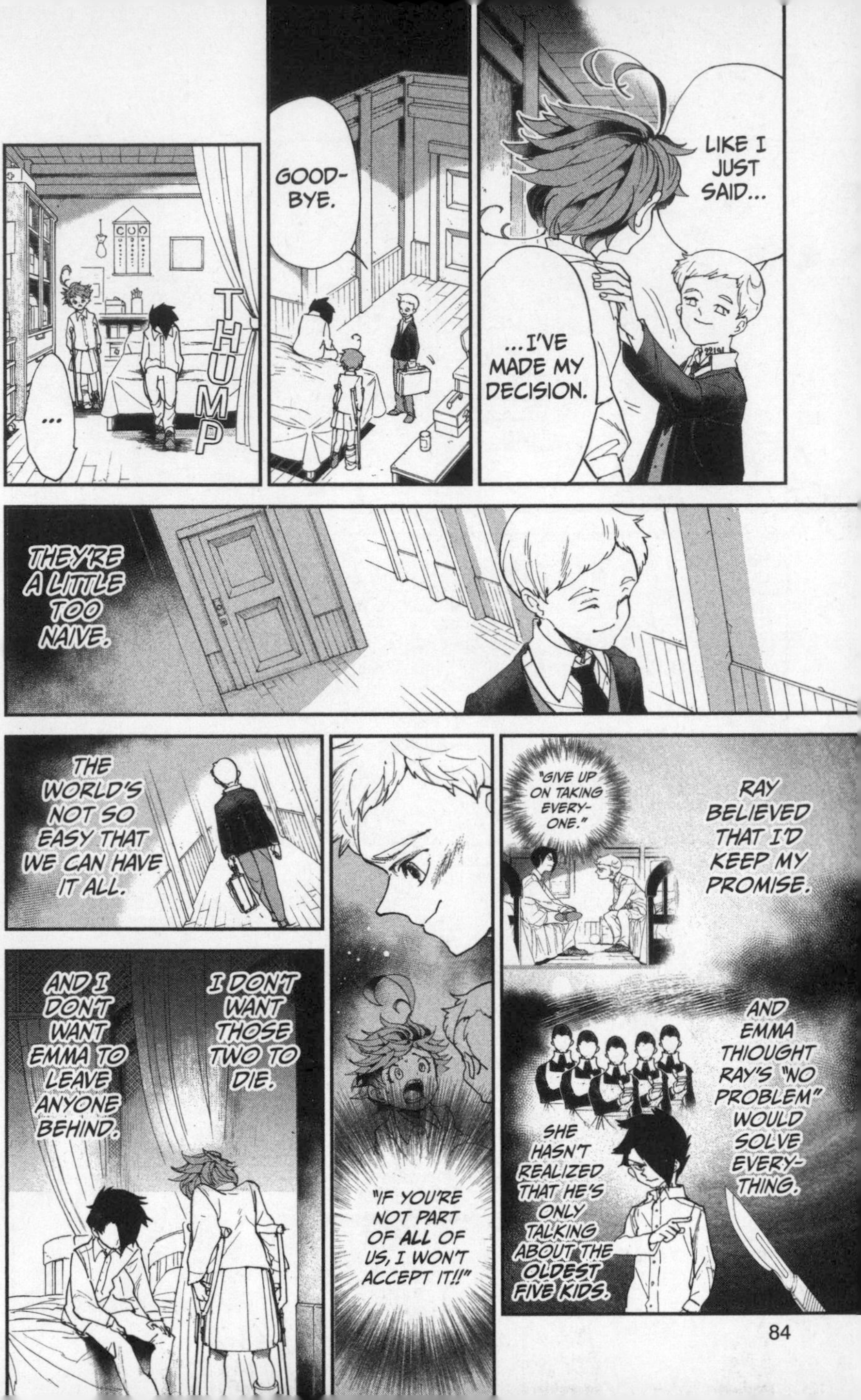
LIKE I JUST SAID...
...I'VE MADE MY DECISION.
GOOD-BYE.
...
THUMP
THEY'RE A LITTLE TOO NAIVE.
RAY BELIEVED THAT I'D KEEP MY PROMISE.
"GIVE UP ON TAKING EVERY-ONE."
AND EMMA THIOUGHT RAY'S "NO PROBLEM" WOULD SOLVE EVERY-THING.
SHE HASN'T REALIZED THAT HE'S ONLY TALKING ABOUT THE OLDEST FIVE KIDS.
"IF YOU'RE NOT PART OF ALL OF US, I WON'T ACCEPT IT!!"
THE WORLD'S NOT SO EASY THAT WE CAN HAVE IT ALL.
I DON'T WANT THOSE TWO TO DIE.
AND I DON'T WANT EMMA TO LEAVE ANYONE BEHIND.

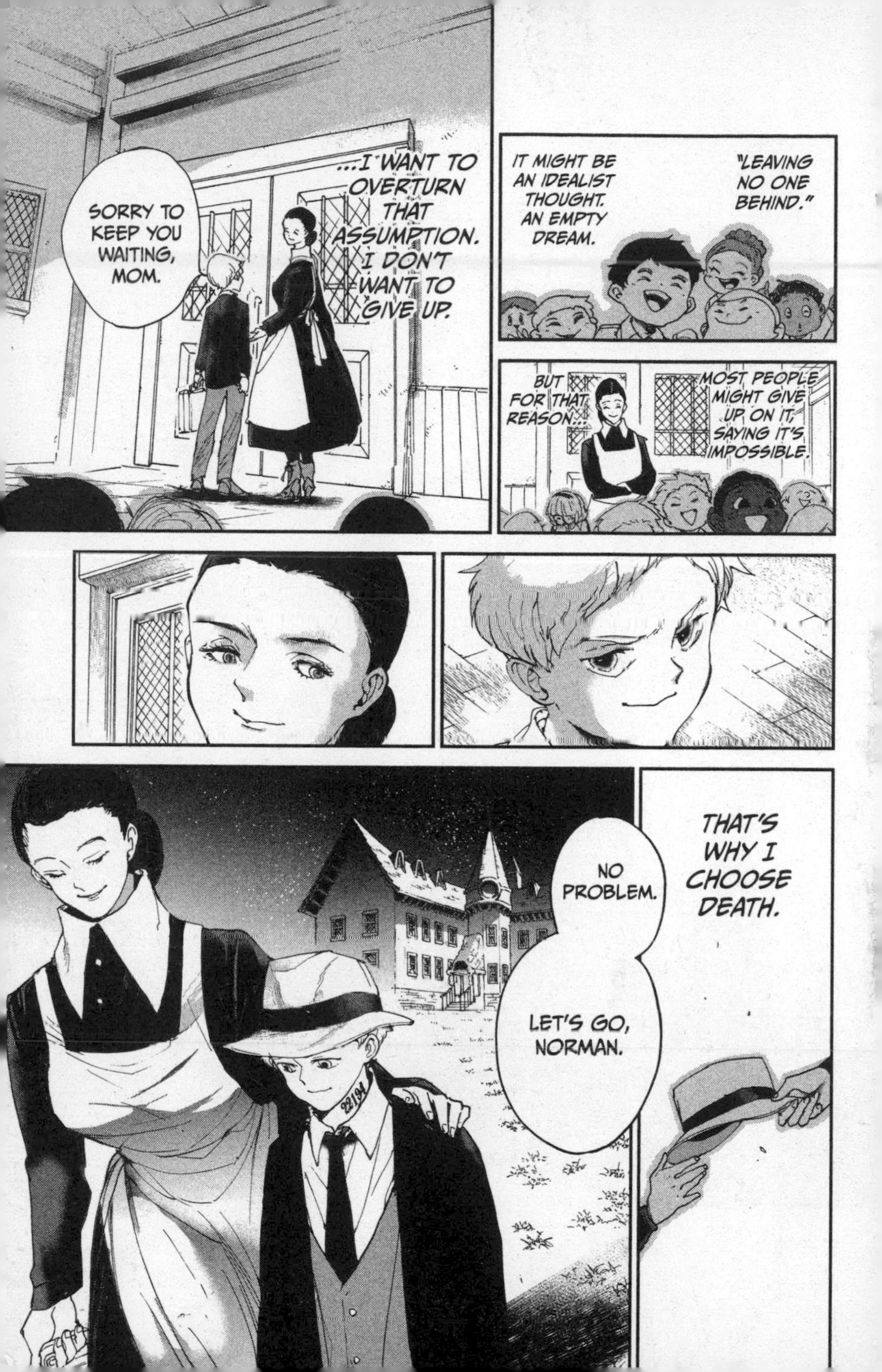
"LEAVING NO ONE BEHIND."
IT MIGHT BE AN IDEALIST THOUGHT. AN EMPTY DREAM.
MOST PEOPLE MIGHT GIVE UP ON IT, SAYING IT'S IMPOSSIBLE.
BUT FOR THAT REASON...
...I WANT TO OVERTURN THAT ASSUMPTION. I DON'T WANT TO GIVE UP.
SORRY TO KEEP YOU WAITING, MOM.
THAT'S WHY I CHOOSE DEATH.
NO PROBLEM.
LET'S GO, NORMAN.
22194

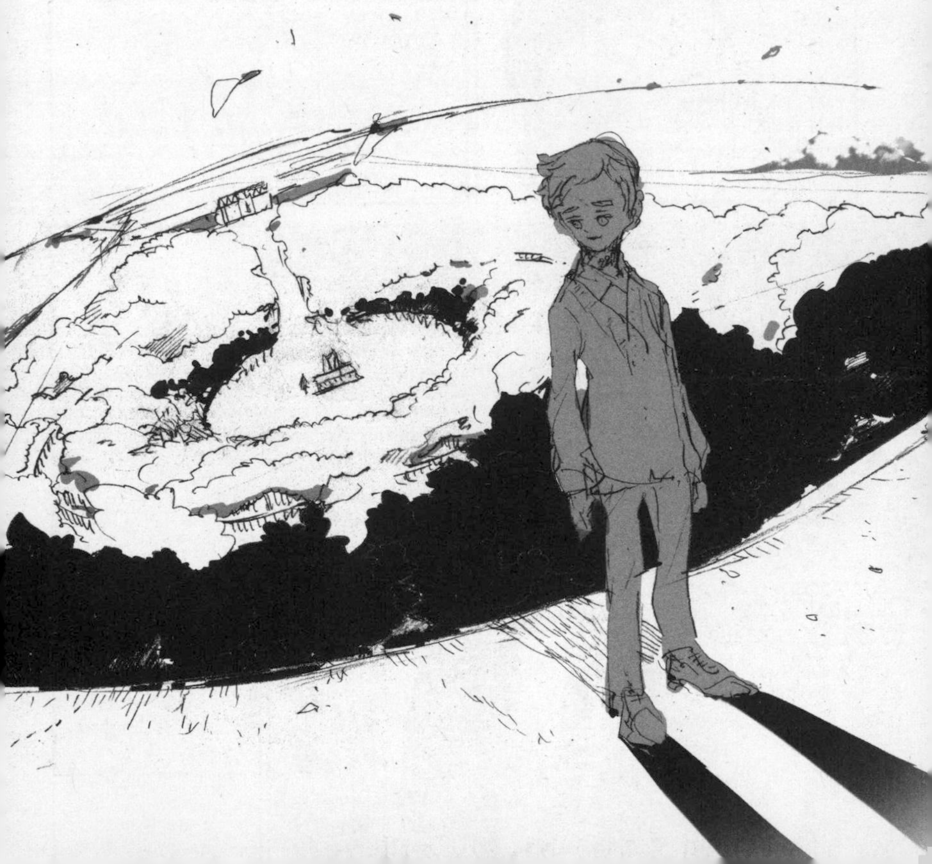

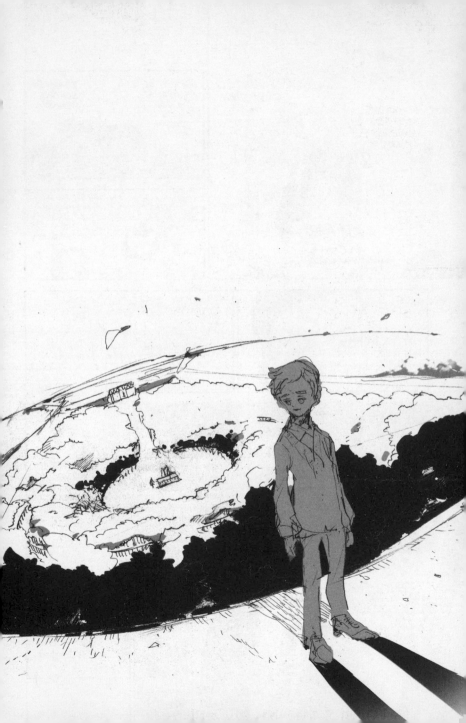

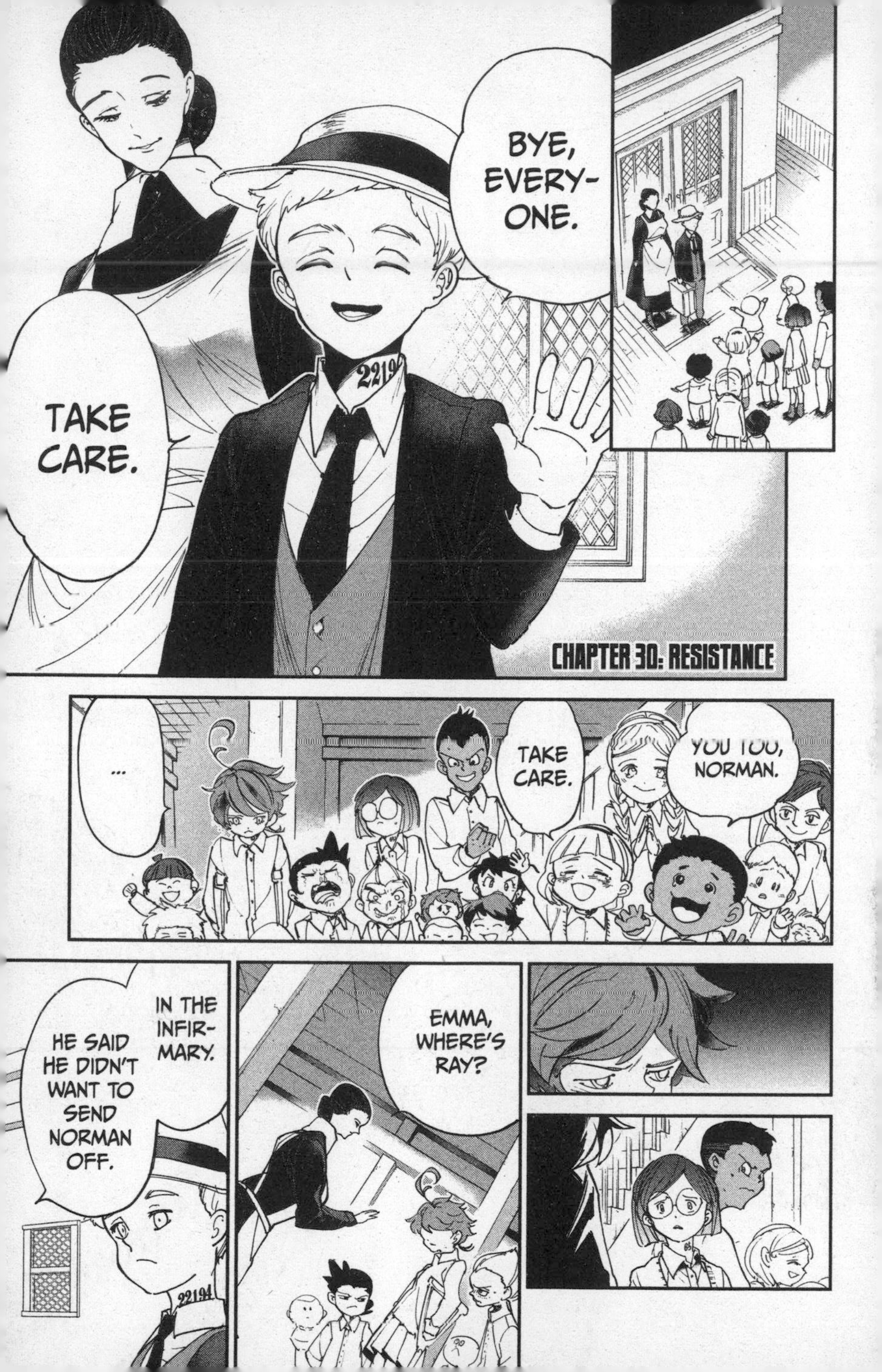
BYE, EVERY-ONE.
TAKE CARE.
CHAPTER 30: RESISTANCE
YOU TOO, NORMAN.
TAKE CARE.
...
EMMA, WHERE'S RAY?
IN THE INFIRMARY.
HE SAID HE DIDN'T WANT TO SEND NORMAN OFF.
22194

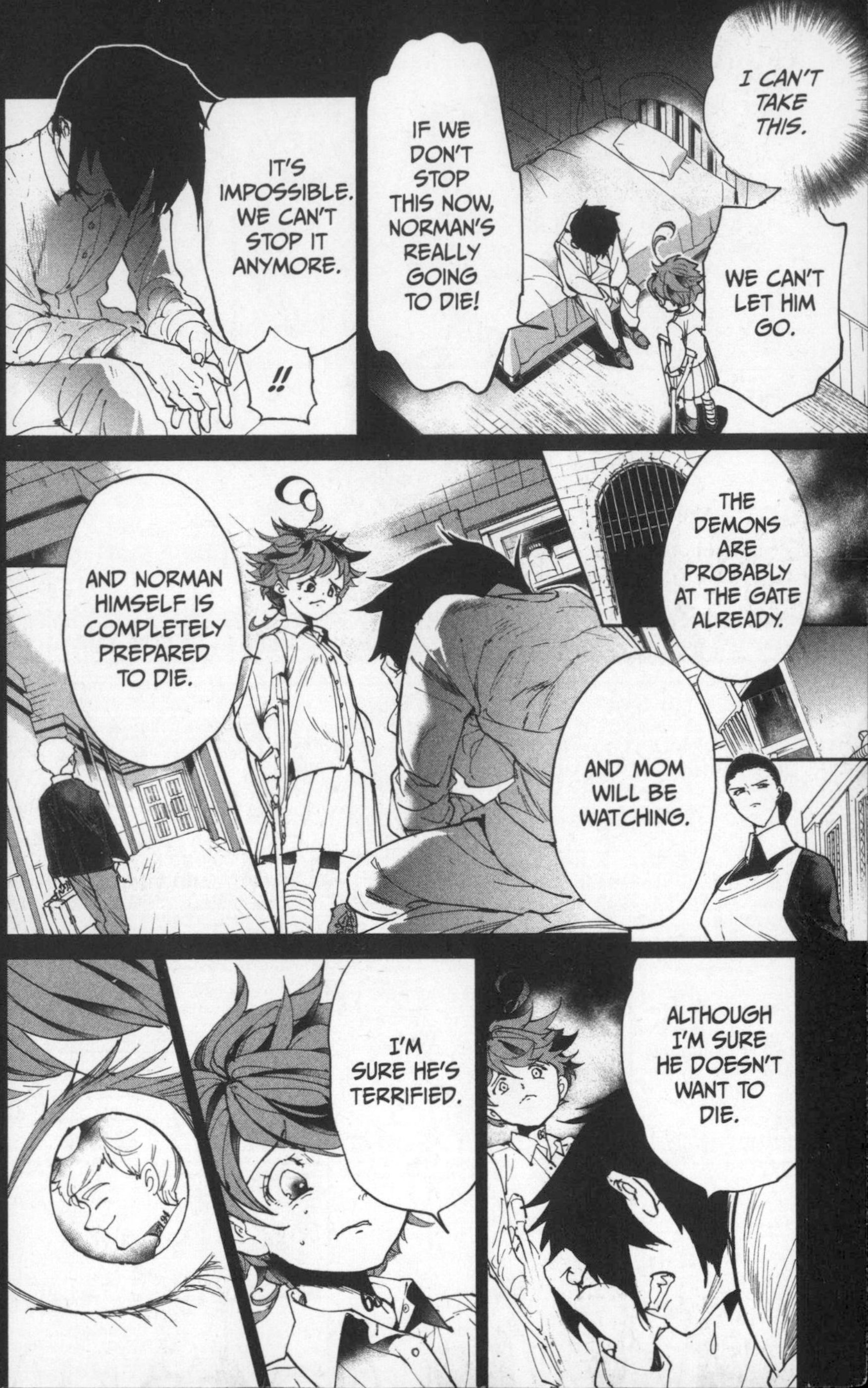
I CAN'T TAKE THIS.
WE CAN'T LET HIM GO.
IF WE DON'T STOP THIS NOW, NORMAN'S REALLY GOING TO DIE!
IT'S IMPOSSIBLE. WE CAN'T STOP IT ANYMORE.
!!
THE DEMONS ARE PROBABLY AT THE GATE ALREADY.
AND MOM WILL BE WATCHING.
AND NORMAN HIMSELF IS COMPLETELY PREPARED TO DIE.
ALTHOUGH I'M SURE HE DOESN'T WANT TO DIE.
I'M SURE HE'S TERRIFIED.

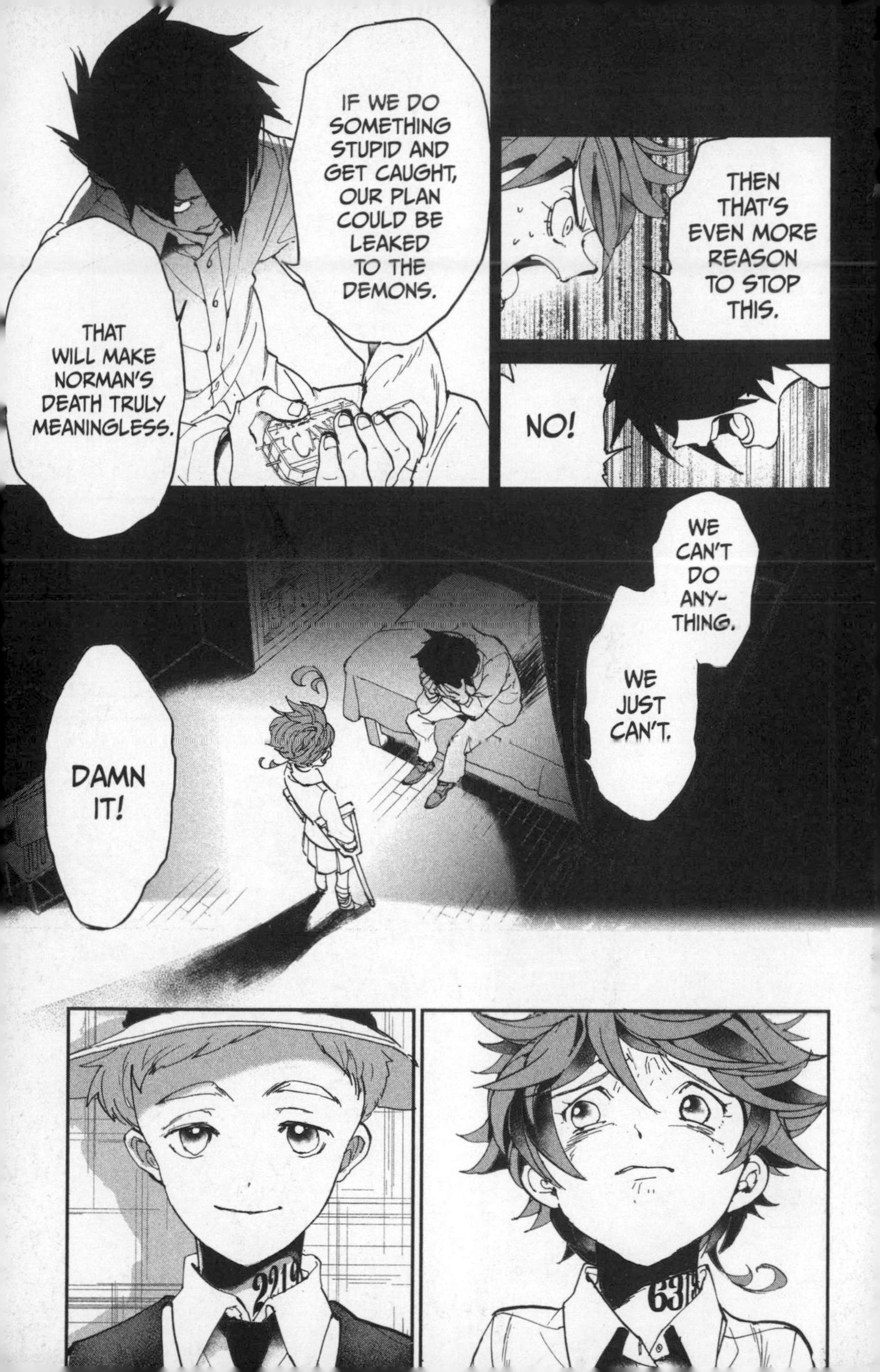
THEN THAT'S EVEN MORE REASON TO STOP THIS.
NO!
IF WE DO SOMETHING STUPID AND GET CAUGHT, OUR PLAN COULD BE LEAKED TO THE DEMONS.
THAT WILL MAKE NORMAN'S DEATH TRULY MEANINGLESS.
WE CAN'T DO ANY-THING.
WE JUST CAN'T.
DAMN IT!

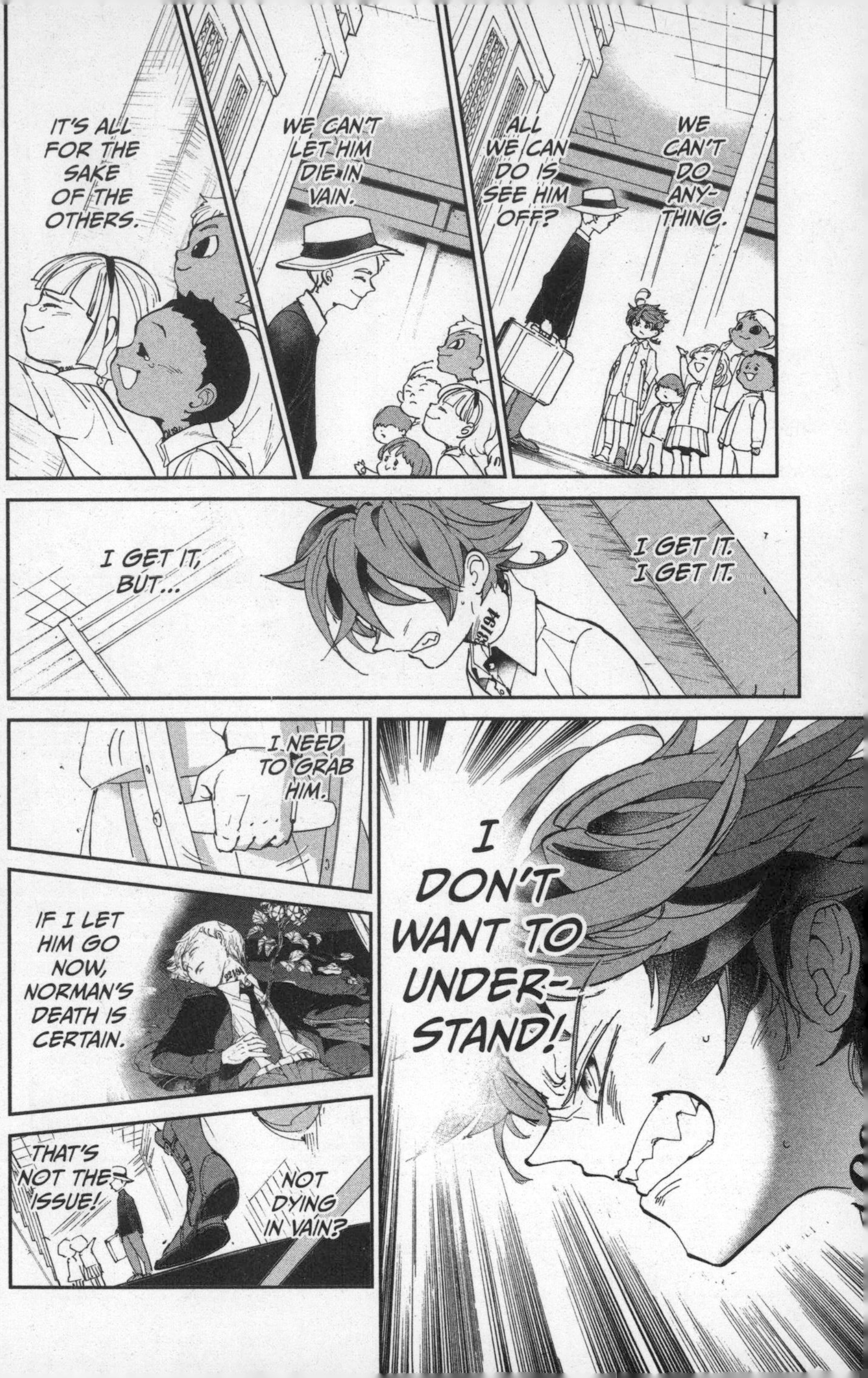
WE CAN'T DO ANY-THING.
ALL WE CAN DO IS SEE HIM OFF?
WE CAN'T LET HIM DIE IN VAIN.
IT'S ALL FOR THE SAKE OF THE OTHERS.
I GET IT. I GET IT.
I GET IT, BUT...
I DON'T WANT TO UNDER-STAND!
I NEED TO GRAB HIM.
IF I LET HIM GO NOW, NORMAN'S DEATH IS CERTAIN.
NOT DYING IN VAIN?
THAT'S NOT THE ISSUE!

NORMAN
!!

I CAN'T LET HIM DIE-- PERIOD.

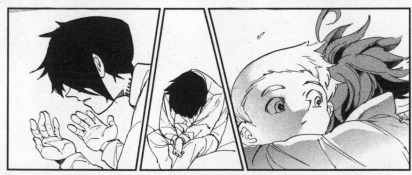

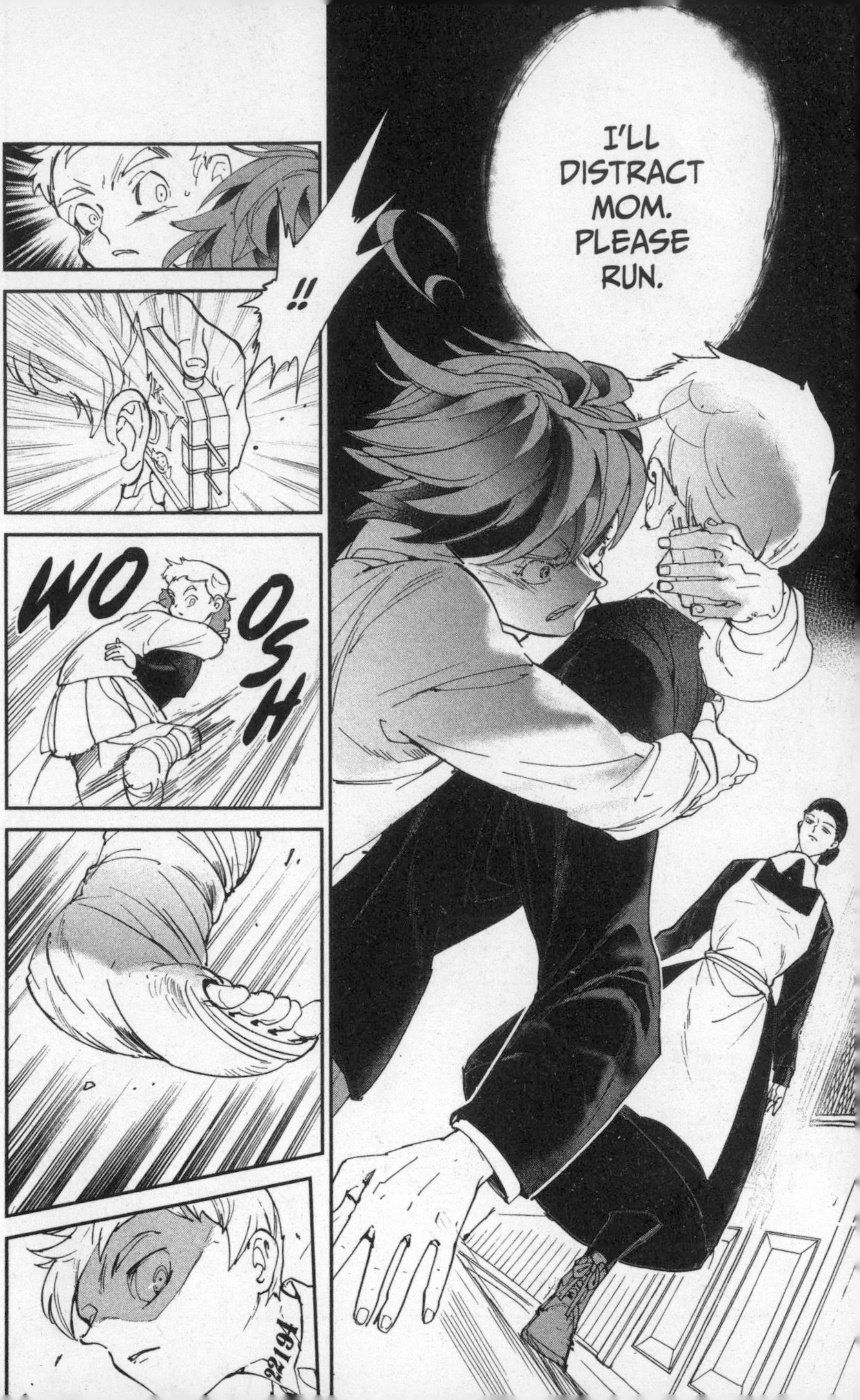
I'LL DISTRACT MOM. PLEASE RUN.
!!
WOOSH
22194

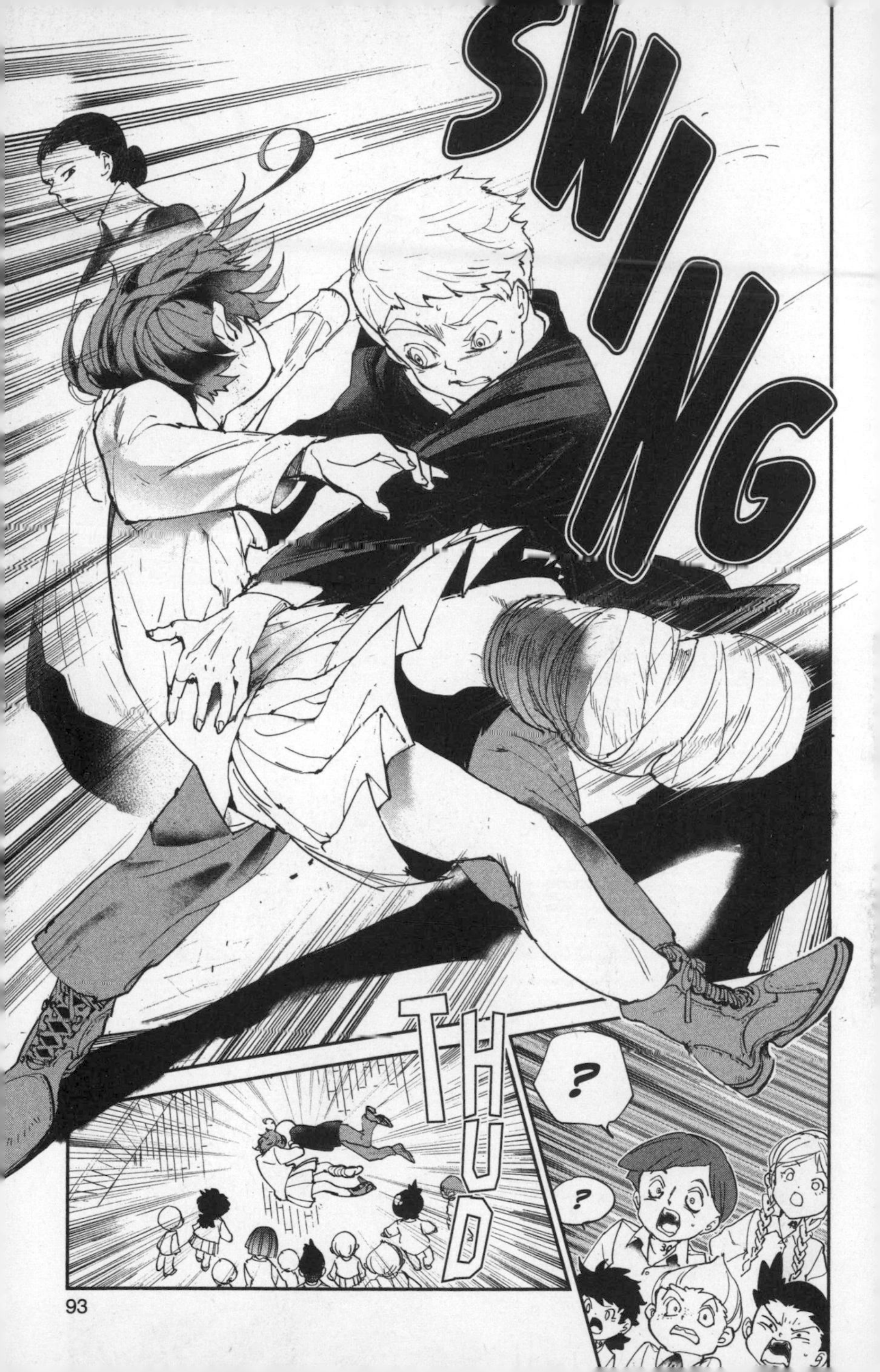
SWING
?
?
THUD

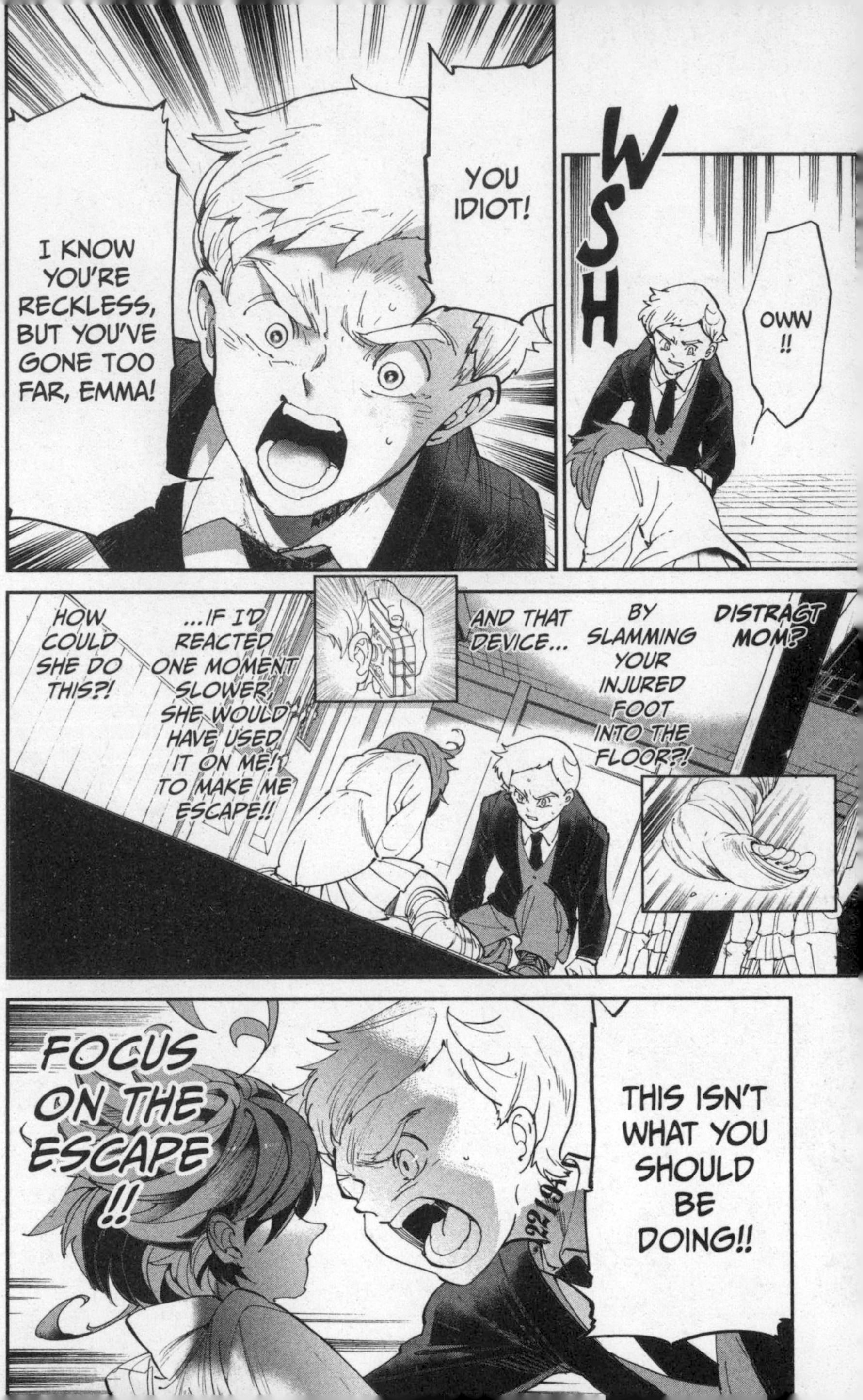
WSH
OWW !!
YOU IDIOT!
I KNOW YOU'RE RECKLESS, BUT YOU'VE GONE TOO FAR, EMMA!
DISTRACT MOM?
BY SLAMMING YOUR INJURED FOOT INTO THE FLOOR?!
AND THAT DEVICE...
...IF I'D REACTED ONE MOMENT SLOWER, SHE WOULD HAVE USED IT ON ME! TO MAKE ME ESCAPE!!
HOW COULD SHE DO THIS?!
THIS ISN'T WHAT YOU SHOULD BE DOING!!
FOCUS ON THE ESCAPE!!

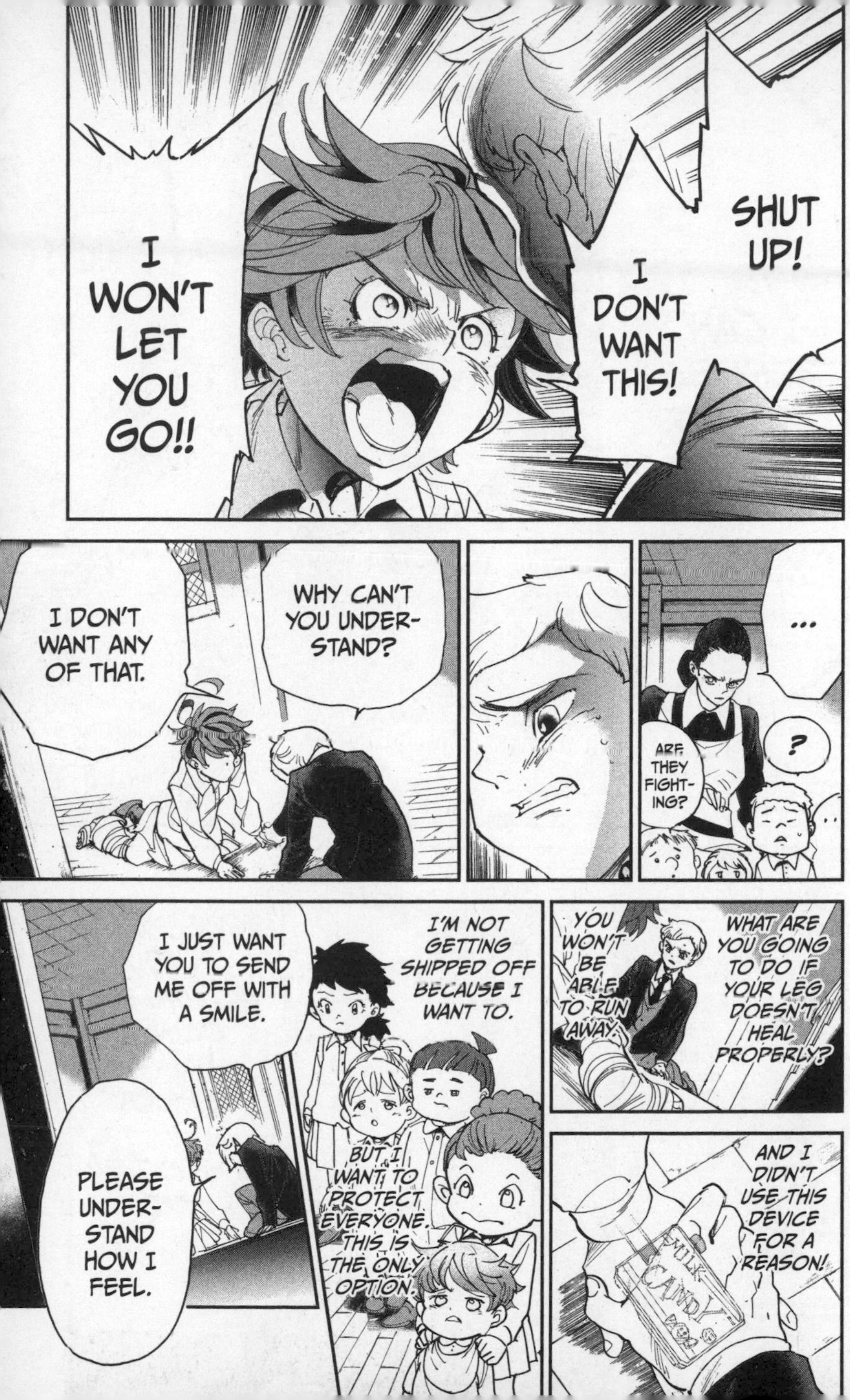
SHUT UP!
I DON'T WANT THIS!
I WON'T LET YOU GO!!
...
?
ARE THEY FIGHTING?
WHY CAN'T YOU UNDERSTAND?
I DON'T WANT ANY OF THAT.
WHAT ARE YOU GOING TO DO IF YOUR LEG DOESN'T HEAL PROPERLY?
YOU WON'T BE ABLE TO RUN AWAY.
AND I DIDN'T USE THIS DEVICE FOR A REASON!
MILK CANDY
I'M NOT GETTING SHIPPED OFF BECAUSE I WANT TO.
I JUST WANT YOU TO SEND ME OFF WITH A SMILE.
BUT I WANT TO PROTECT EVERYONE. THIS IS THE ONLY OPTION.
PLEASE UNDERSTAND HOW I FEEL.

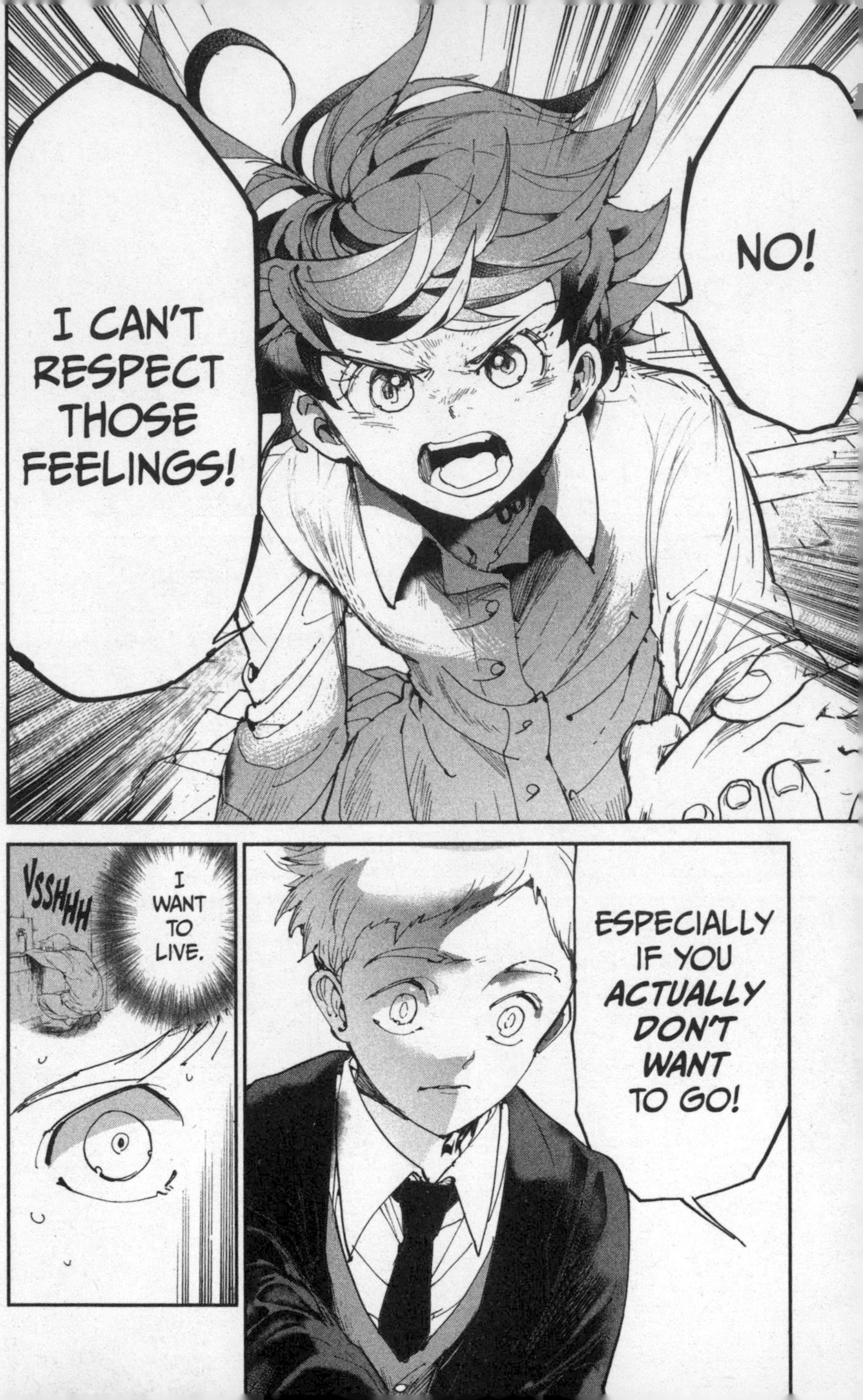
NO!
I CAN'T RESPECT THOSE FEELINGS!
ESPECIALLY IF YOU ACTUALLY DON'T WANT TO GO!
VSSHHH
I WANT TO LIVE.

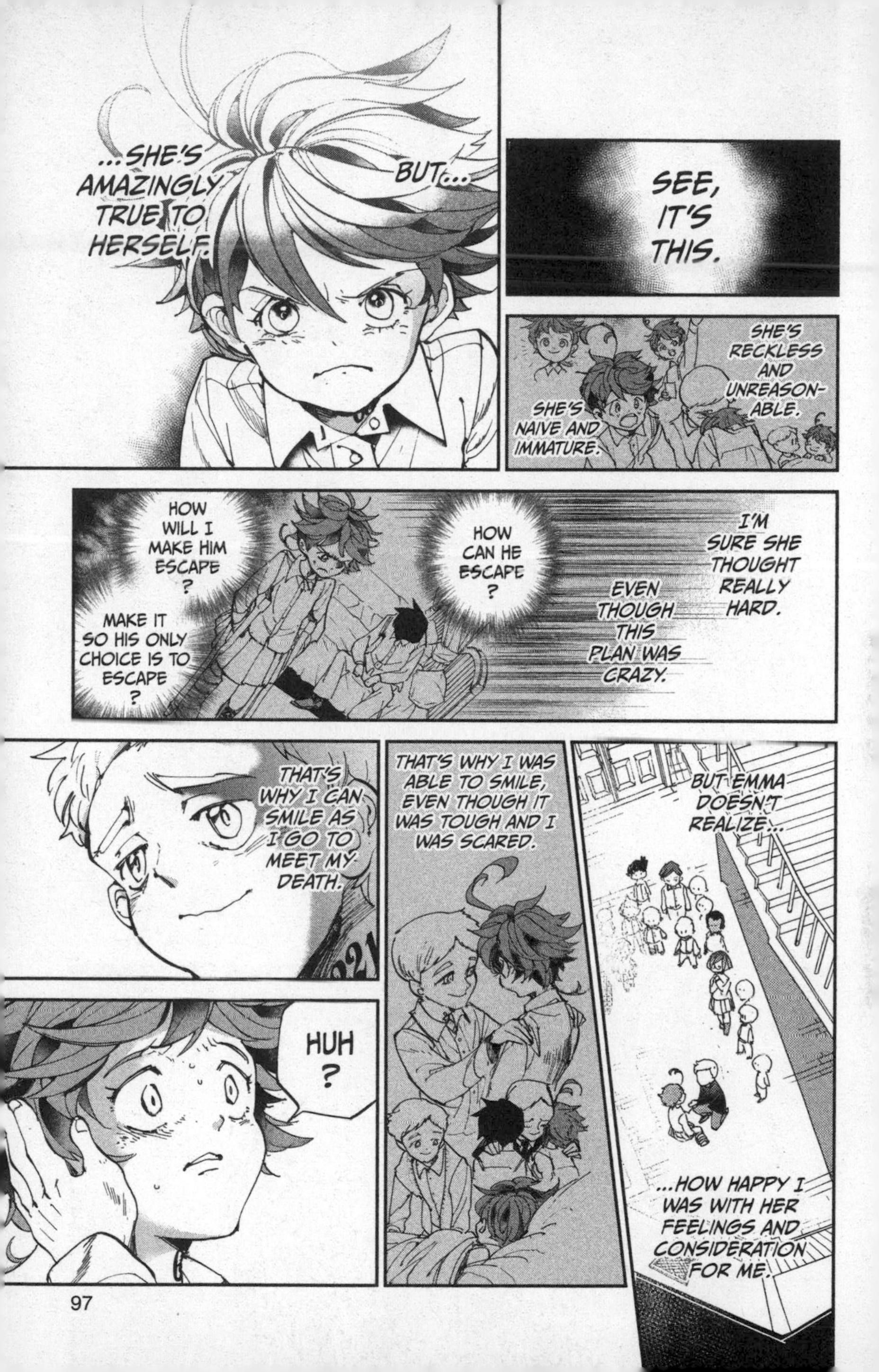
SEE, IT'S THIS.
SHE'S RECKLESS AND UNREASON-ABLE.
SHE'S NAIVE AND IMMATURE.
BUT...
...SHE'S AMAZINGLY TRUE TO HERSELF.
I'M SURE SHE THOUGHT REALLY HARD.
EVEN THOUGH THIS PLAN WAS CRAZY.
HOW CAN HE ESCAPE?
HOW WILL I MAKE HIM ESCAPE?
MAKE IT SO HIS ONLY CHOICE IS TO ESCAPE?
BUT EMMA DOESN'T REALIZE...
...HOW HAPPY I WAS WITH HER FEELINGS AND CONSIDERATION FOR ME.
THAT'S WHY I WAS ABLE TO SMILE, EVEN THOUGH IT WAS TOUGH AND I WAS SCARED.
THAT'S WHY I CAN SMILE AS I GO TO MEET MY DEATH.
HUH?

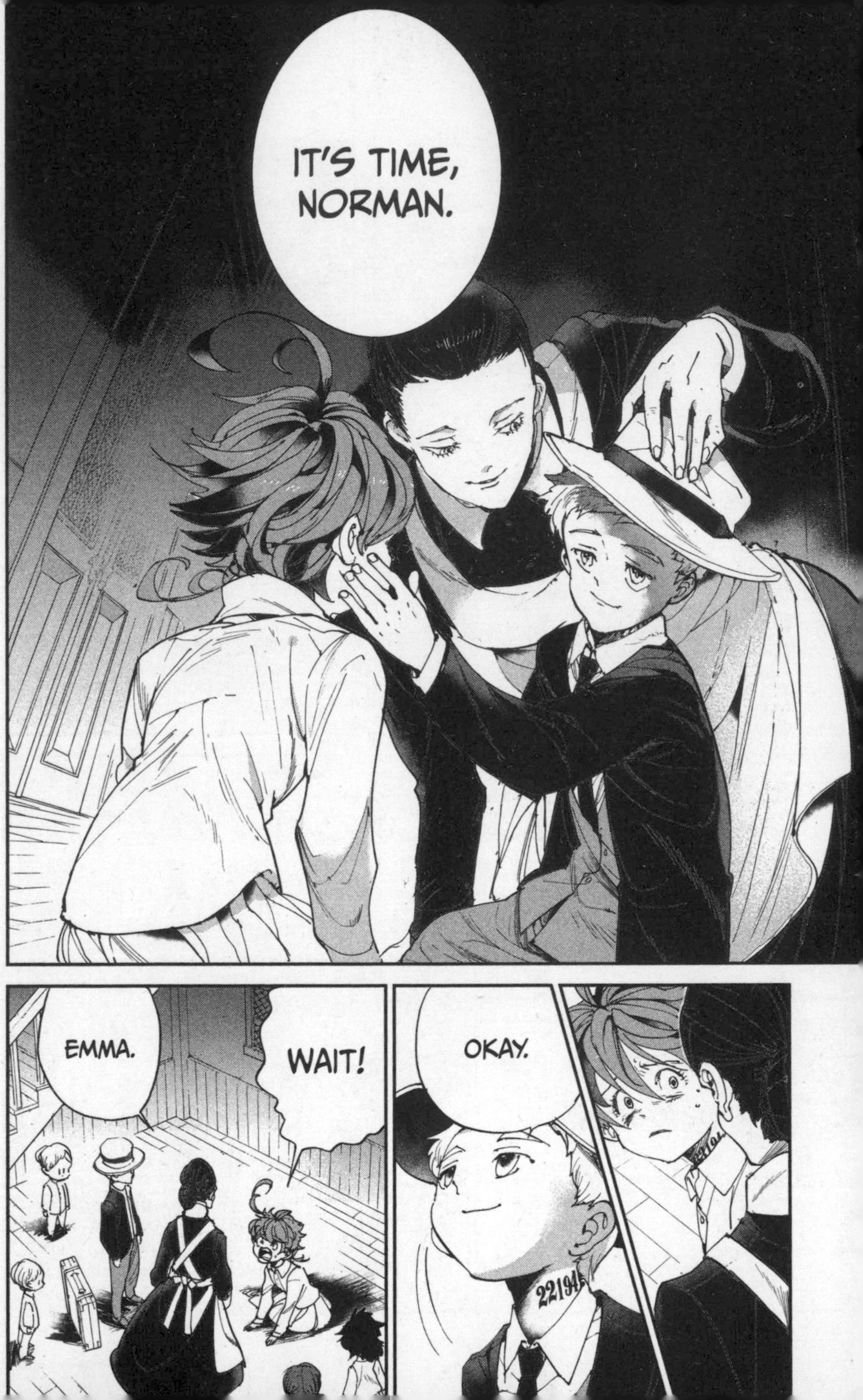
IT'S TIME, NORMAN.
OKAY.
22194
WAIT!
EMMA.

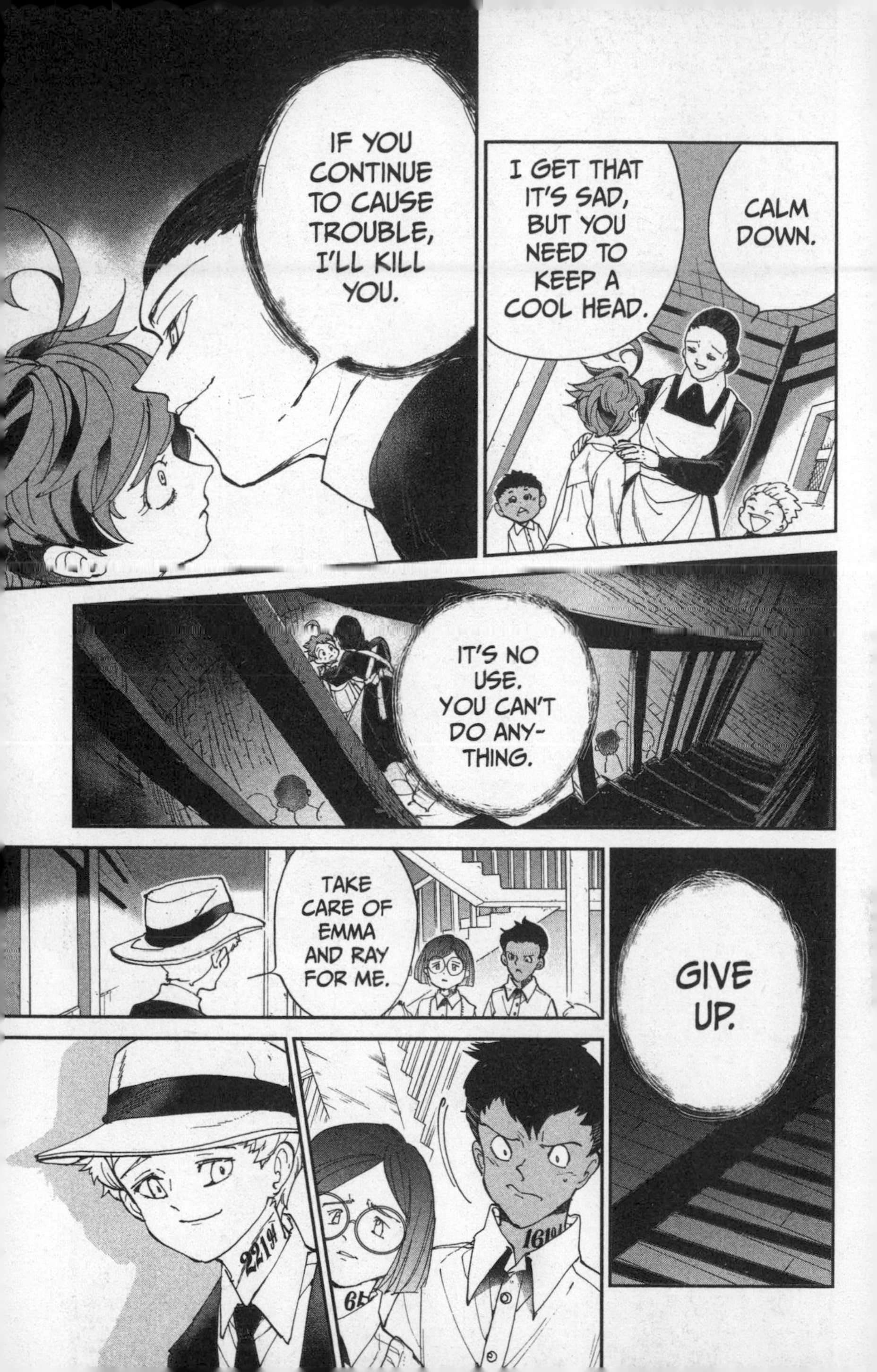
CALM DOWN.
I GET THAT IT'S SAD, BUT YOU NEED TO KEEP A COOL HEAD.
IF YOU CONTINUE TO CAUSE TROUBLE, I'LL KILL YOU.
IT'S NO USE. YOU CAN'T DO ANY-THING.
GIVE UP.
TAKE CARE OF EMMA AND RAY FOR ME.

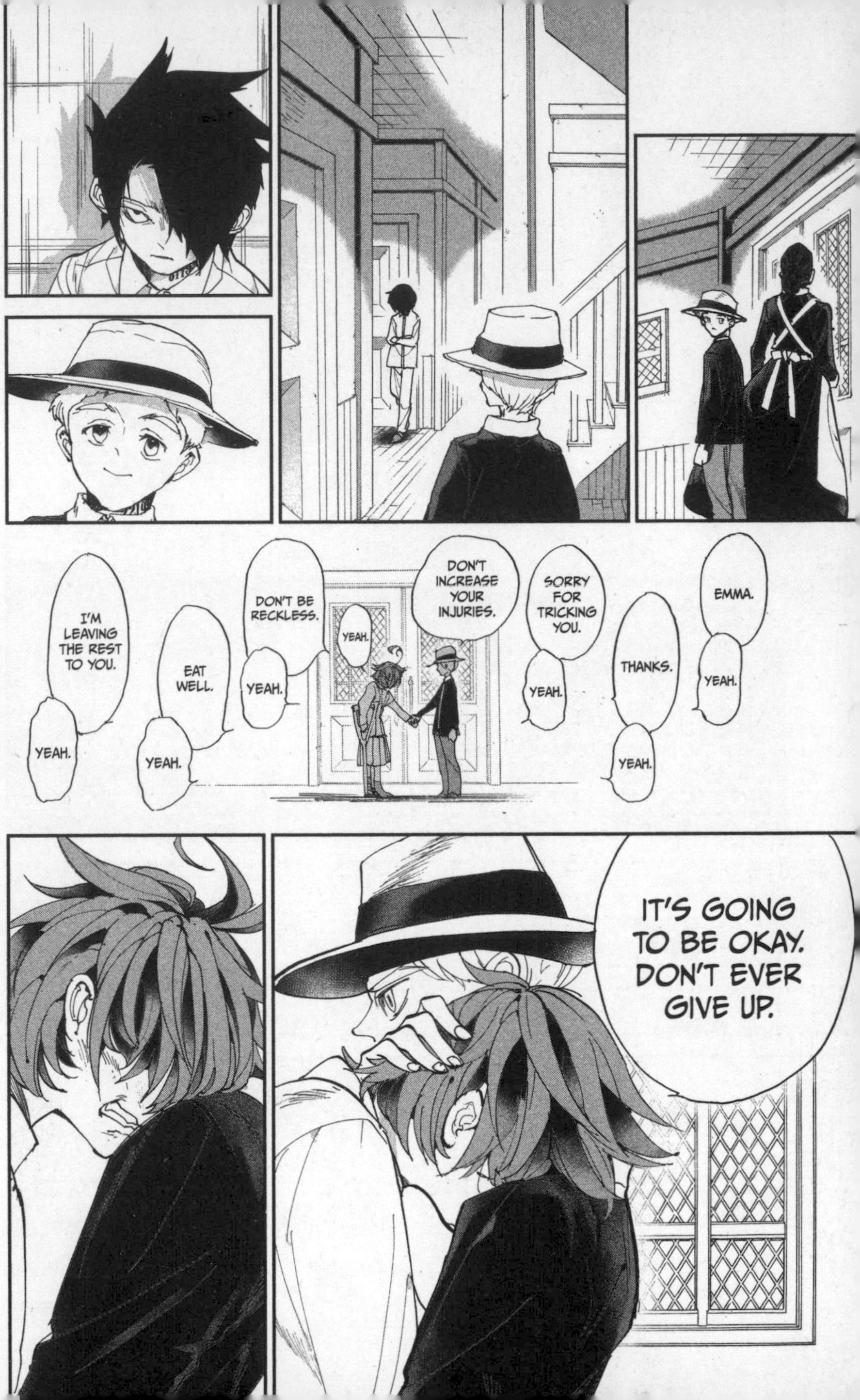
EMMA.
YEAH.
THANKS.
YEAH.
SORRY FOR TRICKING YOU.
YEAH.
DON'T INCREASE YOUR INJURIES.
YEAH.
DON'T BE RECKLESS.
YEAH.
EAT WELL.
YEAH.
I'M LEAVING THE REST TO YOU.
YEAH.
IT'S GOING TO BE OKAY. DON'T EVER GIVE UP.

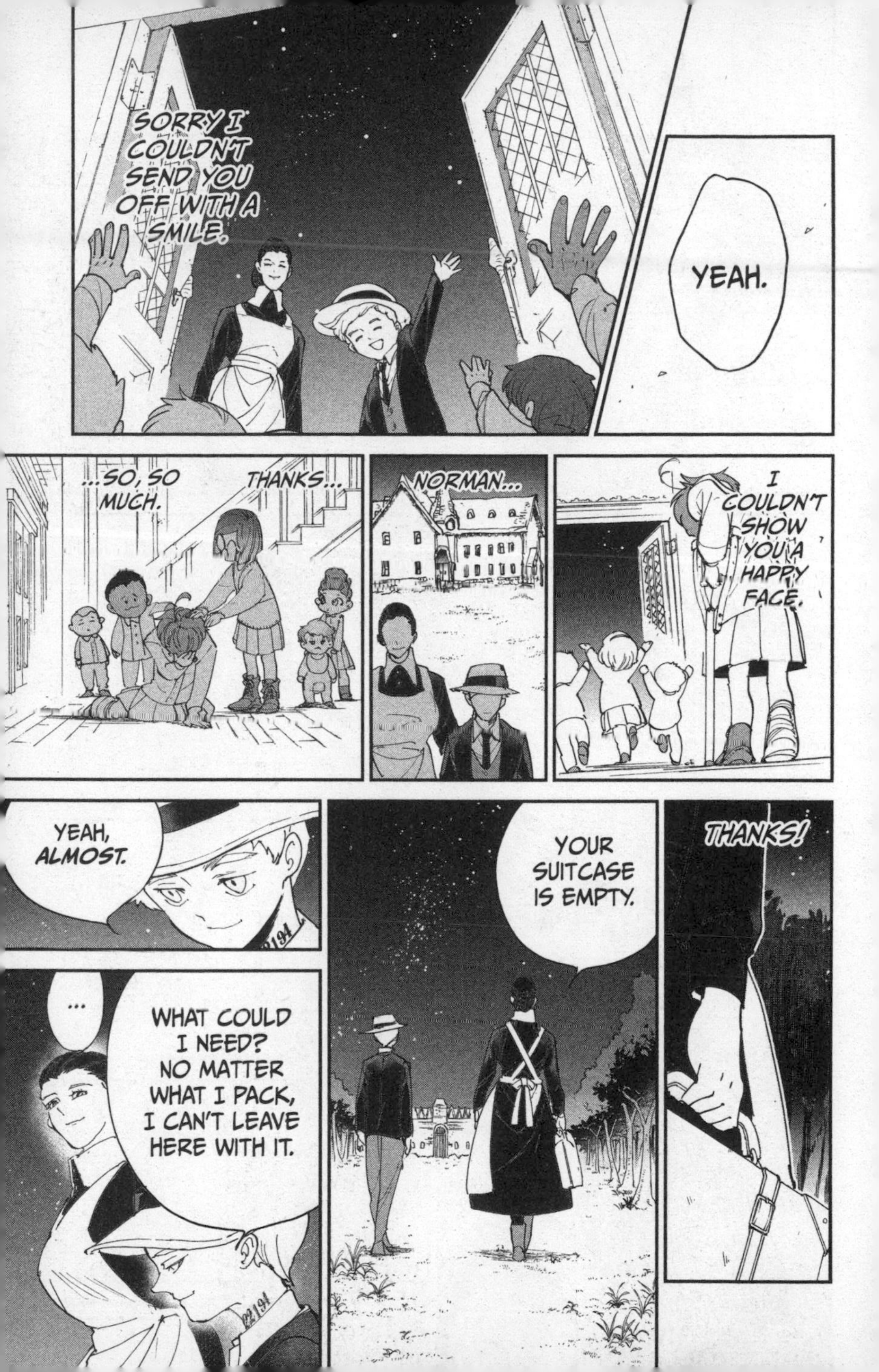
YEAH.
SORRY I COULDN'T SEND YOU OFF WITH A SMILE.
I COULDN'T SHOW YOU A HAPPY FACE.
NORMAN...
THANKS...
...SO, SO MUCH.
THANKS!
YOUR SUITCASE IS EMPTY.
YEAH, ALMOST.
WHAT COULD I NEED? NO MATTER WHAT I PACK, I CAN'T LEAVE HERE WITH IT.
...

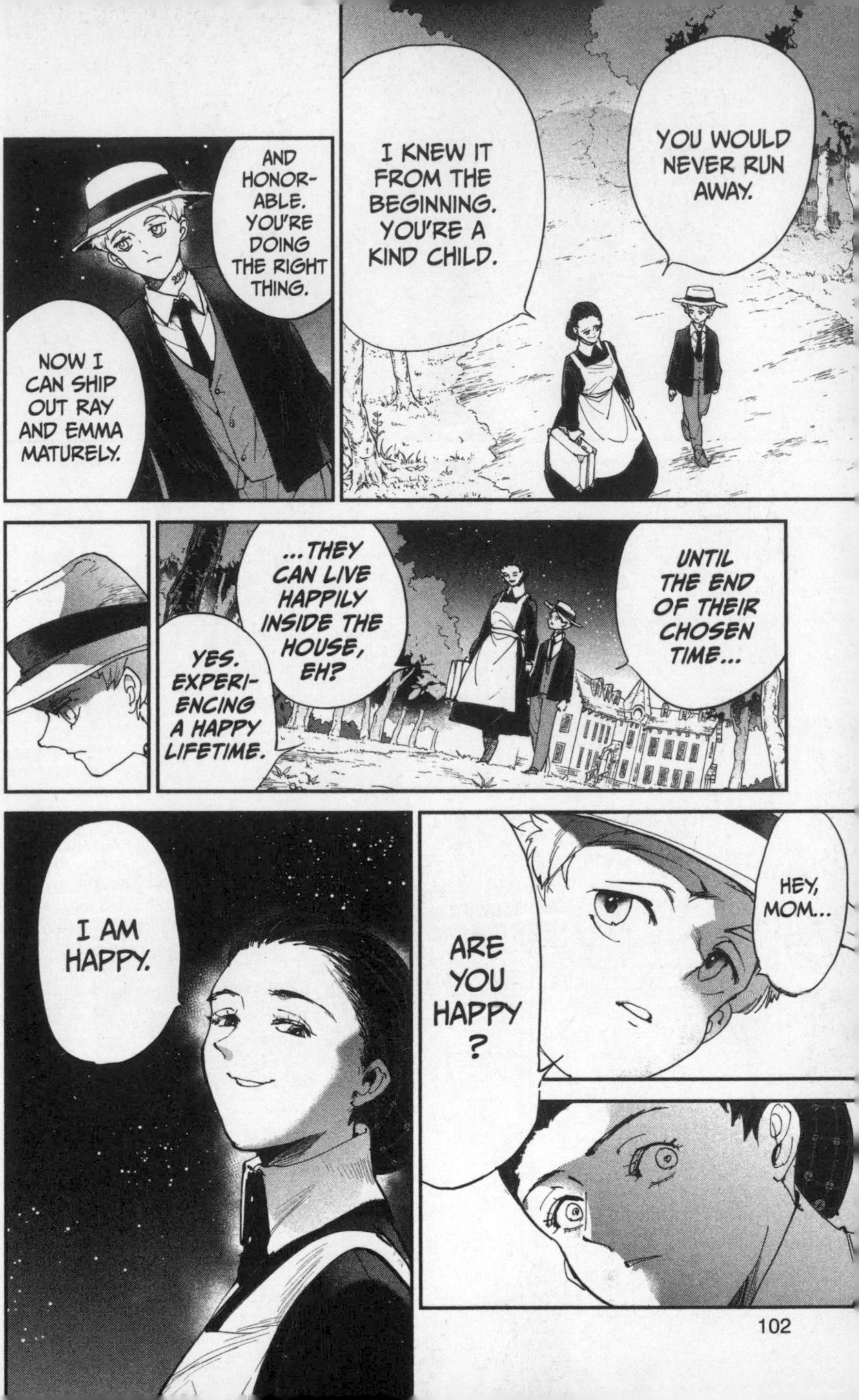
YOU WOULD NEVER RUN AWAY.
I KNEW IT FROM THE BEGINNING. YOU'RE A KIND CHILD.
AND HONOR-ABLE. YOU'RE DOING THE RIGHT THING.
NOW I CAN SHIP OUT RAY AND EMMA MATURELY.
UNTIL THE END OF THEIR CHOSEN TIME...
...THEY CAN LIVE HAPPILY INSIDE THE HOUSE, EH?
YES. EXPERIENCING A HAPPY LIFETIME.
HEY, MOM...
ARE YOU HAPPY?
I AM HAPPY.

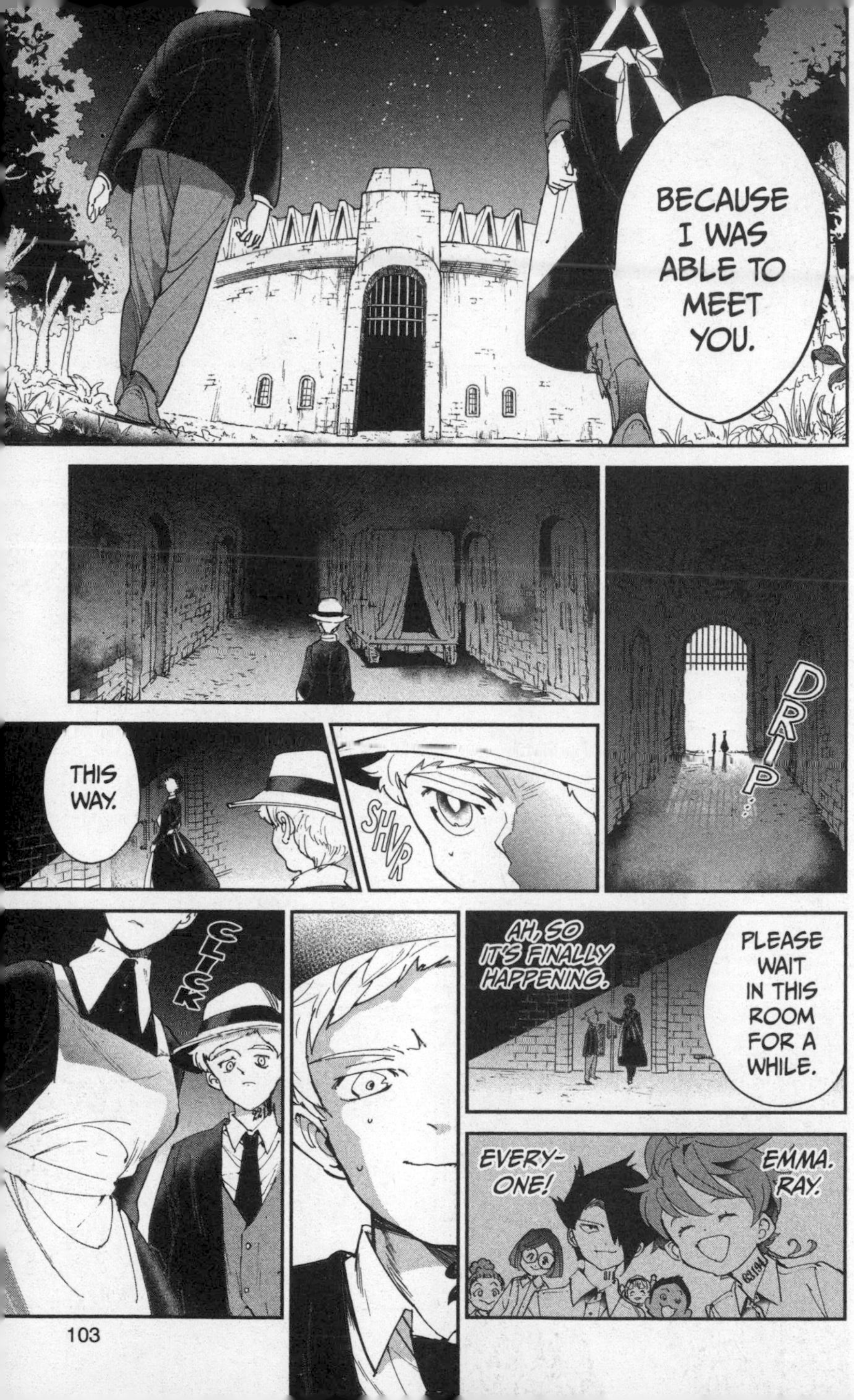
BECAUSE I WAS ABLE TO MEET YOU.
DRIP...
SHVR
THIS WAY.
PLEASE WAIT IN THIS ROOM FOR A WHILE.
AH, SO IT'S FINALLY HAPPENING.
EMMA. RAY.
EVERY-ONE!
CLICK

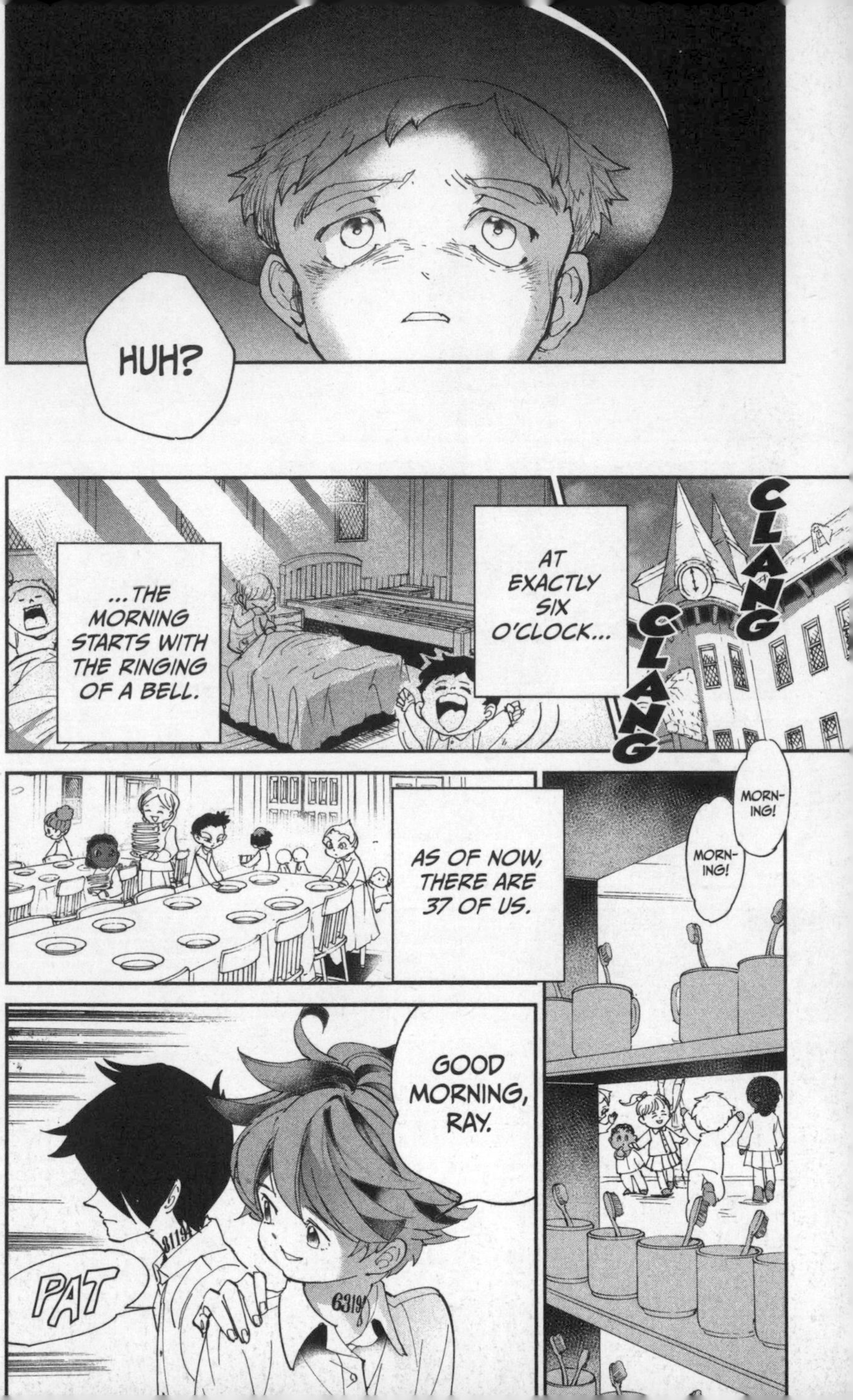
HUH?
CLANG
CLANG
CLANG
AT EXACTLY SIX O'CLOCK...
...THE MORNING STARTS WITH THE RINGING OF A BELL.
MORN-ING!
MORN-ING!
AS OF NOW, THERE ARE 37 OF US.
GOOD MORNING, RAY.
81194
63194
PAT

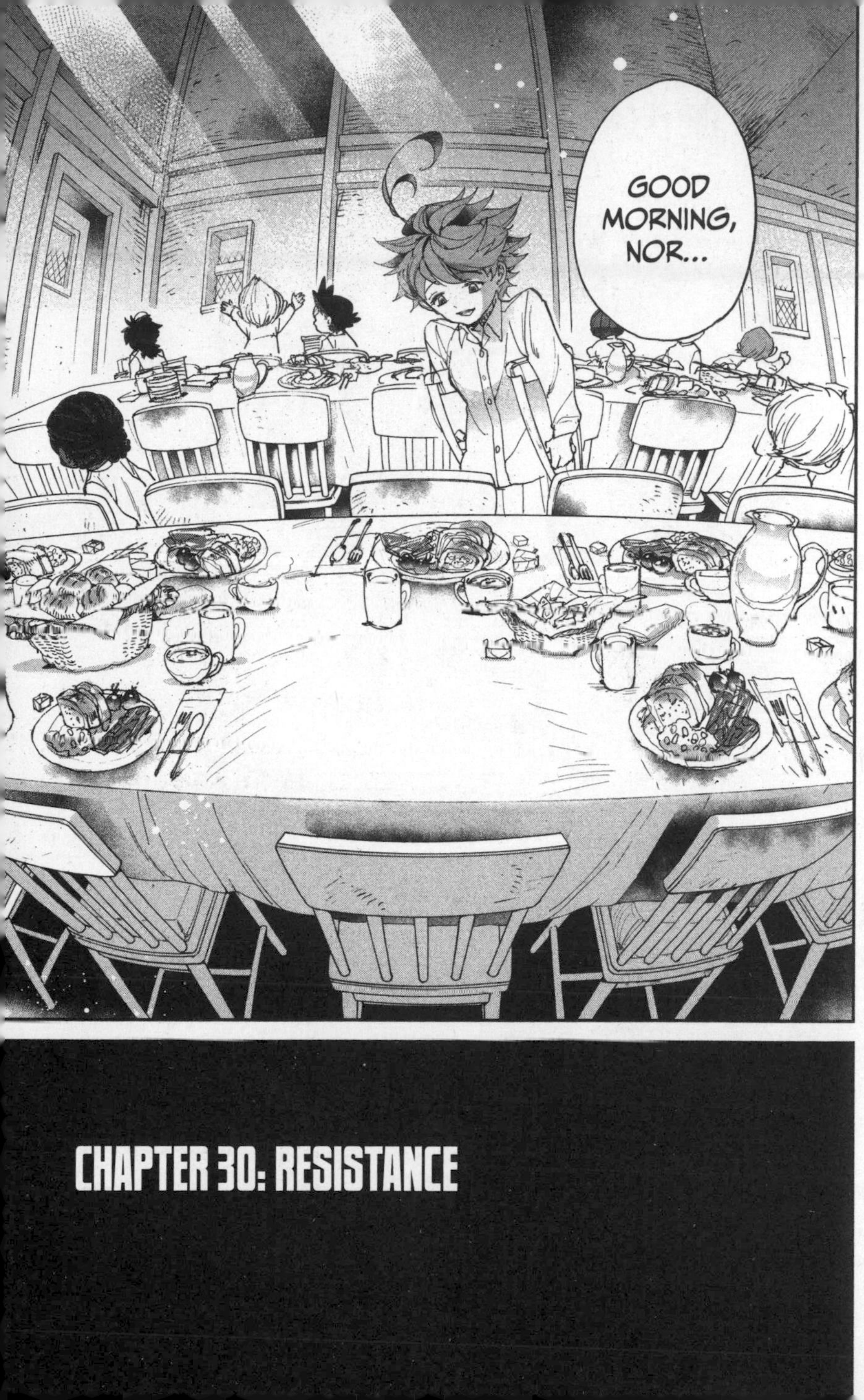
GOOD MORNING, NOR...

CHAPTER 30: RESISTANCE

THE PROMISED NEVERLAND SIDE SCENE 007

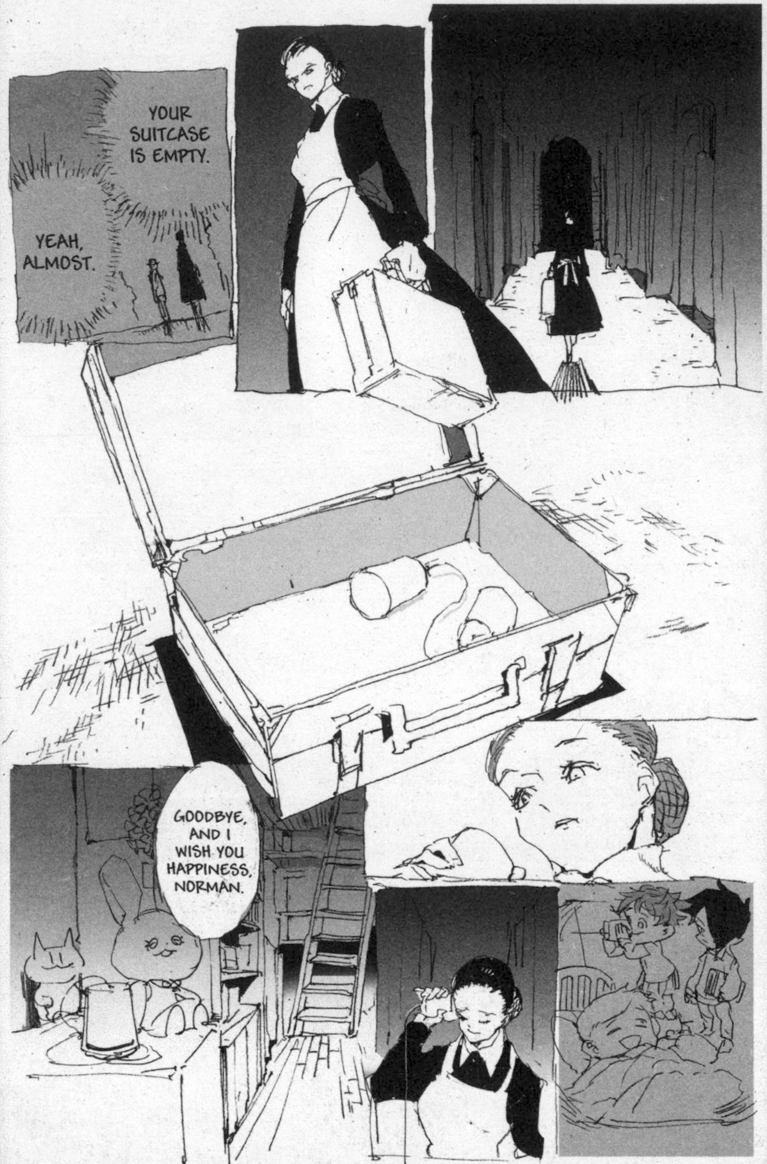
YOUR SUITCASE IS EMPTY.
YEAH, ALMOST.
GOODBYE, AND I WISH YOU HAPPINESS, NORMAN.

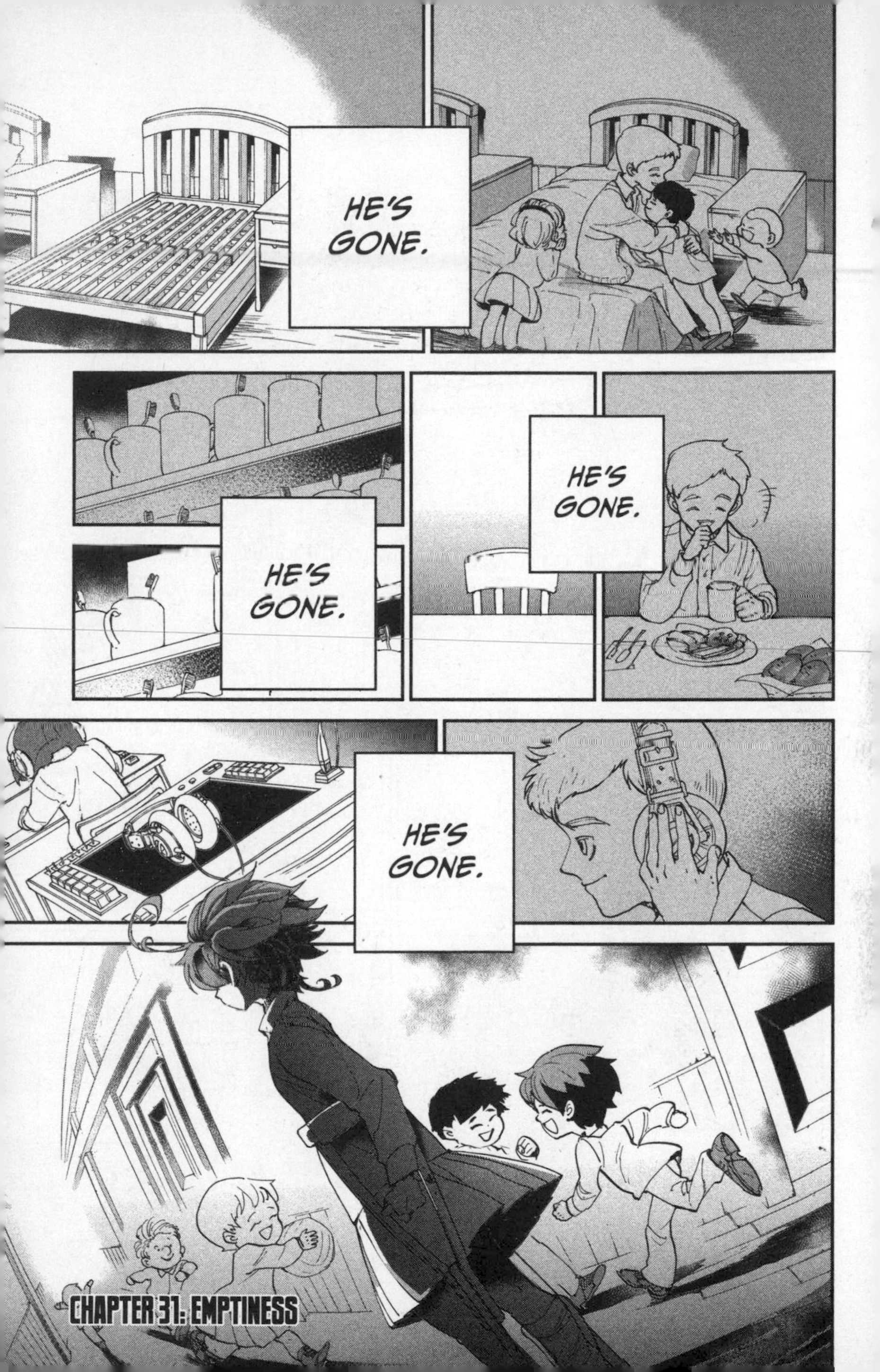
HE'S GONE.
HE'S GONE.
HE'S GONE.
HE'S GONE.
CHAPTER 31: EMPTINESS

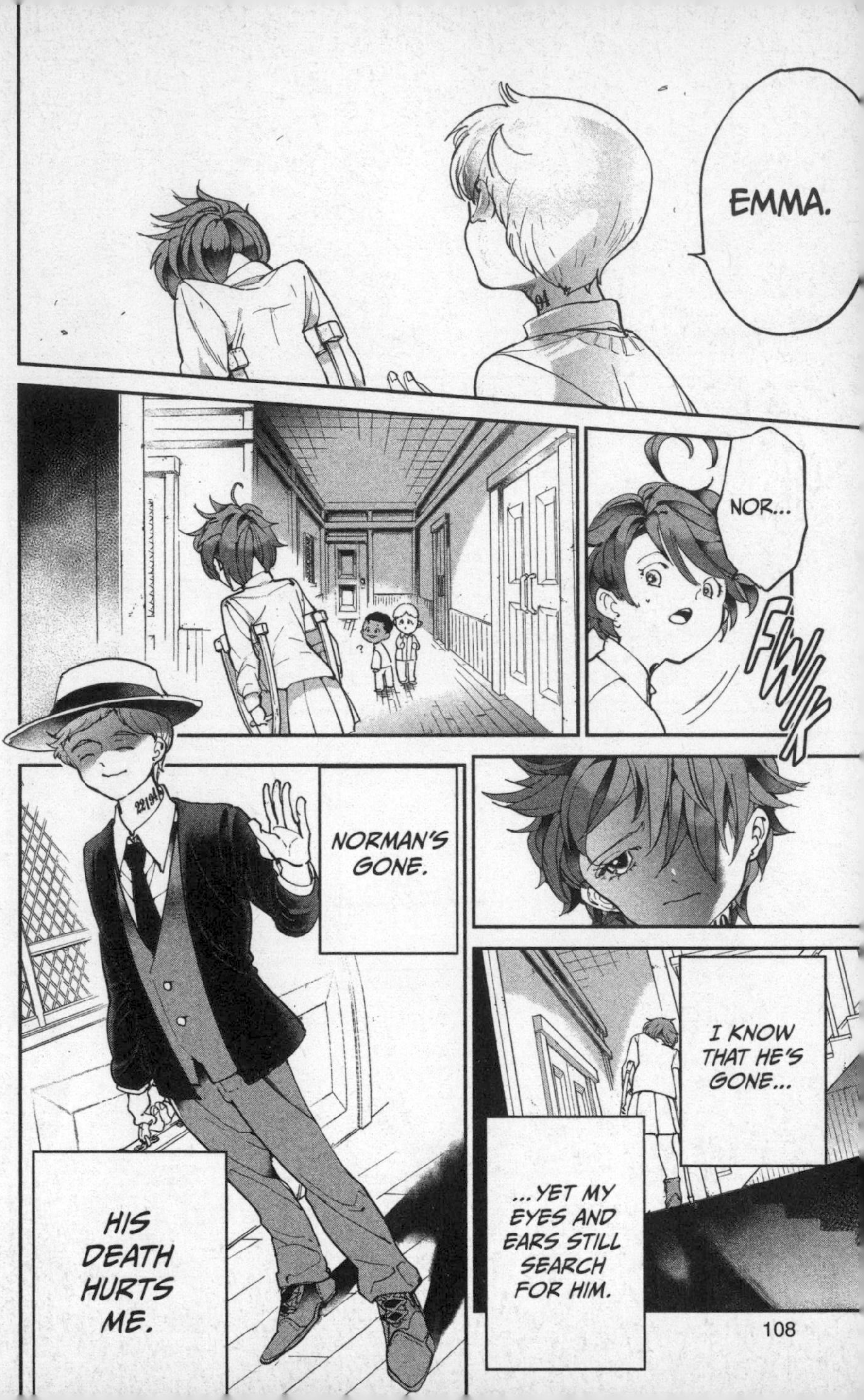
EMMA.
NOR...
FWIK
I KNOW THAT HE'S GONE...
...YET MY EYES AND EARS STILL SEARCH FOR HIM.
NORMAN'S GONE.
HIS DEATH HURTS ME.

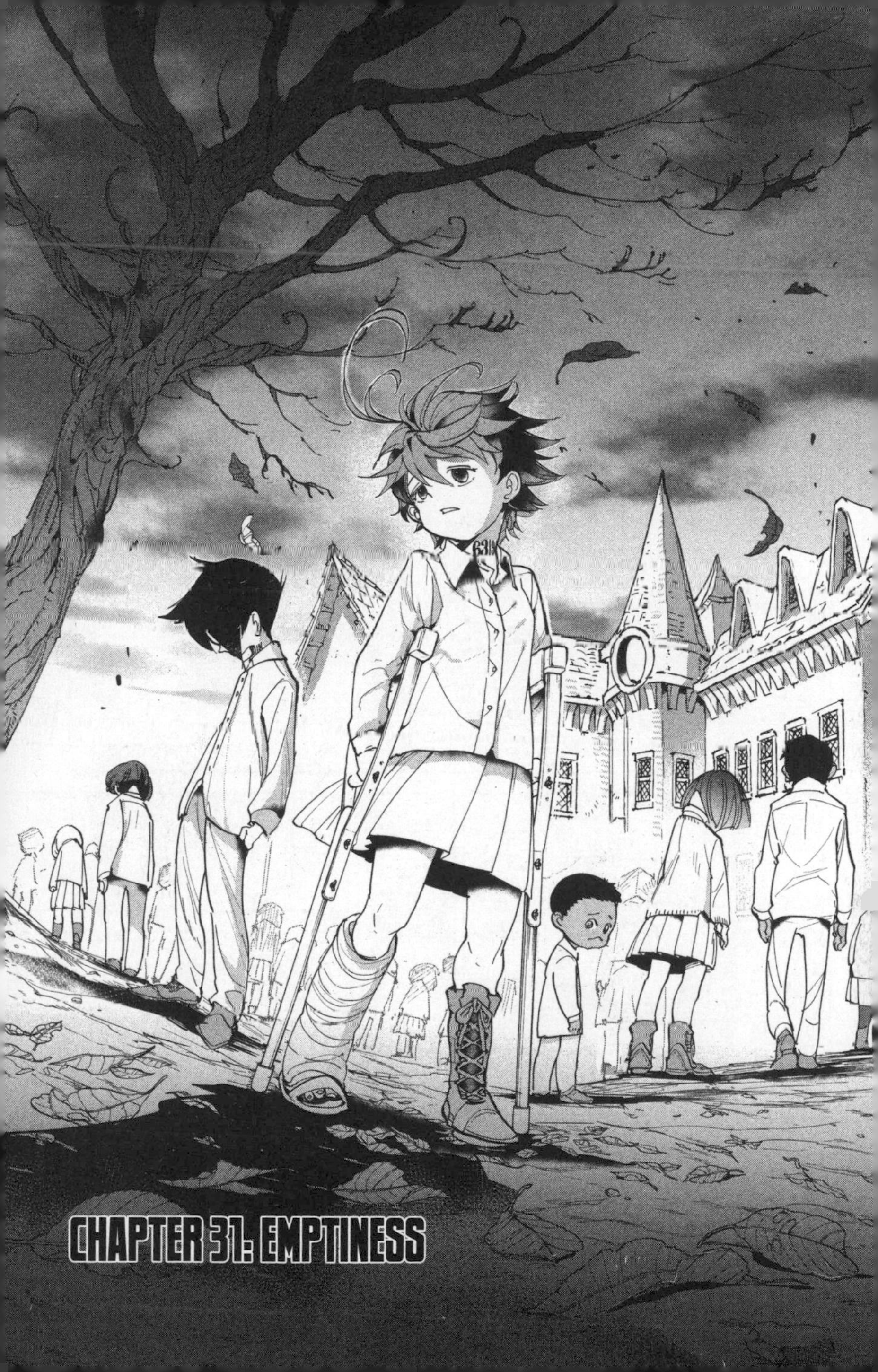
CHAPTER 31: EMPTINESS

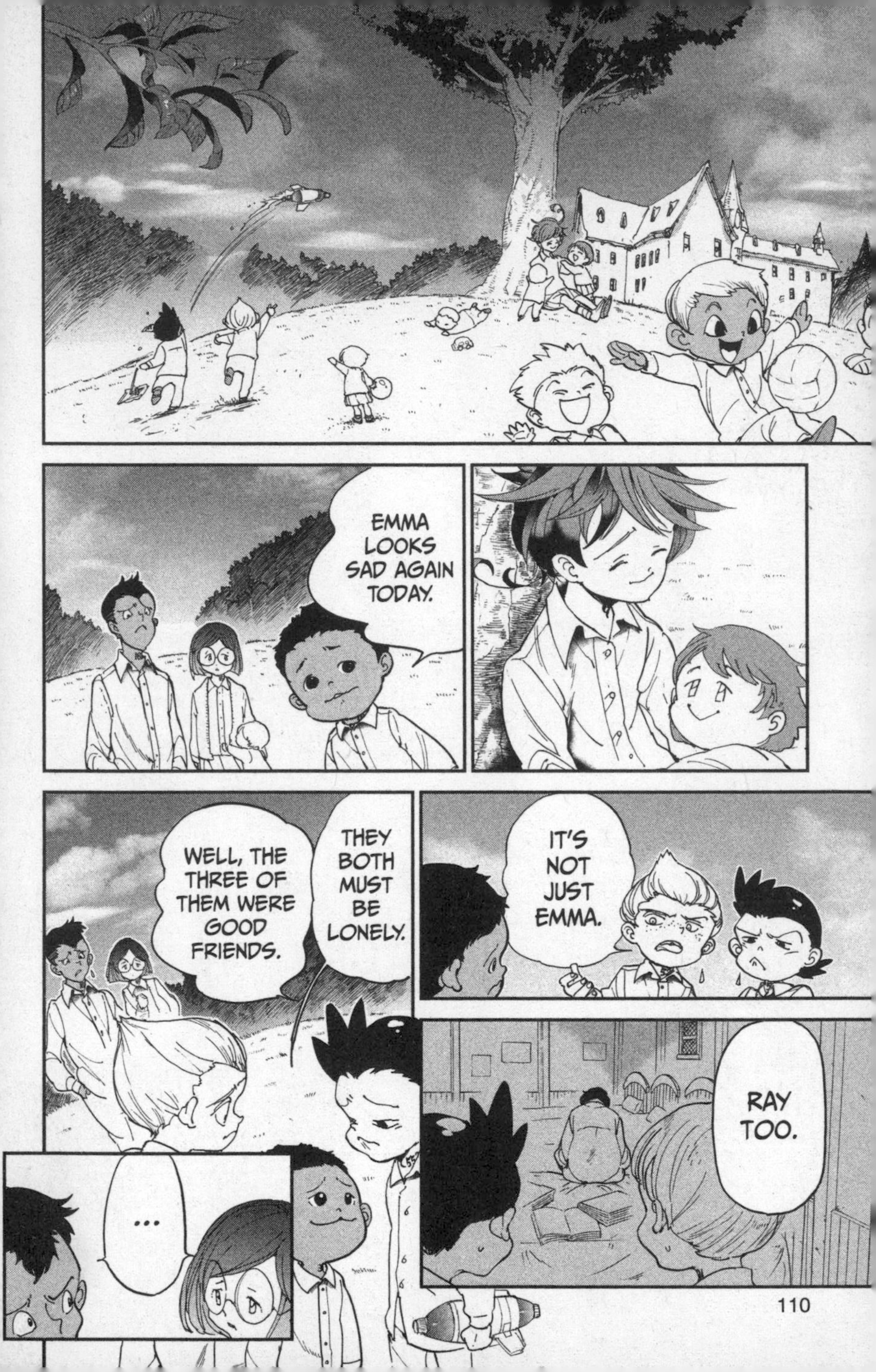
EMMA LOOKS SAD AGAIN TODAY.
IT'S NOT JUST EMMA.
RAY TOO.
THEY BOTH MUST BE LONELY.
WELL, THE THREE OF THEM WERE GOOD FRIENDS.
...

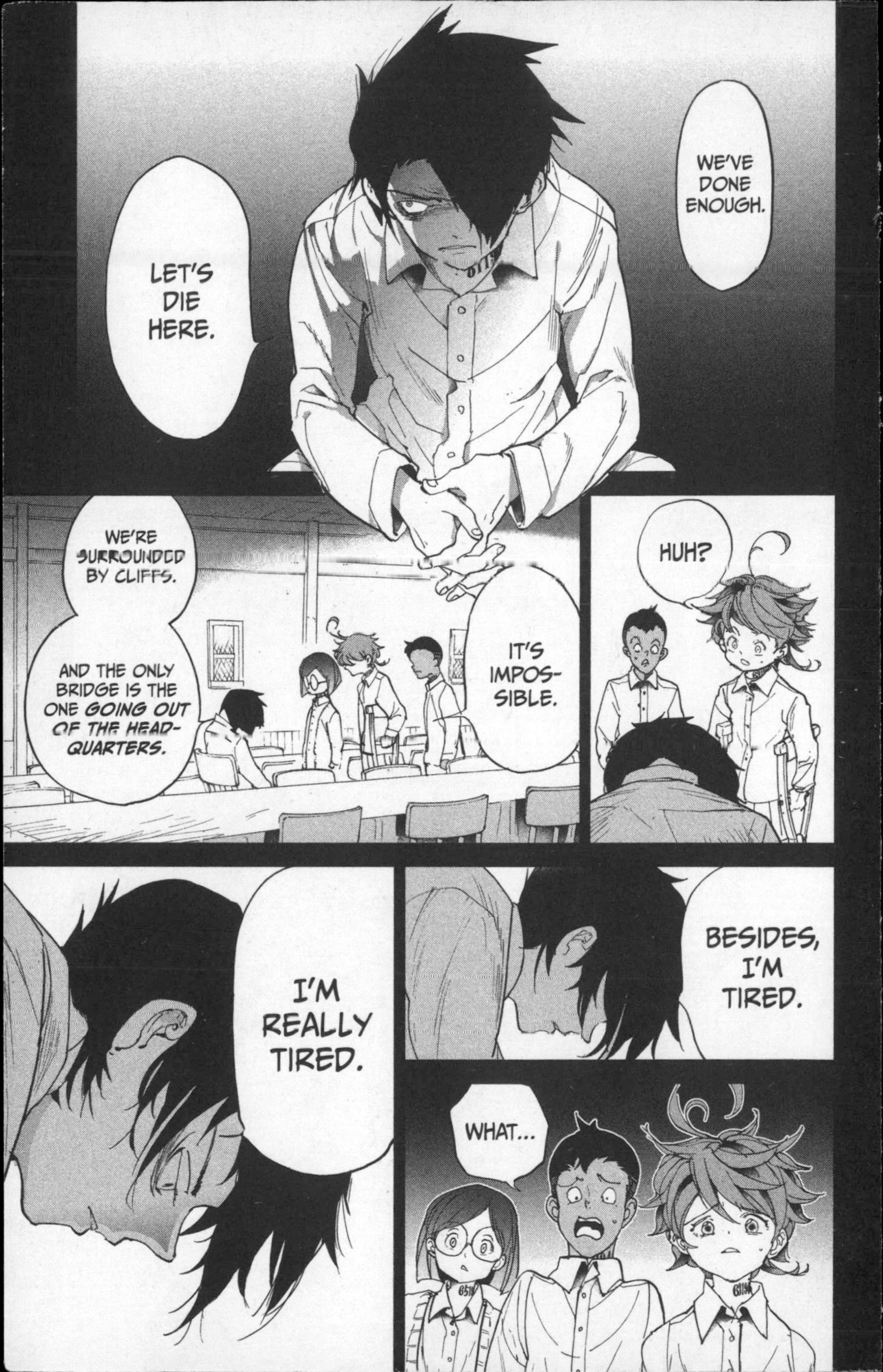
WE'VE DONE ENOUGH.
LET'S DIE HERE.
HUH?
IT'S IMPOSSIBLE.
WE'RE SURROUNDED BY CLIFFS.
AND THE ONLY BRIDGE IS THE ONE GOING OUT OF THE HEADQUARTERS.
BESIDES, I'M TIRED.
WHAT...
I'M REALLY TIRED.

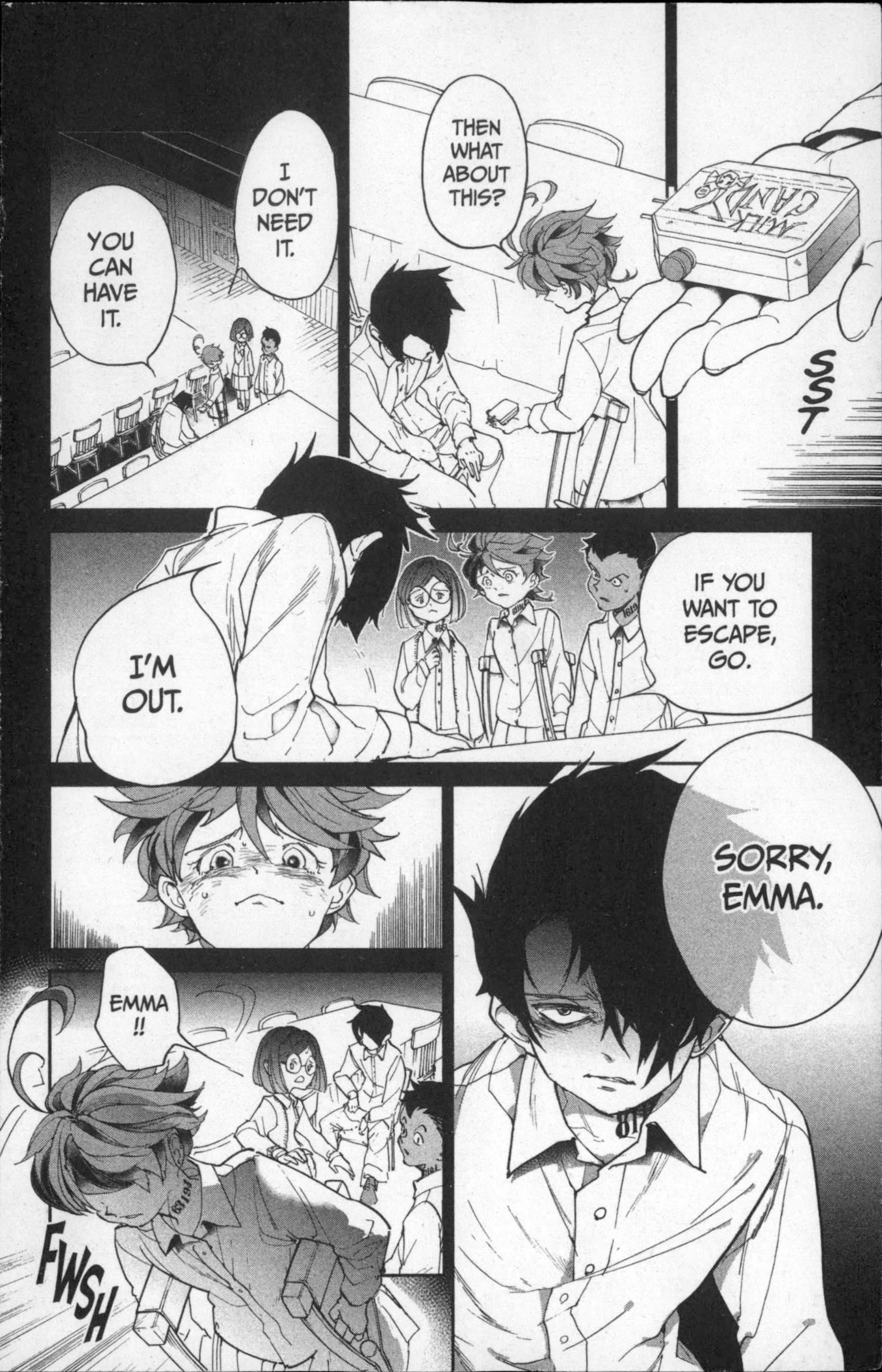
SST
THEN WHAT ABOUT THIS?
I DON'T NEED IT.
YOU CAN HAVE IT.
IF YOU WANT TO ESCAPE, GO.
I'M OUT.
SORRY, EMMA.
EMMA!!
FWSH

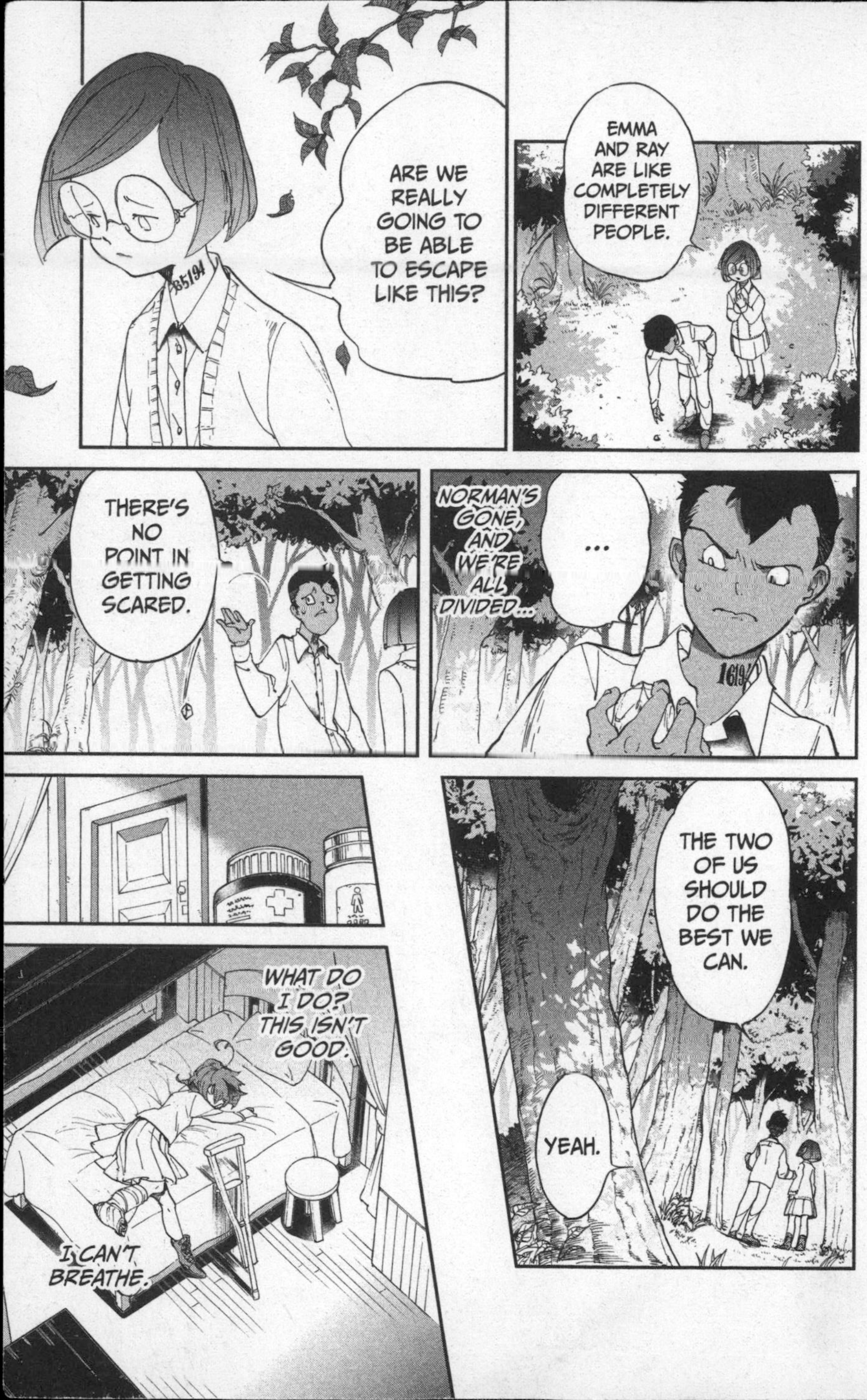
EMMA AND RAY ARE LIKE COMPLETELY DIFFERENT PEOPLE.
ARE WE REALLY GOING TO BE ABLE TO ESCAPE LIKE THIS?
...
NORMAN'S GONE, AND WE'RE ALL DIVIDED...
THERE'S NO POINT IN GETTING SCARED.
THE TWO OF US SHOULD DO THE BEST WE CAN.
YEAH.
WHAT DO I DO? THIS ISN'T GOOD.
I CAN'T BREATHE.

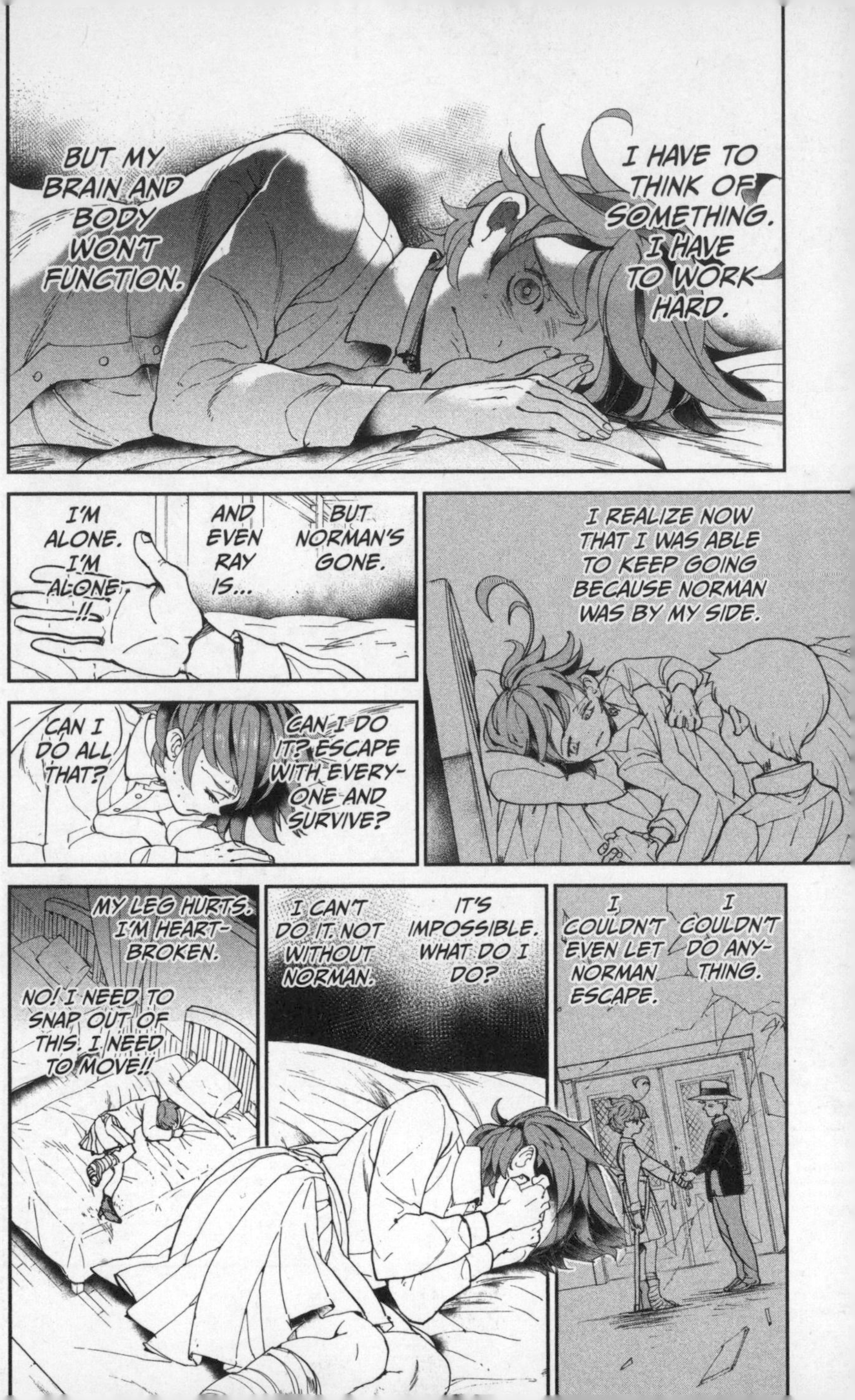
I HAVE TO THINK OF SOMETHING. I HAVE TO WORK HARD.
BUT MY BRAIN AND BODY WON'T FUNCTION.
I REALIZE NOW THAT I WAS ABLE TO KEEP GOING BECAUSE NORMAN WAS BY MY SIDE.
BUT NORMAN'S GONE.
AND EVEN RAY IS...
I'M ALONE. I'M ALONE!!
CAN I DO IT? ESCAPE WITH EVERYONE AND SURVIVE?
CAN I DO ALL THAT?
I COULDN'T DO ANYTHING.
I COULDN'T EVEN LET NORMAN ESCAPE.
IT'S IMPOSSIBLE. WHAT DO I DO?
I CAN'T DO IT. NOT WITHOUT NORMAN.
MY LEG HURTS. I'M HEARTBROKEN.
NO! I NEED TO SNAP OUT OF THIS. I NEED TO MOVE!!

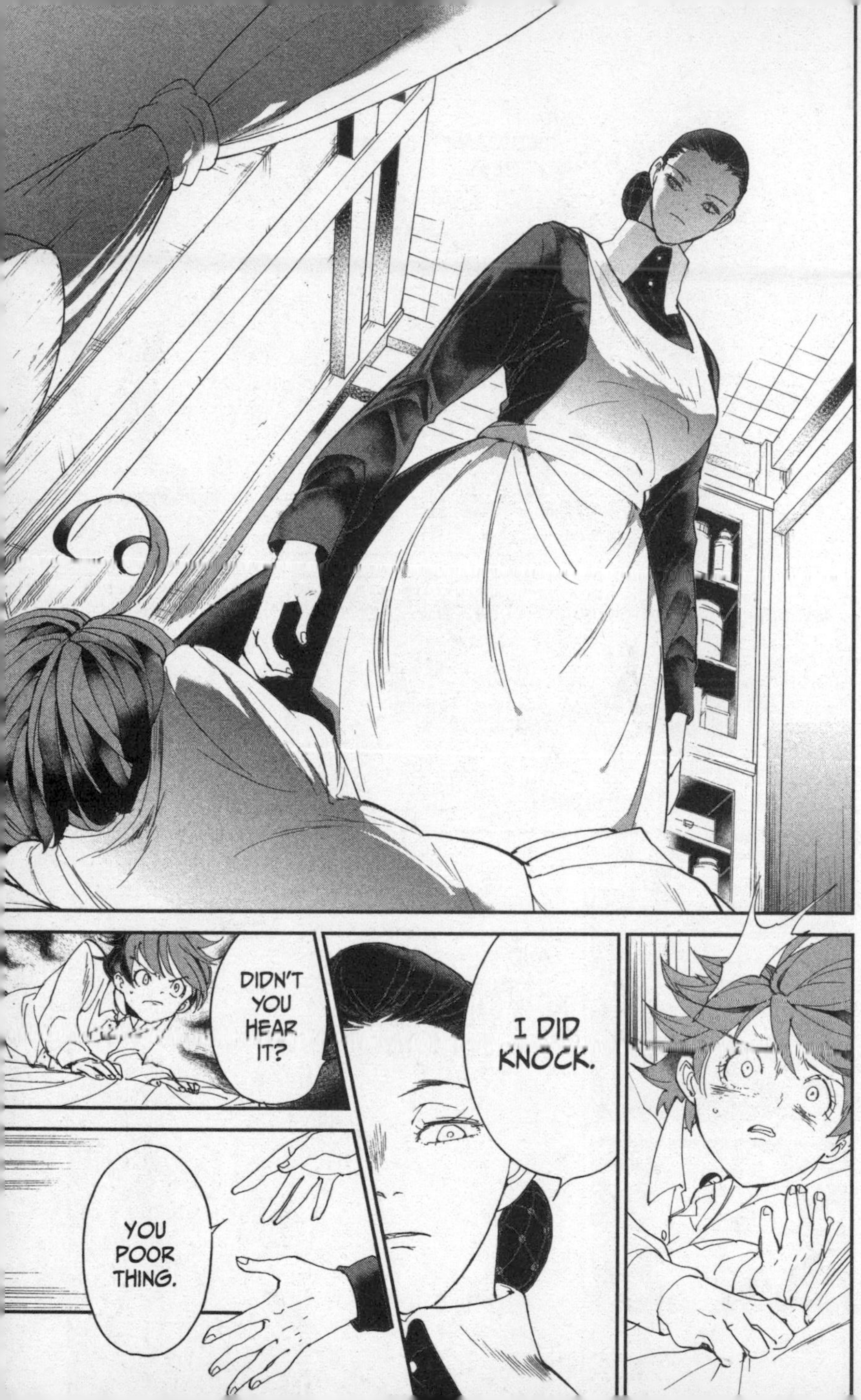
I DID KNOCK.
DIDN'T YOU HEAR IT?
YOU POOR THING.

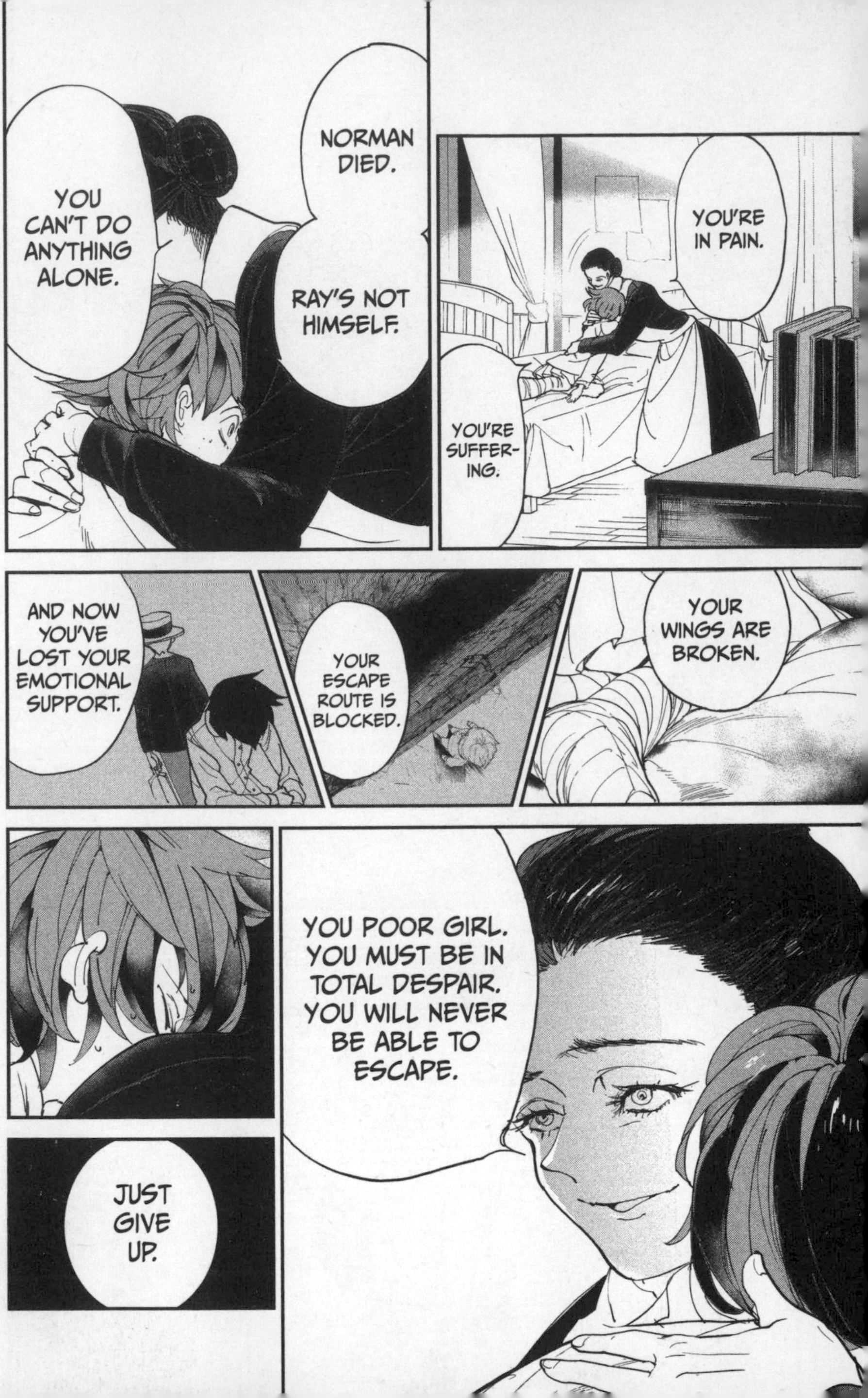
YOU'RE IN PAIN.
YOU'RE SUFFER-ING.
NORMAN DIED.
RAY'S NOT HIMSELF.
YOU CAN'T DO ANYTHING ALONE.
YOUR WINGS ARE BROKEN.
YOUR ESCAPE ROUTE IS BLOCKED.
AND NOW YOU'VE LOST YOUR EMOTIONAL SUPPORT.
YOU POOR GIRL. YOU MUST BE IN TOTAL DESPAIR. YOU WILL NEVER BE ABLE TO ESCAPE.
JUST GIVE UP.

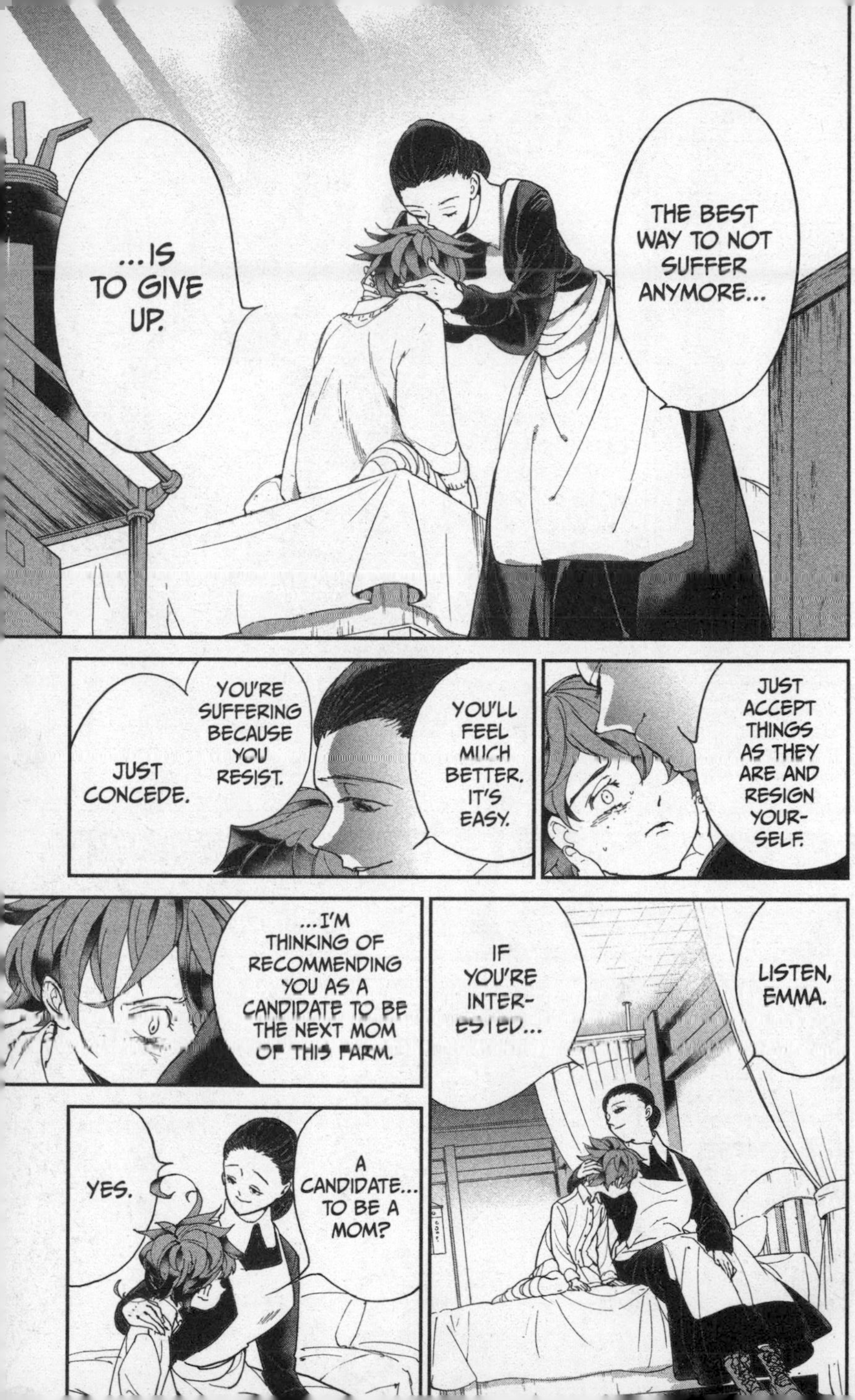
THE BEST WAY TO NOT SUFFER ANYMORE...
...IS TO GIVE UP.
JUST ACCEPT THINGS AS THEY ARE AND RESIGN YOURSELF.
YOU'LL FEEL MUCH BETTER. IT'S EASY.
YOU'RE SUFFERING BECAUSE YOU RESIST.
JUST CONCEDE.
LISTEN, EMMA.
IF YOU'RE INTERESTED...
...I'M THINKING OF RECOMMENDING YOU AS A CANDIDATE TO BE THE NEXT MOM OF THIS FARM.
A CANDIDATE... TO BE A MOM?
YES.

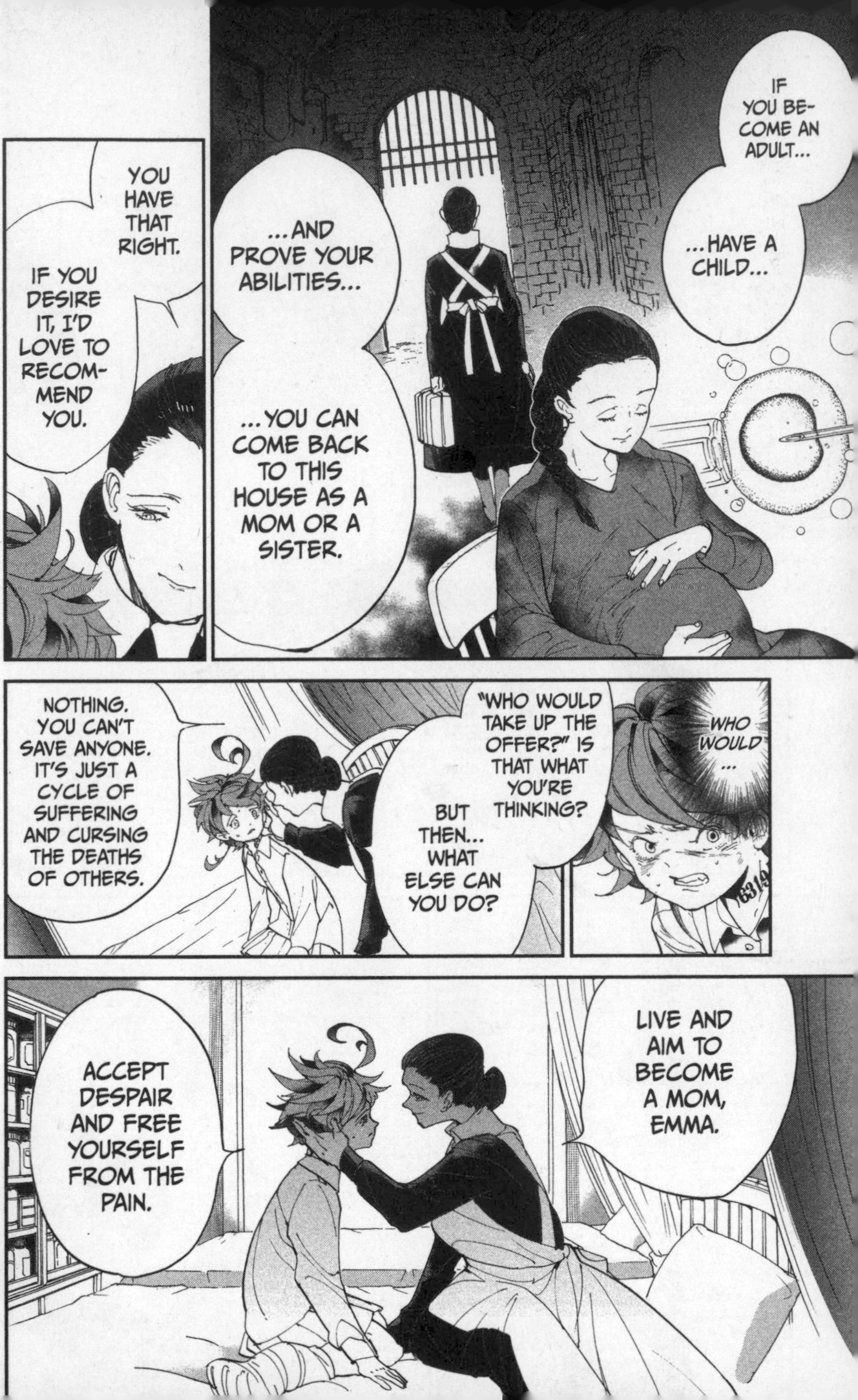
IF YOU BE-COME AN ADULT...
...HAVE A CHILD...
...AND PROVE YOUR ABILITIES...
...YOU CAN COME BACK TO THIS HOUSE AS A MOM OR A SISTER.
YOU HAVE THAT RIGHT.
IF YOU DESIRE IT, I'D LOVE TO RECOM-MEND YOU.
WHO WOULD ...
"WHO WOULD TAKE UP THE OFFER?" IS THAT WHAT YOU'RE THINKING?
BUT THEN... WHAT ELSE CAN YOU DO?
NOTHING. YOU CAN'T SAVE ANYONE. IT'S JUST A CYCLE OF SUFFERING AND CURSING THE DEATHS OF OTHERS.
LIVE AND AIM TO BECOME A MOM, EMMA.
ACCEPT DESPAIR AND FREE YOURSELF FROM THE PAIN.

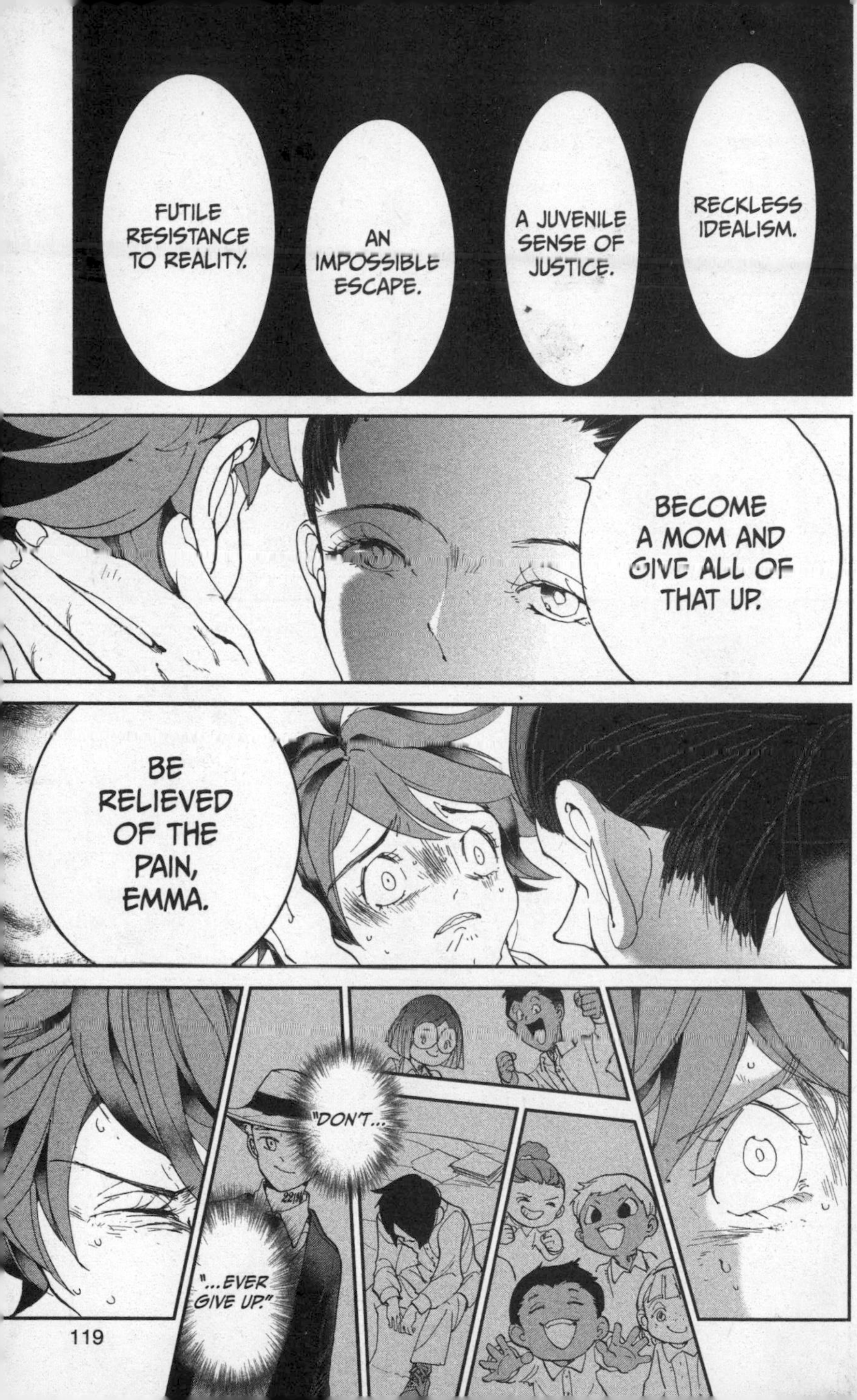
RECKLESS IDEALISM.
A JUVENILE SENSE OF JUSTICE.
AN IMPOSSIBLE ESCAPE.
FUTILE RESISTANCE TO REALITY.
BECOME A MOM AND GIVE ALL OF THAT UP.
BE RELIEVED OF THE PAIN, EMMA.
"DON'T...
"...EVER GIVE UP."

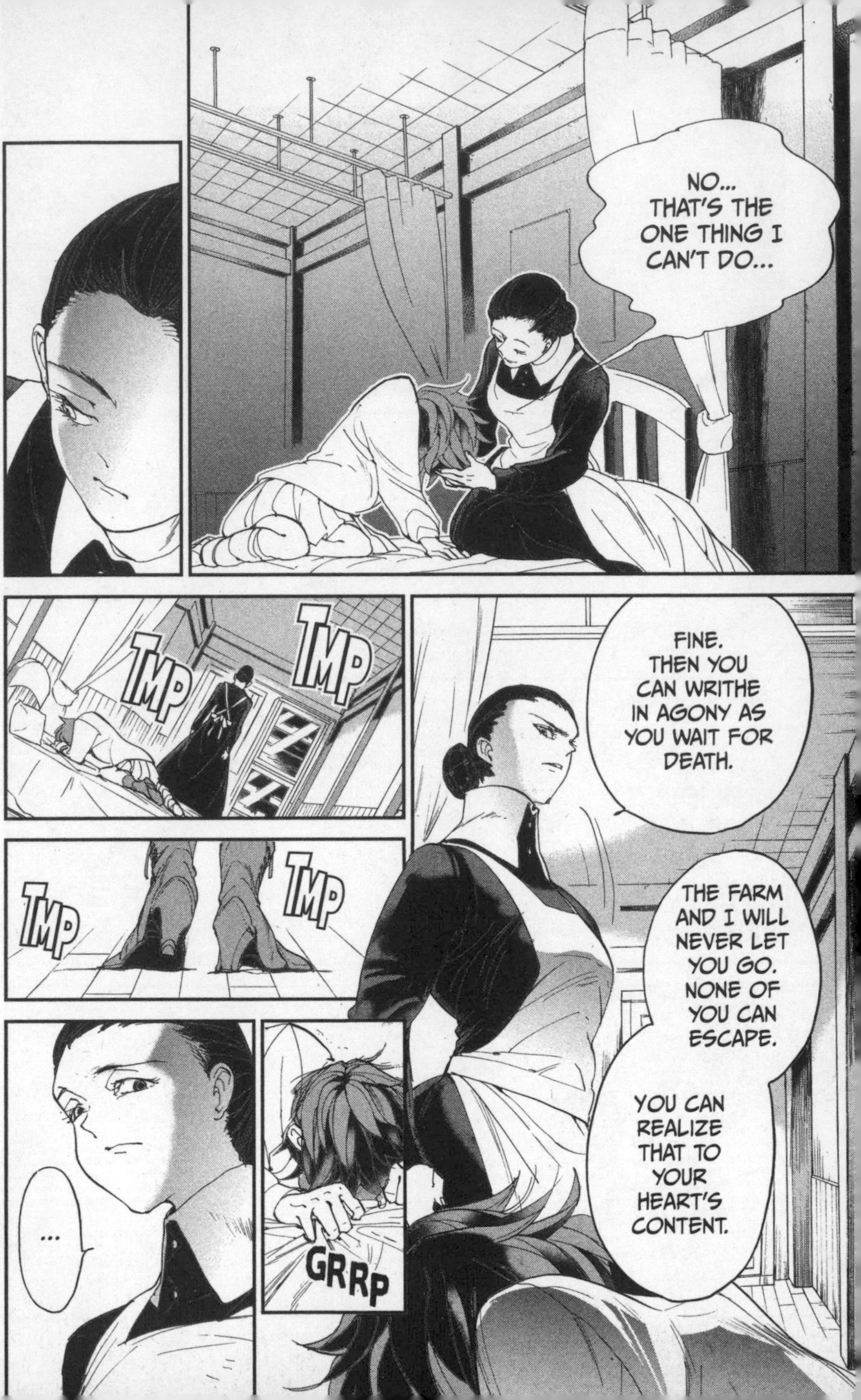
NO... THAT'S THE ONE THING I CAN'T DO...
FINE. THEN YOU CAN WRITHE IN AGONY AS YOU WAIT FOR DEATH.
THE FARM AND I WILL NEVER LET YOU GO. NONE OF YOU CAN ESCAPE.
YOU CAN REALIZE THAT TO YOUR HEART'S CONTENT.
TMP
TMP
TMP
TMP
GRRP
...

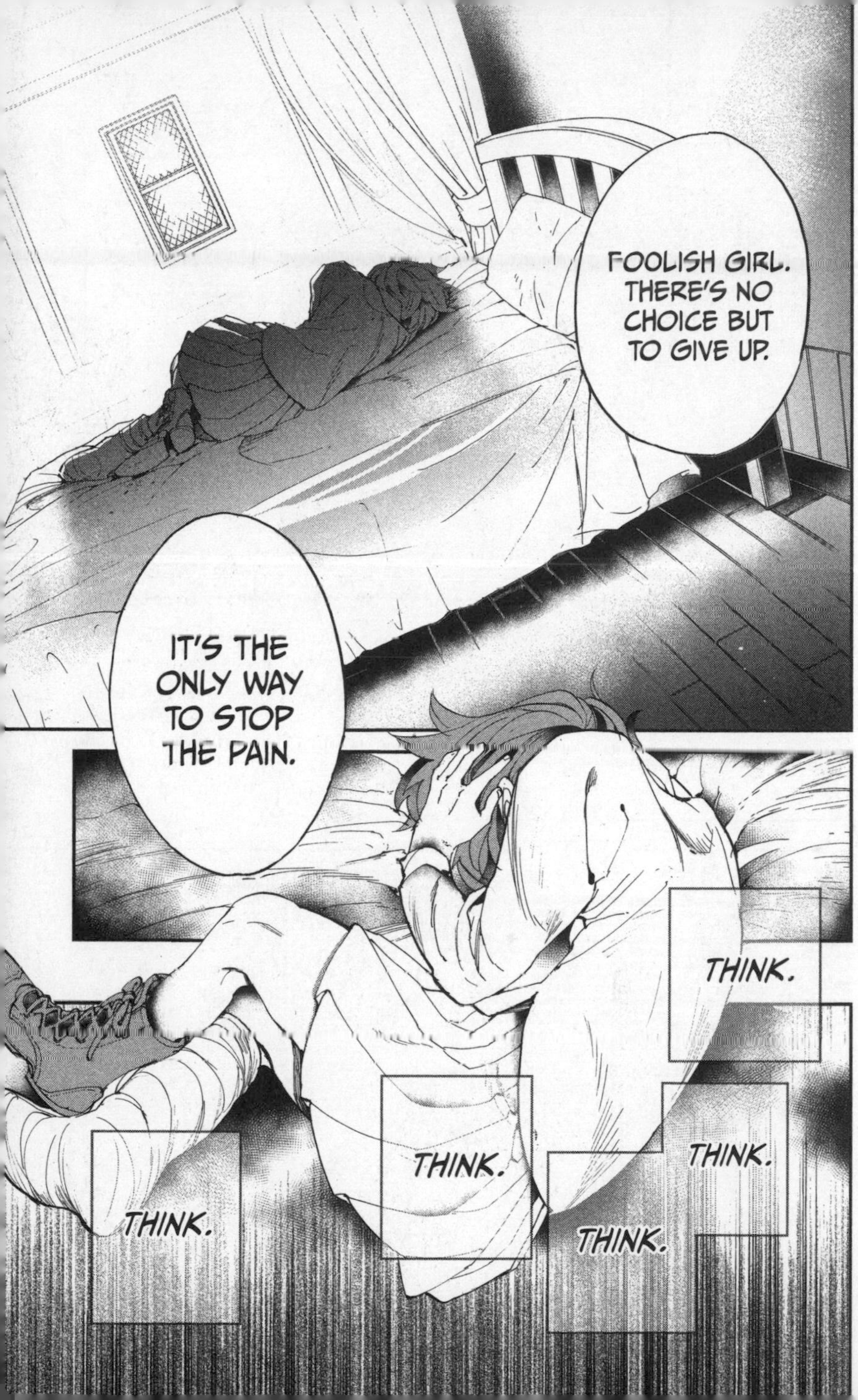
FOOLISH GIRL. THERE'S NO CHOICE BUT TO GIVE UP.
IT'S THE ONLY WAY TO STOP THE PAIN.
THINK.
THINK.
THINK.
THINK.
THINK.

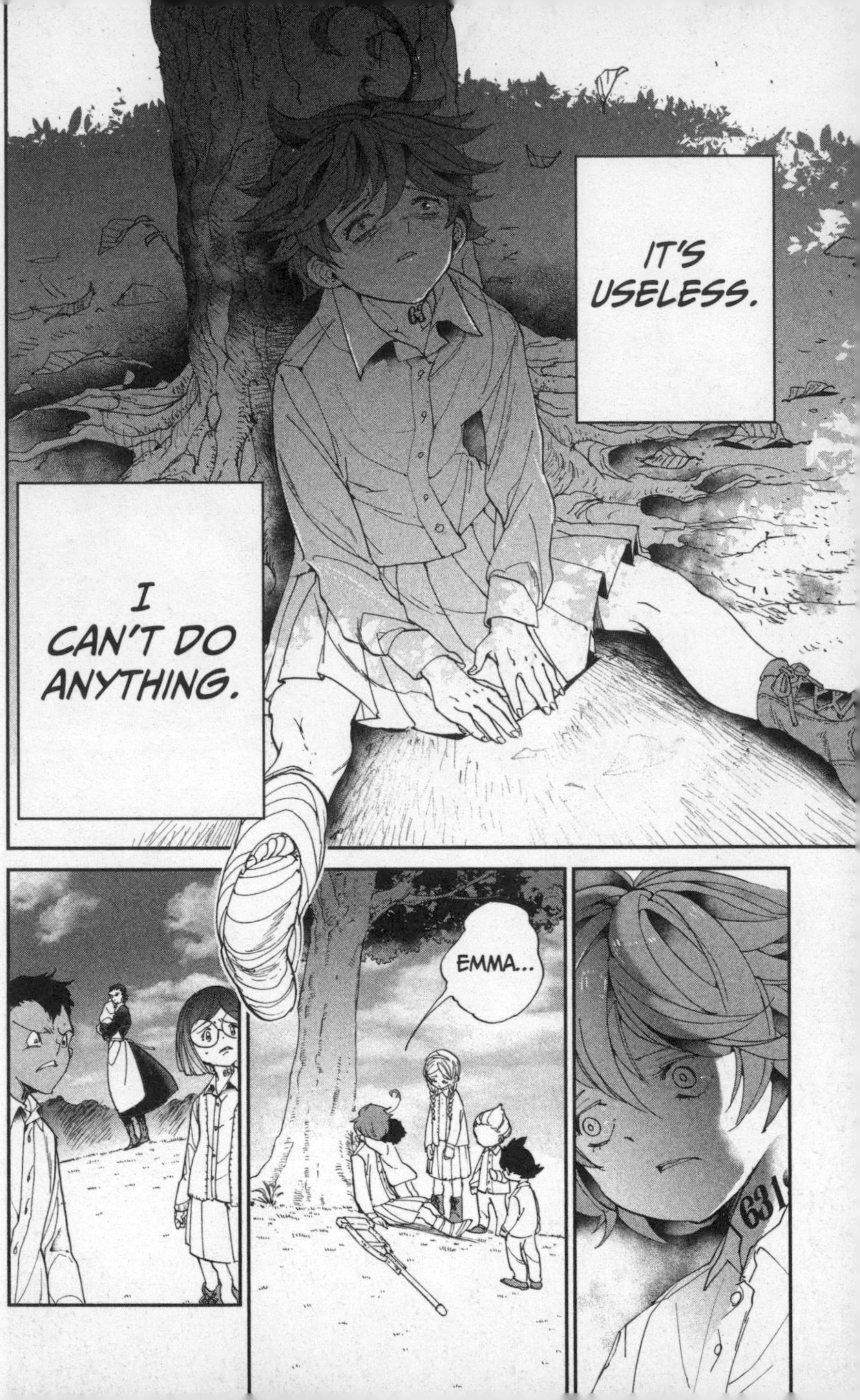

IT'S USELESS.
I CAN'T DO ANYTHING.
EMMA...

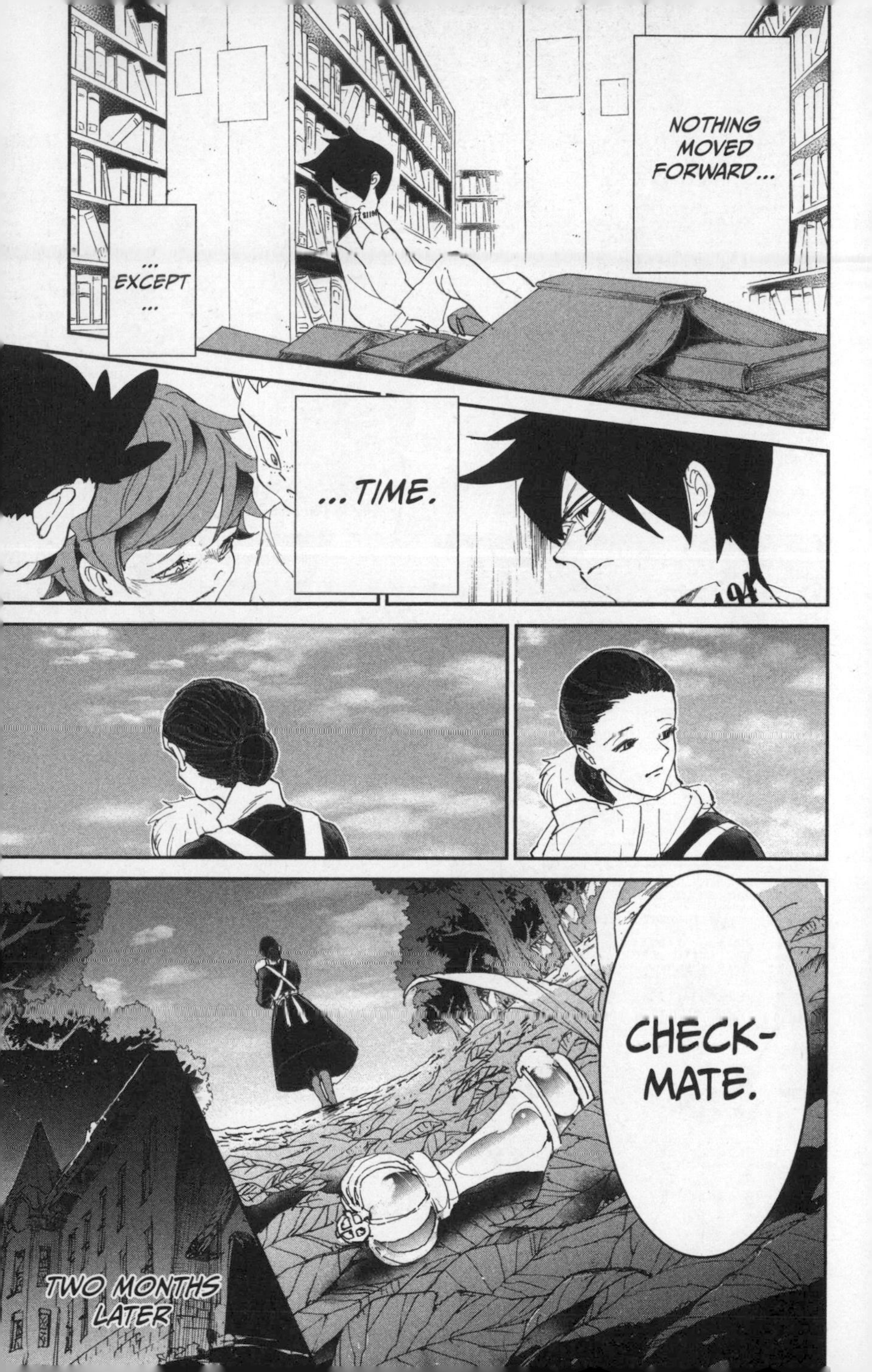
NOTHING MOVED FORWARD...
... EXCEPT ...
... TIME.
CHECK-MATE.
TWO MONTHS LATER

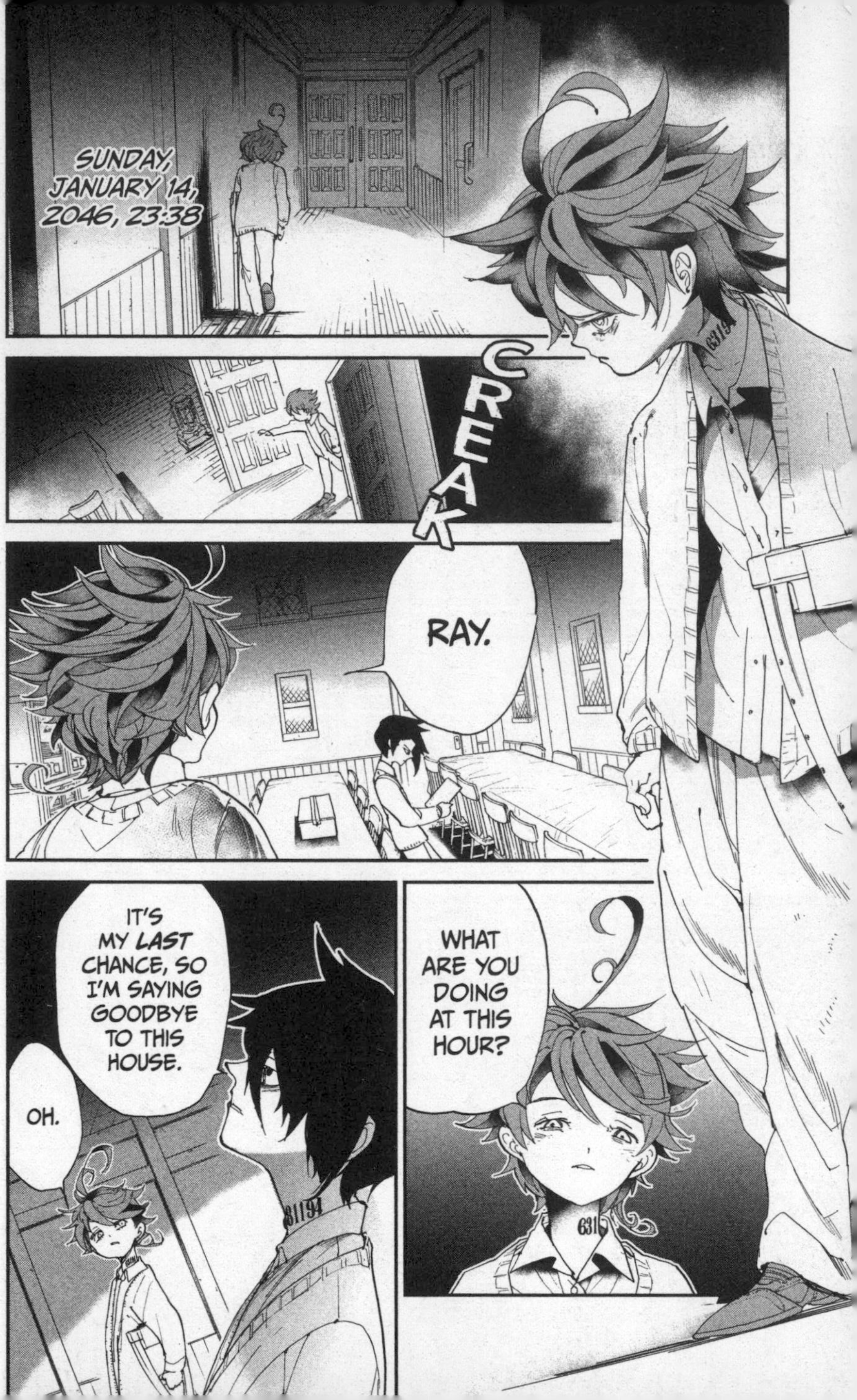
SUNDAY, JANUARY 14, 2046, 23:38
CREAK
RAY.
WHAT ARE YOU DOING AT THIS HOUR?
IT'S MY LAST CHANCE, SO I'M SAYING GOODBYE TO THIS HOUSE.
OH.

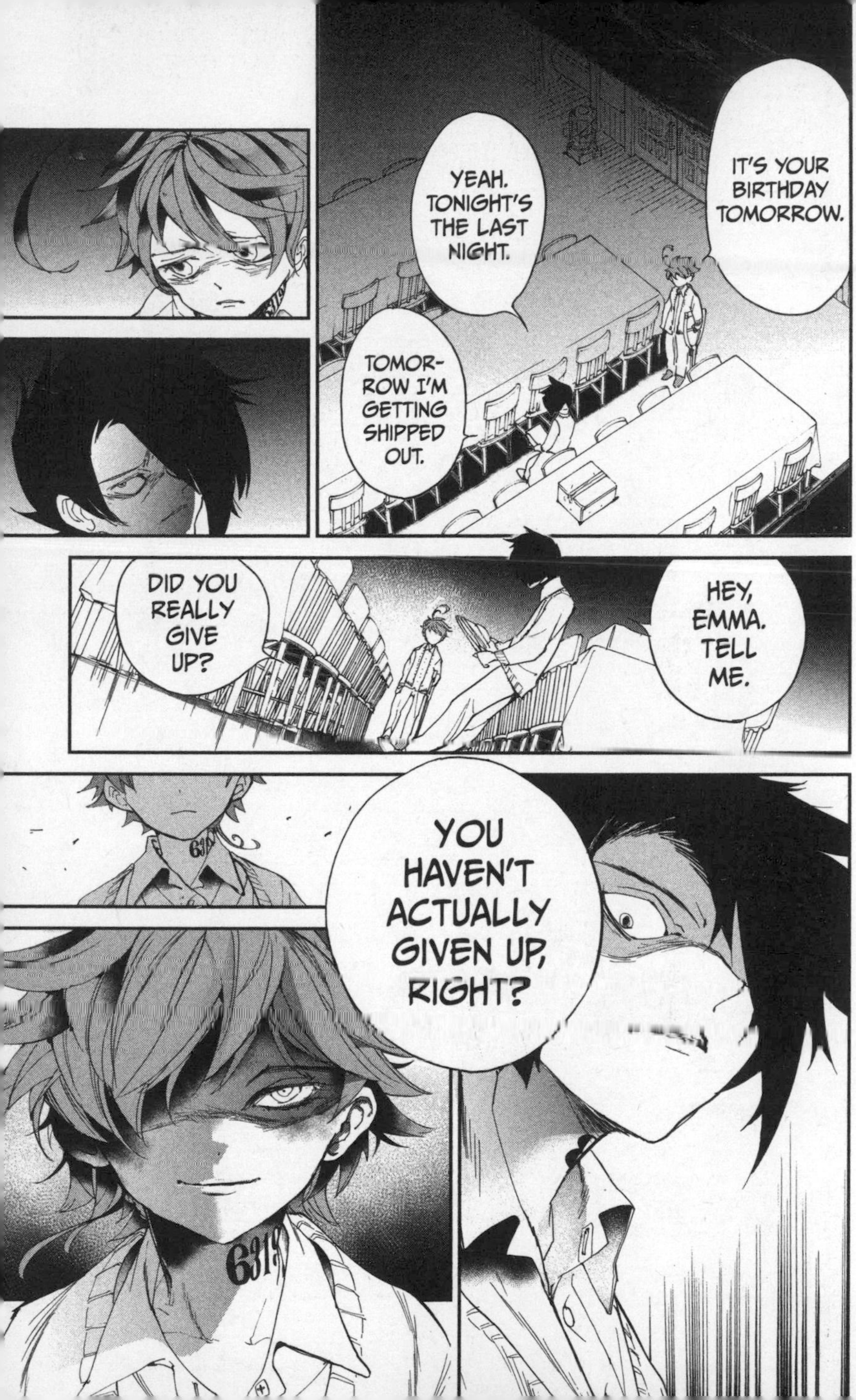
IT'S YOUR BIRTHDAY TOMORROW.
YEAH. TONIGHT'S THE LAST NIGHT.
TOMOR-ROW I'M GETTING SHIPPED OUT.
HEY, EMMA. TELL ME.
DID YOU REALLY GIVE UP?
YOU HAVEN'T ACTUALLY GIVEN UP, RIGHT?

GRACE FIELD HOUSE ART GALLERY

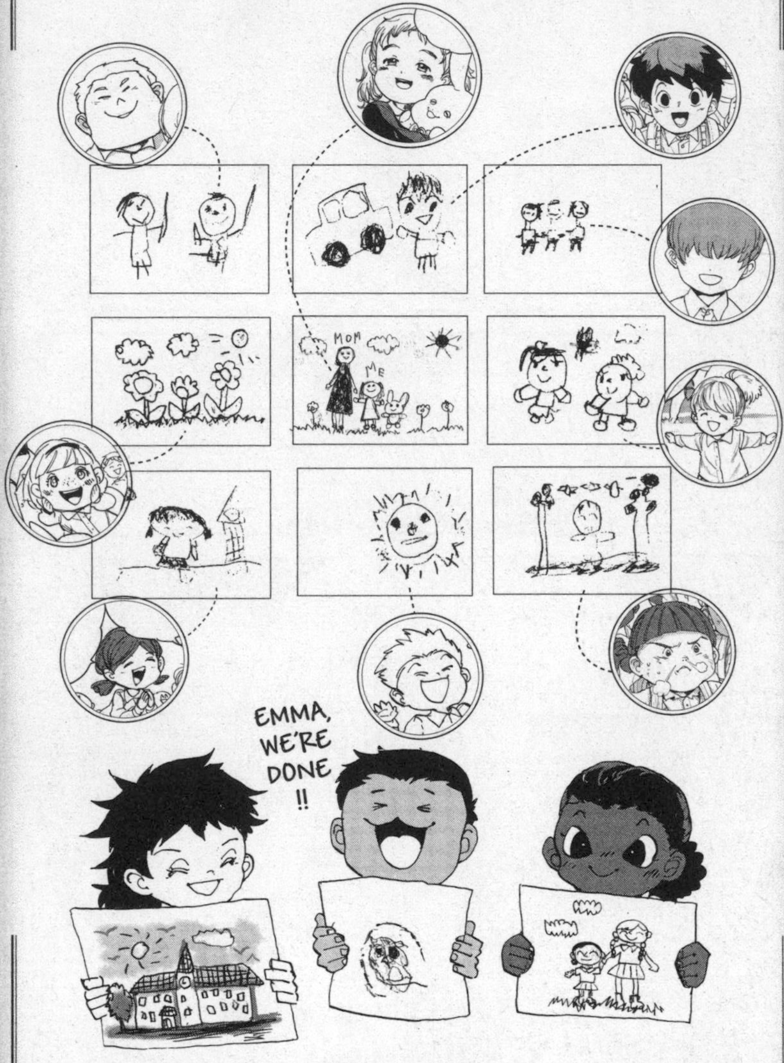
MOM
ME
EMMA, WE'RE DONE !!

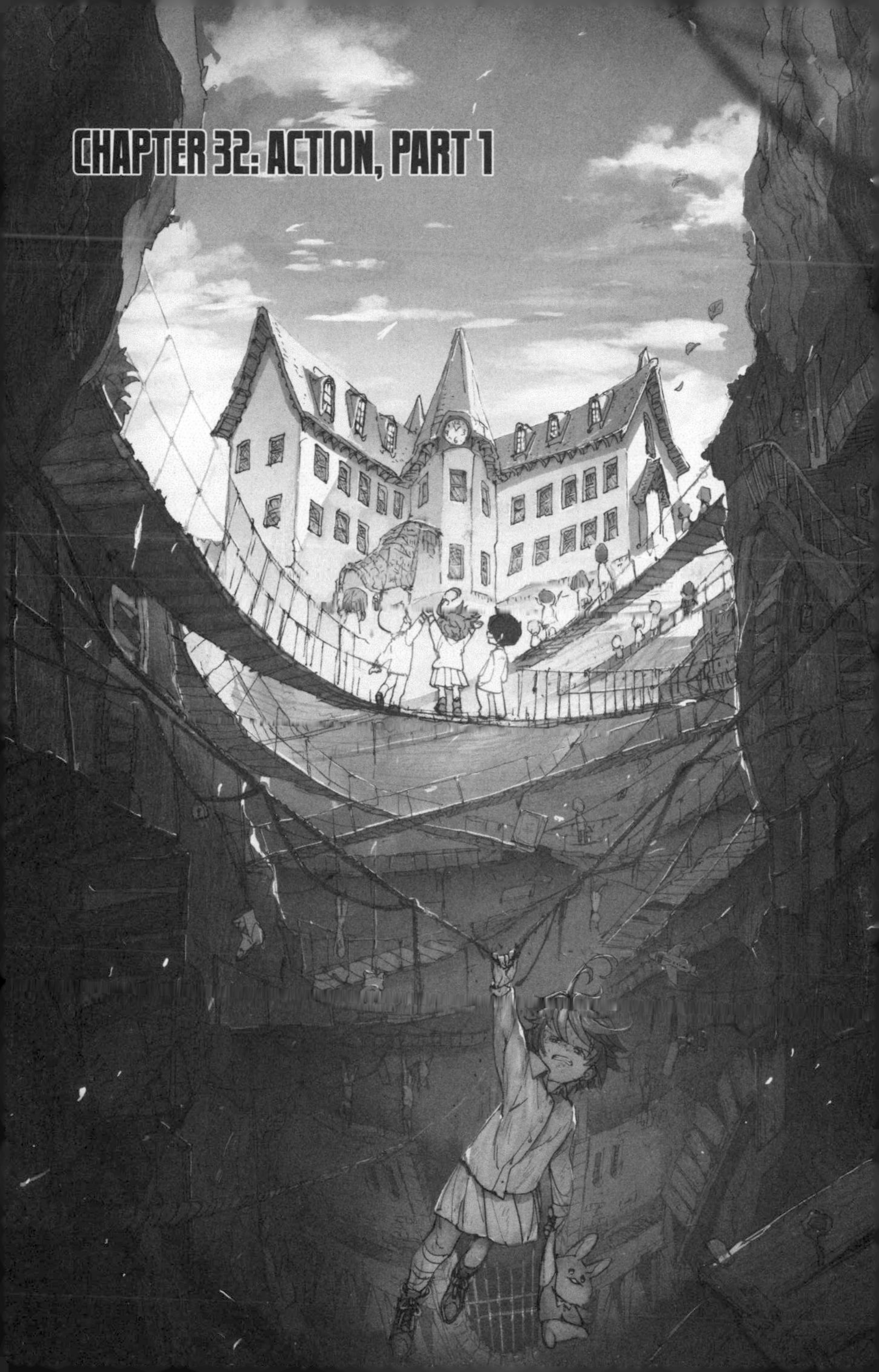
CHAPTER 32: ACTION, PART 1

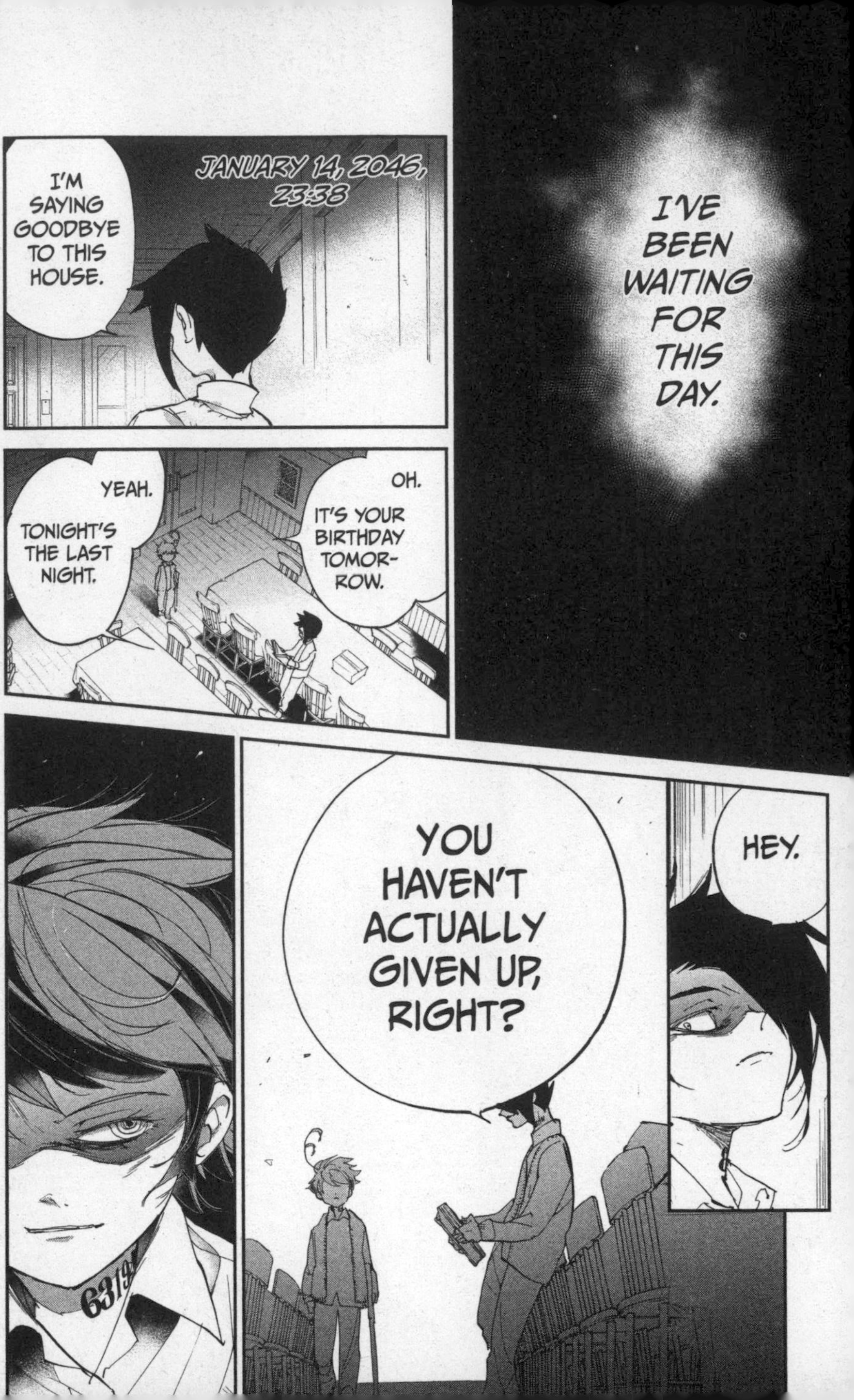
I'VE BEEN WAITING FOR THIS DAY.
JANUARY 14, 2046, 23:38
I'M SAYING GOODBYE TO THIS HOUSE.
OH.
IT'S YOUR BIRTHDAY TOMORROW.
YEAH.
TONIGHT'S THE LAST NIGHT.
HEY.
YOU HAVEN'T ACTUALLY GIVEN UP, RIGHT?

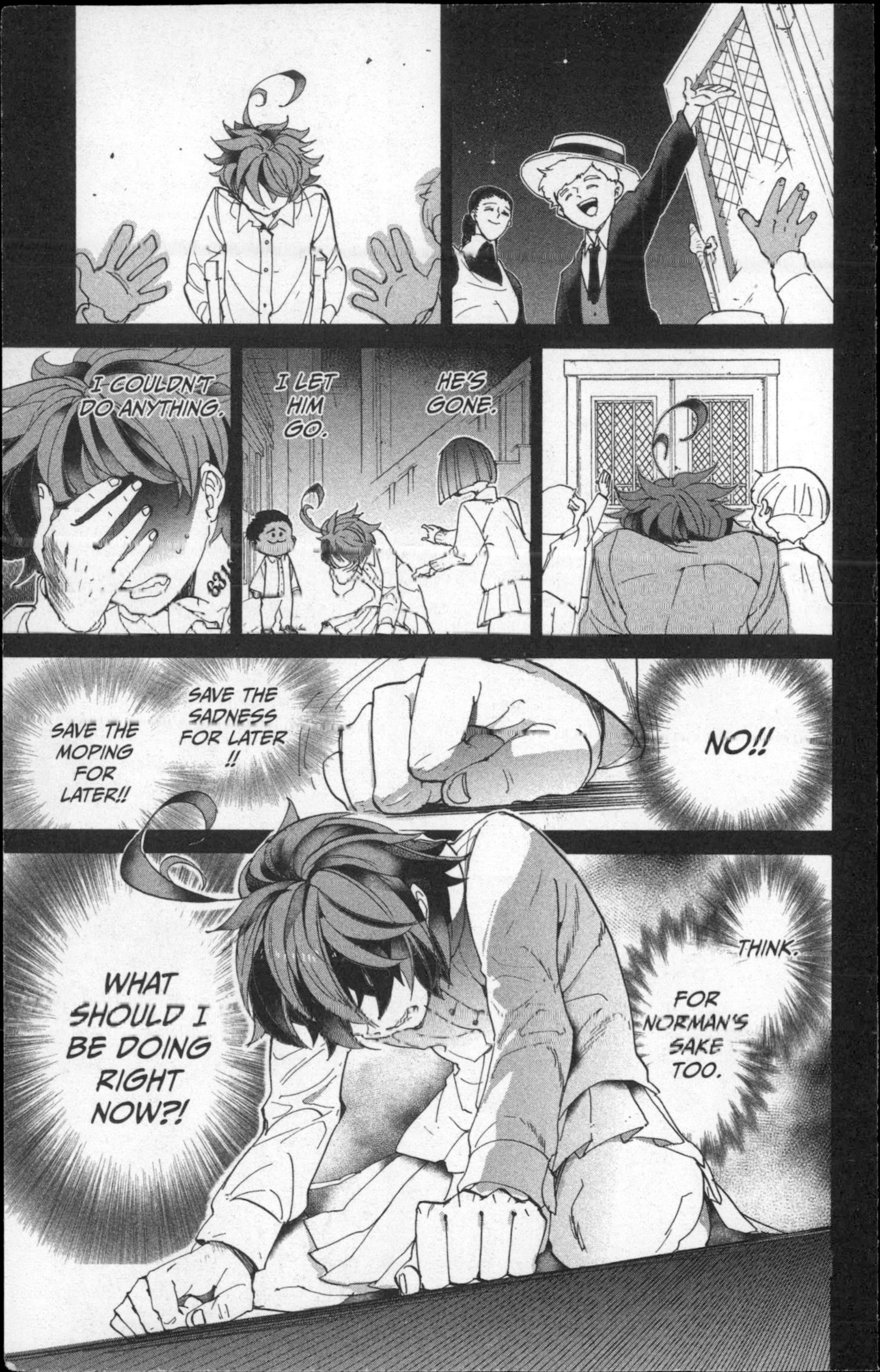
HE'S GONE.
I LET HIM GO.
I COULDN'T DO ANYTHING.
NO!!
SAVE THE SADNESS FOR LATER!!
SAVE THE MOPING FOR LATER!!
THINK.
FOR NORMAN'S SAKE TOO.
WHAT SHOULD I BE DOING RIGHT NOW?!

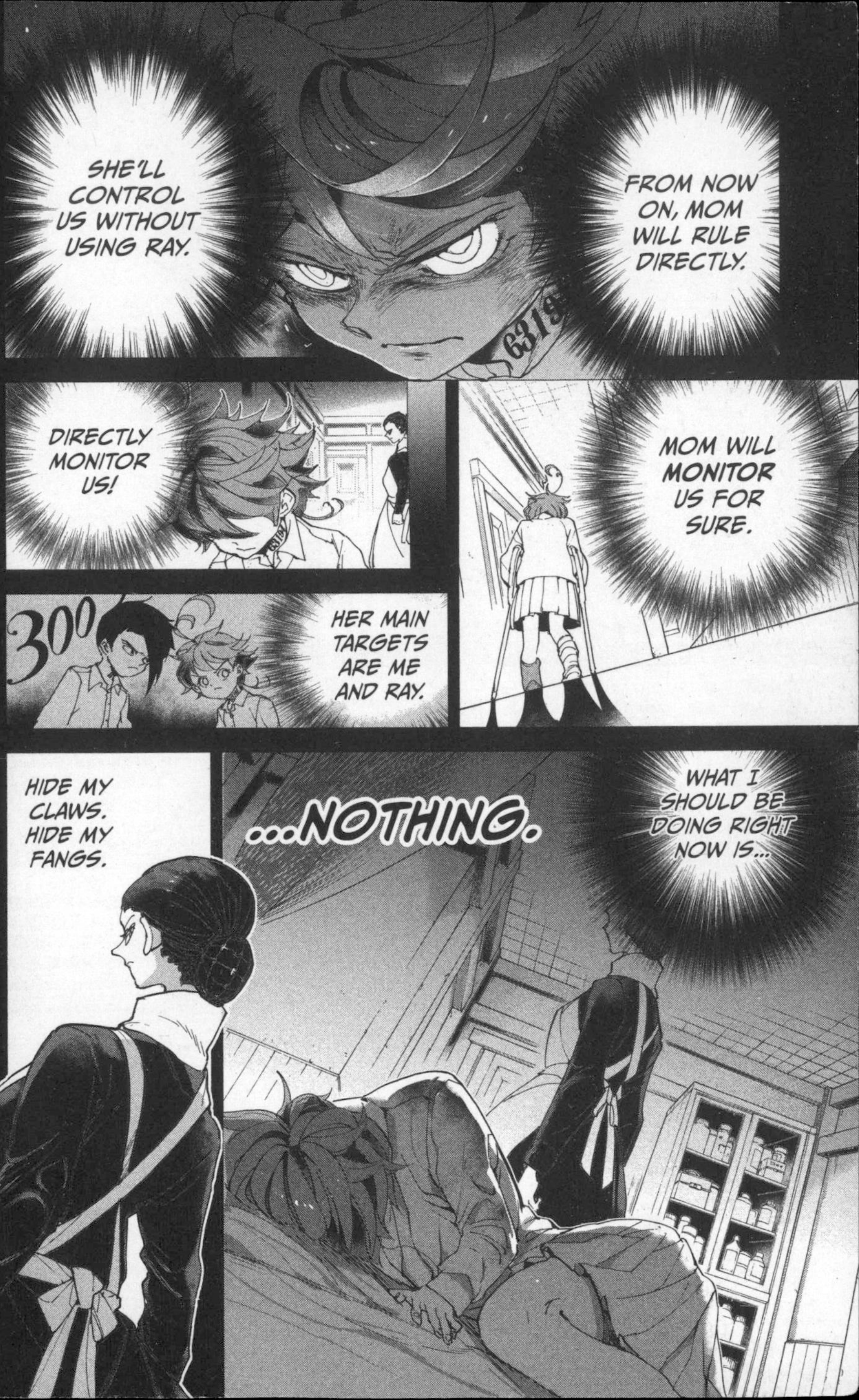
FROM NOW ON, MOM WILL RULE DIRECTLY.
SHE'LL CONTROL US WITHOUT USING RAY.
MOM WILL MONITOR US FOR SURE.
DIRECTLY MONITOR US!
HER MAIN TARGETS ARE ME AND RAY.
300
WHAT I SHOULD BE DOING RIGHT NOW IS...
...NOTHING.
HIDE MY CLAWS. HIDE MY FANGS.

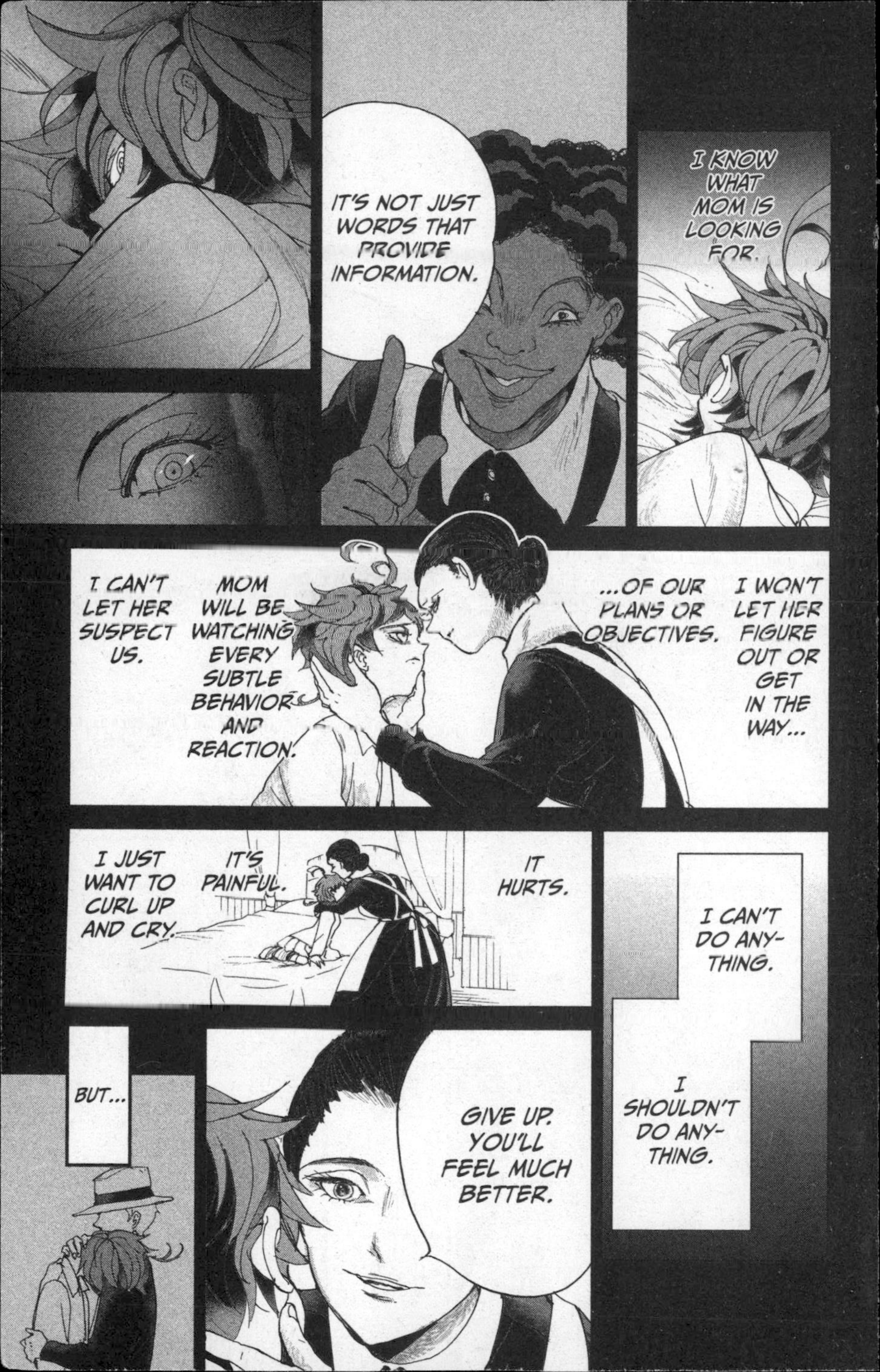
I KNOW WHAT MOM IS LOOKING FOR.
IT'S NOT JUST WORDS THAT PROVIDE INFORMATION.
I WON'T LET HER FIGURE OUT OR GET IN THE WAY...
...OF OUR PLANS OR OBJECTIVES.
MOM WILL BE WATCHING EVERY SUBTLE BEHAVIOR AND REACTION.
I CAN'T LET HER SUSPECT US.
I CAN'T DO ANY-THING.
I SHOULDN'T DO ANY-THING.
IT HURTS.
IT'S PAINFUL.
I JUST WANT TO CURL UP AND CRY.
GIVE UP. YOU'LL FEEL MUCH BETTER.
BUT...

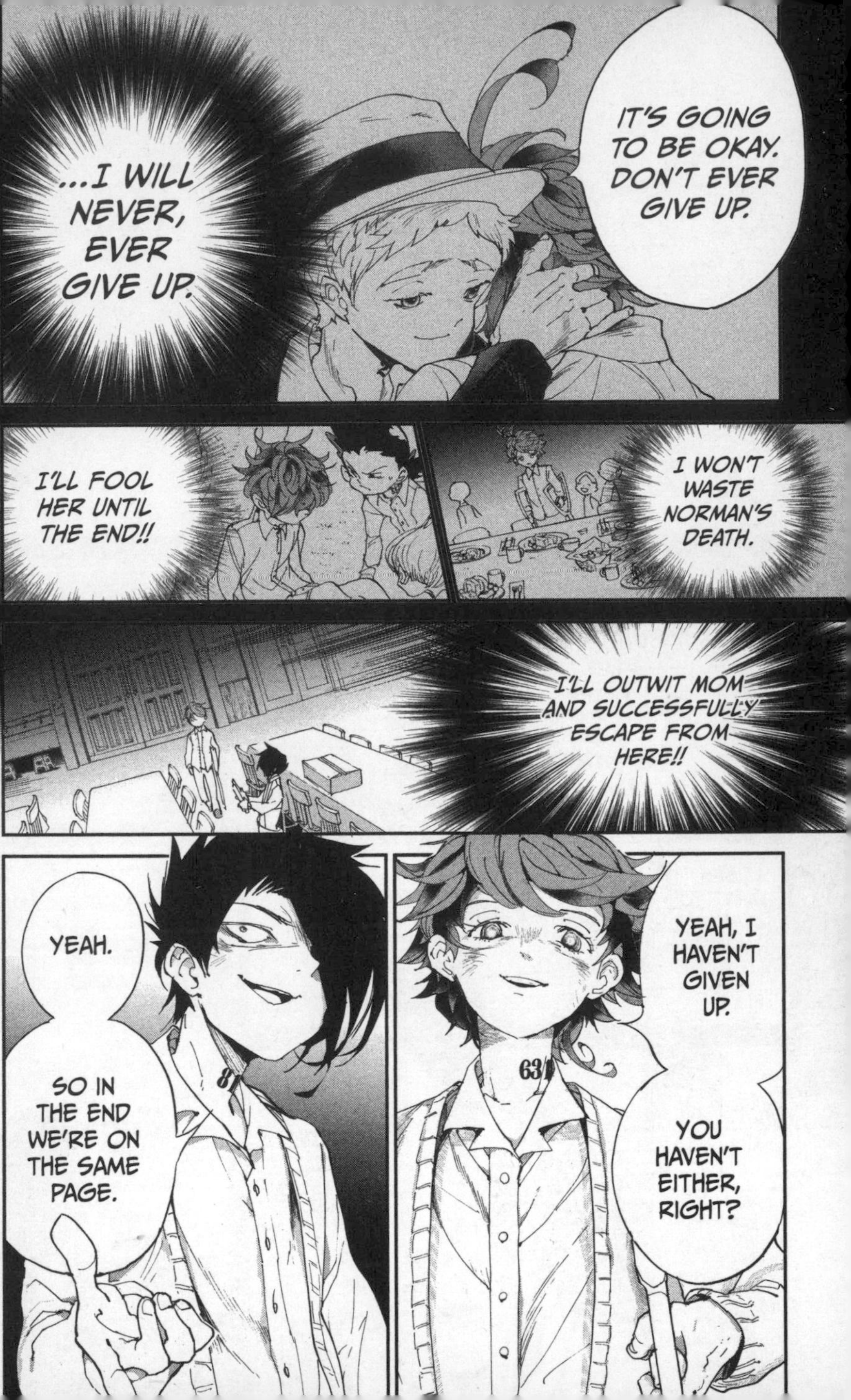
IT'S GOING TO BE OKAY. DON'T EVER GIVE UP.
...I WILL NEVER, EVER GIVE UP.
I WON'T WASTE NORMAN'S DEATH.
I'LL FOOL HER UNTIL THE END!!
I'LL OUTWIT MOM AND SUCCESSFULLY ESCAPE FROM HERE!!
YEAH, I HAVEN'T GIVEN UP.
YOU HAVEN'T EITHER, RIGHT?
YEAH.
SO IN THE END WE'RE ON THE SAME PAGE.

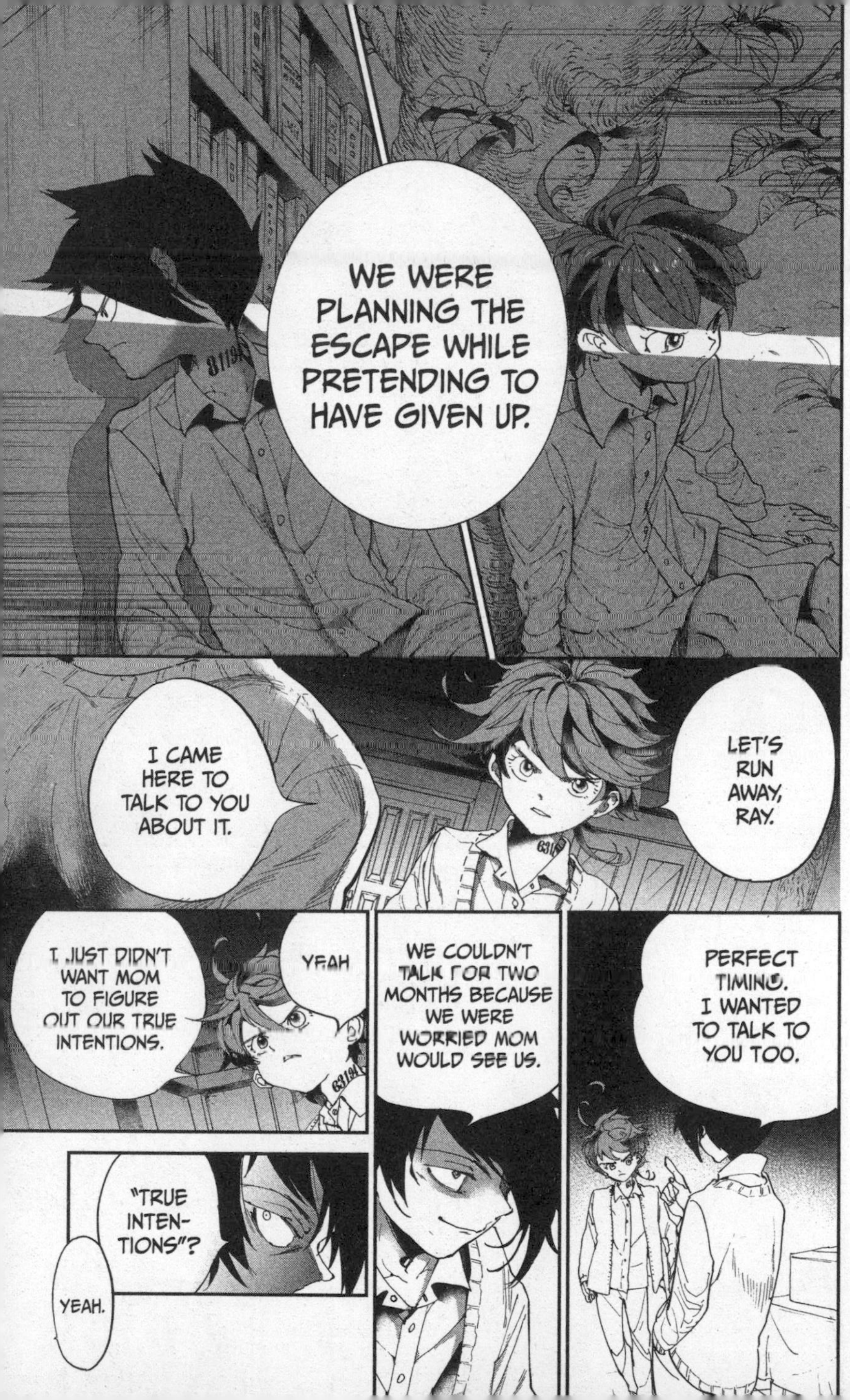
WE WERE PLANNING THE ESCAPE WHILE PRETENDING TO HAVE GIVEN UP.
LET'S RUN AWAY, RAY.
I CAME HERE TO TALK TO YOU ABOUT IT.
PERFECT TIMING. I WANTED TO TALK TO YOU TOO.
WE COULDN'T TALK FOR TWO MONTHS BECAUSE WE WERE WORRIED MOM WOULD SEE US.
YEAH
I JUST DIDN'T WANT MOM TO FIGURE OUT OUR TRUE INTENTIONS.
"TRUE INTEN-TIONS"?
YEAH.

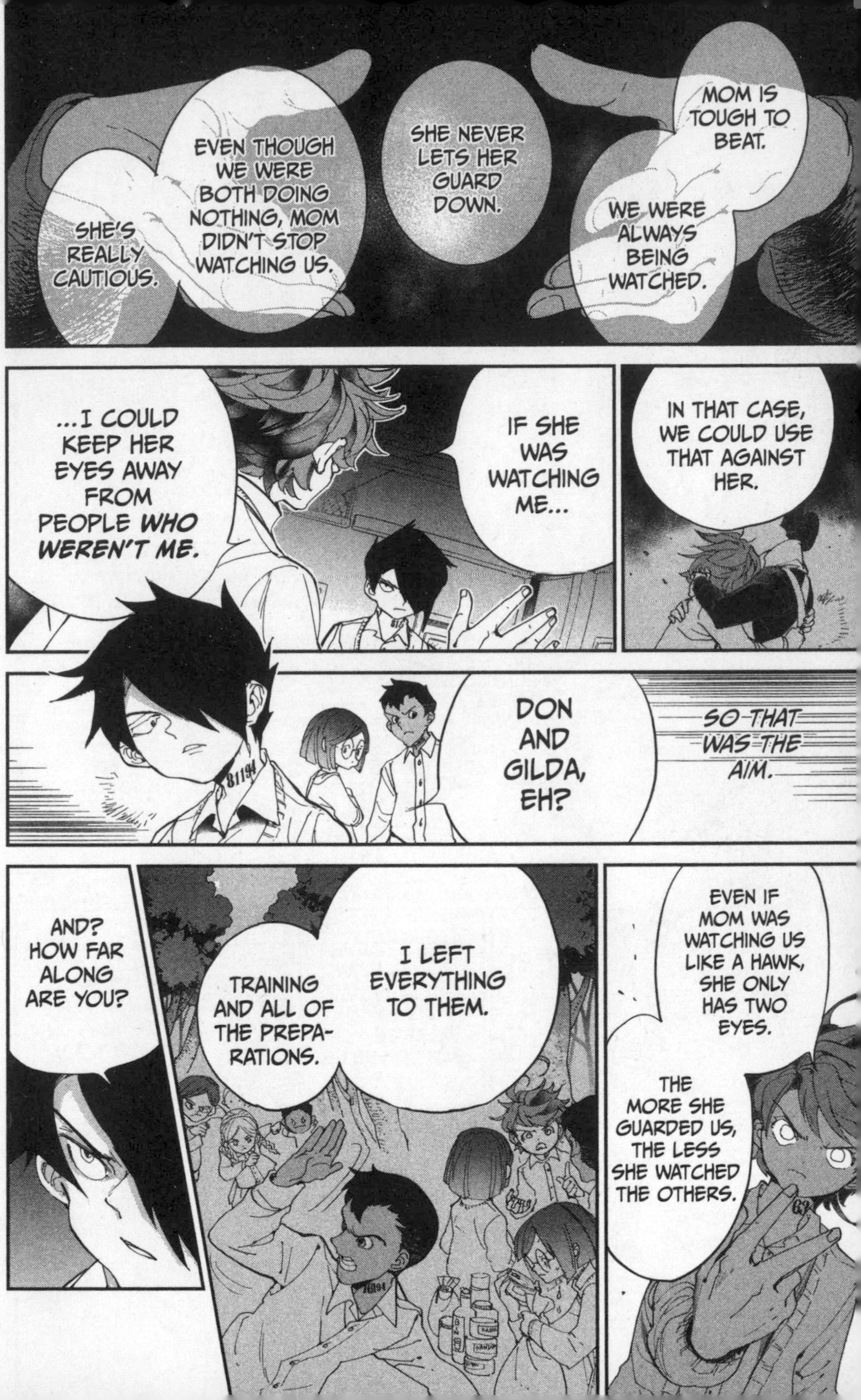
MOM IS TOUGH TO BEAT.
WE WERE ALWAYS BEING WATCHED.
SHE NEVER LETS HER GUARD DOWN.
EVEN THOUGH WE WERE BOTH DOING NOTHING, MOM DIDN'T STOP WATCHING US.
SHE'S REALLY CAUTIOUS.
IN THAT CASE, WE COULD USE THAT AGAINST HER.
IF SHE WAS WATCHING ME...
...I COULD KEEP HER EYES AWAY FROM PEOPLE *WHO WEREN'T ME.*
SO THAT WAS THE AIM.
DON AND GILDA, EH?
EVEN IF MOM WAS WATCHING US LIKE A HAWK, SHE ONLY HAS TWO EYES.
THE MORE SHE GUARDED US, THE LESS SHE WATCHED THE OTHERS.
I LEFT EVERYTHING TO THEM.
TRAINING AND ALL OF THE PREPARATIONS.
AND? HOW FAR ALONG ARE YOU?

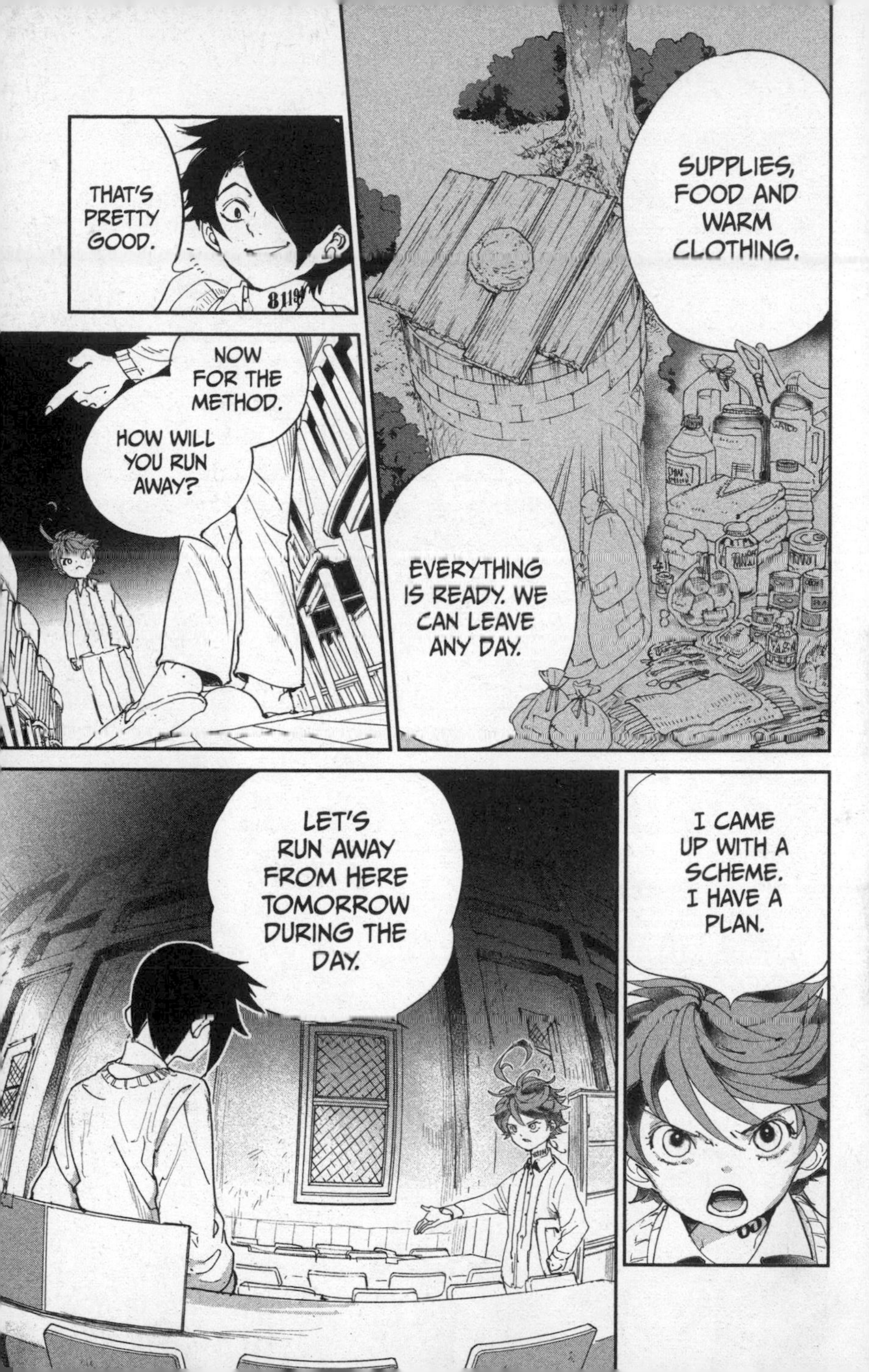
SUPPLIES, FOOD AND WARM CLOTHING.
EVERYTHING IS READY. WE CAN LEAVE ANY DAY.
THAT'S PRETTY GOOD.
NOW FOR THE METHOD.
HOW WILL YOU RUN AWAY?
I CAME UP WITH A SCHEME. I HAVE A PLAN.
LET'S RUN AWAY FROM HERE TOMORROW DURING THE DAY.

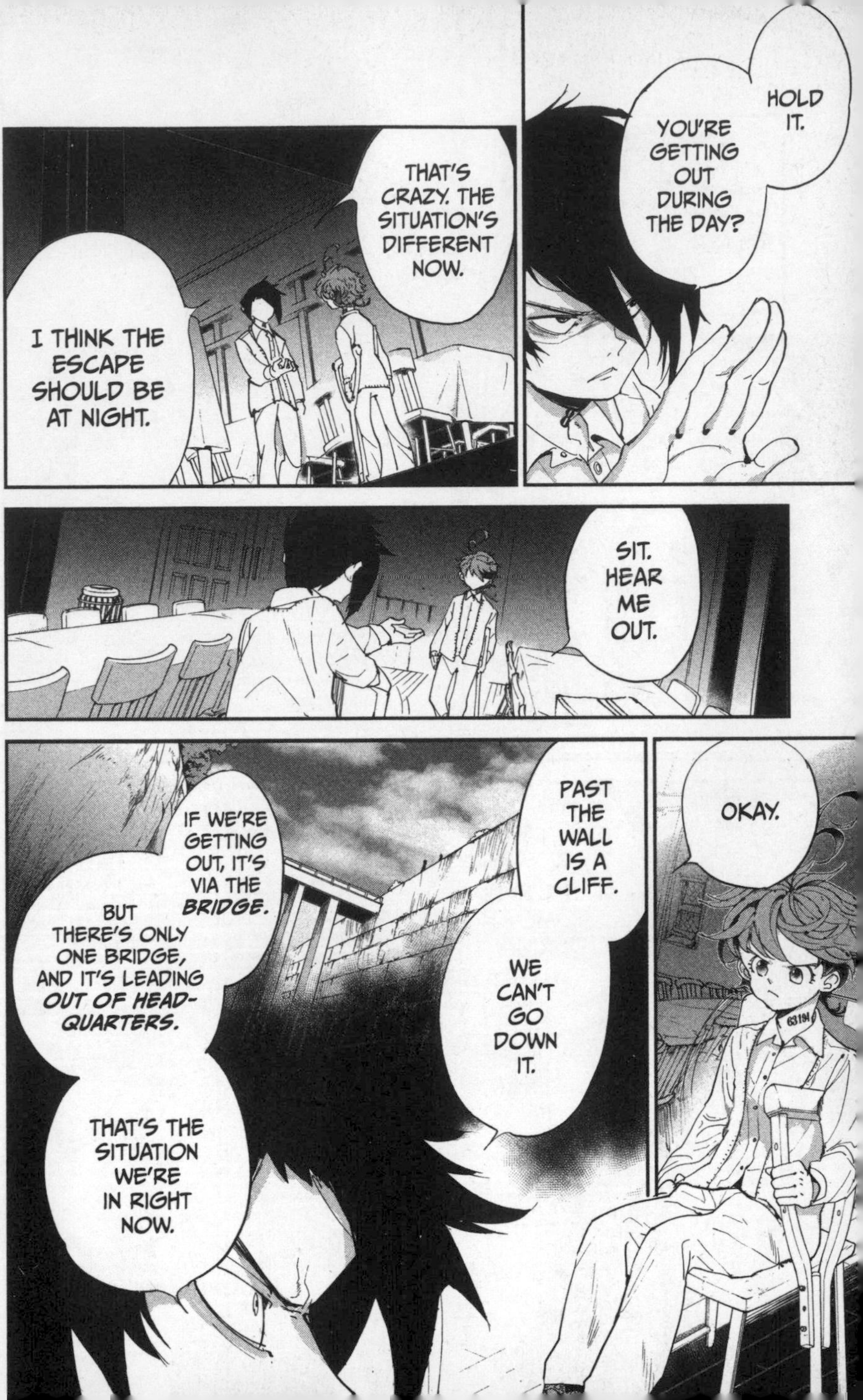
HOLD IT.
YOU'RE GETTING OUT DURING THE DAY?
THAT'S CRAZY. THE SITUATION'S DIFFERENT NOW.
I THINK THE ESCAPE SHOULD BE AT NIGHT.
SIT. HEAR ME OUT.
OKAY.
PAST THE WALL IS A CLIFF.
WE CAN'T GO DOWN IT.
IF WE'RE GETTING OUT, IT'S VIA THE *BRIDGE.*
BUT THERE'S ONLY ONE BRIDGE, AND IT'S LEADING *OUT OF HEAD-QUARTERS.*
THAT'S THE SITUATION WE'RE IN RIGHT NOW.

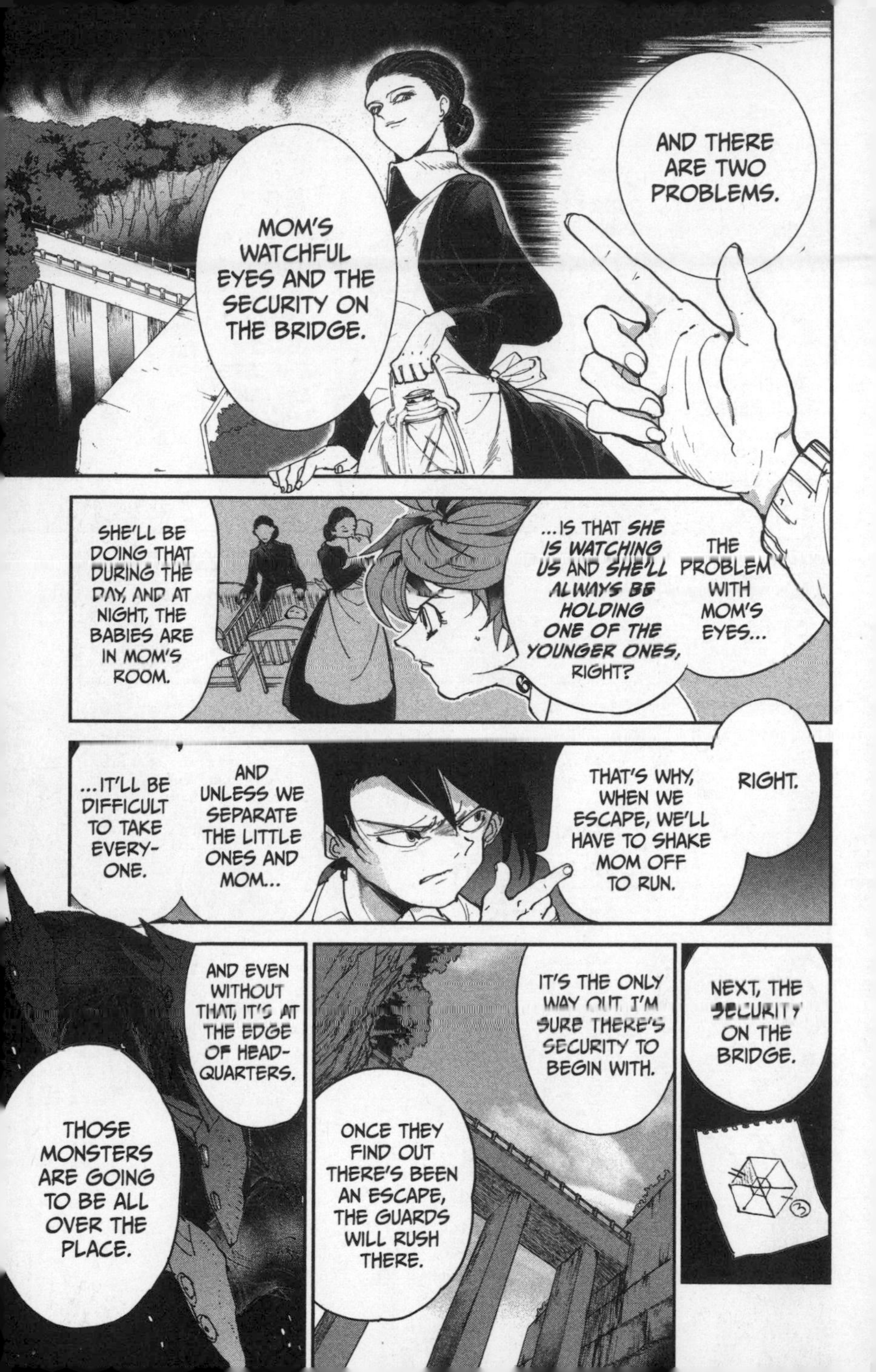
AND THERE ARE TWO PROBLEMS.
MOM'S WATCHFUL EYES AND THE SECURITY ON THE BRIDGE.
THE PROBLEM WITH MOM'S EYES...
...IS THAT SHE IS WATCHING US AND SHE'LL ALWAYS BE HOLDING ONE OF THE YOUNGER ONES, RIGHT?
SHE'LL BE DOING THAT DURING THE DAY, AND AT NIGHT, THE BABIES ARE IN MOM'S ROOM.
RIGHT.
THAT'S WHY, WHEN WE ESCAPE, WE'LL HAVE TO SHAKE MOM OFF TO RUN.
AND UNLESS WE SEPARATE THE LITTLE ONES AND MOM...
...IT'LL BE DIFFICULT TO TAKE EVERY-ONE.
NEXT, THE SECURITY ON THE BRIDGE.
IT'S THE ONLY WAY OUT I'M SURE THERE'S SECURITY TO BEGIN WITH.
ONCE THEY FIND OUT THERE'S BEEN AN ESCAPE, THE GUARDS WILL RUSH THERE.
AND EVEN WITHOUT THAT, IT'S AT THE EDGE OF HEAD-QUARTERS.
THOSE MONSTERS ARE GOING TO BE ALL OVER THE PLACE.

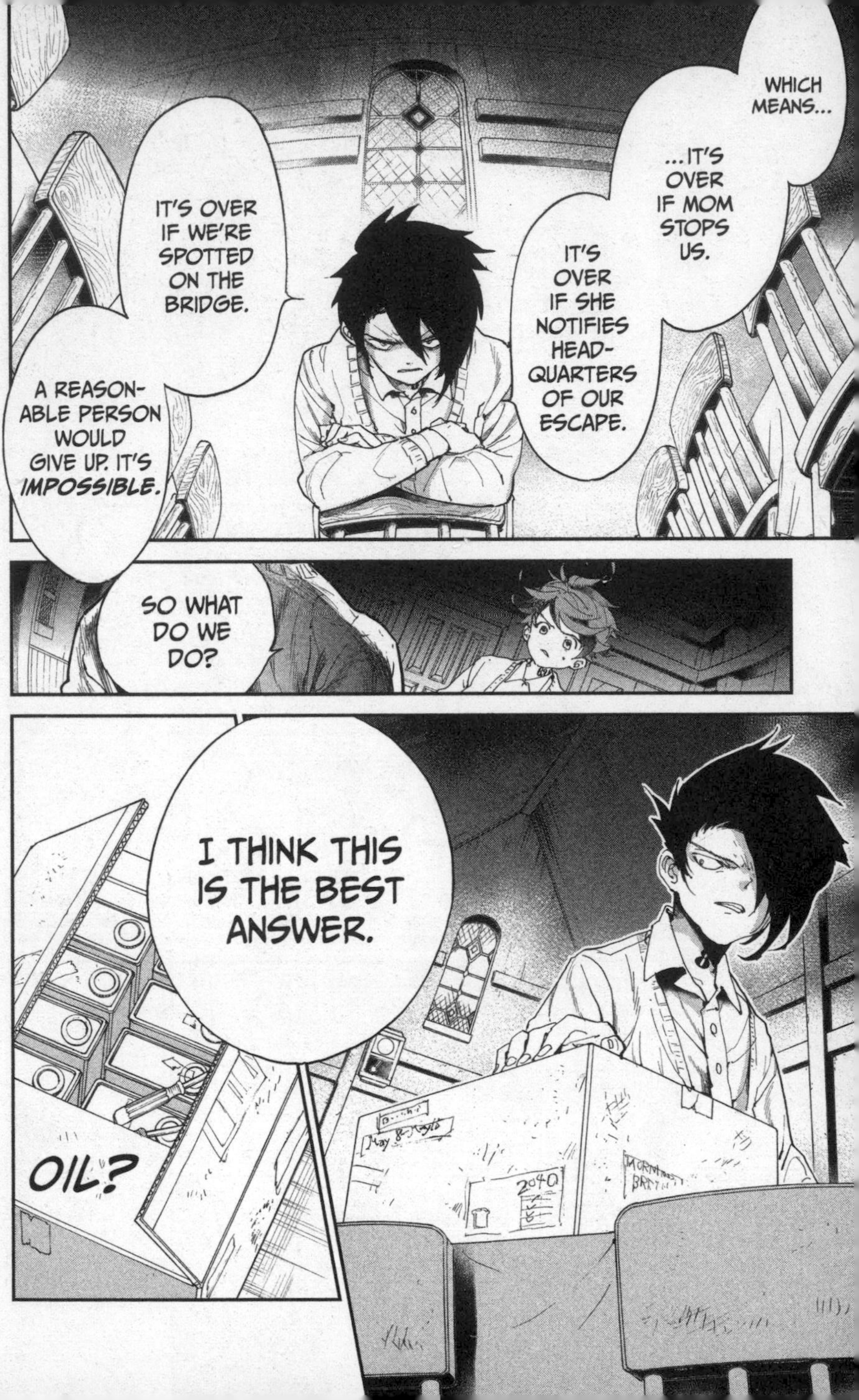
WHICH MEANS...
...IT'S OVER IF MOM STOPS US.
IT'S OVER IF SHE NOTIFIES HEAD-QUARTERS OF OUR ESCAPE.
IT'S OVER IF WE'RE SPOTTED ON THE BRIDGE.
A REASON-ABLE PERSON WOULD GIVE UP. IT'S *IMPOSSIBLE*.
SO WHAT DO WE DO?
I THINK THIS IS THE BEST ANSWER.
2040
OIL?

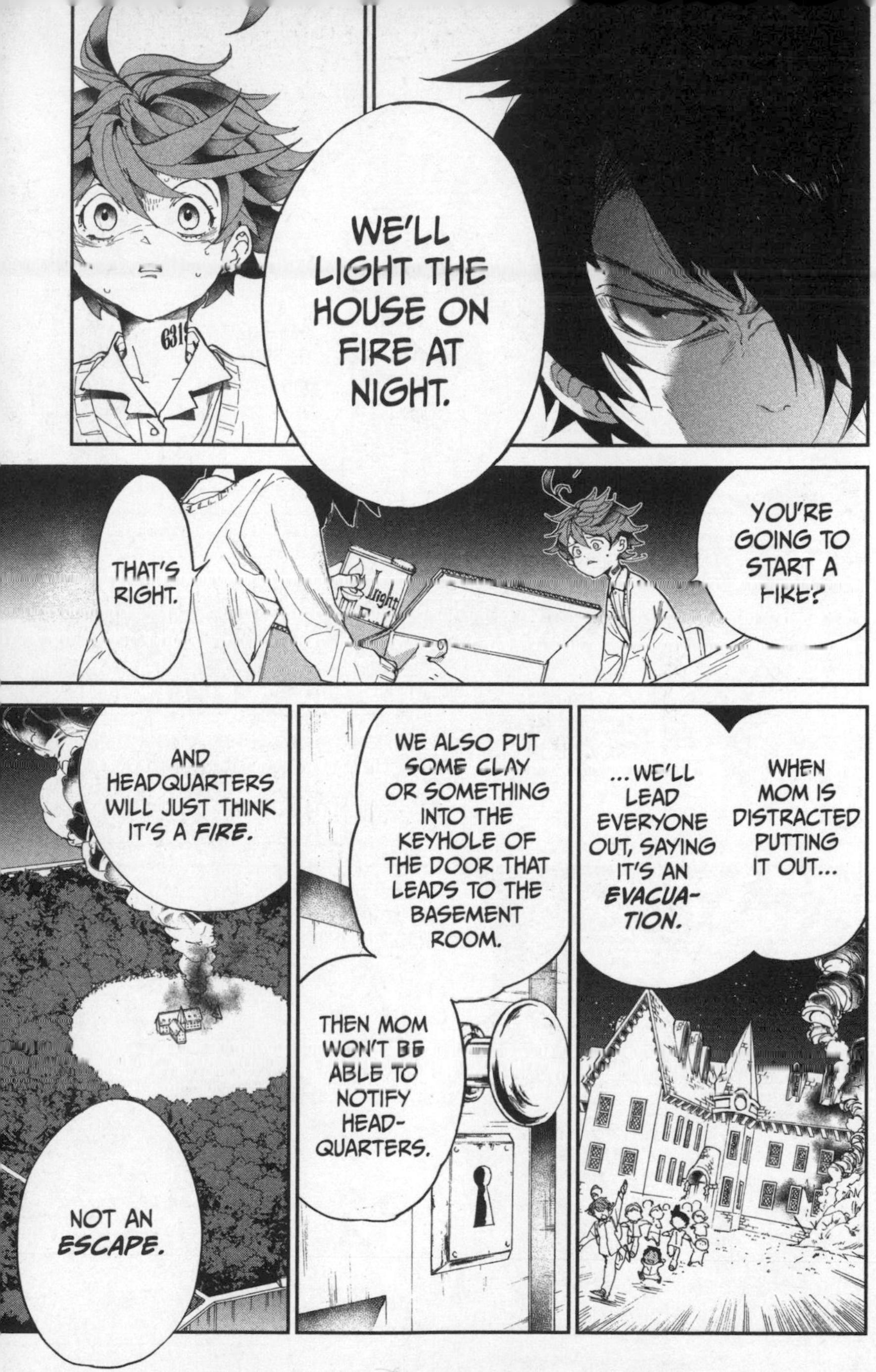
WE'LL LIGHT THE HOUSE ON FIRE AT NIGHT.
YOU'RE GOING TO START A FIRE?
THAT'S RIGHT.
WHEN MOM IS DISTRACTED PUTTING IT OUT...
...WE'LL LEAD EVERYONE OUT, SAYING IT'S AN *EVACUATION.*
WE ALSO PUT SOME CLAY OR SOMETHING INTO THE KEYHOLE OF THE DOOR THAT LEADS TO THE BASEMENT ROOM.
THEN MOM WON'T BE ABLE TO NOTIFY HEAD-QUARTERS.
AND HEADQUARTERS WILL JUST THINK IT'S A *FIRE.*
NOT AN *ESCAPE.*

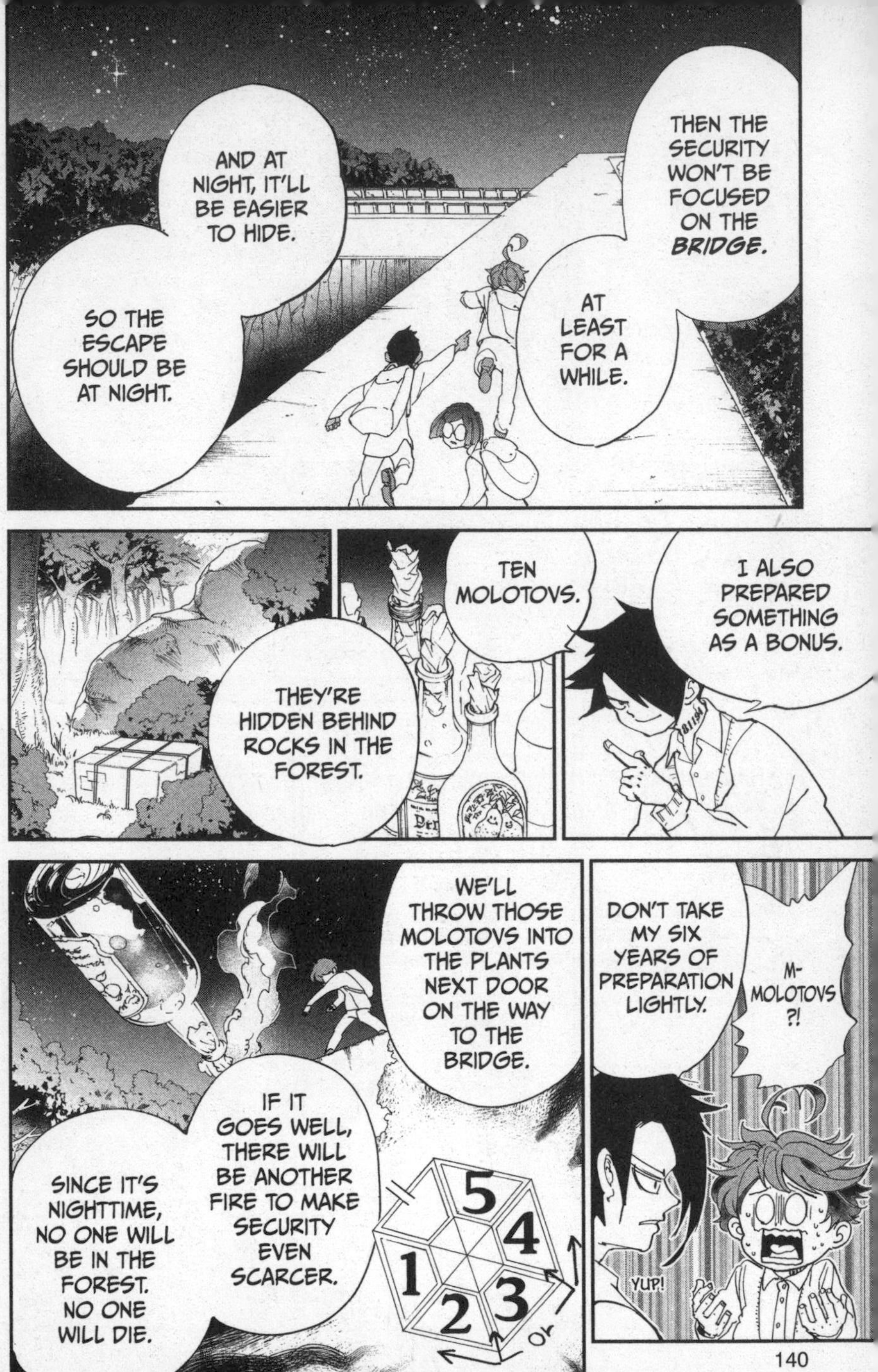
THEN THE SECURITY WON'T BE FOCUSED ON THE BRIDGE.
AT LEAST FOR A WHILE.
AND AT NIGHT, IT'LL BE EASIER TO HIDE.
SO THE ESCAPE SHOULD BE AT NIGHT.
I ALSO PREPARED SOMETHING AS A BONUS.
TEN MOLOTOVS.
THEY'RE HIDDEN BEHIND ROCKS IN THE FOREST.
M-MOLOTOVS?!
DON'T TAKE MY SIX YEARS OF PREPARATION LIGHTLY.
YUP!
WE'LL THROW THOSE MOLOTOVS INTO THE PLANTS NEXT DOOR ON THE WAY TO THE BRIDGE.
IF IT GOES WELL, THERE WILL BE ANOTHER FIRE TO MAKE SECURITY EVEN SCARCER.
SINCE IT'S NIGHTTIME, NO ONE WILL BE IN THE FOREST. NO ONE WILL DIE.
5
4
1
2
3
Or

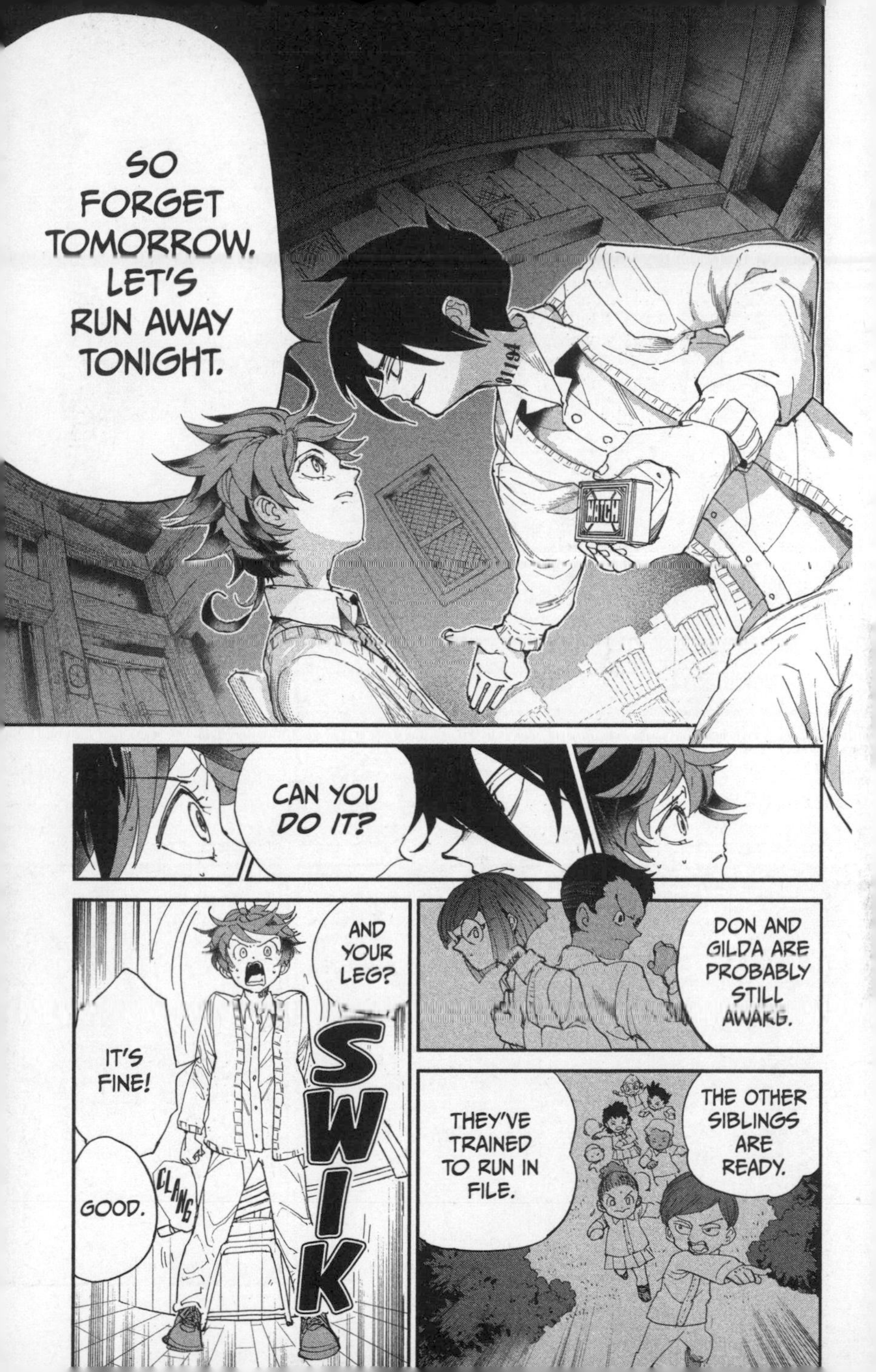
SO FORGET TOMORROW. LET'S RUN AWAY TONIGHT.
MATCH
CAN YOU DO IT?
DON AND GILDA ARE PROBABLY STILL AWAKE.
THE OTHER SIBLINGS ARE READY.
THEY'VE TRAINED TO RUN IN FILE.
AND YOUR LEG?
IT'S FINE!
SWIK
GOOD.
CLANG

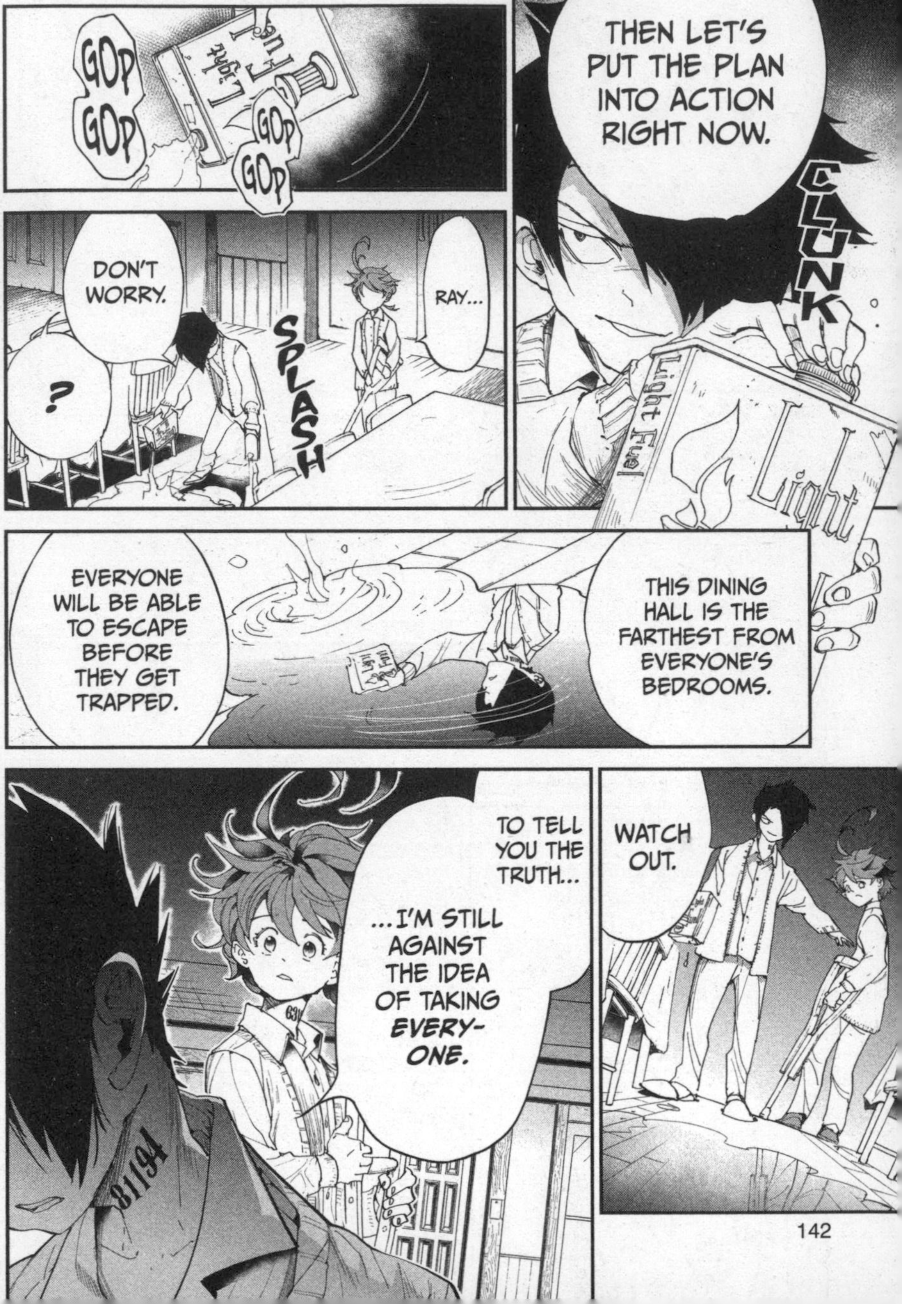
THEN LET'S PUT THE PLAN INTO ACTION RIGHT NOW.
CLUNK
Light Fuel
Light
GOP GOP
GOP GOP
RAY...
SPLASH
DON'T WORRY.
?
THIS DINING HALL IS THE FARTHEST FROM EVERYONE'S BEDROOMS.
EVERYONE WILL BE ABLE TO ESCAPE BEFORE THEY GET TRAPPED.
WATCH OUT.
TO TELL YOU THE TRUTH...
...I'M STILL AGAINST THE IDEA OF TAKING *EVERY-ONE.*

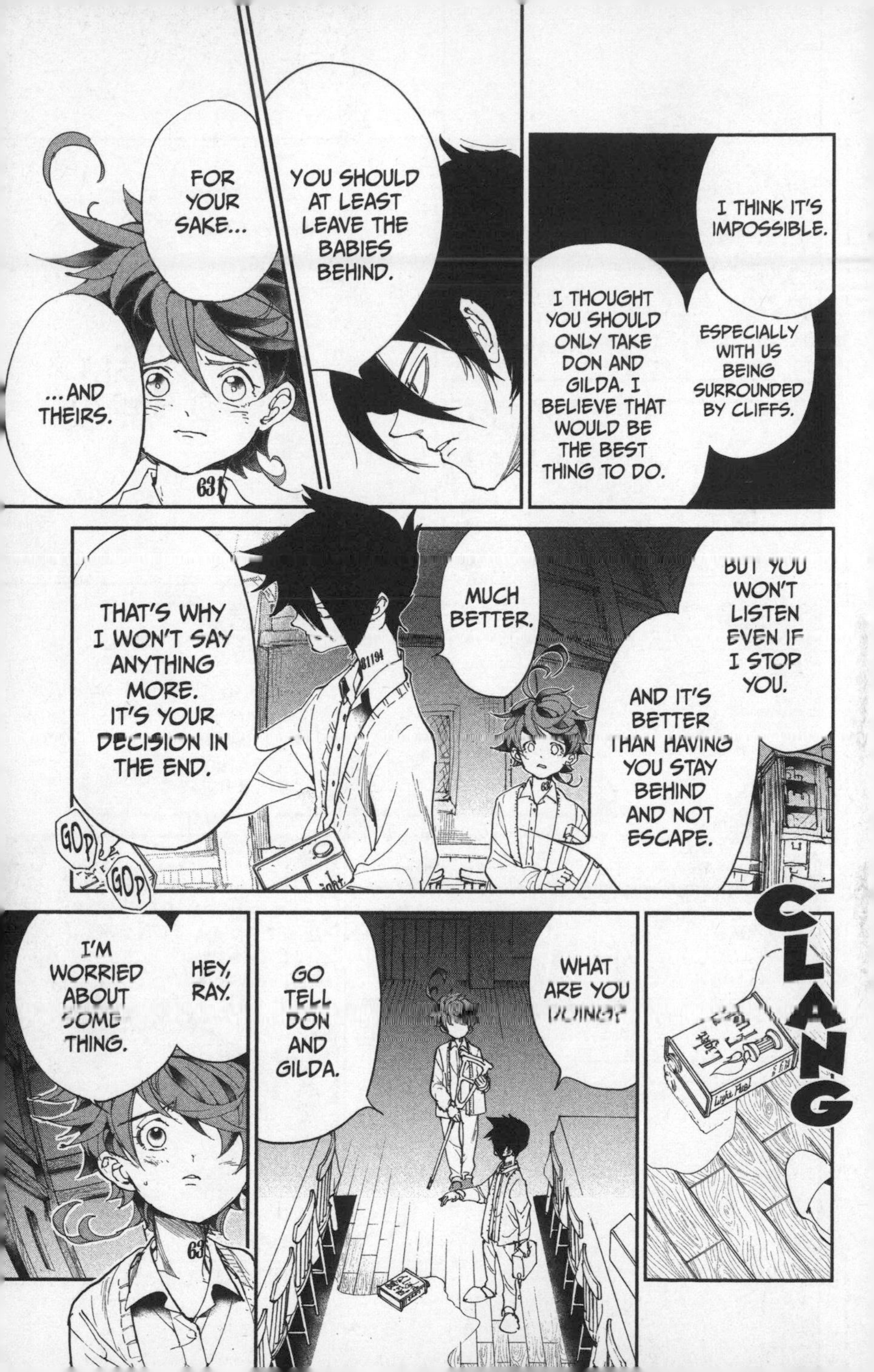
I THINK IT'S IMPOSSIBLE.
ESPECIALLY WITH US BEING SURROUNDED BY CLIFFS.
I THOUGHT YOU SHOULD ONLY TAKE DON AND GILDA. I BELIEVE THAT WOULD BE THE BEST THING TO DO.
YOU SHOULD AT LEAST LEAVE THE BABIES BEHIND.
FOR YOUR SAKE...
...AND THEIRS.
BUT YOU WON'T LISTEN EVEN IF I STOP YOU.
AND IT'S BETTER THAN HAVING YOU STAY BEHIND AND NOT ESCAPE.
MUCH BETTER.
THAT'S WHY I WON'T SAY ANYTHING MORE. IT'S YOUR DECISION IN THE END.
GOP
GOP
CLANG
WHAT ARE YOU DOING?
GO TELL DON AND GILDA.
HEY, RAY.
I'M WORRIED ABOUT SOME THING.

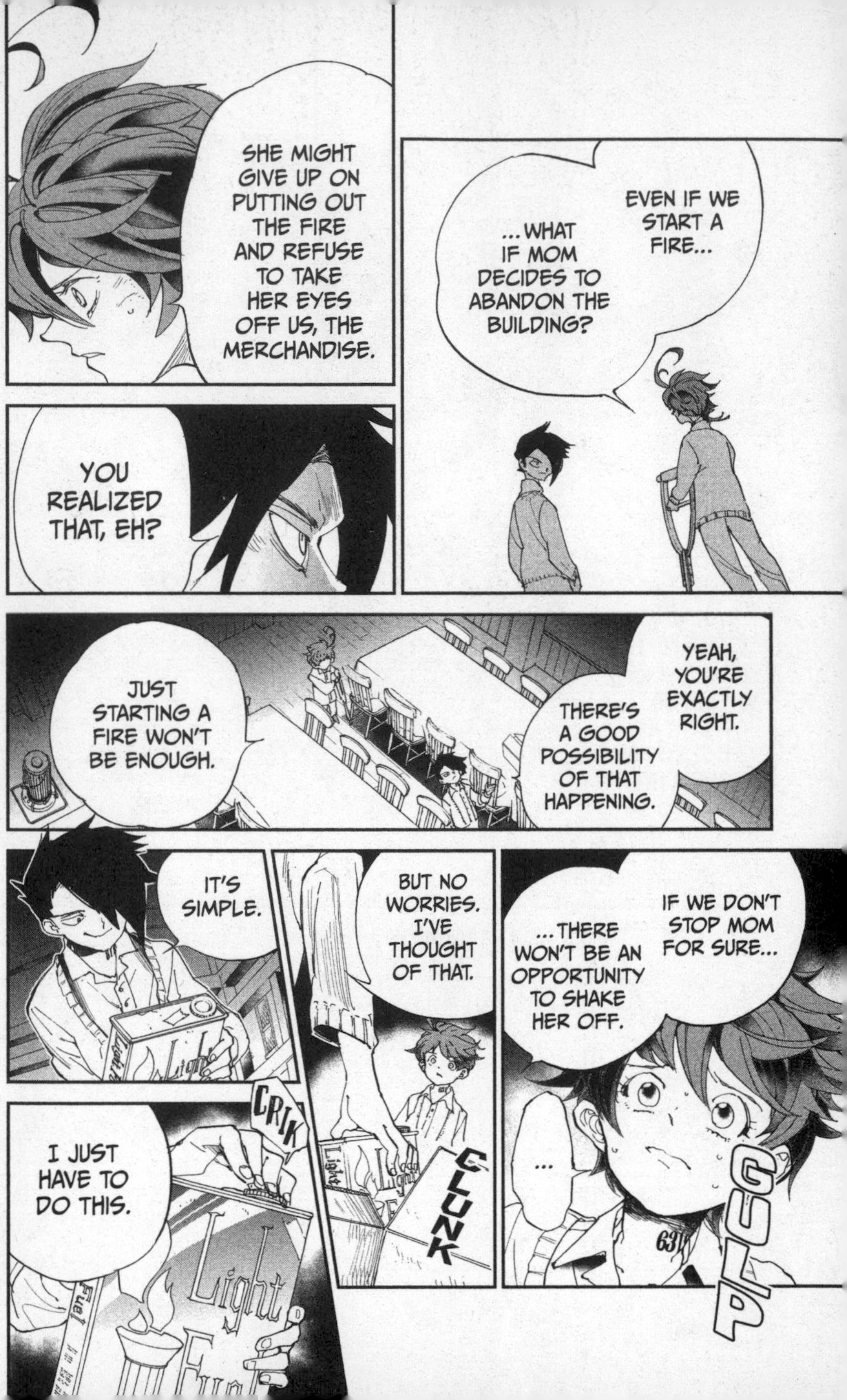
EVEN IF WE START A FIRE...
...WHAT IF MOM DECIDES TO ABANDON THE BUILDING?
SHE MIGHT GIVE UP ON PUTTING OUT THE FIRE AND REFUSE TO TAKE HER EYES OFF US, THE MERCHANDISE.
YOU REALIZED THAT, EH?
YEAH, YOU'RE EXACTLY RIGHT.
THERE'S A GOOD POSSIBILITY OF THAT HAPPENING.
JUST STARTING A FIRE WON'T BE ENOUGH.
IF WE DON'T STOP MOM FOR SURE...
...THERE WON'T BE AN OPPORTUNITY TO SHAKE HER OFF.
...
GULP
BUT NO WORRIES. I'VE THOUGHT OF THAT.
CLUNK
IT'S SIMPLE.
CRIK
I JUST HAVE TO DO THIS.
Light Fuel

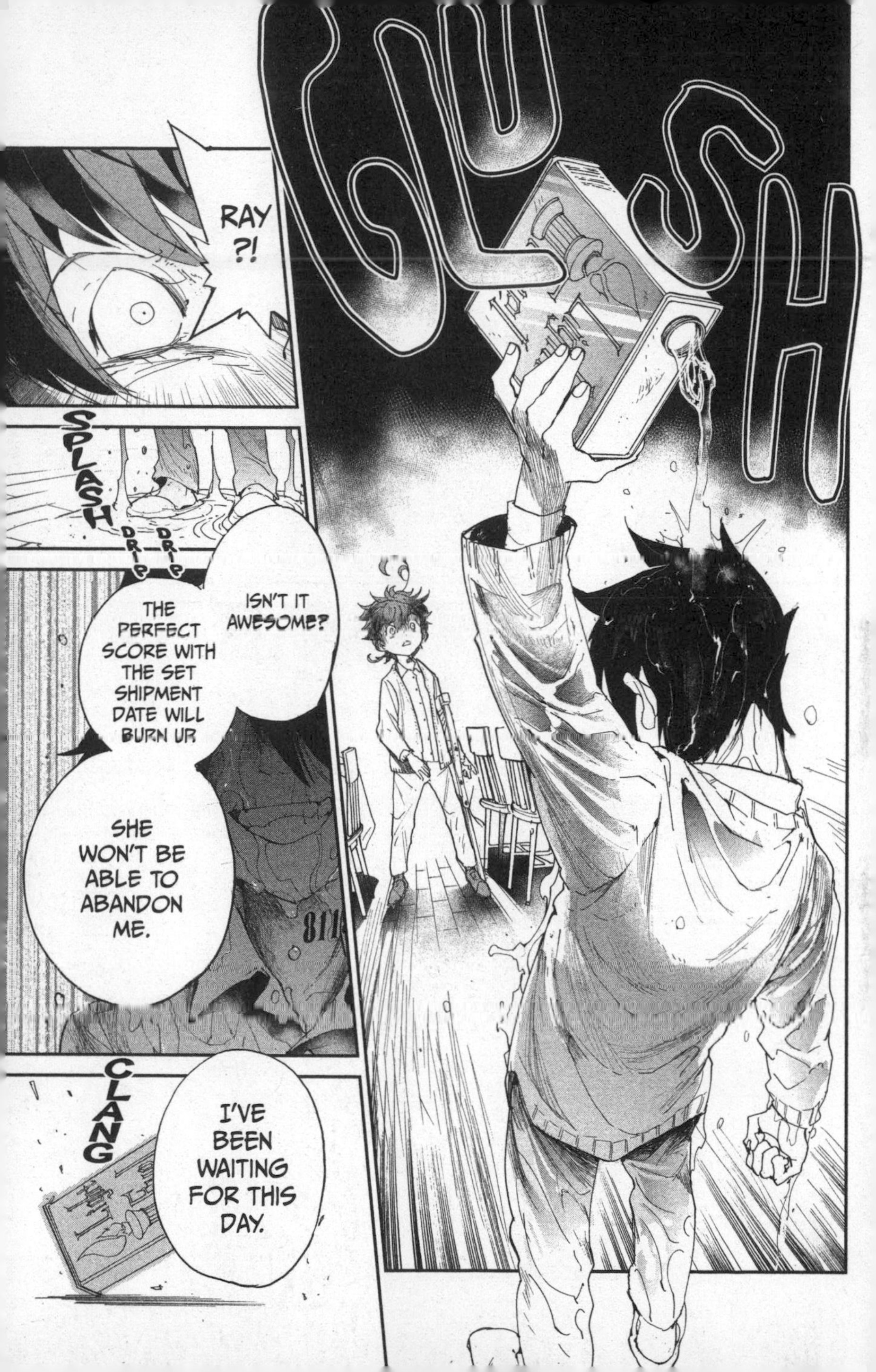
GUSH
RAY ?!
SPLASH
DRIP DRIP
ISN'T IT AWESOME?
THE PERFECT SCORE WITH THE SET SHIPMENT DATE WILL BURN UP
SHE WON'T BE ABLE TO ABANDON ME.
CLANG
I'VE BEEN WAITING FOR THIS DAY.

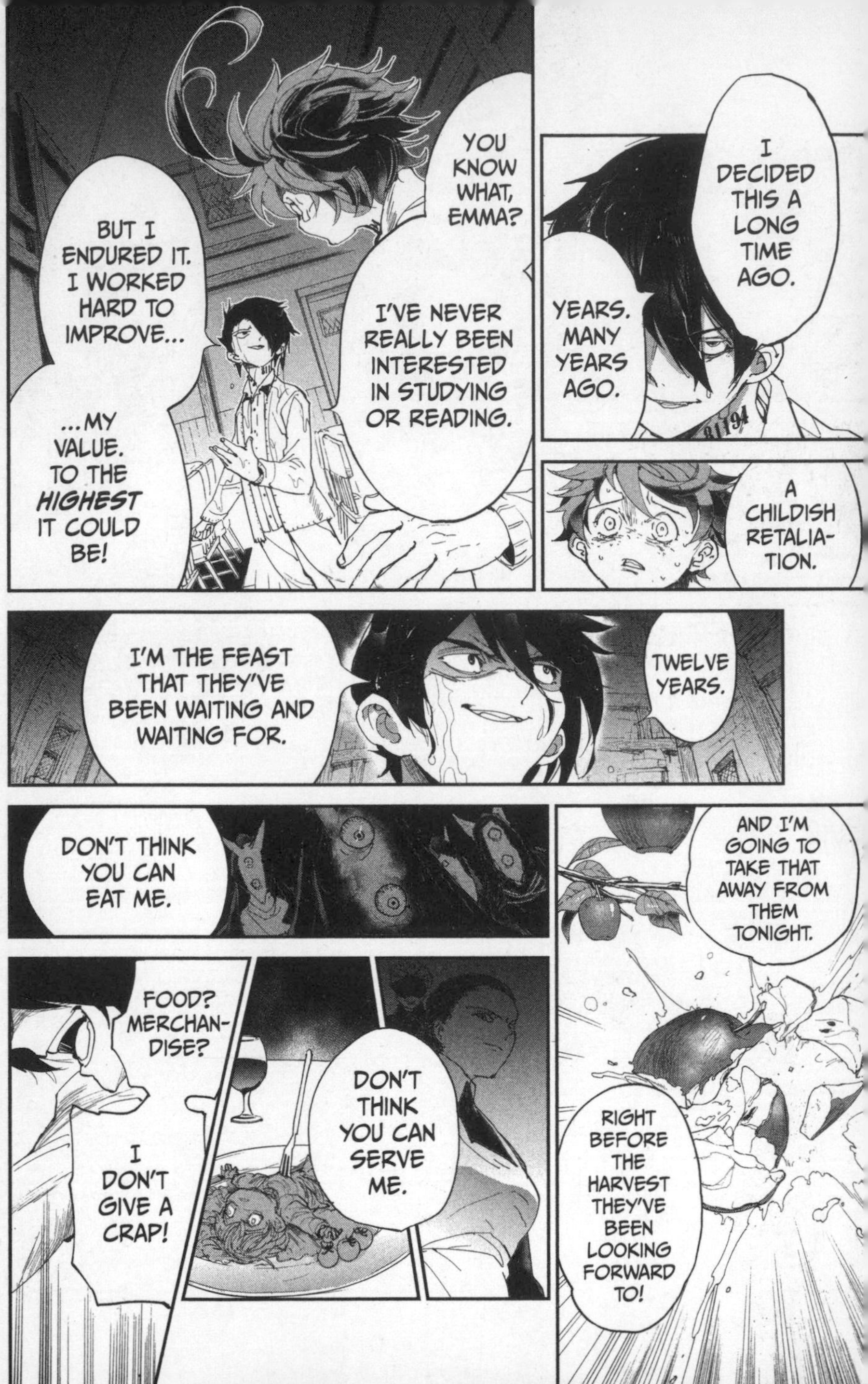
I DECIDED THIS A LONG TIME AGO.
YEARS. MANY YEARS AGO.
A CHILDISH RETALIATION.
YOU KNOW WHAT, EMMA?
I'VE NEVER REALLY BEEN INTERESTED IN STUDYING OR READING.
BUT I ENDURED IT. I WORKED HARD TO IMPROVE...
...MY VALUE. TO THE *HIGHEST* IT COULD BE!
TWELVE YEARS.
I'M THE FEAST THAT THEY'VE BEEN WAITING AND WAITING FOR.
AND I'M GOING TO TAKE THAT AWAY FROM THEM TONIGHT.
RIGHT BEFORE THE HARVEST THEY'VE BEEN LOOKING FORWARD TO!
DON'T THINK YOU CAN EAT ME.
DON'T THINK YOU CAN SERVE ME.
FOOD? MERCHANDISE?
I DON'T GIVE A CRAP!

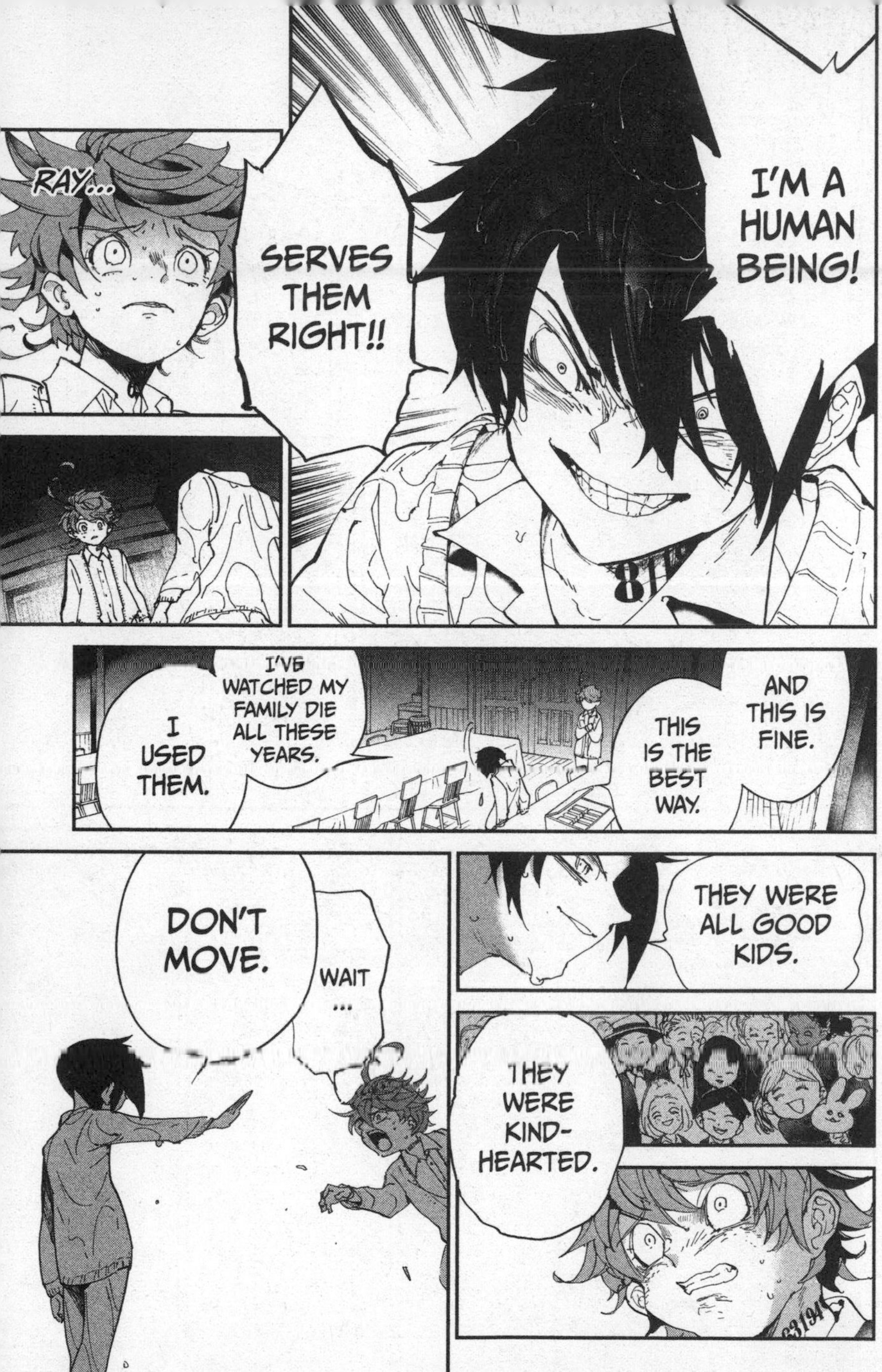
I'M A HUMAN BEING!
SERVES THEM RIGHT!!
RAY...
AND THIS IS FINE.
THIS IS THE BEST WAY.
I'VE WATCHED MY FAMILY DIE ALL THESE YEARS.
I USED THEM.
THEY WERE ALL GOOD KIDS.
THEY WERE KIND-HEARTED.
WAIT...
DON'T MOVE.

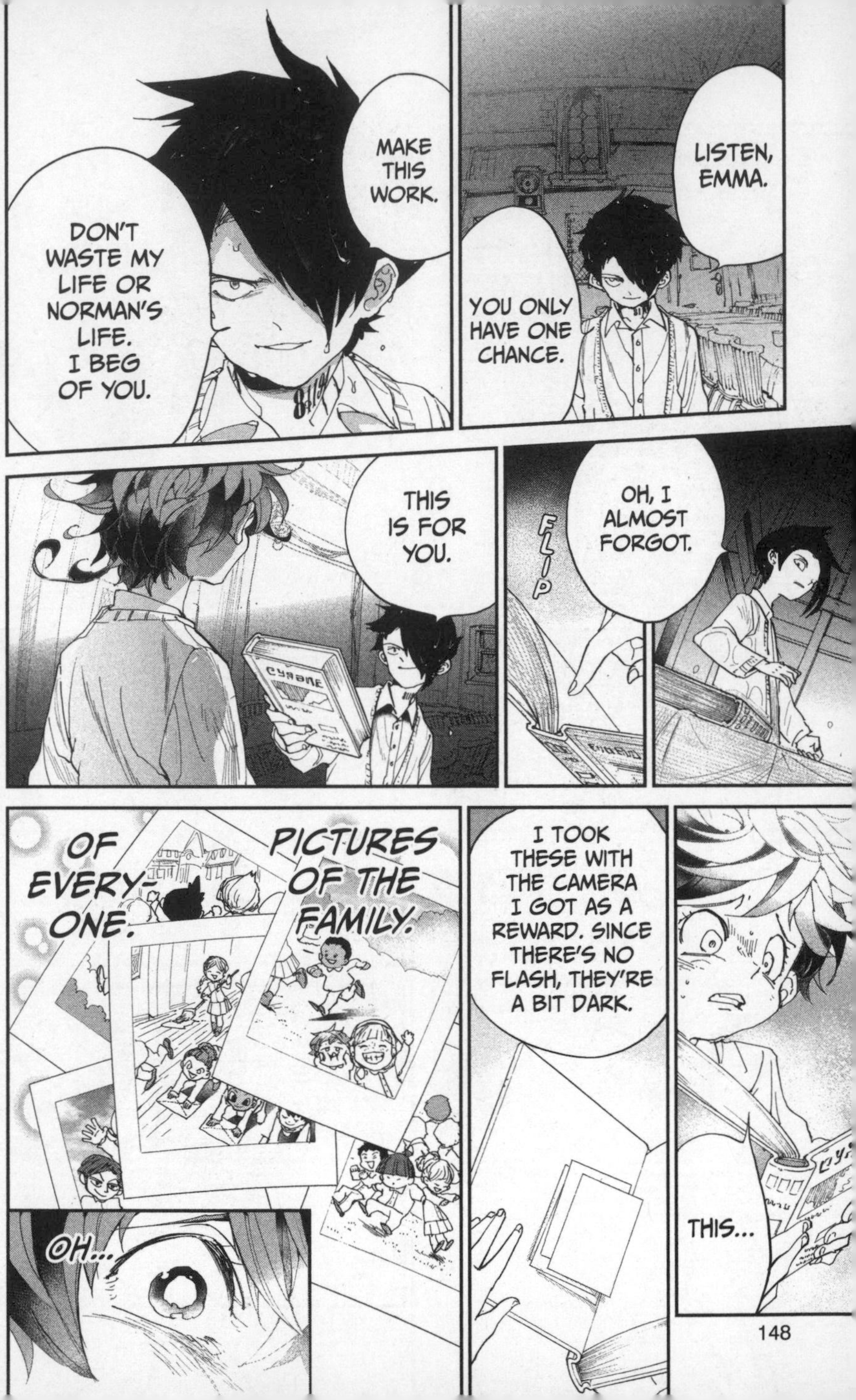
LISTEN, EMMA.
YOU ONLY HAVE ONE CHANCE.
MAKE THIS WORK.
DON'T WASTE MY LIFE OR NORMAN'S LIFE. I BEG OF YOU.
OH, I ALMOST FORGOT.
FLIP
THIS IS FOR YOU.
THIS...
I TOOK THESE WITH THE CAMERA I GOT AS A REWARD. SINCE THERE'S NO FLASH, THEY'RE A BIT DARK.
PICTURES OF THE FAMILY.
OF EVERY-ONE.
OH...

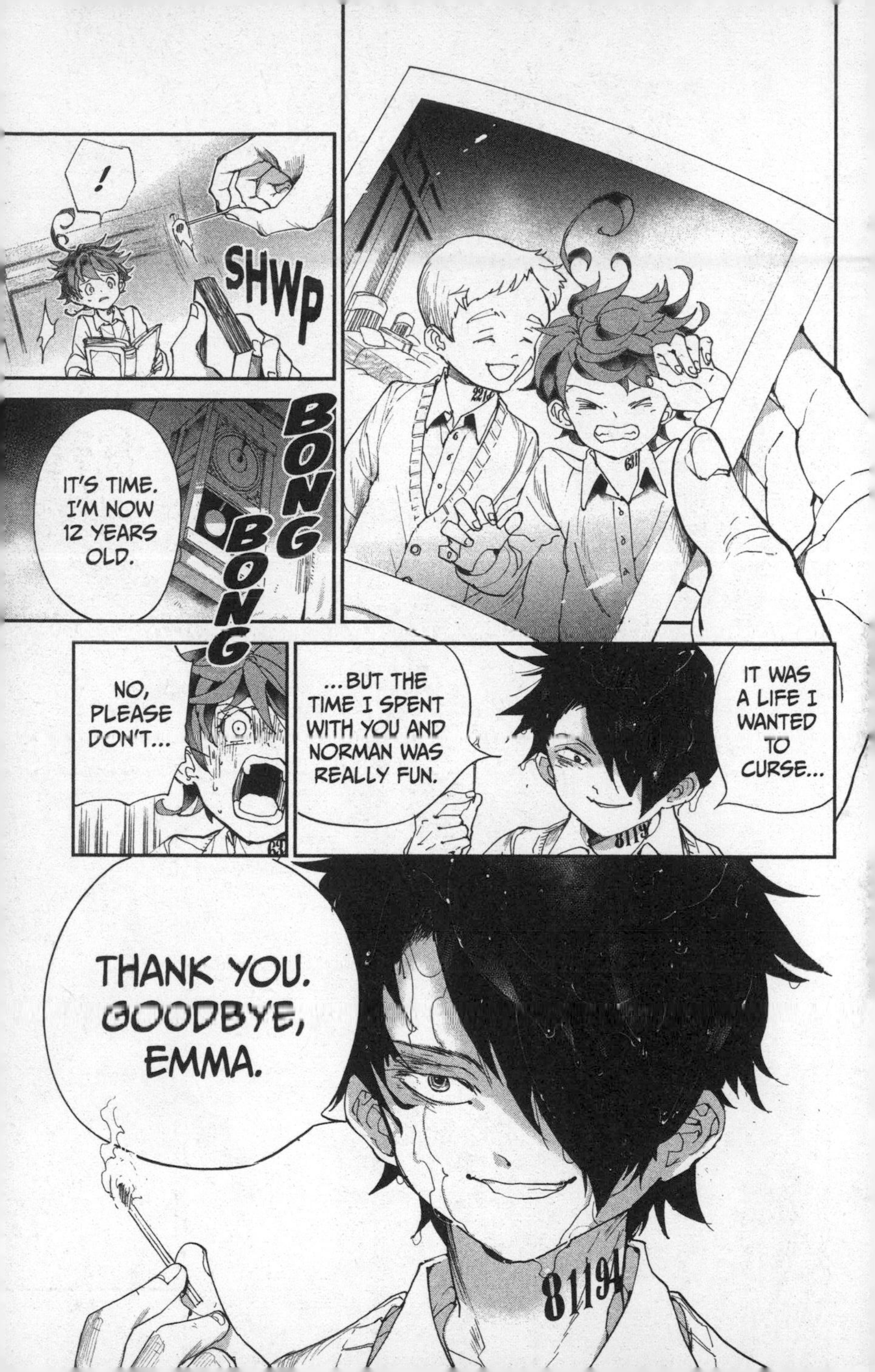
!
SHWP
IT'S TIME. I'M NOW 12 YEARS OLD.
BONG
BONG
IT WAS A LIFE I WANTED TO CURSE...
...BUT THE TIME I SPENT WITH YOU AND NORMAN WAS REALLY FUN.
NO, PLEASE DON'T...
THANK YOU. GOODBYE, EMMA.
81194

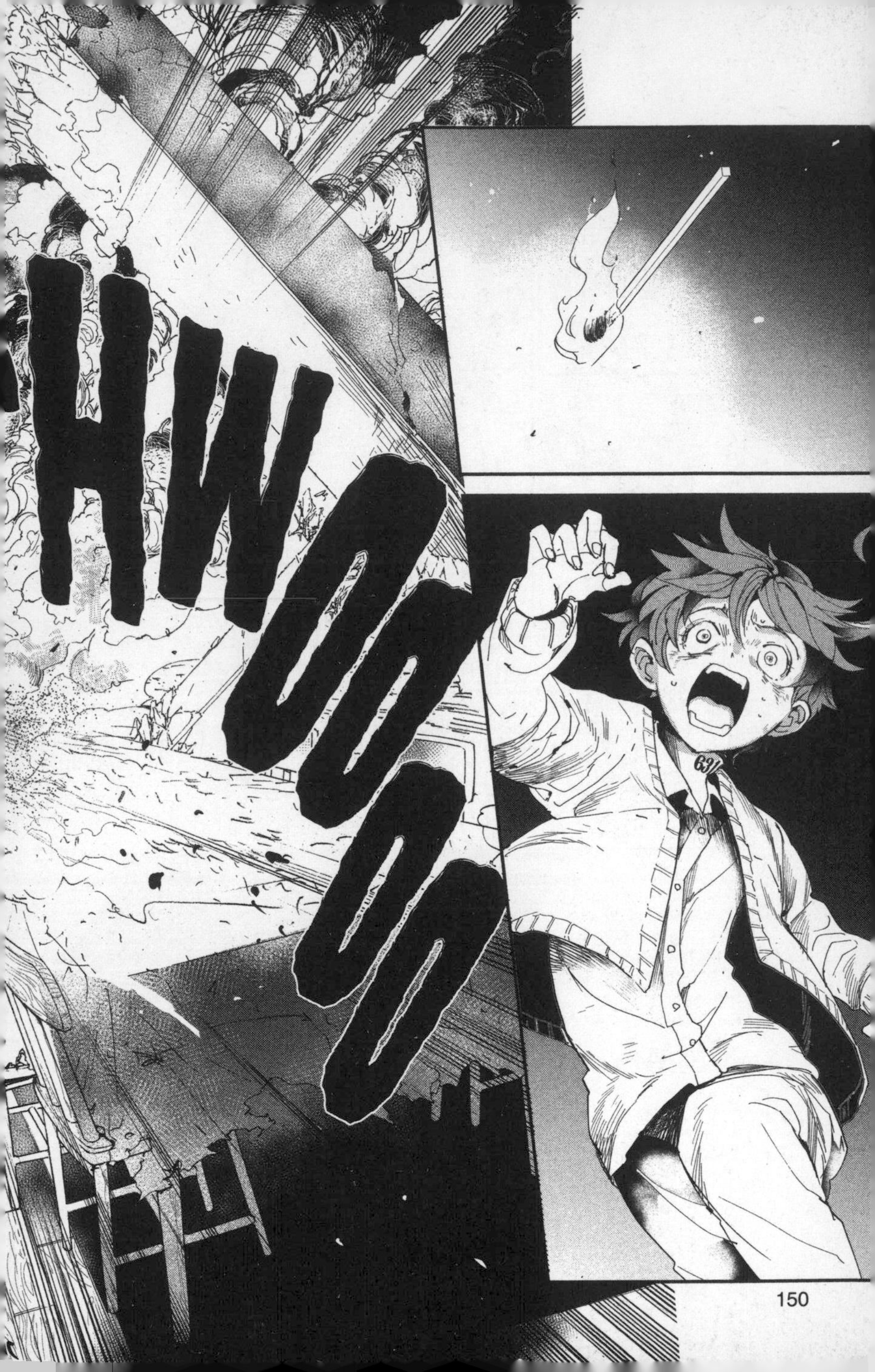
HWOOOO

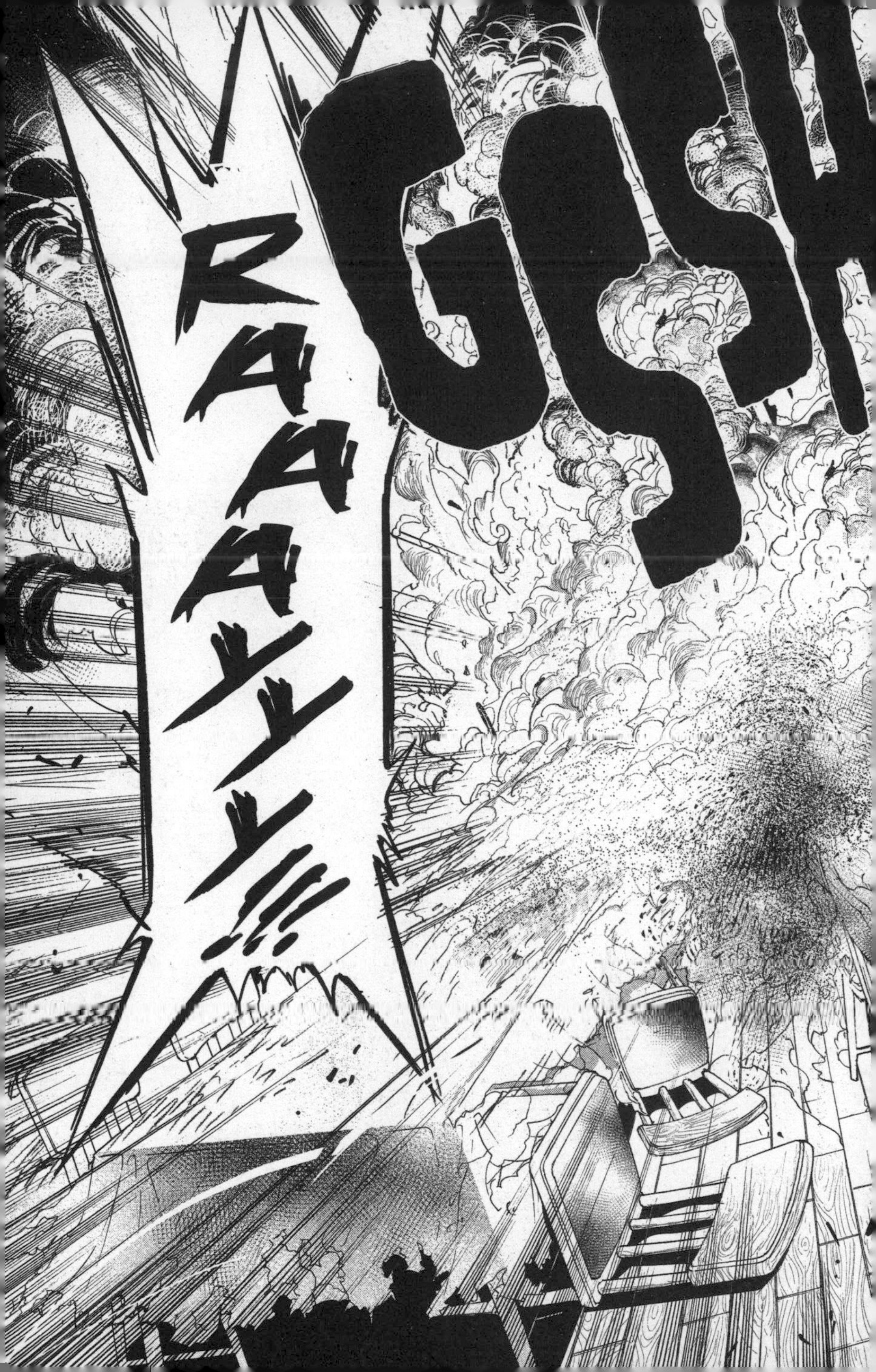
GOSH
RAAAAAA!!!

THE PROMISED NEVERLAND SIDE SCENE 008

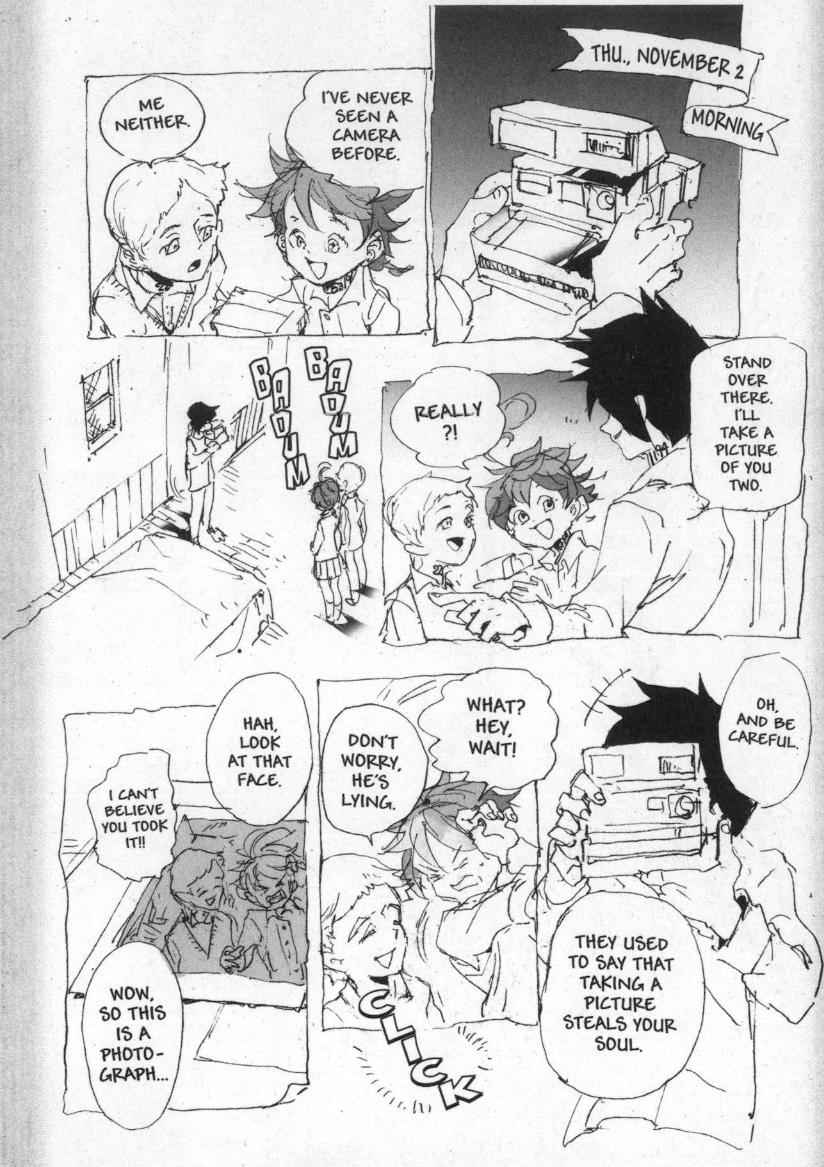
THU., NOVEMBER 2
MORNING
I'VE NEVER SEEN A CAMERA BEFORE.
ME NEITHER.
STAND OVER THERE. I'LL TAKE A PICTURE OF YOU TWO.
REALLY ?!
BADUM
BADUM
OH, AND BE CAREFUL.
THEY USED TO SAY THAT TAKING A PICTURE STEALS YOUR SOUL.
WHAT? HEY, WAIT!
DON'T WORRY, HE'S LYING.
CLICK
HAH, LOOK AT THAT FACE.
I CAN'T BELIEVE YOU TOOK IT!!
WOW, SO THIS IS A PHOTO-GRAPH...

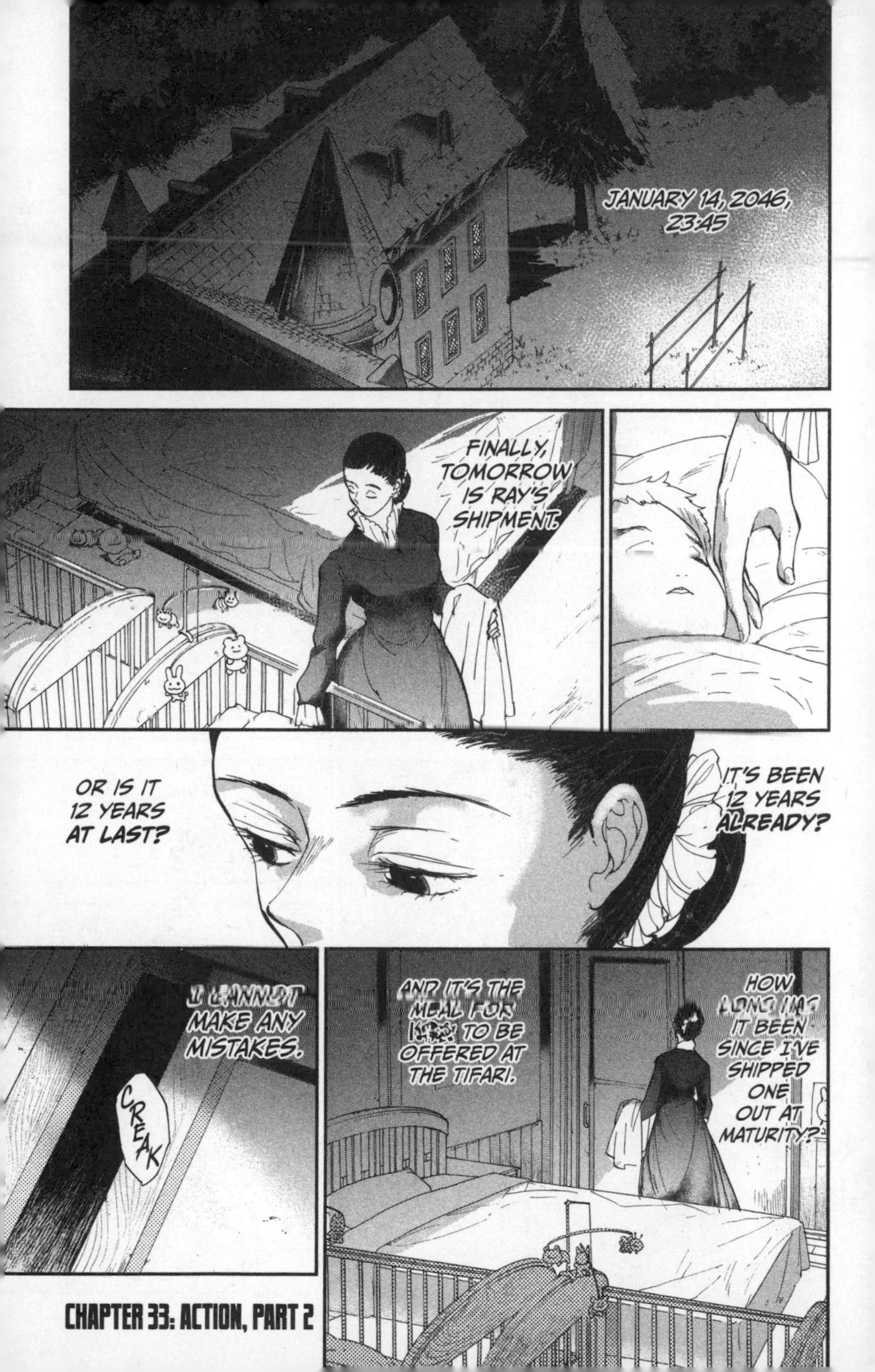
JANUARY 14, 2046, 23:45
FINALLY, TOMORROW IS RAY'S SHIPMENT.
IT'S BEEN 12 YEARS ALREADY?
OR IS IT 12 YEARS AT LAST?
HOW LONG HAS IT BEEN SINCE I'VE SHIPPED ONE OUT AT MATURITY?
AND IT'S THE MEAL FOR TO BE OFFERED AT THE TIFARI.
I CANNOT MAKE ANY MISTAKES.
CREAK

CHAPTER 33: ACTION, PART 2

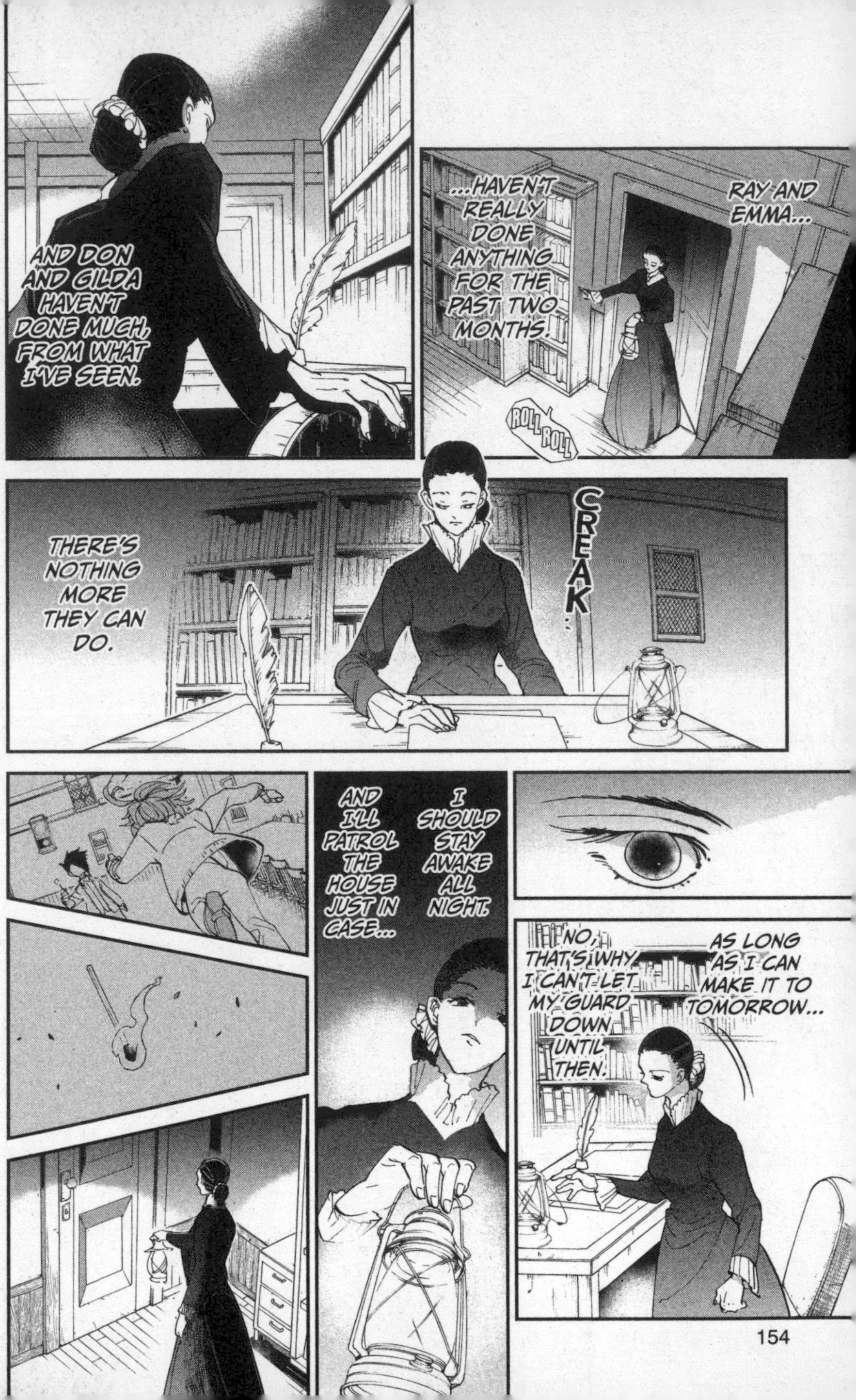
RAY AND EMMA...
...HAVEN'T REALLY DONE ANYTHING FOR THE PAST TWO MONTHS.
ROLL ROLL
AND DON AND GILDA HAVEN'T DONE MUCH, FROM WHAT I'VE SEEN.
CREAK
THERE'S NOTHING MORE THEY CAN DO.
AS LONG AS I CAN MAKE IT TO TOMORROW...
NO, THAT'S WHY I CAN'T LET MY GUARD DOWN UNTIL THEN.
I SHOULD STAY AWAKE ALL NIGHT.
AND I'LL PATROL THE HOUSE JUST IN CASE...

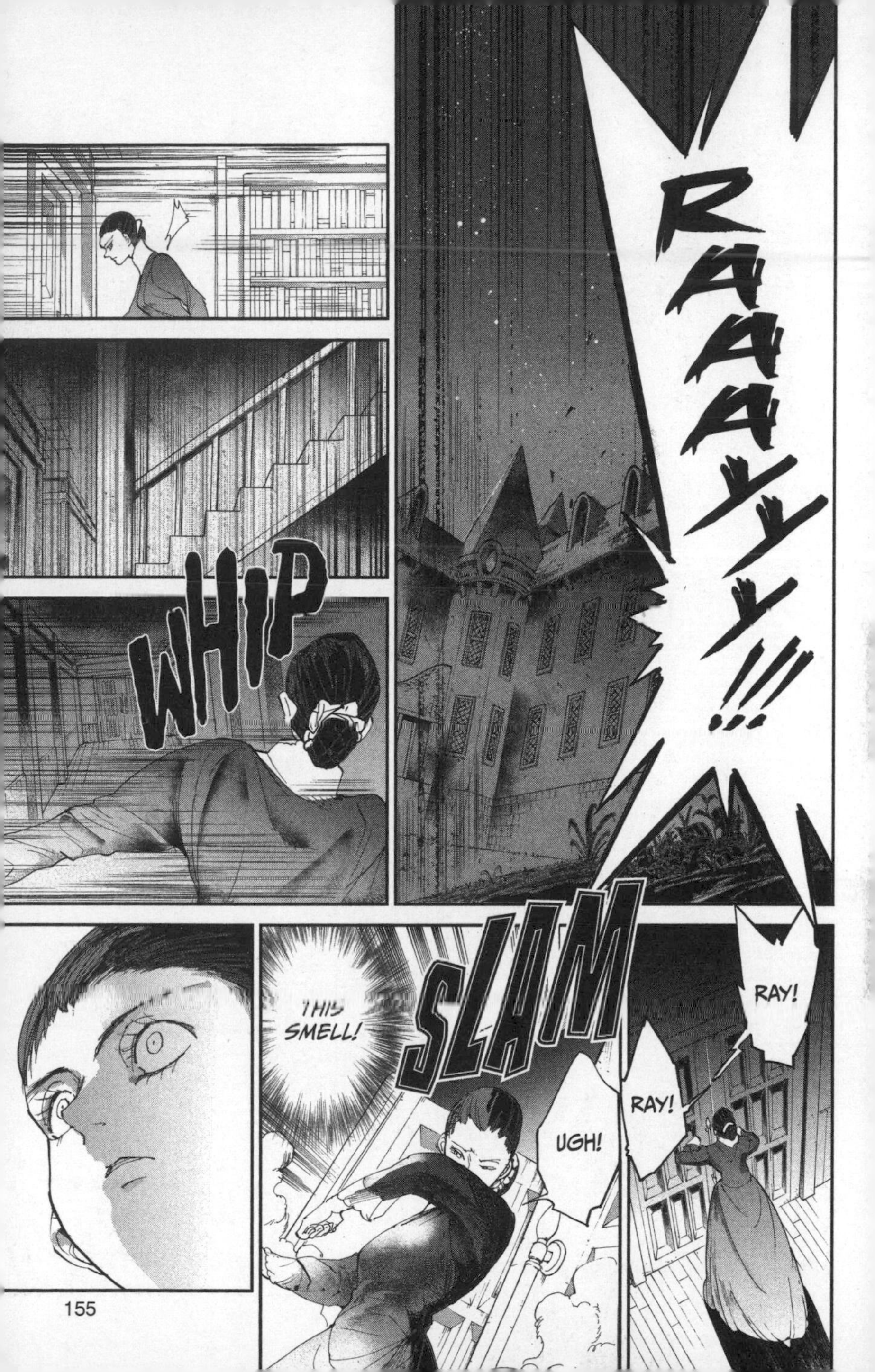
RAAAYYY!!!
WHIP
RAY!
RAY!
UGH!
SLAM
THIS SMELL!

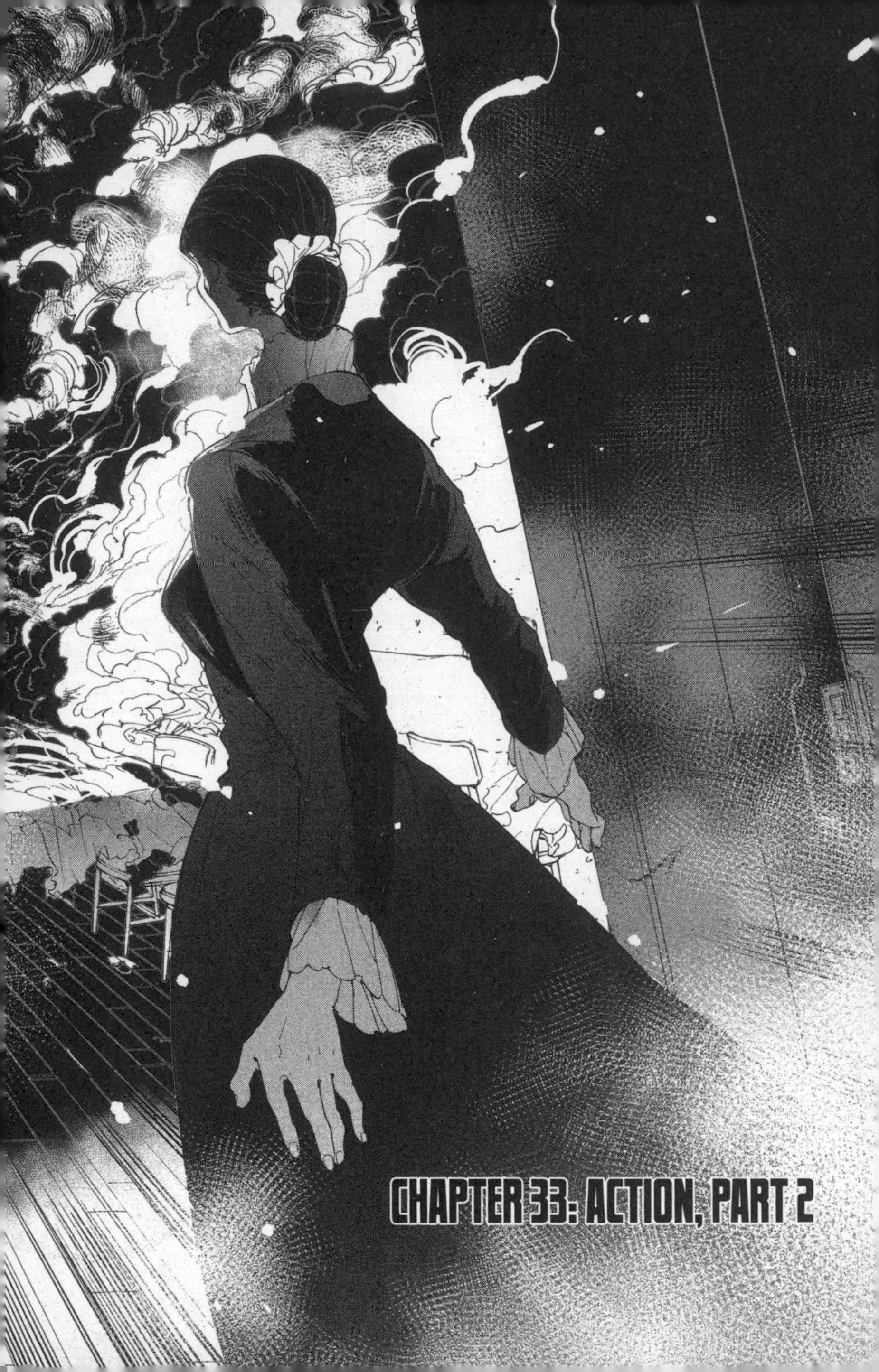
CHAPTER 33: ACTION, PART 2

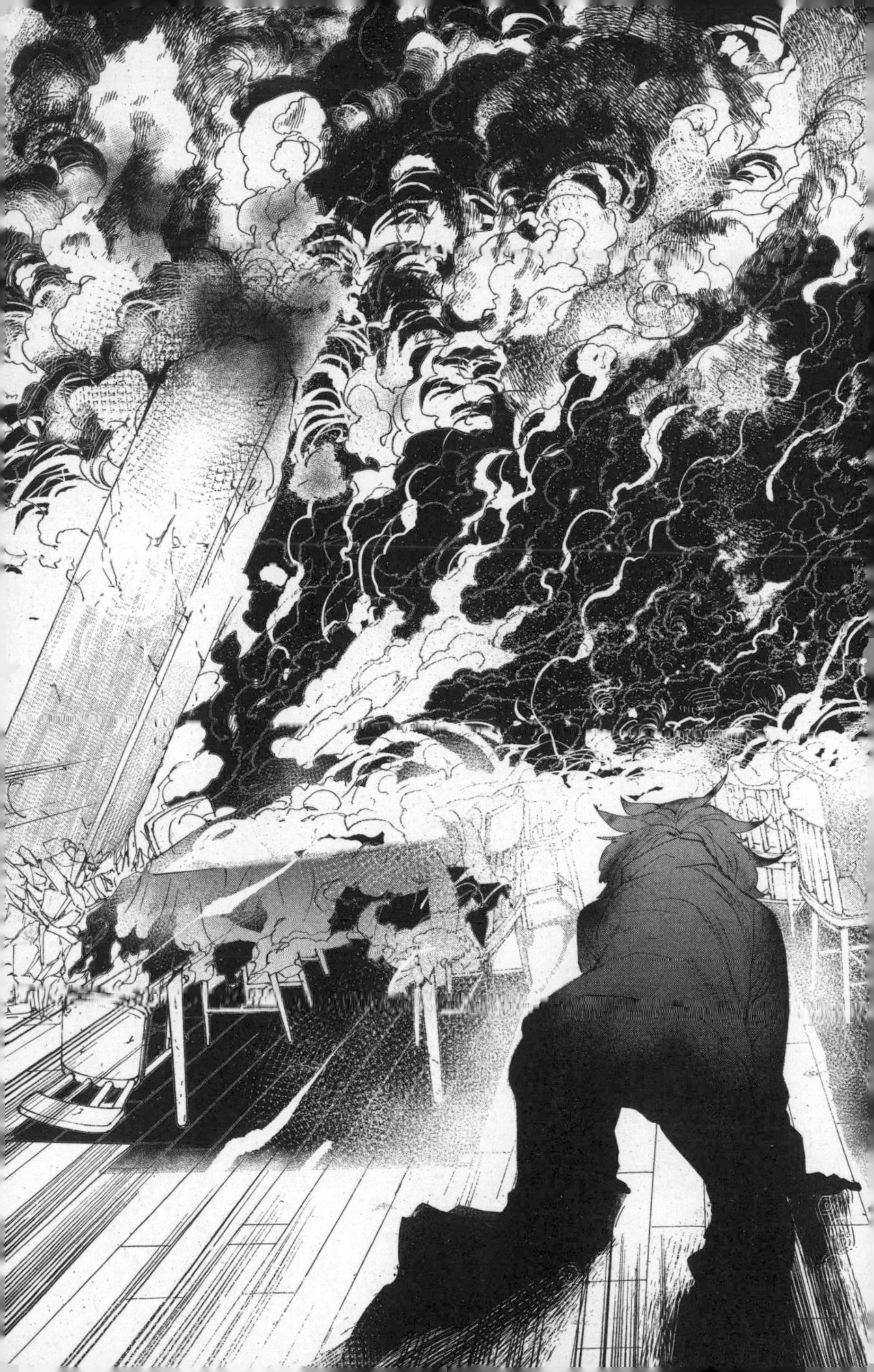

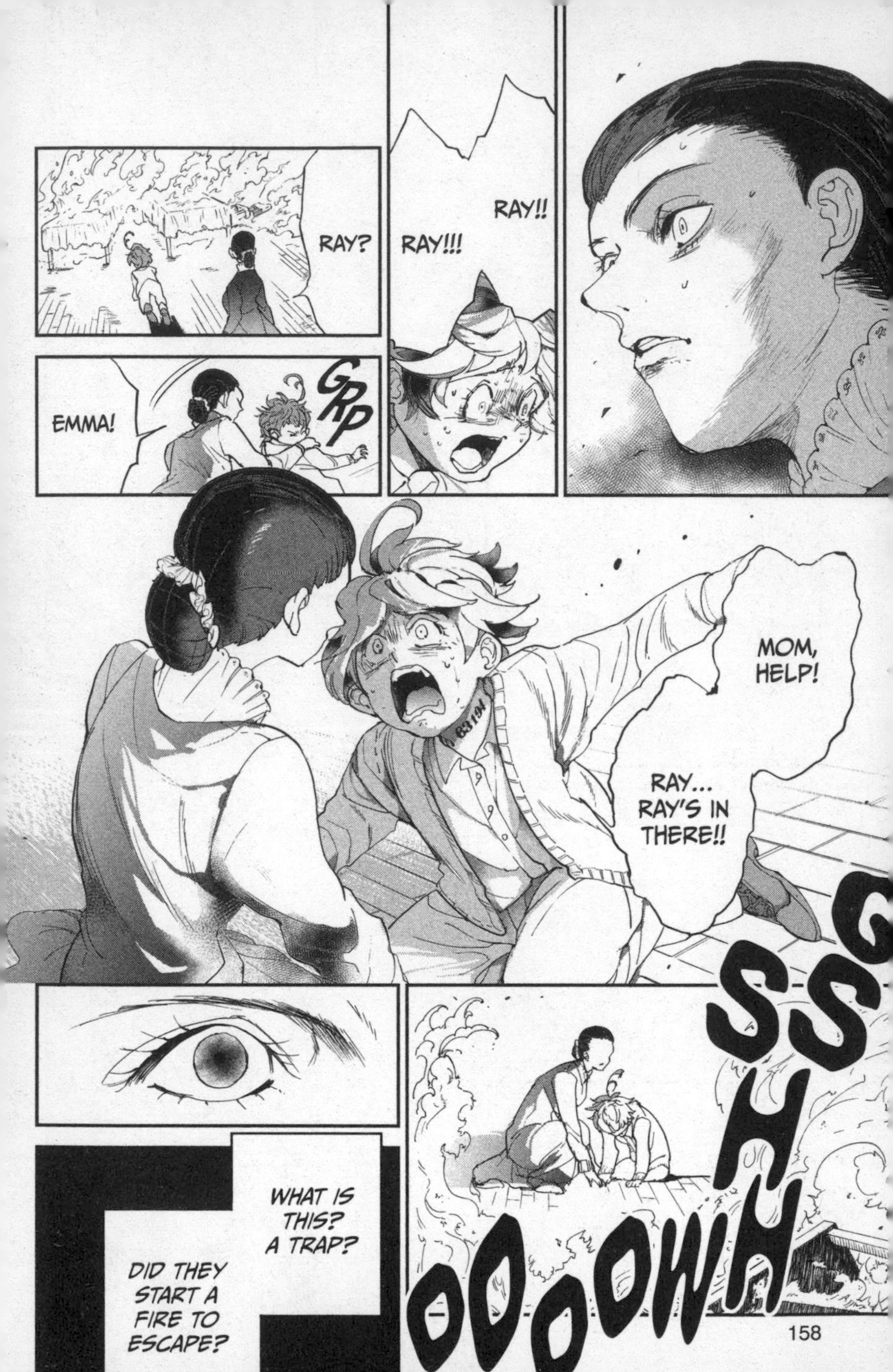
RAY!!
RAY!!!
RAY?
EMMA!
GRP
MOM, HELP!
RAY... RAY'S IN THERE!!
WHAT IS THIS? A TRAP?
DID THEY START A FIRE TO ESCAPE?

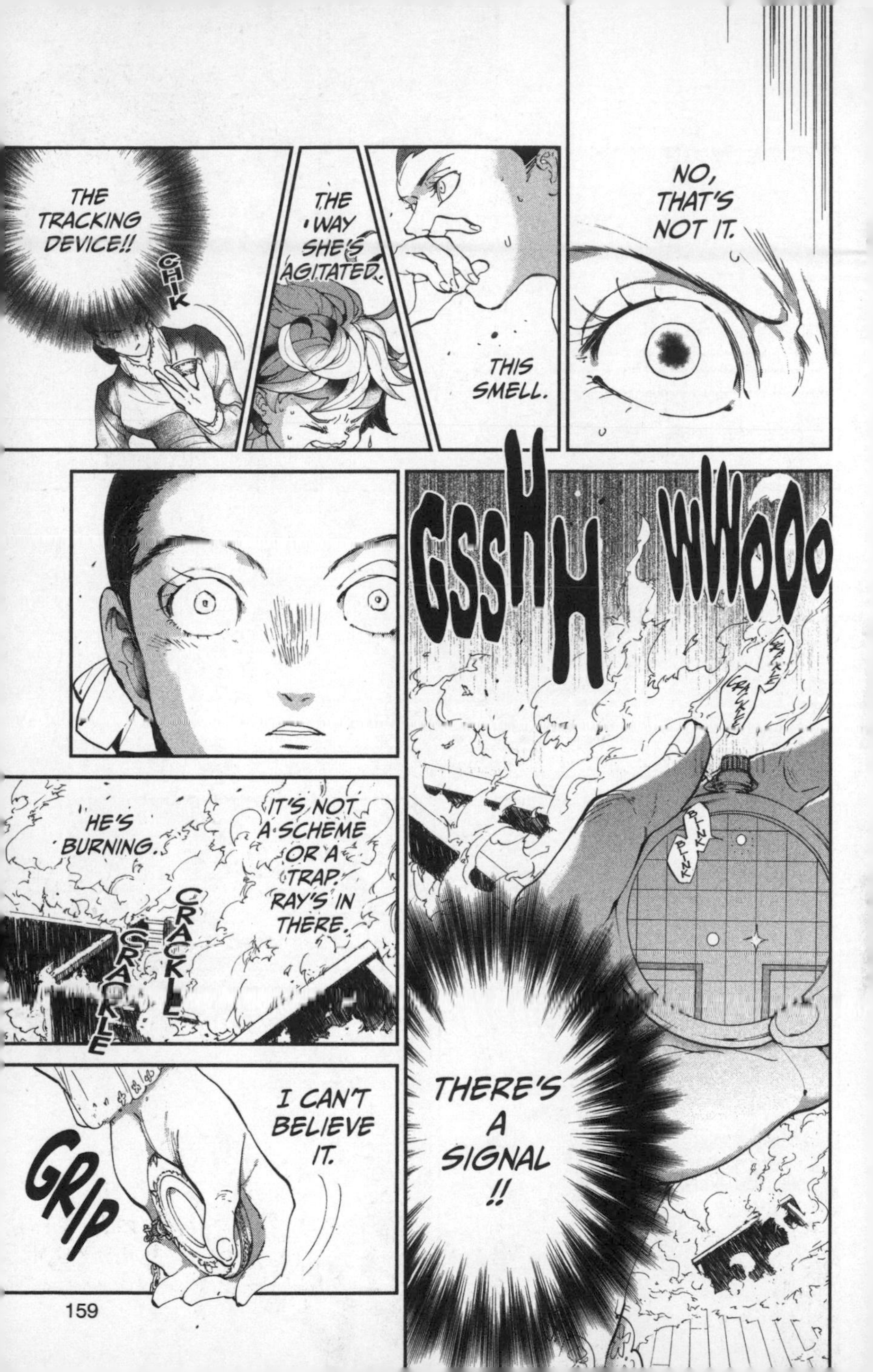
NO, THAT'S NOT IT.
THIS SMELL.
THE WAY SHE'S AGITATED.
THE TRACKING DEVICE!!
CHIK
GSSHH
WWOOO
CRACKLE
CRACKLE
BLINK
BLINK
THERE'S A SIGNAL!!
IT'S NOT A SCHEME OR A TRAP. RAY'S IN THERE.
HE'S BURNING.
CRACKLE
CRACKLE
I CAN'T BELIEVE IT.
GRIP

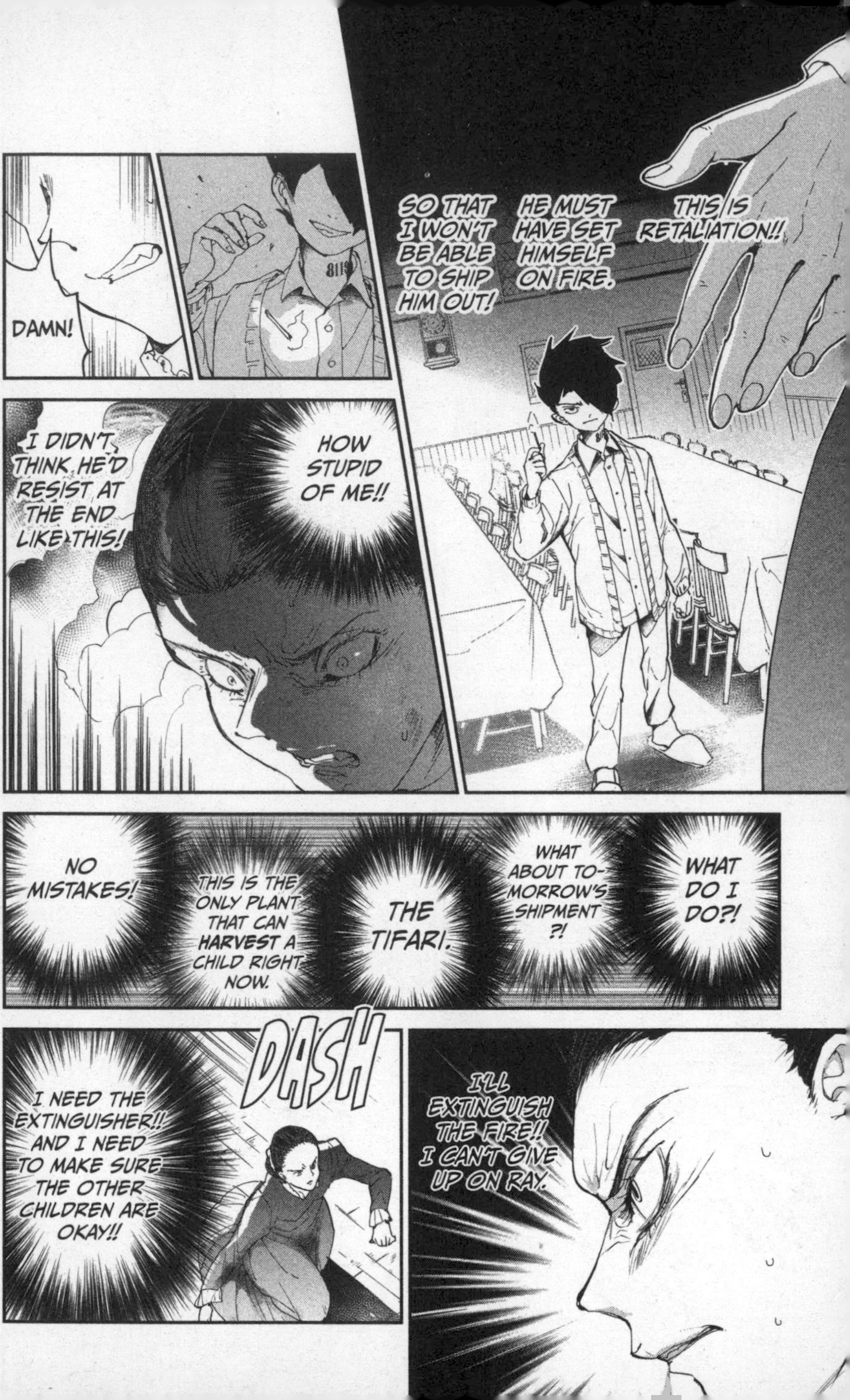
THIS IS RETALIATION!!
HE MUST HAVE SET HIMSELF ON FIRE.
SO THAT I WON'T BE ABLE TO SHIP HIM OUT!
DAMN!
HOW STUPID OF ME!!
I DIDN'T THINK HE'D RESIST AT THE END LIKE THIS!
WHAT DO I DO?!
WHAT ABOUT TO-MORROW'S SHIPMENT ?!
THE TIFARI.
THIS IS THE ONLY PLANT THAT CAN HARVEST A CHILD RIGHT NOW.
NO MISTAKES!
I'LL EXTINGUISH THE FIRE!! I CAN'T GIVE UP ON RAY.
DASH
I NEED THE EXTINGUISHER!! AND I NEED TO MAKE SURE THE OTHER CHILDREN ARE OKAY!!

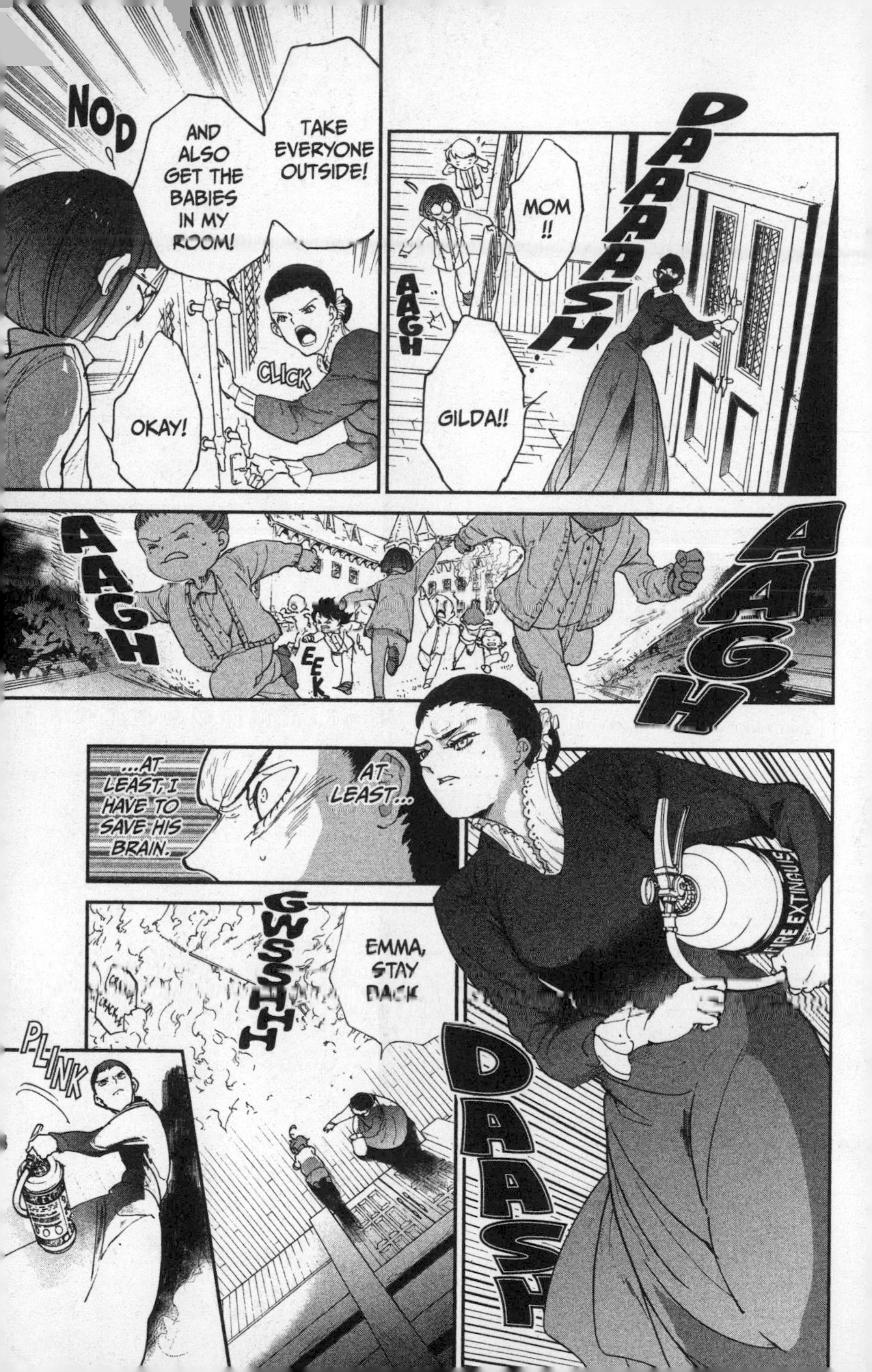
DAARAASH
MOM!!
AAGH
GILDA!!
TAKE EVERYONE OUTSIDE!
AND ALSO GET THE BABIES IN MY ROOM!
NOD
CLICK
OKAY!
AAAGH
EEK
AAGH
DAASH
AT LEAST...
...AT LEAST, I HAVE TO SAVE HIS BRAIN.
EMMA, STAY BACK
GWSSHH
P-LINK

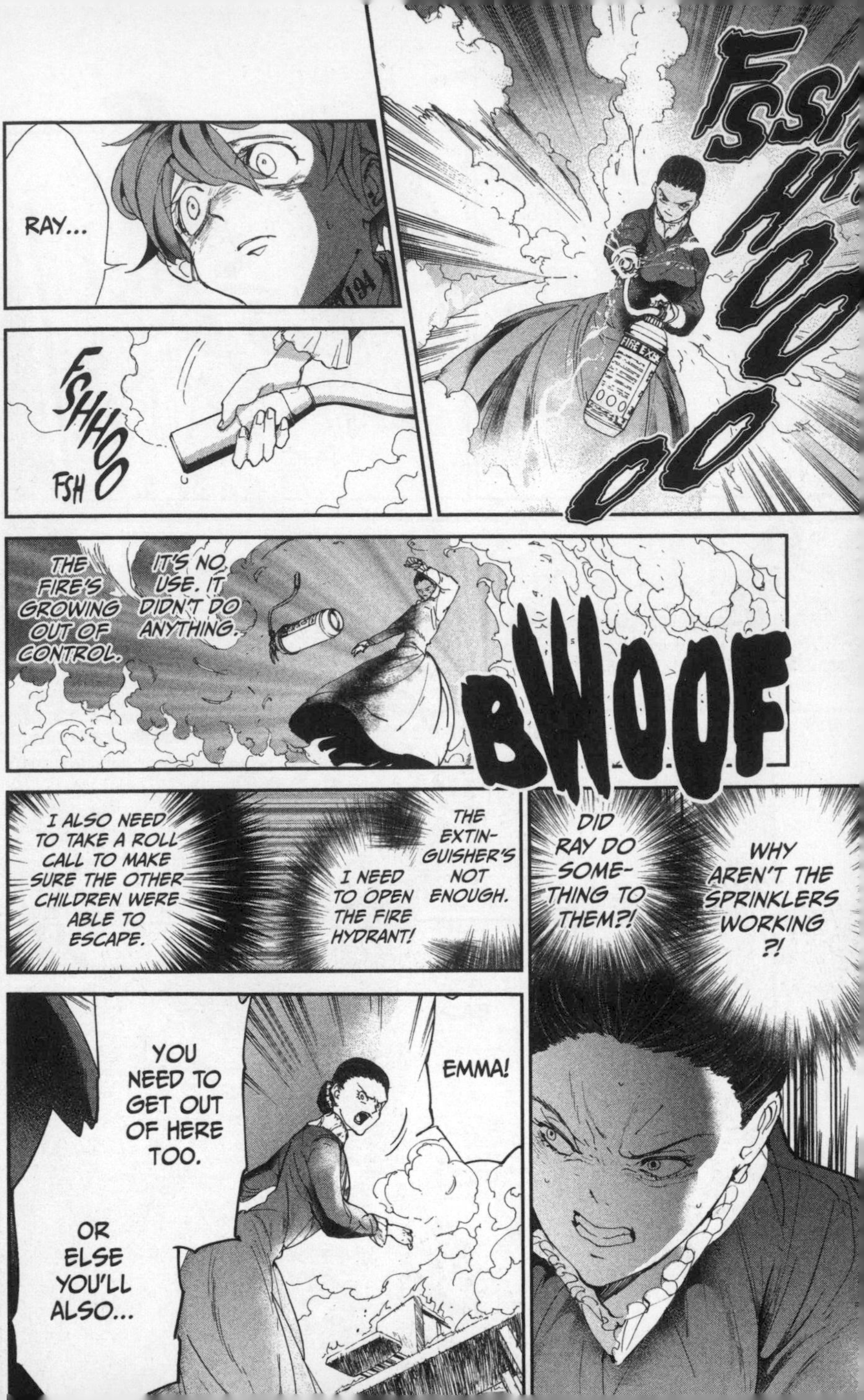
FSSHHOOOOO
RAY...
FSHHOO
FSH
BWOOF
IT'S NO USE. IT DIDN'T DO ANYTHING.
THE FIRE'S GROWING OUT OF CONTROL.
WHY AREN'T THE SPRINKLERS WORKING?!
DID RAY DO SOME-THING TO THEM?!
THE EXTIN-GUISHER'S NOT ENOUGH.
I NEED TO OPEN THE FIRE HYDRANT!
I ALSO NEED TO TAKE A ROLL CALL TO MAKE SURE THE OTHER CHILDREN WERE ABLE TO ESCAPE.
EMMA!
YOU NEED TO GET OUT OF HERE TOO.
OR ELSE YOU'LL ALSO...

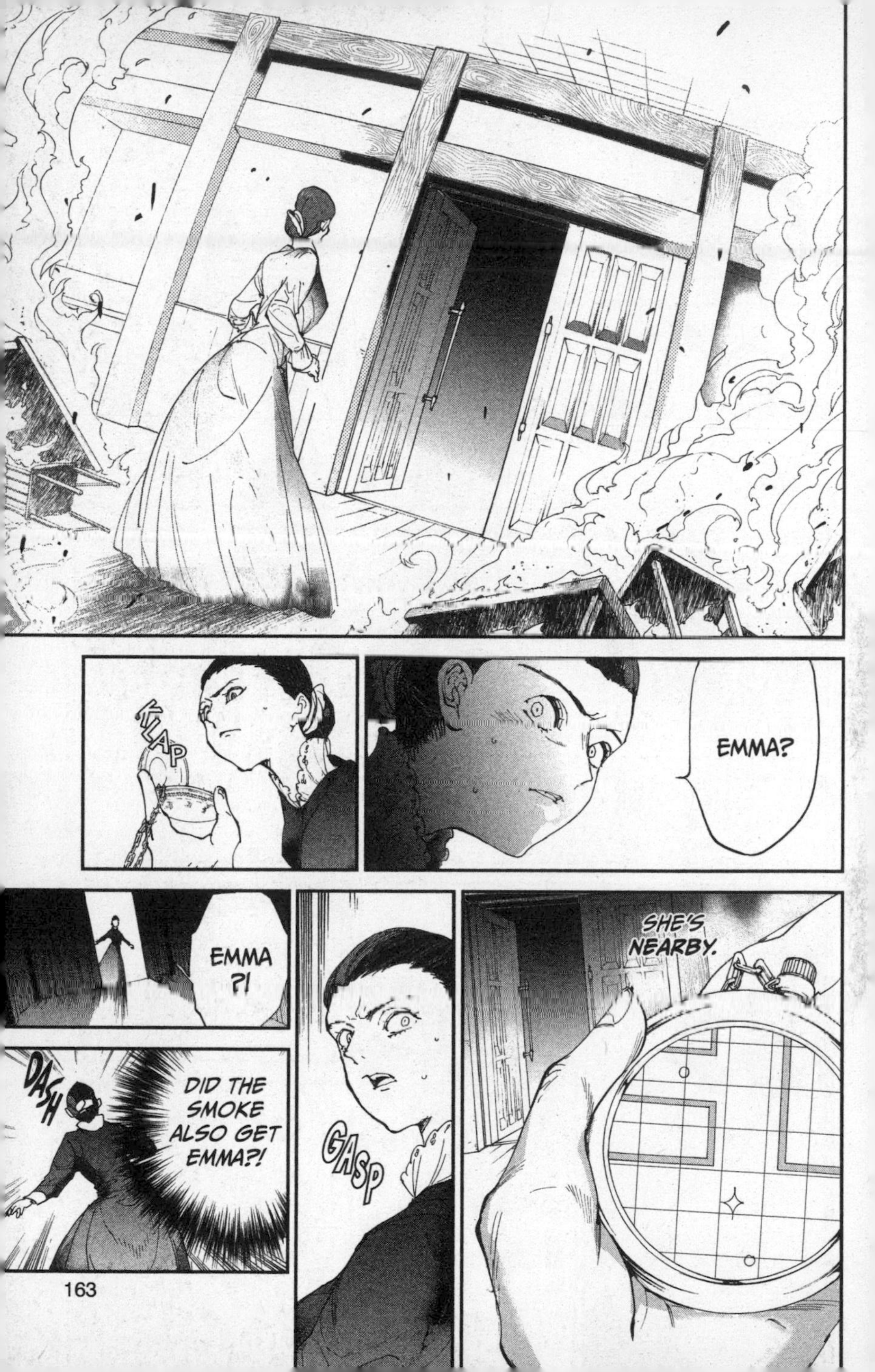
EMMA?
KLAP
SHE'S NEARBY.
GASP
EMMA ?!
DASH
DID THE SMOKE ALSO GET EMMA?!

...

EMMA!!

CRINKLE

EMMA...?

CLANG

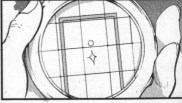

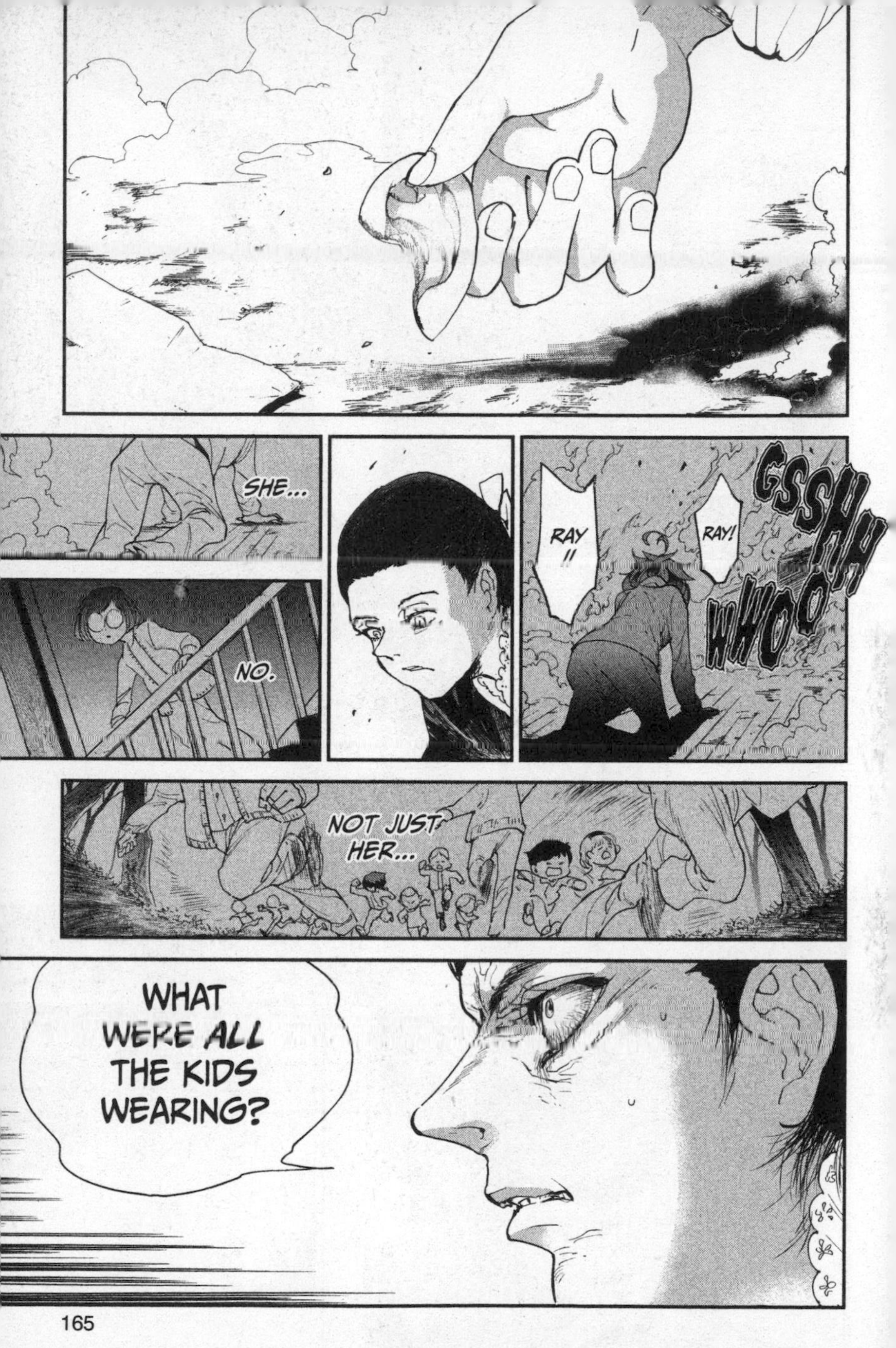
GSSHH
WHOO
RAY!
RAY !!
SHE...
NO.
NOT JUST HER...
WHAT WERE ALL THE KIDS WEARING?

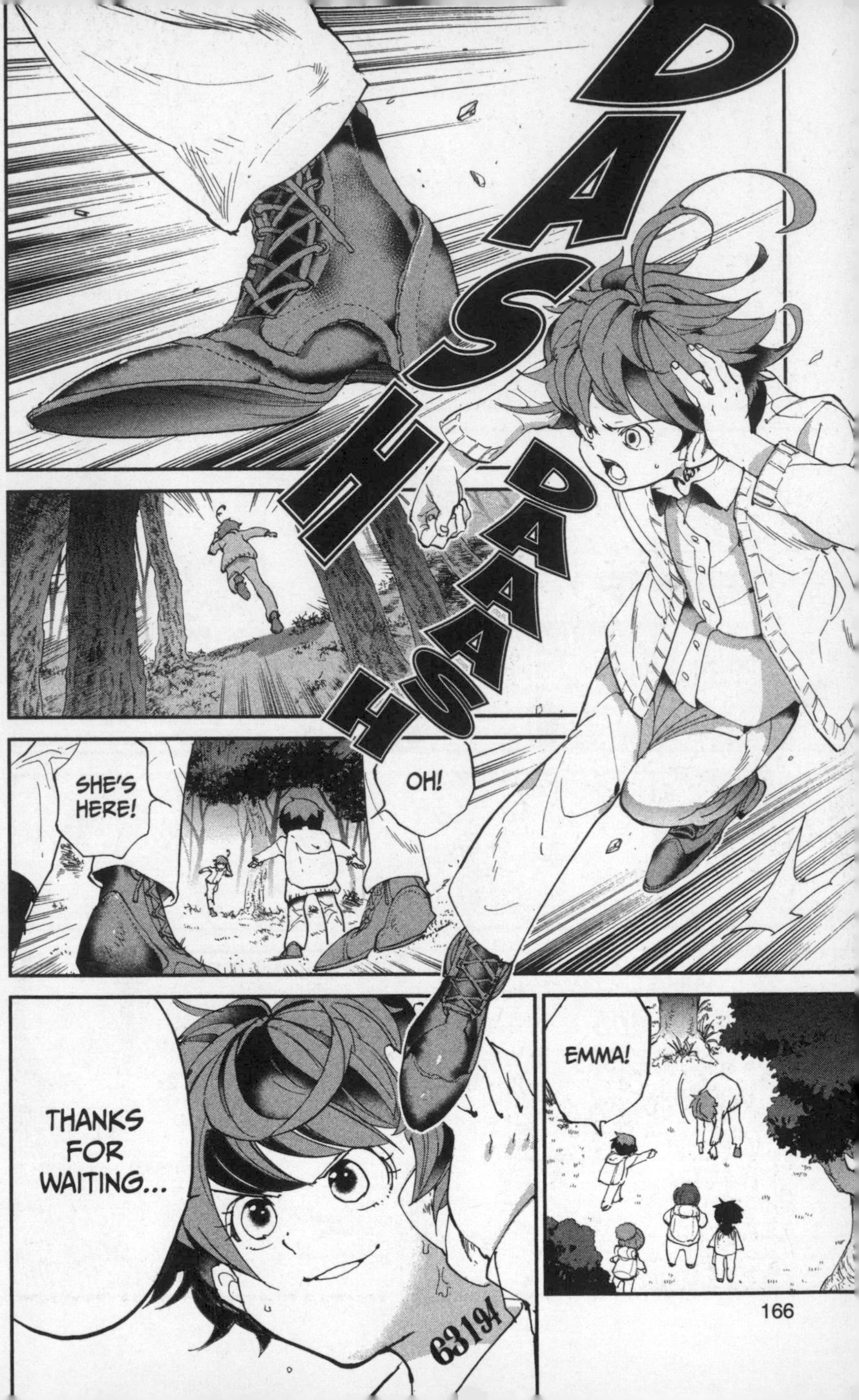
DASH
DAAASH
OH!
SHE'S HERE!
EMMA!
THANKS FOR WAITING...
63194

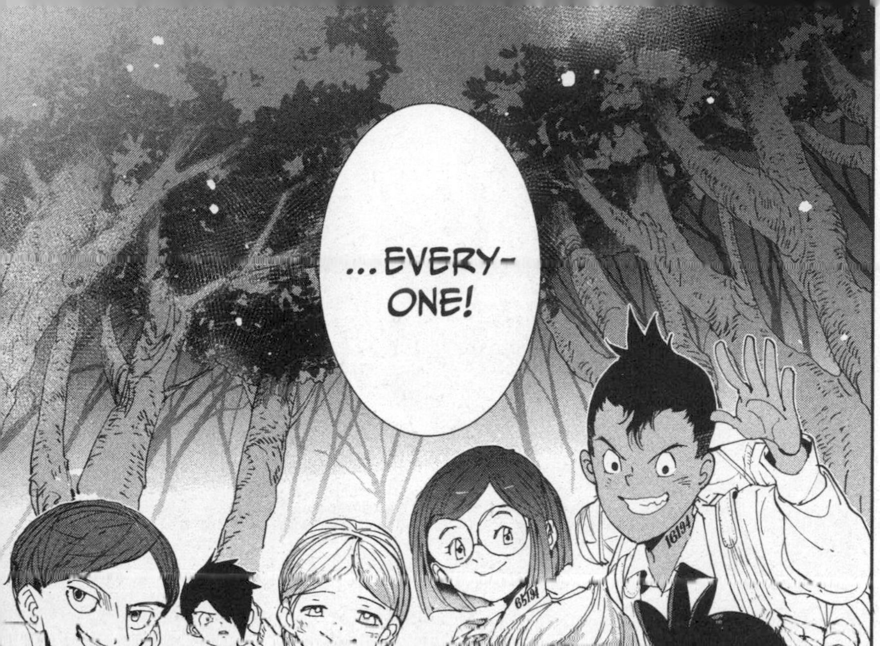
...EVERY-ONE!
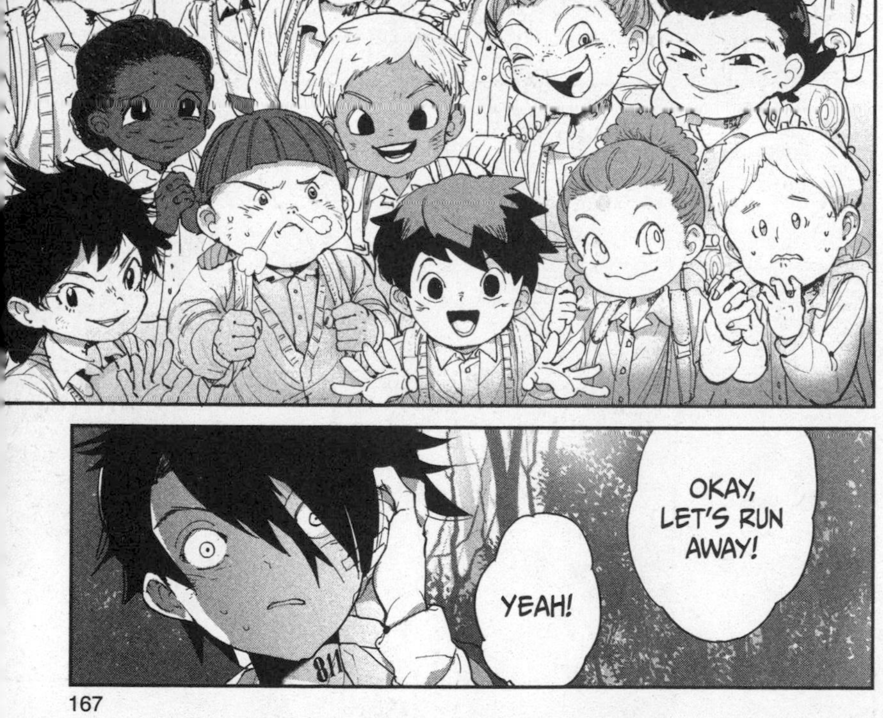
OKAY, LET'S RUN AWAY!
YEAH!

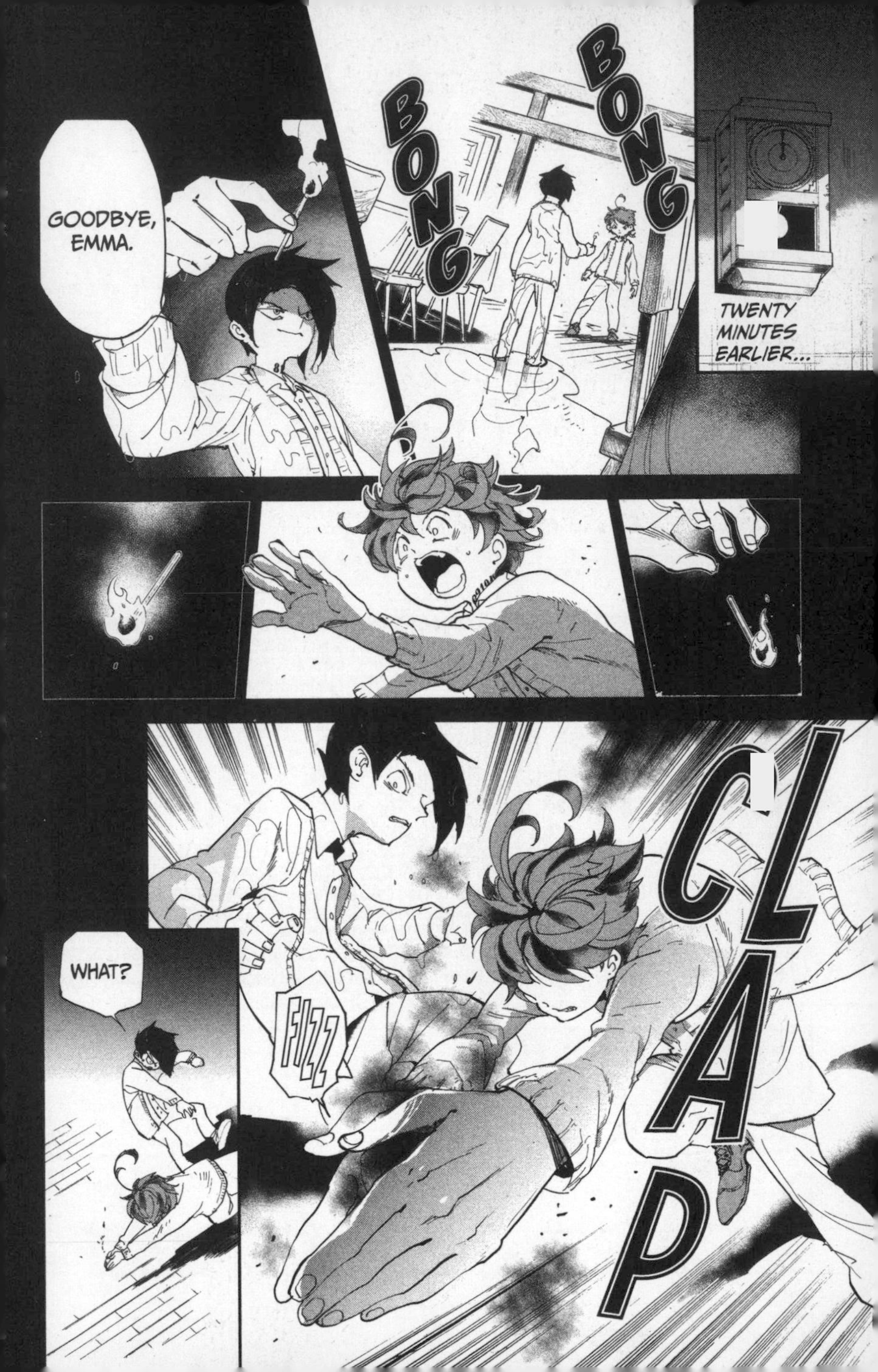
TWENTY MINUTES EARLIER...
BONG
BONG
GOODBYE, EMMA.
CLAP
FIZZ
WHAT?

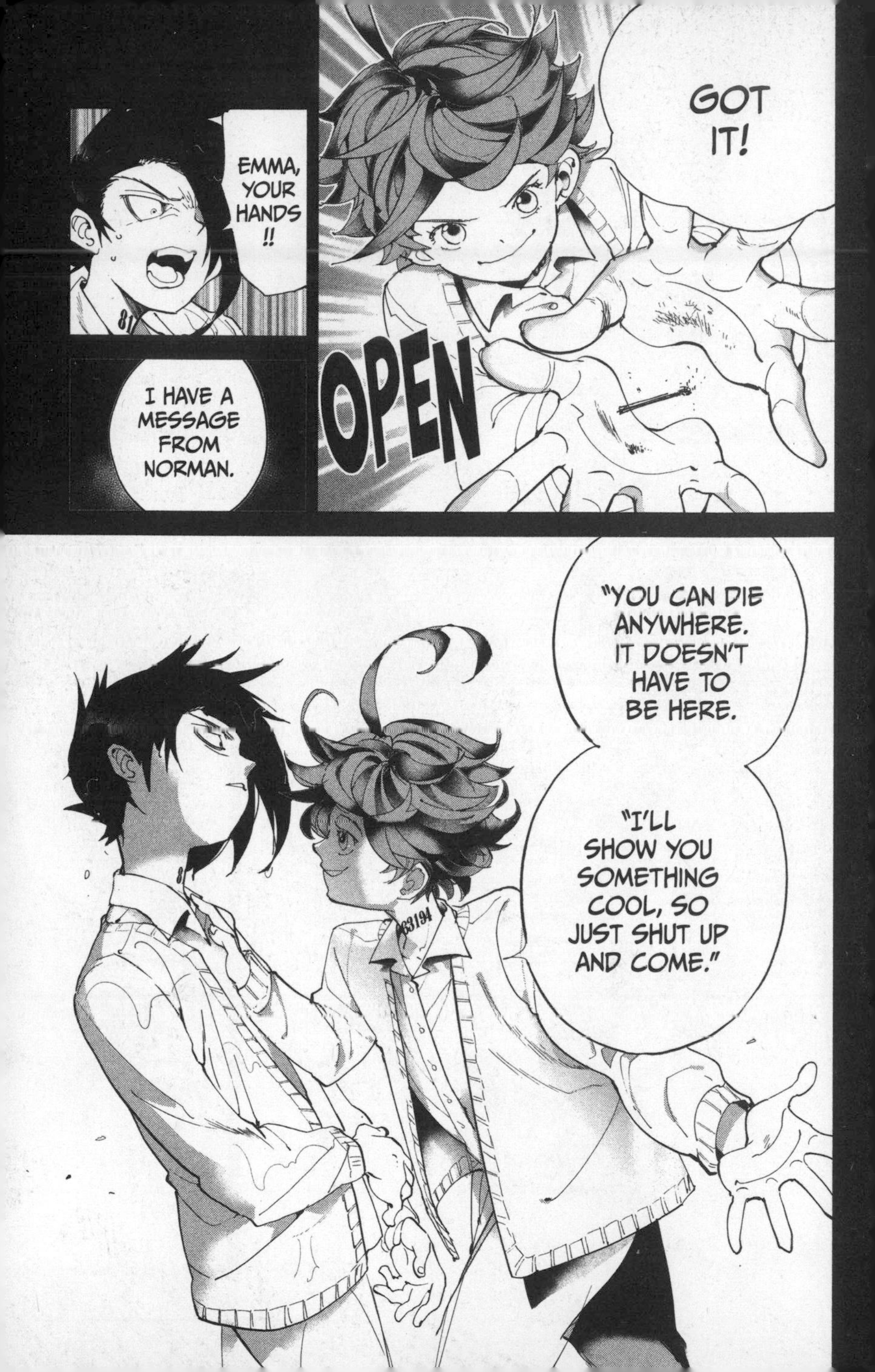
GOT IT!
OPEN
EMMA, YOUR HANDS!!
I HAVE A MESSAGE FROM NORMAN.
"YOU CAN DIE ANYWHERE. IT DOESN'T HAVE TO BE HERE.
"I'LL SHOW YOU SOMETHING COOL, SO JUST SHUT UP AND COME."

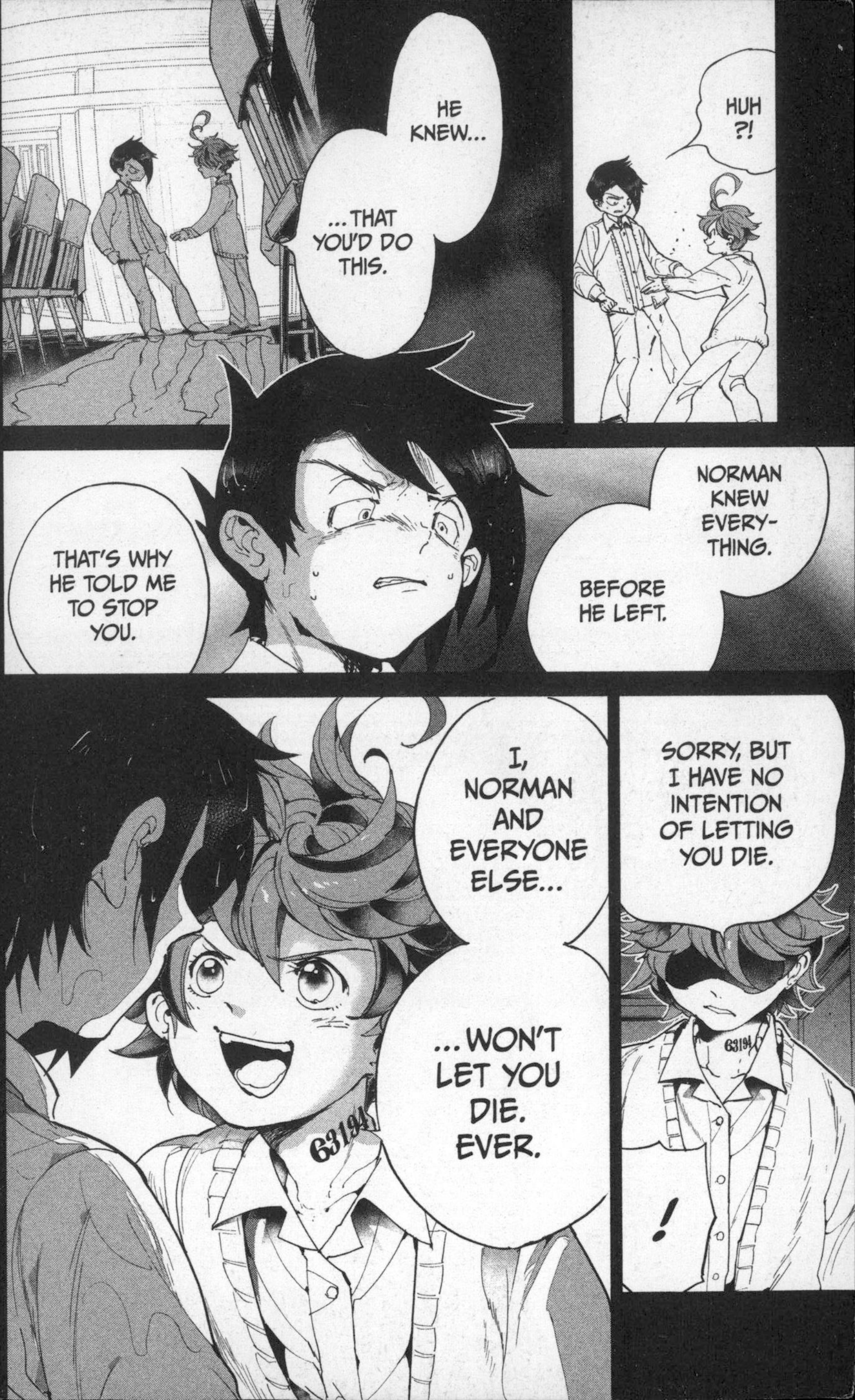
HUH ?!
HE KNEW...
...THAT YOU'D DO THIS.
NORMAN KNEW EVERY-THING.
BEFORE HE LEFT.
THAT'S WHY HE TOLD ME TO STOP YOU.
SORRY, BUT I HAVE NO INTENTION OF LETTING YOU DIE.
!
I, NORMAN AND EVERYONE ELSE...
...WON'T LET YOU DIE. EVER.

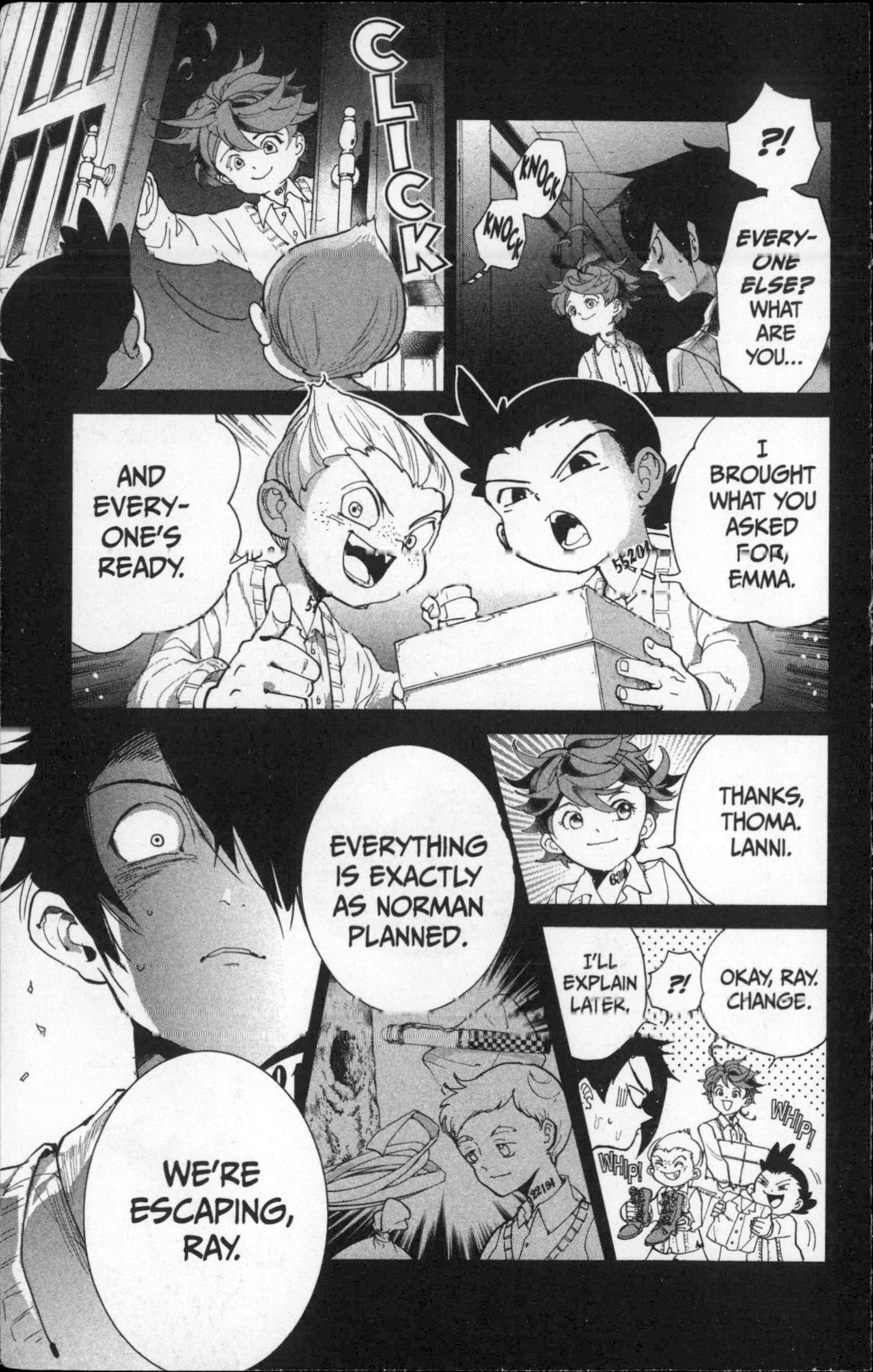
?!
EVERY-ONE ELSE? WHAT ARE YOU...
KNOCK
KNOCK
CLICK
I BROUGHT WHAT YOU ASKED FOR, EMMA.
AND EVERY-ONE'S READY.
THANKS, THOMA. LANNI.
OKAY, RAY. CHANGE.
?!
I'LL EXPLAIN LATER.
WHIP!
WHIP!
EVERYTHING IS EXACTLY AS NORMAN PLANNED.
WE'RE ESCAPING, RAY.

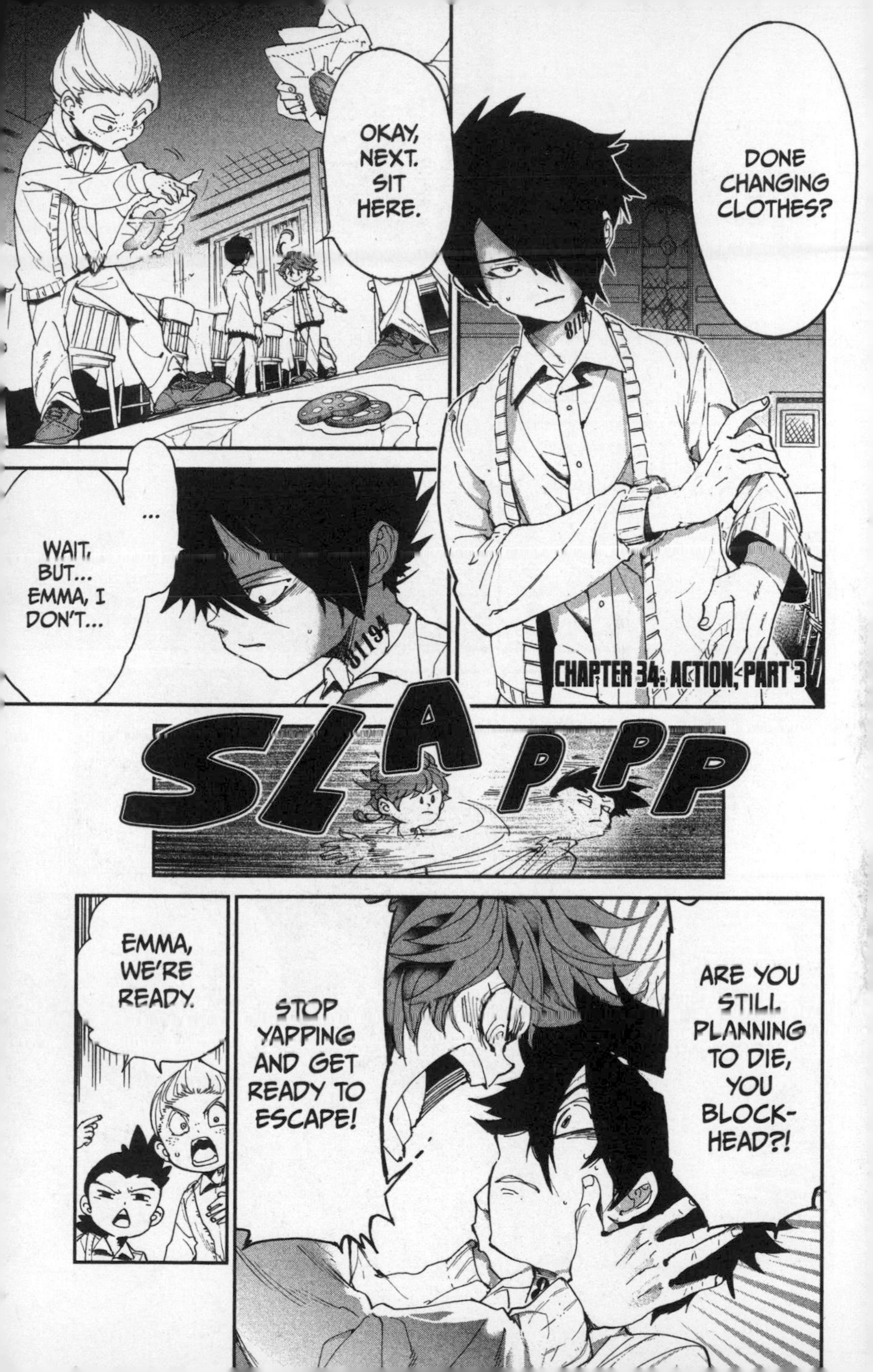
DONE CHANGING CLOTHES?
CHAPTER 34: ACTION, PART 3
OKAY, NEXT. SIT HERE.
...
WAIT, BUT... EMMA, I DON'T...
SLAPPP
ARE YOU STILL PLANNING TO DIE, YOU BLOCK-HEAD?!
STOP YAPPING AND GET READY TO ESCAPE!
EMMA, WE'RE READY.

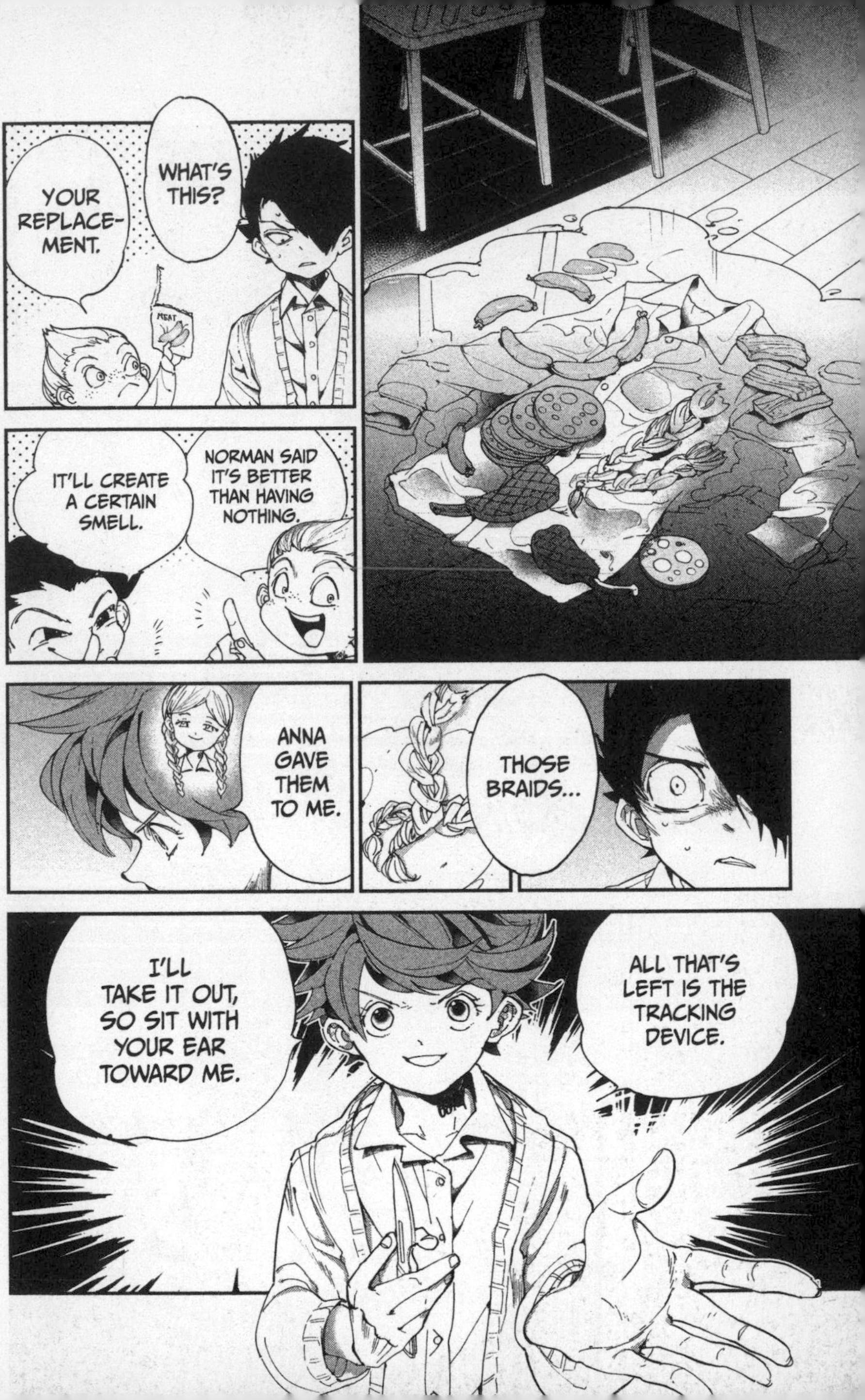
WHAT'S THIS?
YOUR REPLACEMENT.
NORMAN SAID IT'S BETTER THAN HAVING NOTHING.
IT'LL CREATE A CERTAIN SMELL.
THOSE BRAIDS...
ANNA GAVE THEM TO ME.
ALL THAT'S LEFT IS THE TRACKING DEVICE.
I'LL TAKE IT OUT, SO SIT WITH YOUR EAR TOWARD ME.

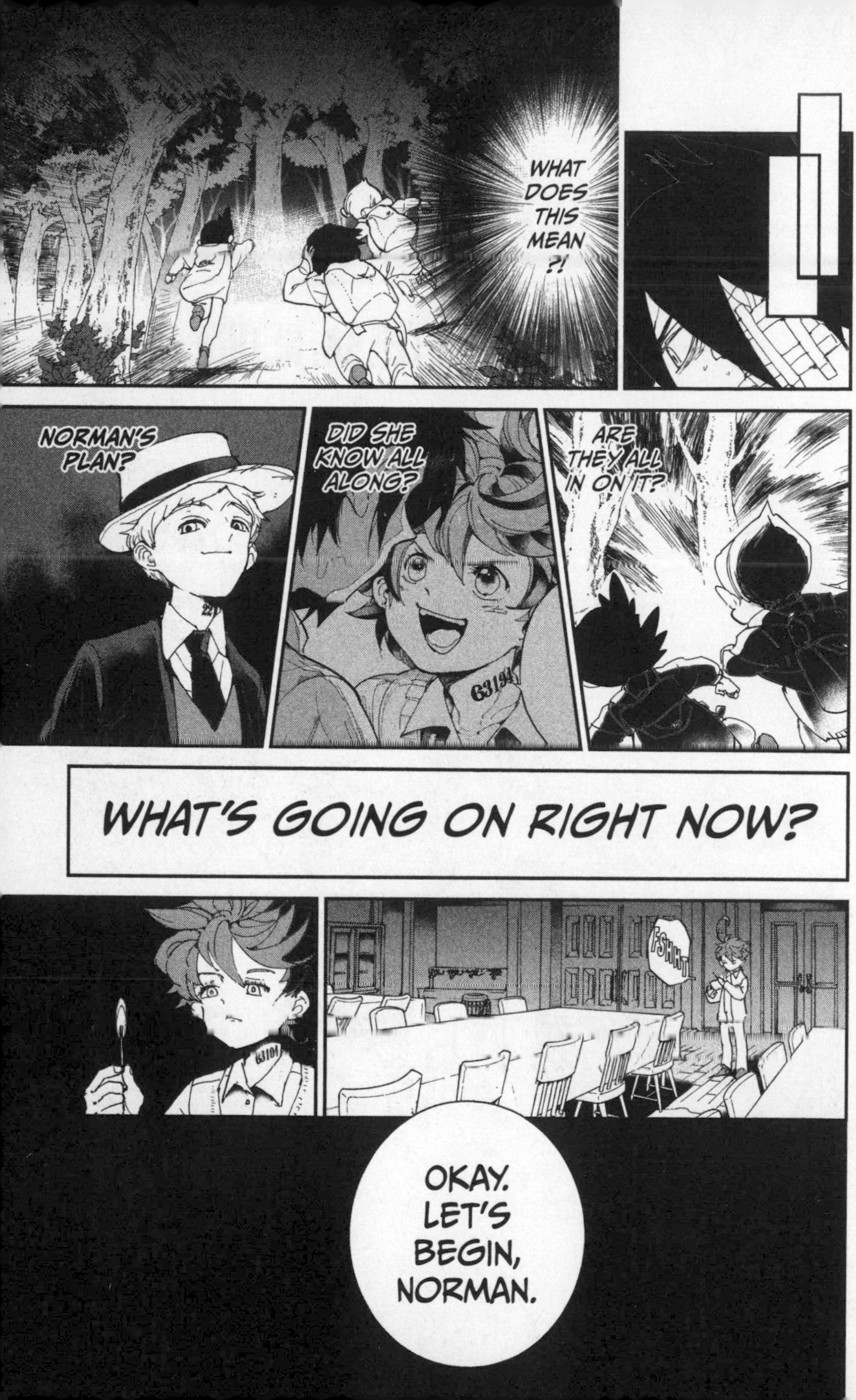
WHAT DOES THIS MEAN ?!
ARE THEY ALL IN ON IT?
DID SHE KNOW ALL ALONG?
NORMAN'S PLAN?
WHAT'S GOING ON RIGHT NOW?
FSHHT
OKAY. LET'S BEGIN, NORMAN.

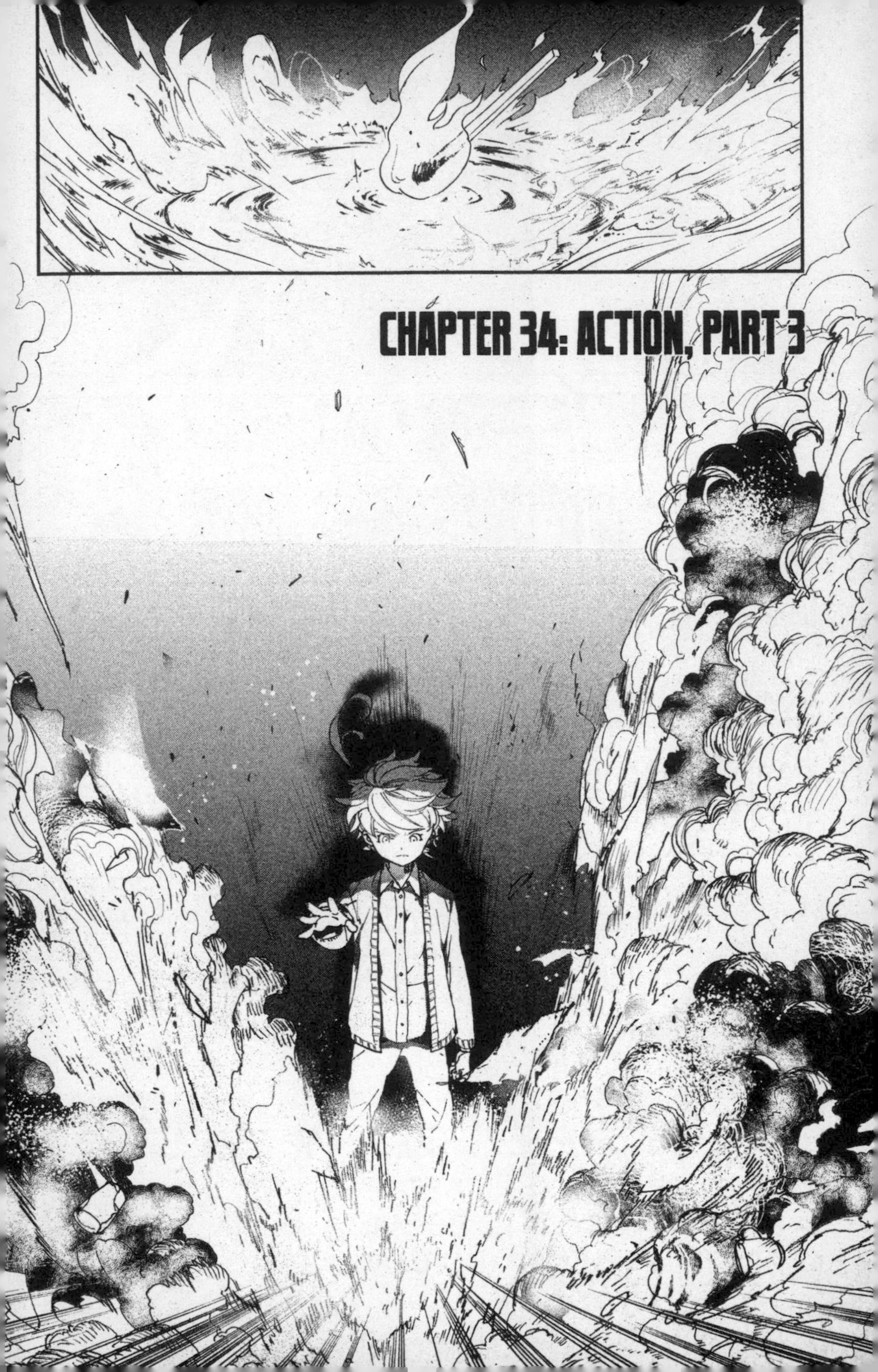
CHAPTER 34: ACTION, PART 3

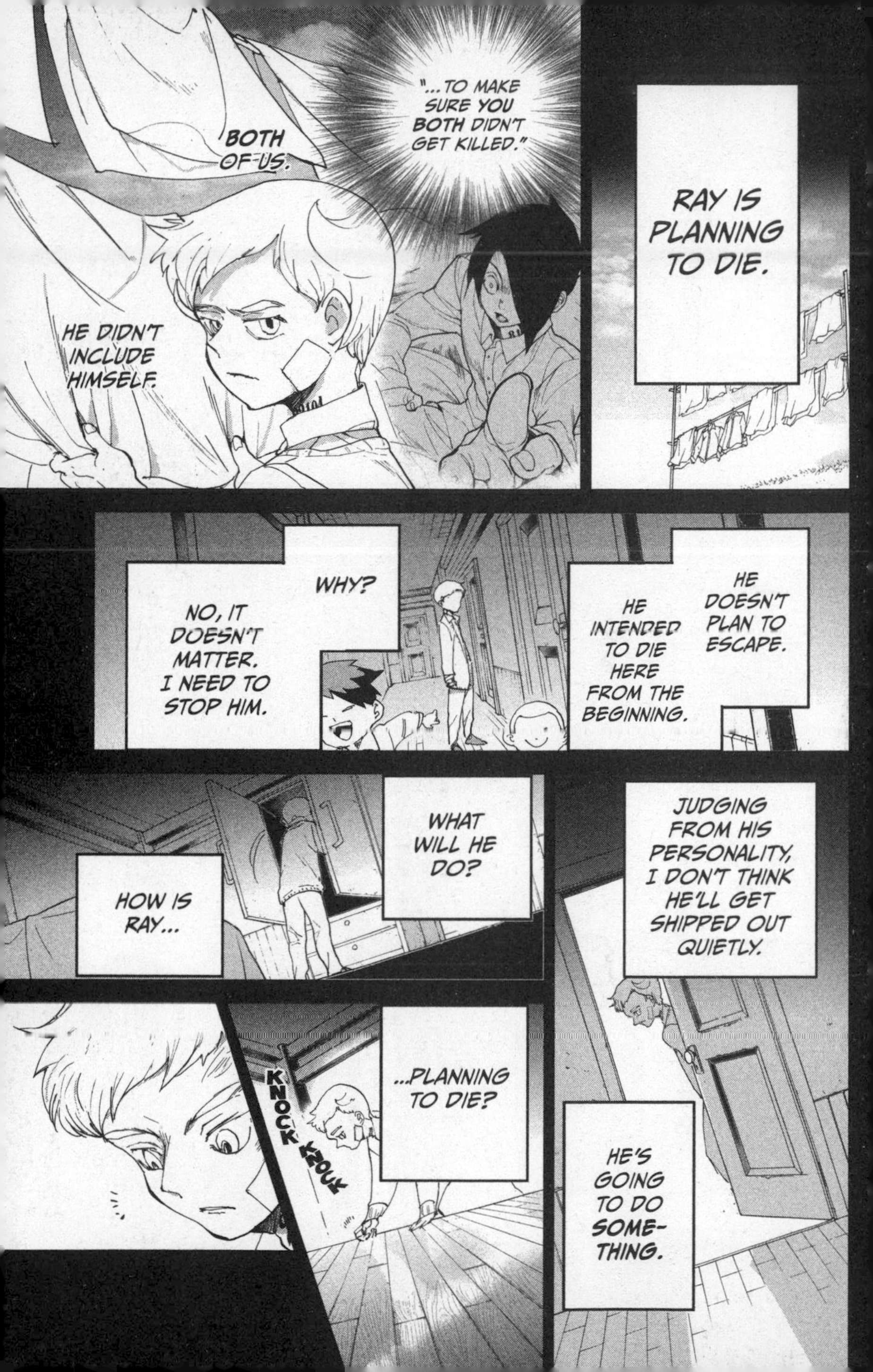
RAY IS PLANNING TO DIE.
"...TO MAKE SURE YOU BOTH DIDN'T GET KILLED."
BOTH OF US.
HE DIDN'T INCLUDE HIMSELF.
HE DOESN'T PLAN TO ESCAPE.
HE INTENDED TO DIE HERE FROM THE BEGINNING.
WHY?
NO, IT DOESN'T MATTER. I NEED TO STOP HIM.
JUDGING FROM HIS PERSONALITY, I DON'T THINK HE'LL GET SHIPPED OUT QUIETLY.
HE'S GOING TO DO SOME-THING.
WHAT WILL HE DO?
HOW IS RAY...
...PLANNING TO DIE?
KNOCK
KNOCK

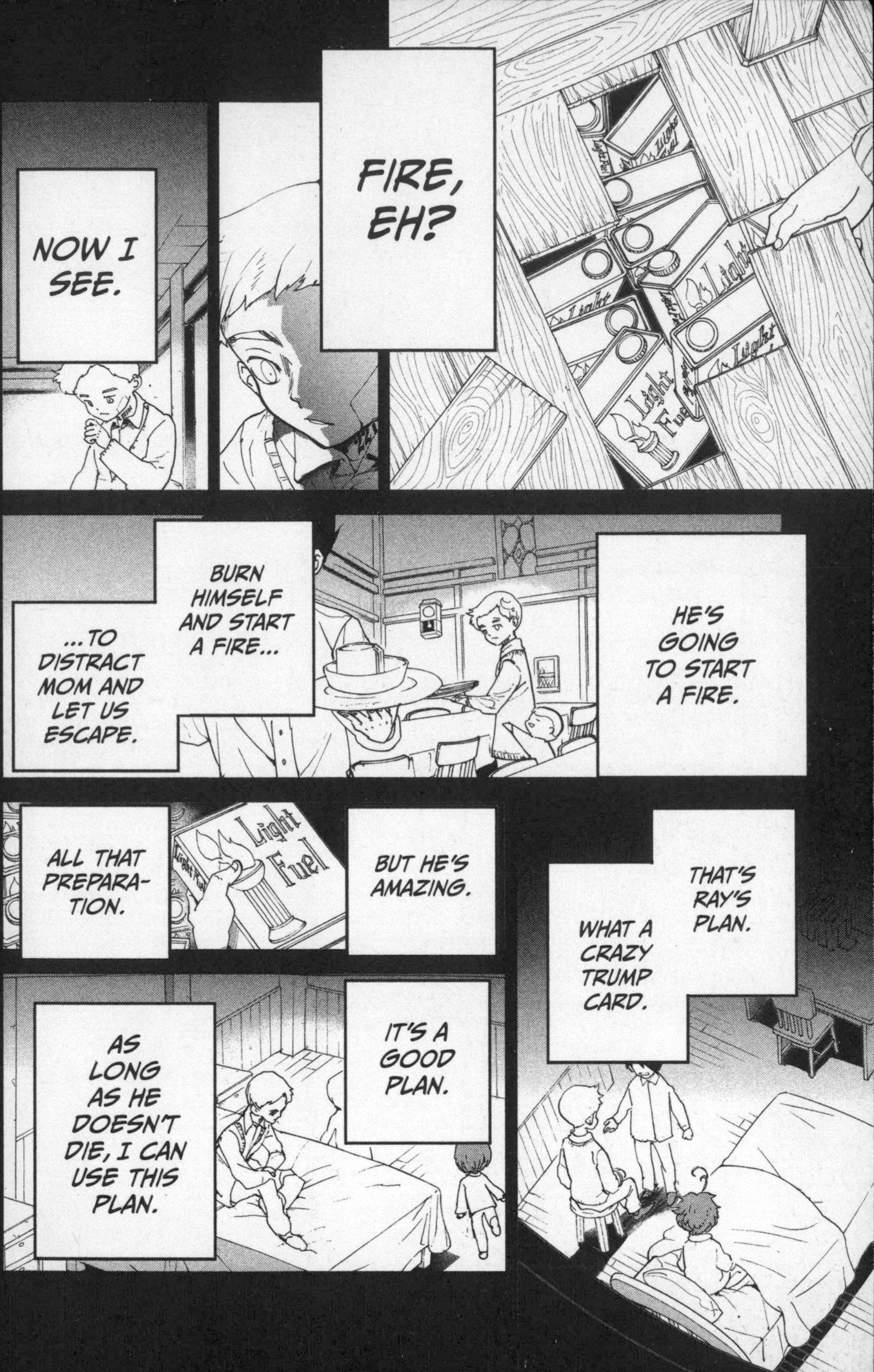
FIRE, EH?
NOW I SEE.
HE'S GOING TO START A FIRE.
BURN HIMSELF AND START A FIRE...
...TO DISTRACT MOM AND LET US ESCAPE.
THAT'S RAY'S PLAN.
WHAT A CRAZY TRUMP CARD.
BUT HE'S AMAZING.
ALL THAT PREPARATION.
Light Fuel
IT'S A GOOD PLAN.
AS LONG AS HE DOESN'T DIE, I CAN USE THIS PLAN.

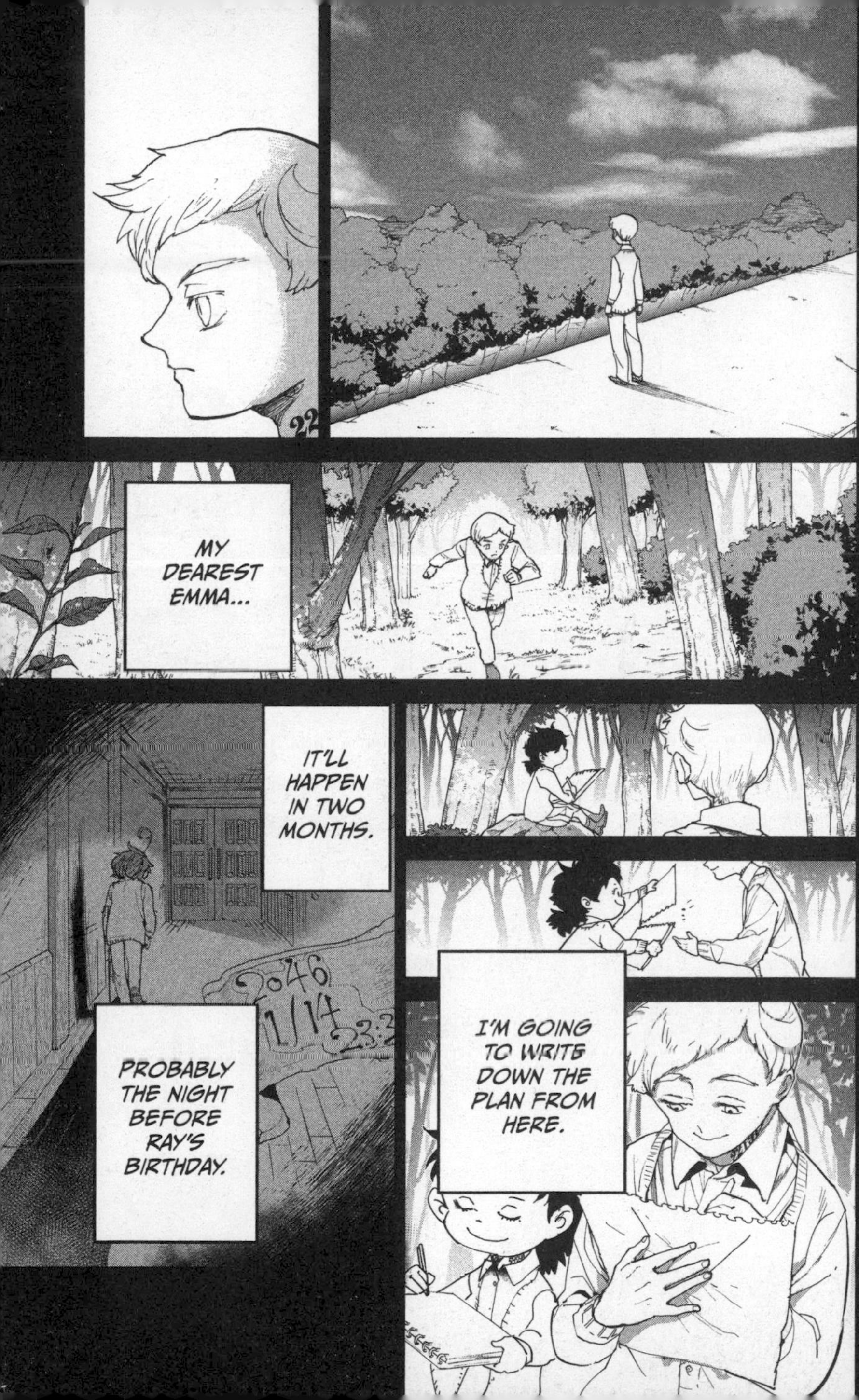
MY DEAREST EMMA...
I'M GOING TO WRITE DOWN THE PLAN FROM HERE.
IT'LL HAPPEN IN TWO MONTHS.
PROBABLY THE NIGHT BEFORE RAY'S BIRTHDAY.

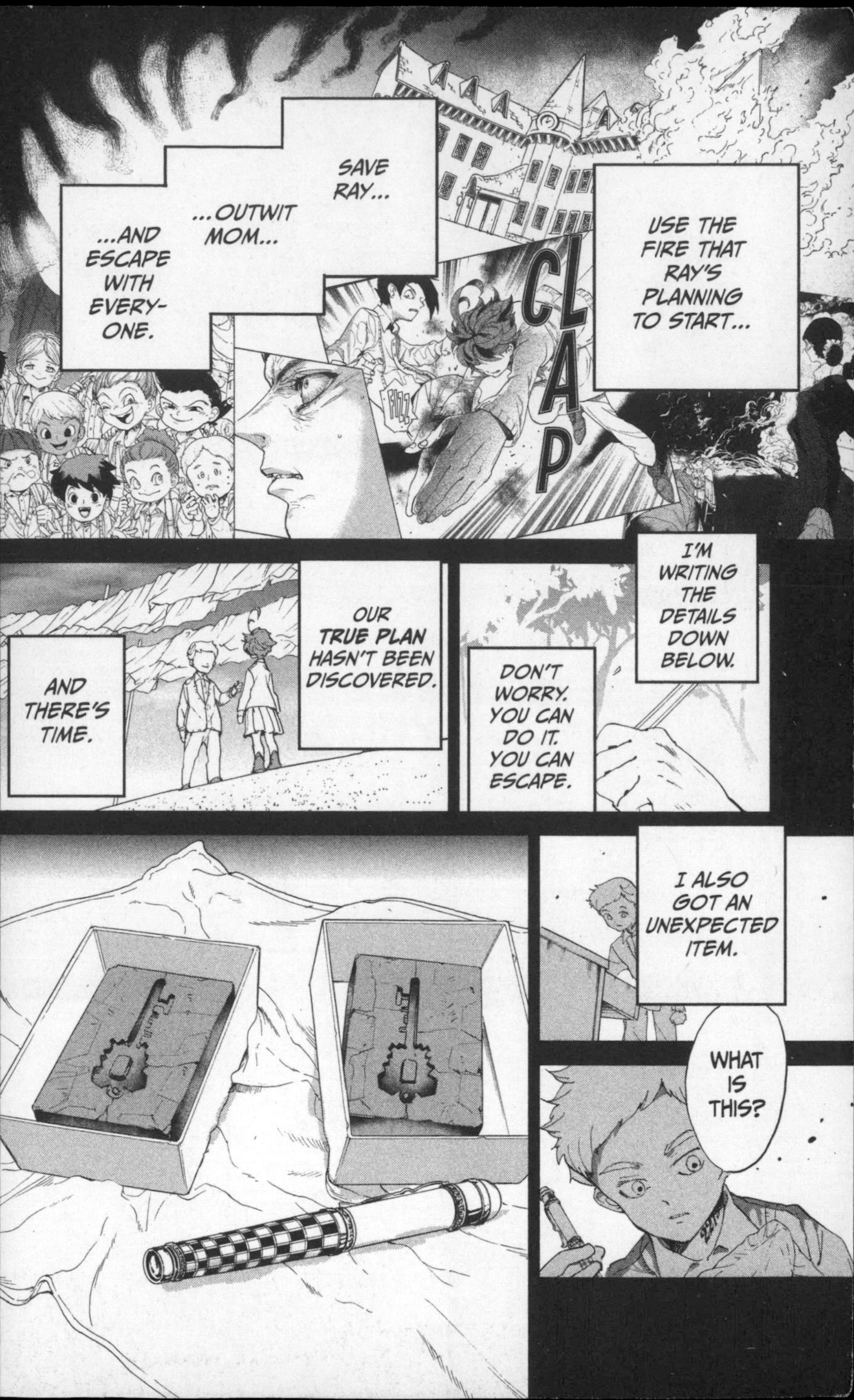
USE THE FIRE THAT RAY'S PLANNING TO START...
CLAP
FIZZ
SAVE RAY...
...OUTWIT MOM...
...AND ESCAPE WITH EVERY-ONE.
I'M WRITING THE DETAILS DOWN BELOW.
DON'T WORRY. YOU CAN DO IT. YOU CAN ESCAPE.
OUR TRUE PLAN HASN'T BEEN DISCOVERED.
AND THERE'S TIME.
I ALSO GOT AN UNEXPECTED ITEM.
WHAT IS THIS?

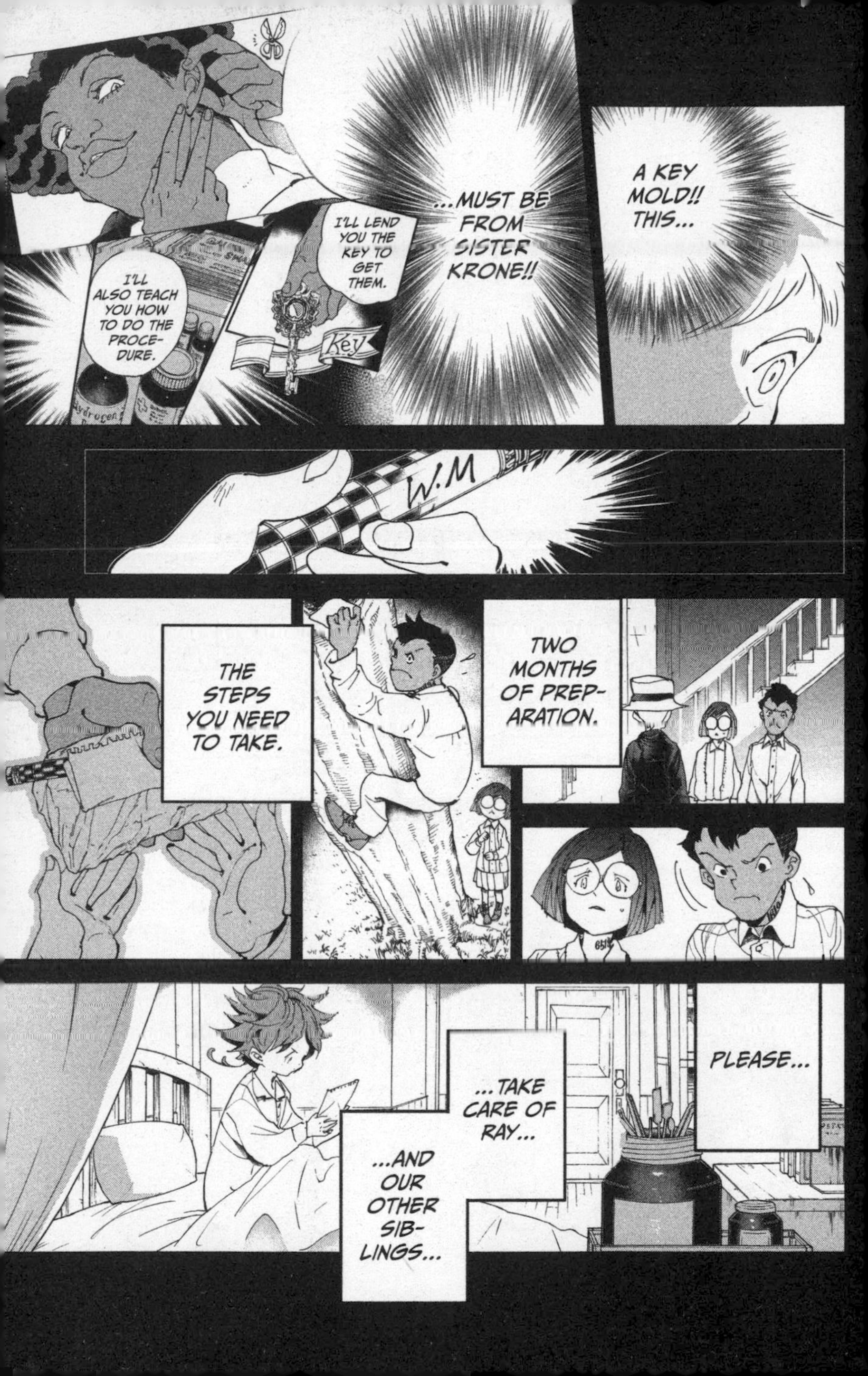
A KEY MOLD!! THIS...
...MUST BE FROM SISTER KRONE!!
I'LL LEND YOU THE KEY TO GET THEM.
I'LL ALSO TEACH YOU HOW TO DO THE PROCE-DURE.
Key
W.M
TWO MONTHS OF PREP-ARATION.
THE STEPS YOU NEED TO TAKE.
PLEASE...
...TAKE CARE OF RAY...
...AND OUR OTHER SIB-LINGS...

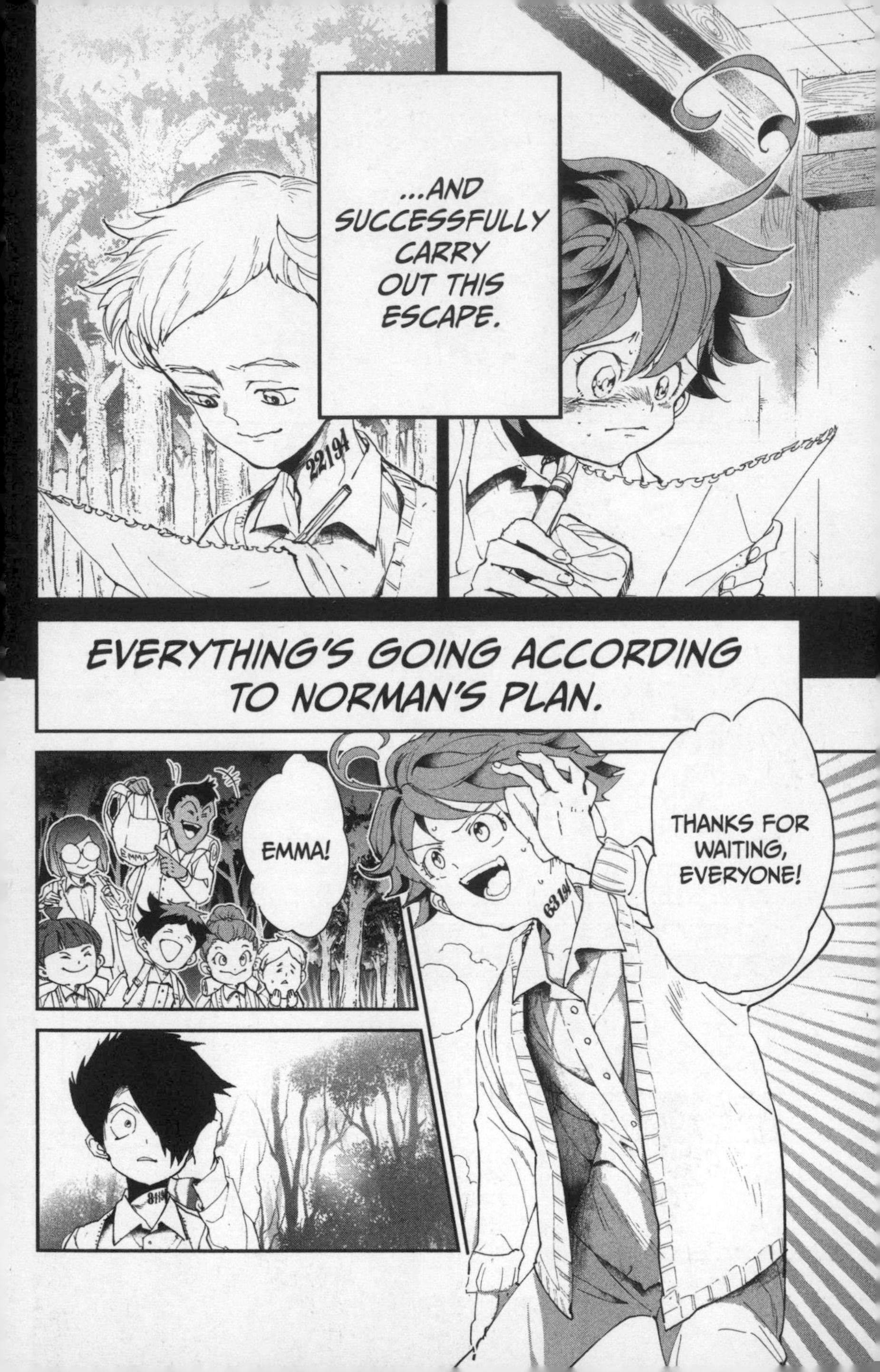
...AND SUCCESSFULLY CARRY OUT THIS ESCAPE.
EVERYTHING'S GOING ACCORDING TO NORMAN'S PLAN.
THANKS FOR WAITING, EVERYONE!
EMMA!

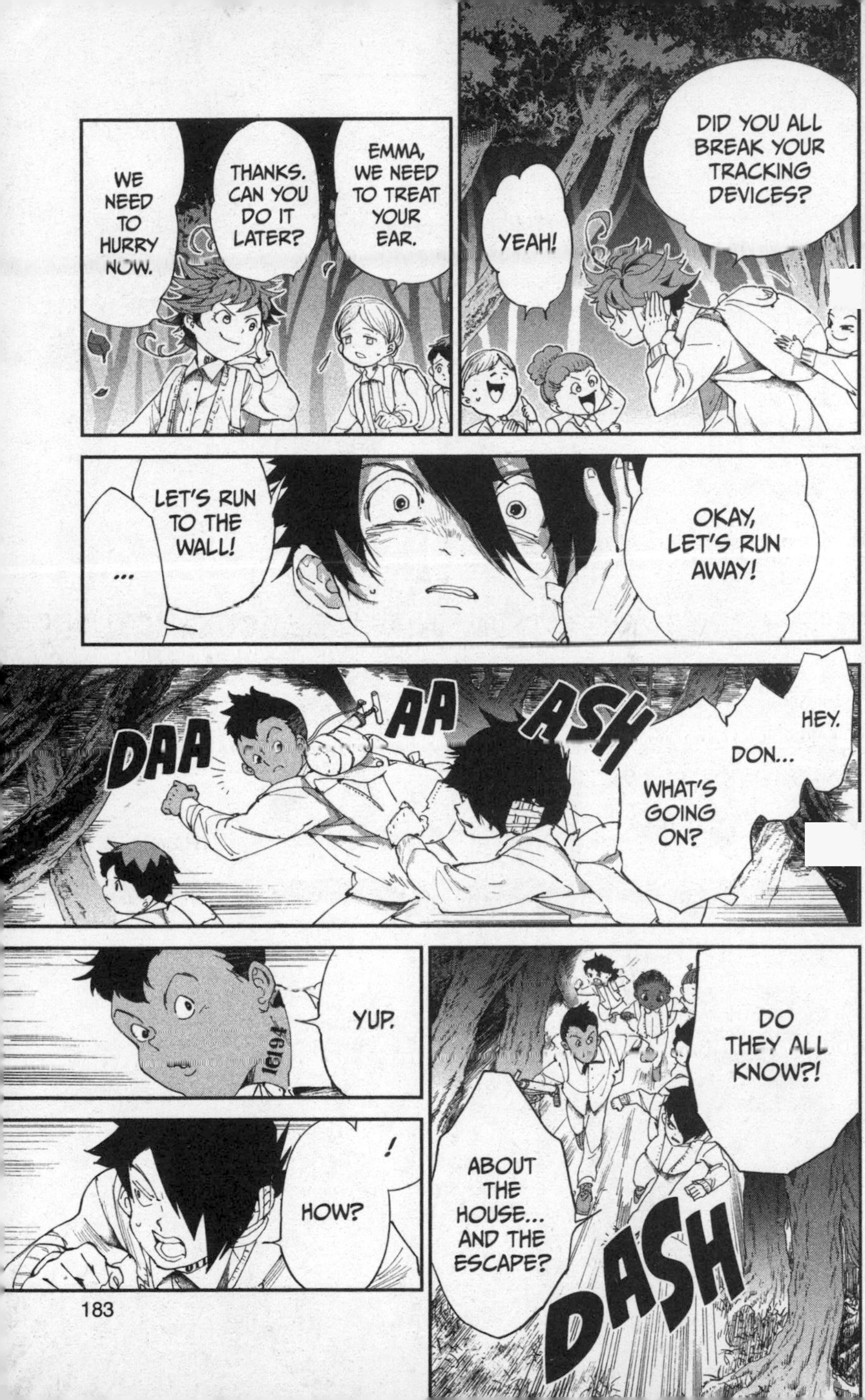
DID YOU ALL BREAK YOUR TRACKING DEVICES?
YEAH!
EMMA, WE NEED TO TREAT YOUR EAR.
THANKS. CAN YOU DO IT LATER?
WE NEED TO HURRY NOW.
OKAY, LET'S RUN AWAY!
LET'S RUN TO THE WALL!
...
HEY.
DON...
WHAT'S GOING ON?
DAA AA ASH
DO THEY ALL KNOW?!
ABOUT THE HOUSE... AND THE ESCAPE?
DASH
YUP.
16194
!
HOW?

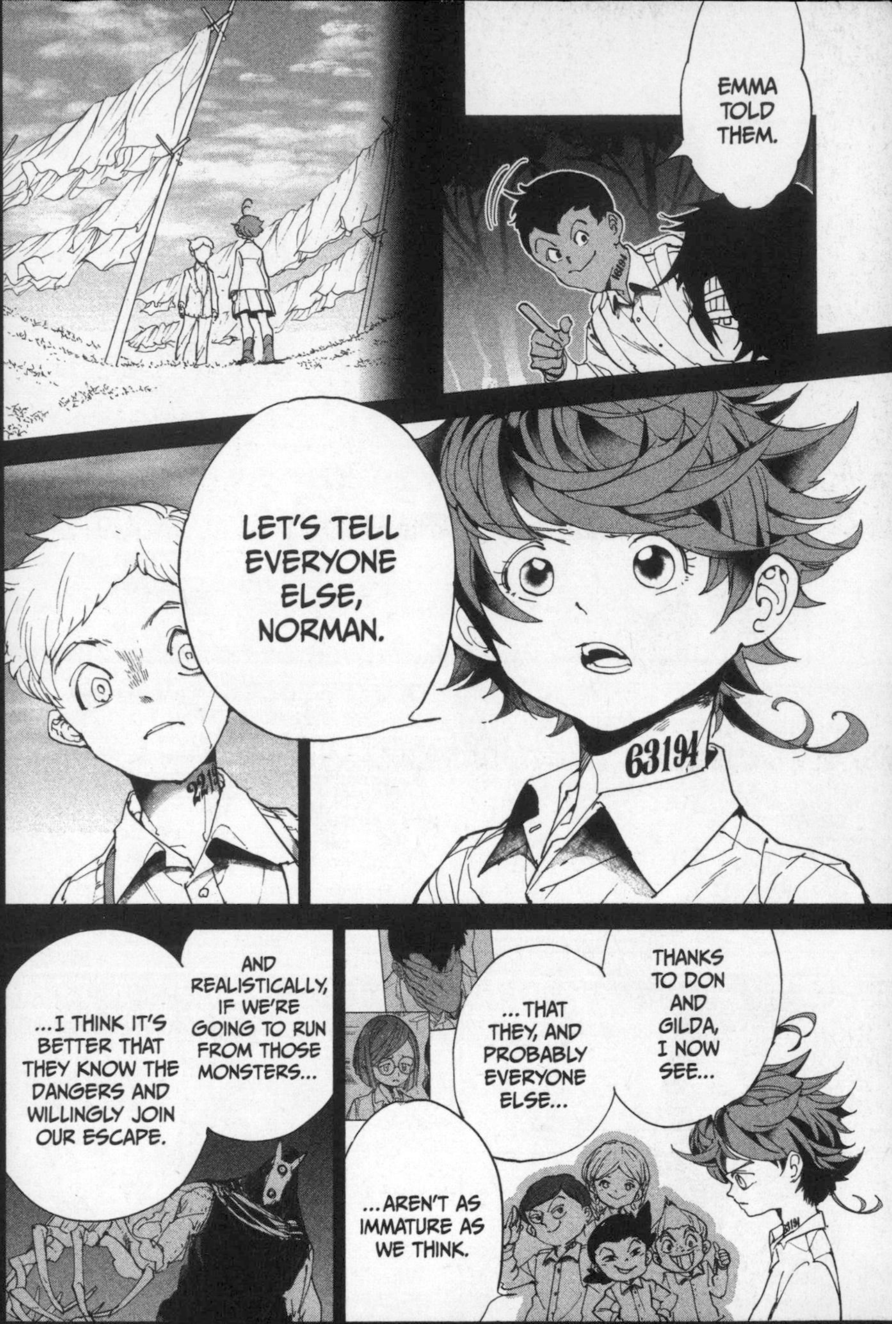
EMMA TOLD THEM.
LET'S TELL EVERYONE ELSE, NORMAN.
63194
THANKS TO DON AND GILDA, I NOW SEE...
...THAT THEY, AND PROBABLY EVERYONE ELSE...
...AREN'T AS IMMATURE AS WE THINK.
AND REALISTICALLY, IF WE'RE GOING TO RUN FROM THOSE MONSTERS...
...I THINK IT'S BETTER THAT THEY KNOW THE DANGERS AND WILLINGLY JOIN OUR ESCAPE.

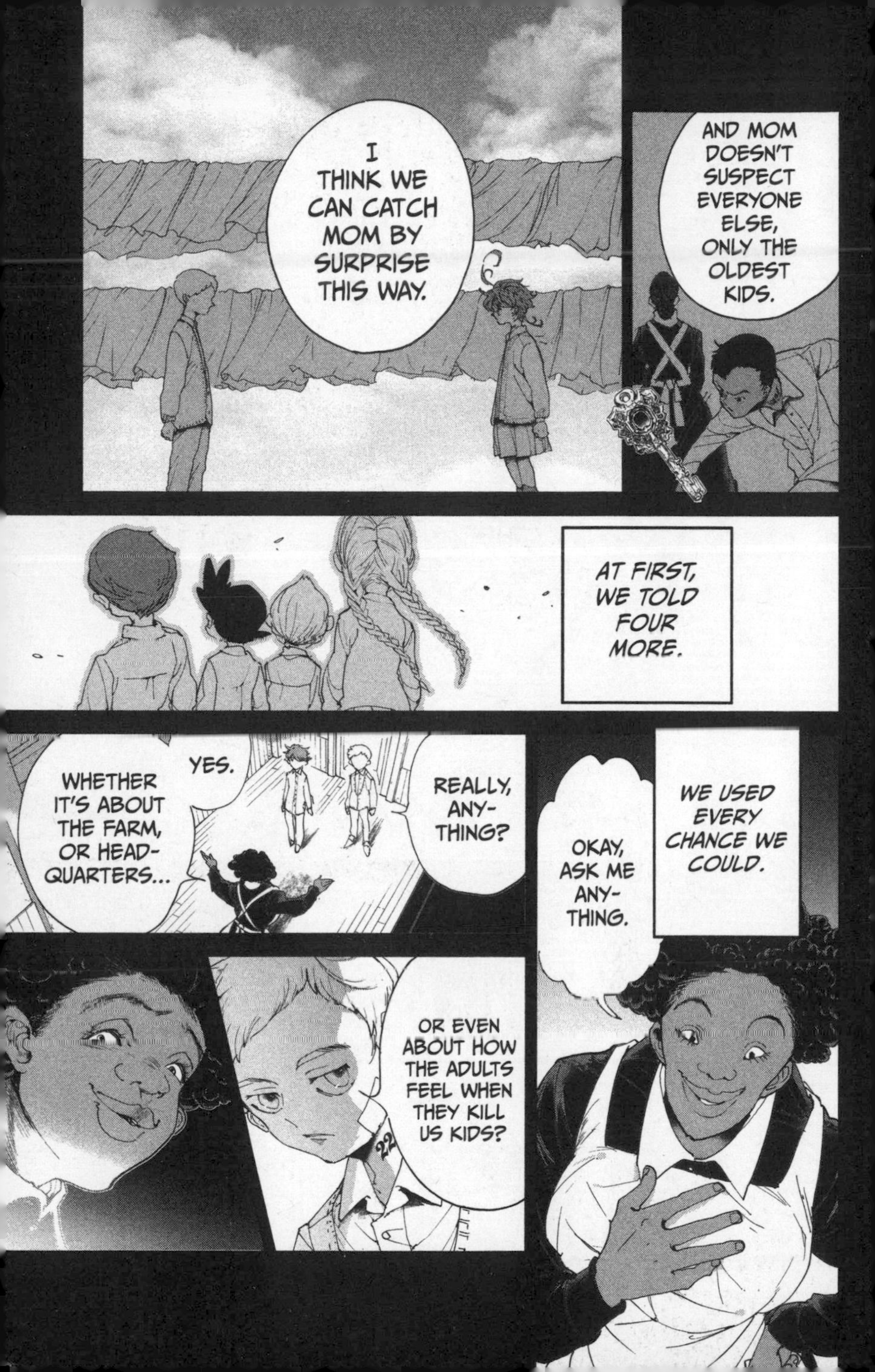
AND MOM DOESN'T SUSPECT EVERYONE ELSE, ONLY THE OLDEST KIDS.
I THINK WE CAN CATCH MOM BY SURPRISE THIS WAY.
AT FIRST, WE TOLD FOUR MORE.
WE USED EVERY CHANCE WE COULD.
OKAY, ASK ME ANYTHING.
REALLY, ANYTHING?
YES.
WHETHER IT'S ABOUT THE FARM, OR HEAD-QUARTERS...
OR EVEN ABOUT HOW THE ADULTS FEEL WHEN THEY KILL US KIDS?

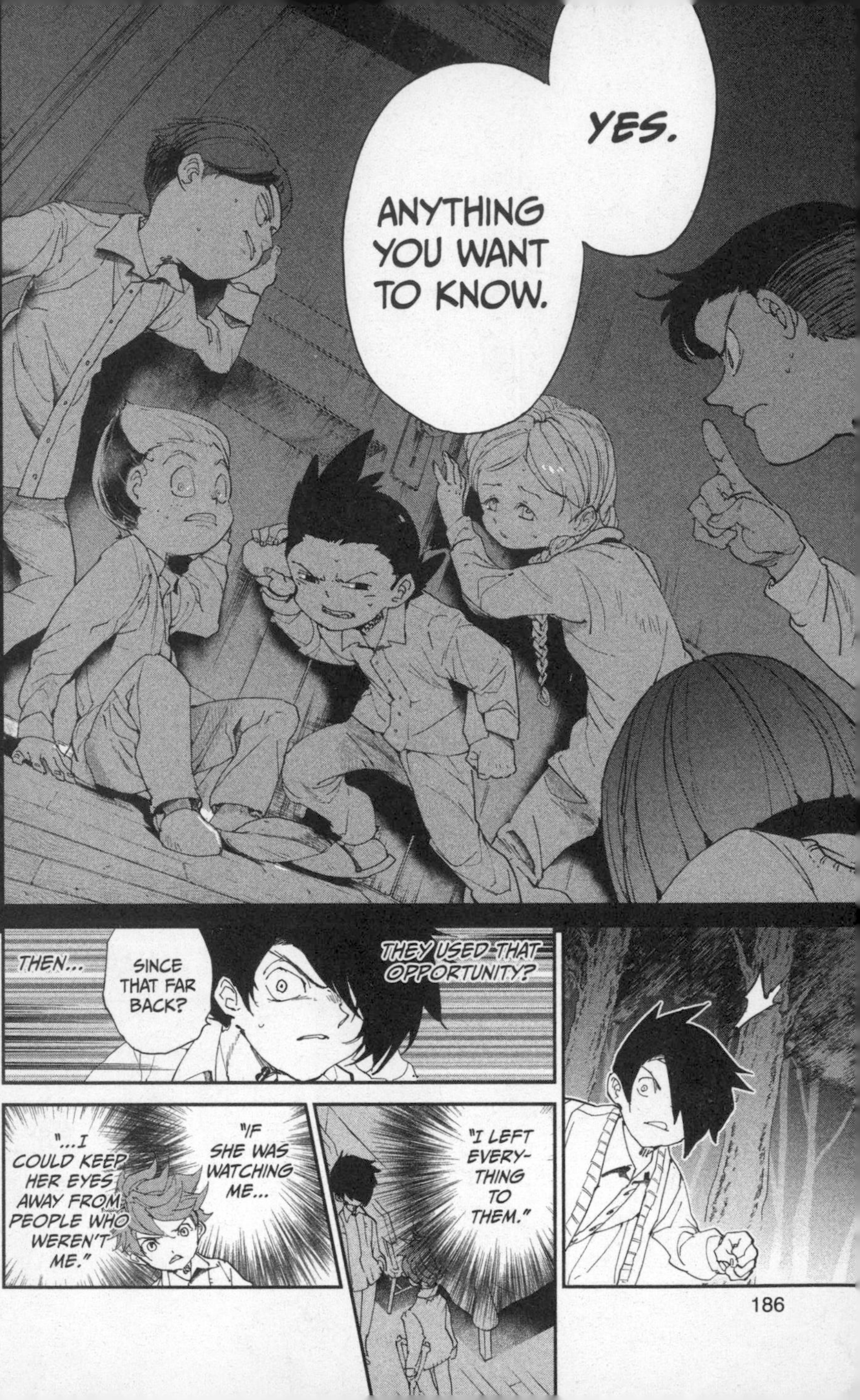
YES.
ANYTHING YOU WANT TO KNOW.
THEY USED THAT OPPORTUNITY?
SINCE THAT FAR BACK?
THEN...
"I LEFT EVERY-THING TO THEM."
"IF SHE WAS WATCHING ME...
"...I COULD KEEP HER EYES AWAY FROM PEOPLE WHO WEREN'T ME."

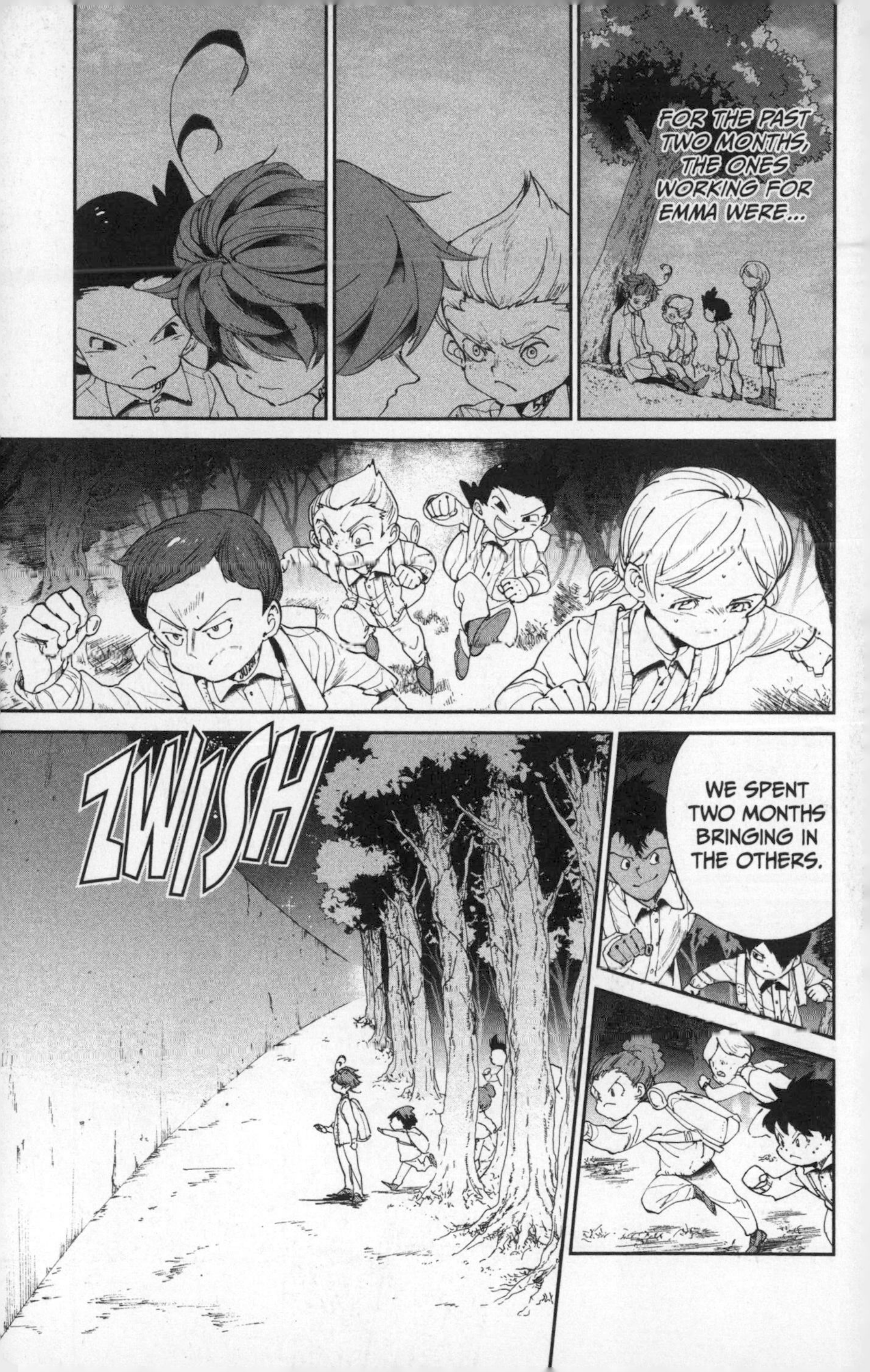
FOR THE PAST TWO MONTHS, THE ONES WORKING FOR EMMA WERE...
WE SPENT TWO MONTHS BRINGING IN THE OTHERS.
ZWISH

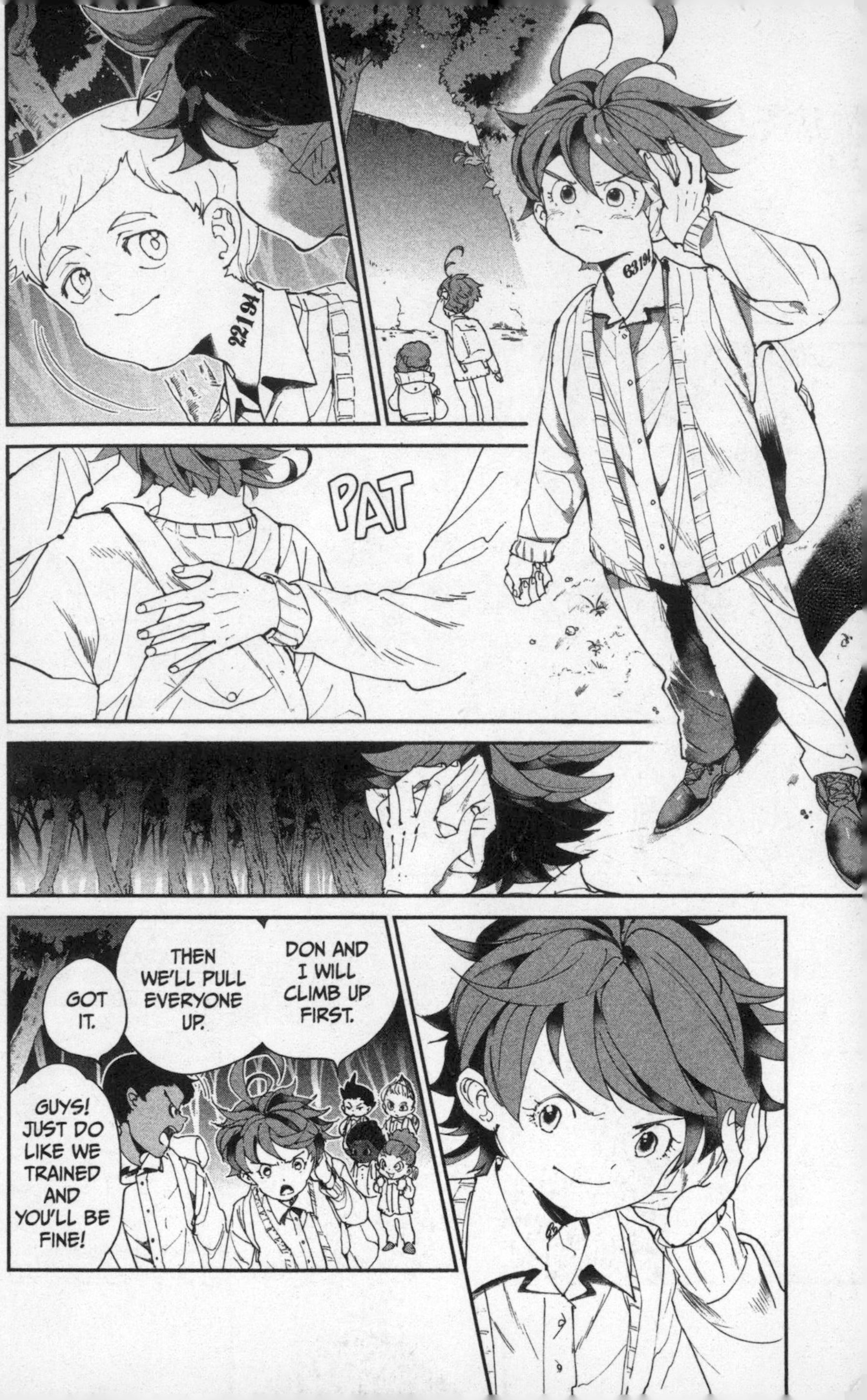
PAT
DON AND I WILL CLIMB UP FIRST.
THEN WE'LL PULL EVERYONE UP.
GOT IT.
GUYS! JUST DO LIKE WE TRAINED AND YOU'LL BE FINE!

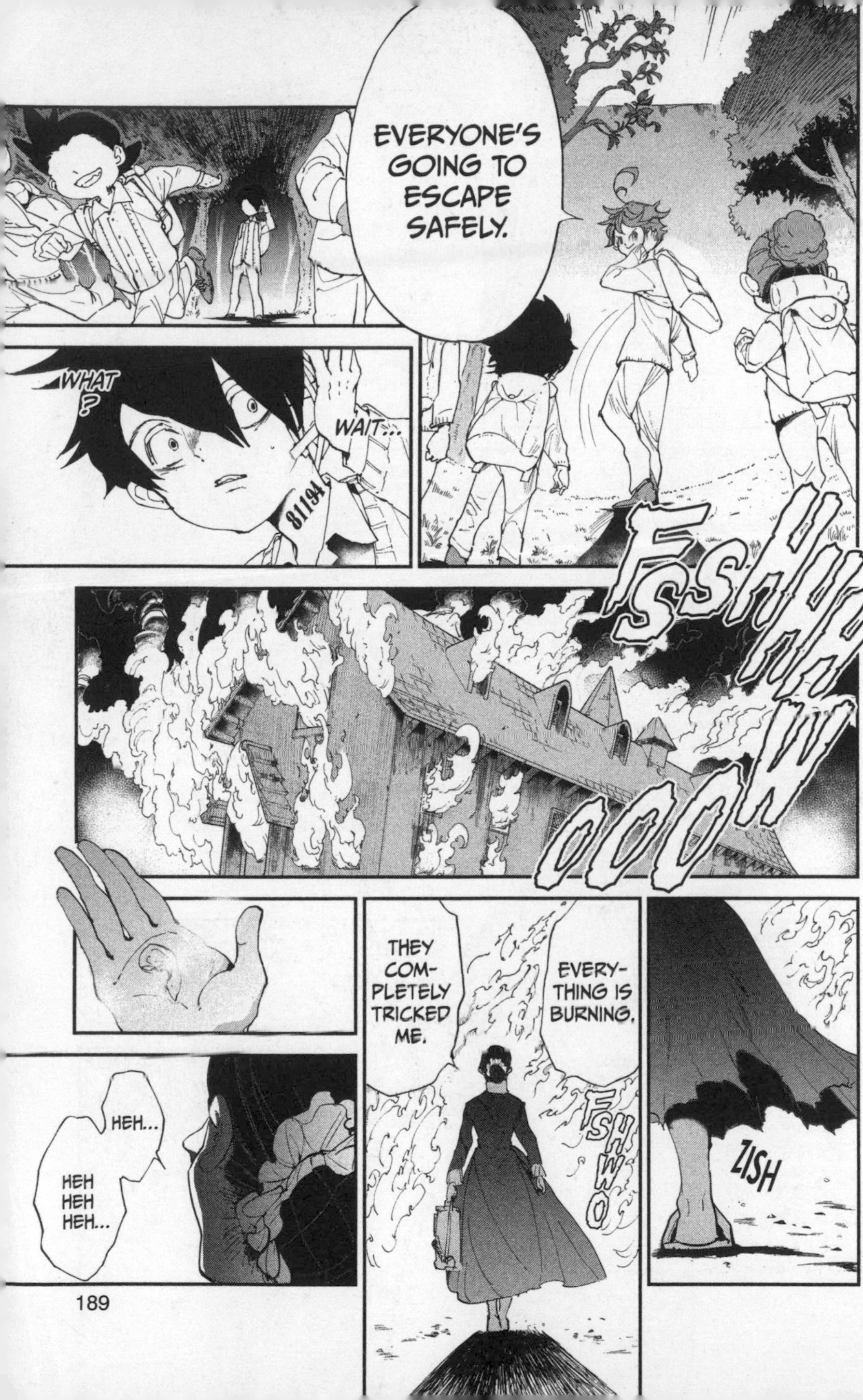
EVERYONE'S GOING TO ESCAPE SAFELY.
WAIT...
WHAT?
81194
FSSHHHHWOOOOW
ZISH
EVERY-THING IS BURNING.
THEY COM-PLETELY TRICKED ME.
FSHWO
HEH...
HEH HEH HEH...

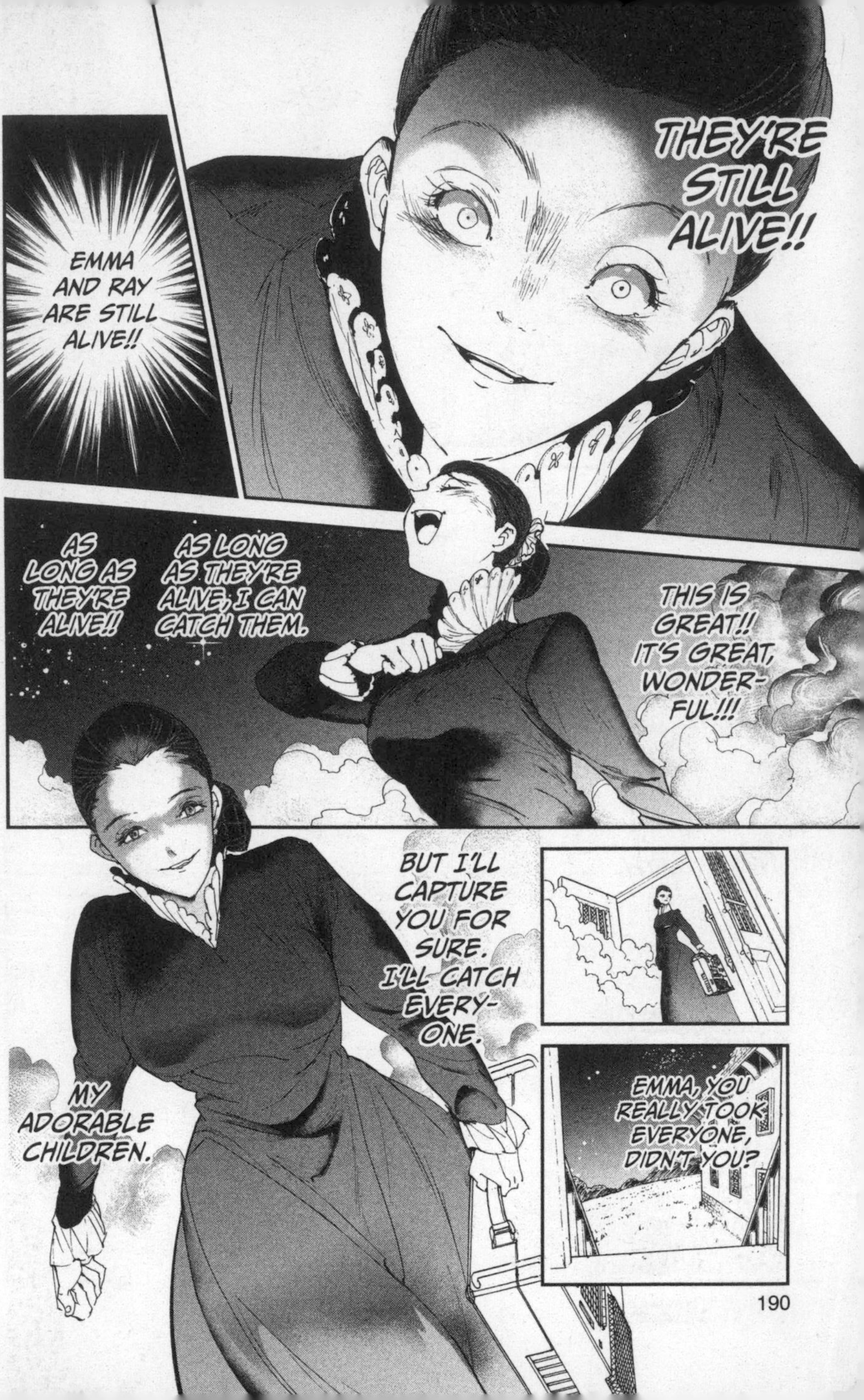
THEY'RE STILL ALIVE!!
EMMA AND RAY ARE STILL ALIVE!!
THIS IS GREAT!! IT'S GREAT, WONDERFUL!!!
AS LONG AS THEY'RE ALIVE, I CAN CATCH THEM.
AS LONG AS THEY'RE ALIVE!!
EMMA, YOU REALLY TOOK EVERYONE, DIDN'T YOU?
BUT I'LL CAPTURE YOU FOR SURE. I'LL CATCH EVERYONE.
MY ADORABLE CHILDREN.

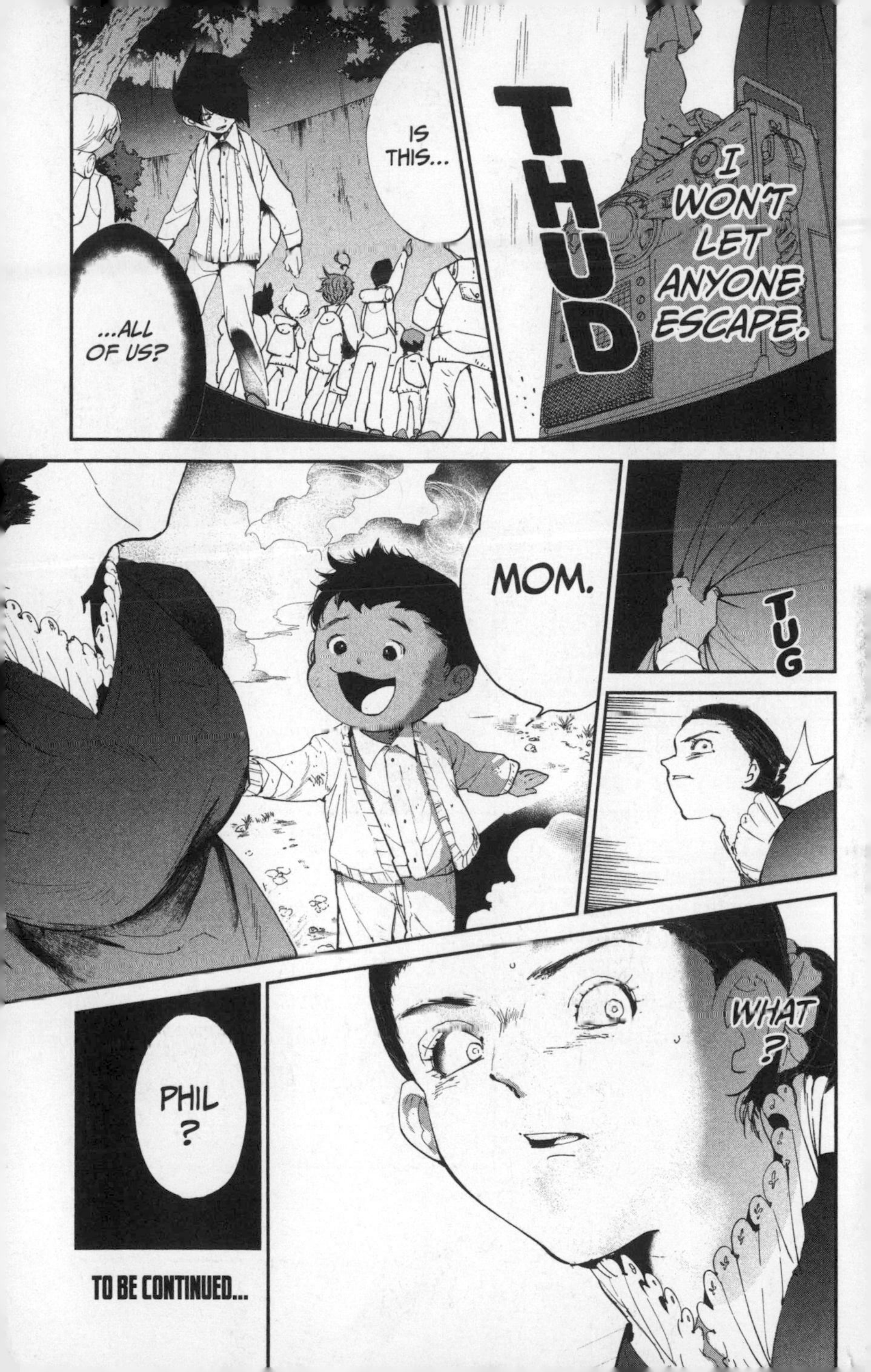
THUD
I WON'T LET ANYONE ESCAPE.
IS THIS...
...ALL OF US?
TUG
MOM.
WHAT?
PHIL?
TO BE CONTINUED...

YOU'RE READING THE **WRONG WAY!**

The Promised Neverland reads from right to left, starting in the upper-right corner. Japanese is read from right to left, meaning that action, sound effects and word-balloon order are completely reversed from English order.